Reparations for Slavery in International Law

Reparations for Slavery in International Law

Transatlantic Enslavement, the Maangamizi, *and the Making of International Law*

KATARINA SCHWARZ

OXFORD
UNIVERSITY PRESS

OXFORD
UNIVERSITY PRESS

Oxford University Press is a department of the University of Oxford. It furthers the University's objective of excellence in research, scholarship, and education by publishing worldwide. Oxford is a registered trade mark of Oxford University Press in the UK and certain other countries.

Published in the United States of America by Oxford University Press
198 Madison Avenue, New York, NY 10016, United States of America.

Library of Congress Cataloging-in-Publication Data
Names: Schwarz, Katarina, author.
Title: Reparations for slavery in international law : transatlantic enslavement, the maangamizi, and the making of international law / Katarina Schwarz.
Description: New York : Oxford University Press, 2022. |
Includes bibliographical references and index.
Identifiers: LCCN 2021056089 (print) | LCCN 2021056090 (ebook) | ISBN 9780197636398 (hardback) | ISBN 9780197636411 (epub) | ISBN 9780197636404 (updf) | ISBN 9780197636428 (online)
Subjects: LCSH: Slavery—Law and legislation—History. | Reparations for historical injustices. | Restorative justice.
Classification: LCC K3267 .S39 2022 (print) | LCC K3267 (ebook) |
DDC 342.08/7—dc23/eng/20220331
LC record available at https://lccn.loc.gov/2021056089
LC ebook record available at https://lccn.loc.gov/2021056090

DOI: 10.1093/oso/9780197636398.001.0001

1 3 5 7 9 8 6 4 2

Printed by Integrated Books International, United States of America

To the grassroots. To the marginalized voices of past, present, and future speaking truth to power and fighting for change even when justice is far from reach.

Contents

Acknowledgments

This topic belongs not to institution academia but to the grassroots—to the local and global movements for reparatory justice who have spoken to this issue for centuries and will continue to do so until their message is no longer marginal. Thus, I would first like to acknowledge those activists and scholars who give life to the quest for reparatory justice every day and who push us to be better scholars, better citizens, and better human beings. In particular, to the International Network of Scholars and Activists for Afrikan Reparations—to those activists and scholars with whom I have spoken, and the many more to whom I have listened—and to all those speaking truth to power, often at significant personal cost.

Positionality and representation matter in this work, and I acknowledge that my own position contributed to the privilege of pursuing this research. I am grateful to have had the opportunity to pursue this work but recognize that the legacies of racialization continue to shape academia, bearing on who has access to the "ivory tower," what topics are advanced, how they are addressed, and whose knowledge is respected. My hope is that this work will be of service to those advancing reparatory justice debates and help contribute to changing the face of legal research in ways that bring the marginal to the center. The duty to change these structures rests with all of us.

This work has developed over many years. It began its life as an undergraduate dissertation at the University of Otago and grew through my doctoral research at Queen's University Belfast and the University of Nottingham, funded by the Arts and Humanities Research Council through the Care for the Future grant "The Antislavery Usable Past." I am thankful for this support, which made the research possible, and for the project team who provided encouragement and a wealth of opportunities for development.

Over almost eight years, this research has benefited from the insights, support, and encouragement of a wonderful and diverse network of individuals and communities. All these people know me to not be one for high sentiment. Thus, brevity here should not be taken as a lack of appreciation for all those who made this research not only possible but also a joy.

My sincerest thanks to Jean Allain for a blind email, endless opportunities, insightful critique, and an open mind—for bringing me halfway around the world and even for leaving to that half of the world yourself.

To Luke Moffett for opening this project to a new world of research, placing justice for victims at the heart of academic inquiry, and supporting a research agenda and not just a project.

To Kevin Bales and David Fraser for their unanticipated but greatly appreciated supervision. To have benefited from the insights of four entirely different but equally learned perspectives made my doctoral thesis, and therefore this book, what it is.

To the PhD communities at Queen's University Belfast and the University of Nottingham for making halfway around the world welcoming and for solidarity always.

To my friends "on the outside" for life beyond—sanity demands it.

To my family, who encouraged me to say yes to a blind email from halfway around the world and made it possible.

And finally, to Christian, who sacrificed 12,000 miles for 100,000 words.

Note on Language

Language matters in reparatory justice. Where representation has played a role in the wrongs identified—including in their normalization in law, politics, and society—the language and representations employed in reparations discourse are of direct concern.

The language used to describe the wrongs committed against African people and people of African descent in connection with the system of transatlantic chattel enslavement or the "transatlantic slave trade" is heavily contested. Legal frameworks have developed specific concepts, each with prescribed definitions, to describe different practices associated with the treatment and exploitation of human beings as property. Dominant framing across scholarship on the subject likewise ascribes to a set of meanings associated to the terms, creating an orthodoxy in language.

However, reparations advocates challenge the use of language in this domain as perpetuating wrongs and reinforcing the assumptions and hierarchies that justified enslavement. In many spaces, these assumptions continue to block serious discussion of the possibility of a case for reparations.

This text engages in a conscious process of reframing language used rather than simply relying on dominant discourse within academic writing. This is explained further in the introductory chapter.

Broadly, the language of enslavement is used over "slavery" and "slave trade," except when required for specificity, or in referring to relevant legal frameworks and preexisting commentaries. The text therefore refers to the system of transatlantic chattel enslavement or, in brief, transatlantic enslavement rather than the "transatlantic slave trade." It refers to enslaved persons rather than "slaves," recognizing the humanity of those persons irrespective of how they were treated (by others or by the law).

The use of the term "victim" to describe those persons who experience abuses, as well as more broadly, is recognized to be problematic. The term is therefore only utilized in its legal sense, to describe the category of persons who have experienced violations of law and should not be taken as descriptive of those persons more broadly.

At various points in the drafting and review of this text, commentators have taken issue with this reframing or suggested reverting to the orthodox language already employed in academic commentary. Some see the language of enslavement as inappropriate to describe the ongoing institution, seeing this label as describing only the moment at which a person is reduced to the condition of slavery and not the continuation of such. This is further complicated by the specific international legal positioning of "enslavement" as a concept of international criminal law.

These legal developments and framings are not overlooked in the text. For instance, section 2.3 specifically addresses the distinction between the developing prohibitions of "slave trade" and "slavery" in international law. However, the power dynamics embedded in the language are also not ignored.

The current language employed is not neutral. The text therefore seeks to adopt language that does not reaffirm preexisting power imbalances and presumptions about legality, that recognizes slavery as involving ongoing perpetration at all stages rather than as an institution that exists absent conscious human action, and that affirms the humanity of those enslaved.

Table of Cases

INTERNATIONAL COURTS

International Court of Justice

Permanent Court of International Justice

European Court of Human Rights

Inter-American Court of Human Rights

Other international tribunals

DOMESTIC COURTS

Australia

United States

United Kingdom

South Africa

Table of Legislation

NATIONAL LAWS

Argentina

Brazil

Chile

Colombia

Czech and Slovak Federative Republic

United Kingdom

United States

South Africa

Introduction

The Reparations Debate and International Law

The debate over reparations for transatlantic enslavement is not new. The movement for redress has a pedigree predating legal emancipation to the years of enslavement. It finds voice at the grassroots and filters up.[1] It speaks through Belinda's 1783 petition to the Massachusetts legislature for an annual pension from the estate of her ex-captor.[2] It underlies the thousands of signatures penned by previously enslaved persons on petitions demanding pensions for their years of unfree labor.[3] It is written in André Rebouças' 1875 *Democracia Rural Brazileira* and in Brazil's 1884 Dantas Bill (No 48) calling for the granting of land to freed populations.[4] It suffuses the continuing history of the transatlantic system of chattel enslavement from its inception. It is a persistent struggle championed by the subaltern against mainstream denials.

While the debate over reparations for transatlantic enslavement is far from new, a palpable shift in public attitudes toward the commemoration of historic events has occurred since the mid-twentieth century.[5] This, in turn, supported the growth of a body of scholarship concerning collective and public memory and an increased awareness of contested histories.[6] The

[1] Rhonda Magee, "The Master's Tools, from the Bottom Up: Responses to African-American Reparations Theory in Mainstream and Outsider Remedies Discourse" (1993) 79 Virginia Law Review 863, 913.

[2] See Roy E Finkenbine, "Belinda's Petition: Reparations for Slavery in Revolutionary Massachusetts" (2007) 64(1) William and Mary Quarterly 95.

[3] See Mary Frances Berry, *My Face Is Black Is True: Callie House and the Struggle for Ex-Slave Reparations* (Alfred A Knopf 2005).

[4] Ana Lucia Araujo, *Reparations for Slavery and the Slave Trade: A Transnational and Comparative History* (Bloomsbury Academic 2017) 77, 80.

[5] See Ana Lucia Araujo, *Public Memory of Slavery: Victims and Perpetrators in the South Atlantic* (Cambria Press 2010); Patrick Finney, "The Ubiquitous Presence of the Past? Collective Memory and International History" (2014) 36(3) The International History Review 443; Chris Weedon and Glenn Jordan, "Collective Memory: Theory and Politics" (2012) 22(2) Social Semiotics 143.

[6] This first wave of growth in recognition of public memory is closely tied to the memorialization of the Shoah. See, for instance, David Lowenthal, "On Arraigning Ancestors: A Critique of Historical Contrition" (2009) 87(3) North Carolina Law Review 901, 905.

Reparations for Slavery in International Law. Katarina Schwarz, Oxford University Press. © Oxford University Press 2022.
DOI: 10.1093/oso/9780197636398.003.0001

past three decades have seen a significant increase in memorialization efforts related to enslavement in the Americas, Europe, and Africa; increased engagement with historical injustices; and a rising tide of political, media, and academic attention on the case for reparations for transatlantic enslavement.[7]

From the early 1990s through the first two decades of the new millennium, the global movement for reparations surfaced in public discourse. In 1992, the Organization of African Unity established the Group of Eminent Persons to consider reparations for the damage done to Africa and the African diaspora as a result of enslavement, colonialism, and neocolonialism.[8] In 1993, the Abuja Proclamation arising from the First Pan-African Conference on Reparations affirmed the international legal grounding of the claim for reparations and called for a range of measures, from internal action in Africa to reparatory action by states in Europe and the Americas, and the restructuring of the international system in pursuit of justice.[9]

In 2014, the promulgation of the CARICOM (Caribbean Community) Ten Point Plan for Reparatory Justice highlighted persistent harm and suffering connected to the history of transatlantic chattel enslavement, colonialism, and racial apartheid in the Caribbean and the obligation on European governments to participate in remedying such.[10] Three months later, Ta-Nehesi Coates' "The Case for Reparations" sparked a new wave of media attention and public discussion of the issue of redress for African Americans for the history of chattel enslavement and the continuum of racialized injustice that followed in the United States.[11] In 2021, H.R. 40—a bill to

[7] On the increase in memorialization from the 1990s, see Ana Lucia Araujo, *Shadows of the Slave Past: Memory, Heritage, and Slavery* (Routledge 2014). See also Alan Rice and Johanna C Kardux, "Confronting the Ghostly Legacies of Slavery: The Politics of Black Bodies, Embodied Memories and Memorial Landscapes" (2012) 9(3) Atlantic Studies 245; John Oldfield, *"Chords of Freedom": Commemoration, Ritual and British Transatlantic Slavery* (Manchester UP 2007); Nicola Frith, "Saving the Republic: State Nostalgia and Slavery Reparations in Media and Political Discourses" (2015) 23(2) Modern and Contemporary France 213.

[8] See Rhoda Howard-Hassmann, "Reparations to Africa and the Group of Eminent Persons" (2004) 173–74 Cahiers d'études africanes 81.

[9] "The Abuja Proclamation" adopted at the Abuja Pan-African Conference on Reparations for African Enslavement, Colonisation and Neo-colonialism (Abuja, April 27–29, 1993) <www.ncobraonline.org/the-abuja-proclamation/> accessed May 22, 2018. The conference was sponsored by the Group of Eminent Persons, the Commission for Reparations of the Organisation of African Unity, and the Nigerian Government.

[10] "CARICOM Ten Point Plan for Reparatory Justice" (*CARICOM*, March 2014) <www.caricom.org/caricom-ten-point-plan-for-reparatory-justice/> accessed June 1, 2018; "CARICOM Nations Unanimously Approve 10 Point Plan for Slavery Reparations" (*Leigh Day*, March 11, 2014) <www.leighday.co.uk/News/2014/March-2014/CARICOM-nations-unanimously-approve-10-point-plan> accessed June 1, 2018.

[11] Ta-Nehisi Coates, "The Case for Reparations" *The Atlantic* (Washington DC, June 2014) <www.theatlantic.com/magazine/archive/2014/06/the-case-for-reparations/361631/> accessed June 1, 2018.

establish a Commission to Study and Develop Reparation Proposals for African Americans—cleared committee for the first time after over thirty years of repetitive introduction.[12]

The landscape of reparations debate has shifted substantially in the past decade. With this new wave of attention on reparations for transatlantic enslavement comes increasing attention on the legal, political, and moral dimensions of the case. Yet, despite the rising prominence of the issue, a raft of uncertainties remain. The question of whether reparations should be made—either as a matter of legal or moral obligation—is at the heart of these debates. However, the form of reparations is also a central concern. Understandings of what reparations look like influence conclusions on whether they ought to be made, and significant issues can arise in moving from the recognition of a wrong to the construction of appropriate redress. The reparations debate therefore raises issues of both principle and practice.

Legal arguments on these questions frequently blur the lines between law, politics, and philosophy through false analogies or assertions of precedent, introduction of nonlegal factors into legal analysis, and the conflation of law and justice.[13] Thus, the increased visibility of the reparations debate has not yet delivered theoretical clarity on the legal dimensions of the issue, particularly in relation to international legal frameworks and their application. This is the controversial and contested ground on which considerations of reparations for historical enslavement rest and to which international legal arguments are central.

Conclusions on the reparatory obligation often turn on a limited set of concerns: the legality of enslavement "at the time"; the responsibility of current generations for the "sins of the past"; the connection of people alive today to the harms of enslavement; and the practicalities of redress for widescale "historical" abuses. Debate on each of these issues is polarized between reparations advocates and detractors. In the quest for clarity in public

[12] See Rep Sheila Jackson Lee, "H.R. 40 Is Not a Symbolic Act. It's a Path to Restorative Justice" (*ACLU*, May 22, 2020) <https://www.aclu.org/news/racial-justice/h-r-40-is-not-a-symbolic-act-its-a-path-to-restorative-justice/> accessed July 27, 2021; Cristy Lytal, "The Complex Case for Reparations as H.R. 40 Advances" (*USCPrice*, June 18, 2021) <https://priceschool.usc.edu/usc-price-faculty-consider-the-complex-case-for-reparations/> accessed July 27, 2021.

[13] See, for instance, Lord Anthony Gifford, "The Legal Basis of the Claim for Reparations" First Pan-African Congress on Reparations (Abuja, April 1993) <www.shaka.mistral.co.uk/legalbasis.htm> accessed June 4, 2018. Despite limitations in the legal argumentation, Gifford's conclusions have served as the basis for many other commentators' views on the question of legality—see, for instance, Hilary Beckles, *Britain's Black Debt: Reparations for Caribbean Slavery and Native Genocide* (University of West Indies Press 2013).

debate, there is often little room for recognition of the nuances and complexities of the international legal frameworks underpinning these points.

Each of these core issues is deconstructed in this text, seeking to bring clarity to the international legal rules, principles, and norms that underpin the discussion. The text leans into the complexities of the international legal frameworks as they evolved over time and the principles guiding the question of whether, and what, reparations are due under international law. It finds a contested legal ground that makes space for both obligation and denial. However, it also provides a framework of reparatory justice—both in theory and in practice—that can shape reparations discourse and delivery.

I.1. International law in reparations debates

In 1997, Antonio Cassese suggested that international criminal tribunals were the most "directly effective and radical" mechanisms of human rights for their aims of "prosecuting and punishing the very authors of serious offences against human dignity."[14] Cassese, then president of the International Criminal Tribunal for the former Yugoslavia, framed prosecution and punishment of individual offenders as protective measures targeted toward victims, with the objective of halting and redressing crimes. Yet, the comparison between criminal trials directly engaging the perpetrators and human rights mechanisms addressing the conduct of states omits an important consideration in its assessment of direct effectiveness and radicalness—that the impact of justice processes on perpetrators is not the sole indicator of either metric.

Particularly where justice for victims is identified as a driving force of judicial processes, the outcomes available to those individuals must be taken into account. Reparations are victim-centered measures of redress that alter the lens through which violations are viewed from a focus on the wrongfulness of the perpetrators' conduct to place the harms suffered by victims in the foreground.[15] At least for victims, they are often the most directly effective

[14] Antonio Cassese, "The International Criminal Tribunal for the former Yugoslavia and Human Rights" Lecture delivered to the British Institute of Human Rights on May 1, 1997, published in European Human Rights Law Review (1997) 4 329, 332.

[15] See Luke Moffett, "Transitional Justice and Reparations: Remedying the Past?" in Cheryl Lawther, Luke Moffett, and Dov Jacobs (eds), *Research Handbook in Transitional Justice* (Edward Elgar Publishing 2017) 377; Pablo de Greiff, "Repairing the Past: Compensation for Victims of Human Rights Violations" in Pablo de Greiff (ed), *The Handbook of Reparations* (OUP 2006) 1, 2.

mechanisms of human rights and international justice, as well as the most sought after.[16]

In the case of historical enslavement, individual criminality is no longer justiciable, the abolition of "slavery" and the "slave trade" failed to effect meaningful change for many previously enslaved persons, and their descendants continue to live with the legacies of the system.[17] Although in domestic settings reparationists often avert to more general domestic laws, particularly equity and tort law, to formulate a legal claim in relation to historical enslavement, these are limited by the technicalities of national legal systems, such as rules of prescription, state immunity, and political question doctrines.[18] Furthermore, the capacity of such frameworks to capture injustice in their totality is critiqued.

Brooks labels domestic tort law "morally deficient" in decrying the full experience of chattel enslavement, Sebok argues that unjust enrichment claims render an "impoverished understanding of slavery" by framing claims involving a complex series of harms as primarily about uncompensated labor, and Sherwin suggests that the juridification of issues of enormous public controversy through restitution claims is divisive and likely to result in resentment rather than repair.[19] Additionally, domestic laws are unable or unlikely to capture the international dimensions of transatlantic chattel enslavement central to understanding the injustice and formulating relevant claims, including relationships between colonizing states and their

[16] de Greiff (n 15).

[17] Although some reparations activists continue to call for the case of historical enslavement to be tried at the International Criminal Court, this is precluded by the individualized nature of criminal responsibility, the principle of non-retroactivity, and the temporal jurisdiction of the court. See UNGA Rome Statute of the International Criminal Court (adopted July 17, 1998, entered into force July 1, 2002) 2187 UNTS 90, arts 11, 22, 24, and 25.

[18] See, in the American context, *Re African-American Slave Descendants Litigation* 375 F Supp 2d 721 (ND Ill 2005); *Re African-American Slave Descendants Litigation* (2006) 471 F Supp 3d 754 (7th Cir); *Cato v United States* (1995) 70 F Supp 3d 1103 (9th Cir).

[19] Roy Brooks, *Atonement and Forgiveness: A New Model for Black Reparations* (University of California Press 2004); Anthony Sebok, "Two Concepts of Injustice in Restitution for Slavery" (2004) 84 Boston University Law Review 1405; Emily Sherwin, "Reparations and Unjust Enrichment" (2004) 84 Boston University Law Review 1443. This critique may also be levied against the juridification of claims relating to transatlantic enslavement in international law, although the affective dimensions of justice at the international level may vary from domestic law. On the other hand, Klimchuk and Dagan support the moral-expressive content of domestic tort claims, suggesting that it is an appropriate framework for reparatory justice. Dennis Klimchuk, "Unjust Enrichment and Reparations for Slavery" (2004) 84 Boston University Law Review 1257, 1275; Hanoch Dagan, "Restitution and Slavery: On Incomplete Commodification, Intergenerational Justice, and Legal Transitions" (2004) 84 Boston University Law Review 1139. However, Dagan recognizes that these should not be the sole measures adopted.

ex-colonies, making international law an integral feature of many potential claims.[20]

The 2001 World Conference against Racism held in Durban marked a landmark moment for reparations in the context of international law. The declaration that "slavery and the slave trade are a crime against humanity and should always have been so" stops short of recognizing transatlantic enslavement to have been internationally unlawful in its time. However, the partnering affirmation that Africans and people of African descent were victims of "slavery and the slave trade" and "continue to be victims of their consequences" connects contemporary suffering to the history of enslavement.[21] Yet, the leap from the Durban Declaration to Anthony Gifford's contention that enslavement is a crime against humanity and always was so leaves several crucial links undeveloped.[22] The critical difference between the Durban Declaration and Gifford's conclusion is that Durban reaches a moral conclusion as to the way law should have been at the time, whereas Gifford asserts that the legal frameworks governing crimes against humanity were in force. This clash continues to manifest in political, activist, and academic discourse on the subject.[23]

[20] Key identified perpetrators are states in many cases, and victims are often formulated as foreign citizens, collectives, or other states. This means that domestic law failures to capture much of the wrongdoing identified. Some claims might nonetheless take place within the national jurisdiction, as is the case with domestic claims within the United States. However, the US claim context cannot be transplanted in many of the contexts in which reparations are an issue because claims exist between former colonies and European colonial powers. Moreover, the domestic US case does not capture the pre-independence conduct of colonial powers in that territory.

[21] "Durban Declaration and Plan of Action, Adopted at the World Conference against Racism, Racial Discrimination, Xenophobia and Related Intolerance" (Durban, September 8, 2001). The Durban Declaration was endorsed by the United Nations General Assembly in UNGA Res 56/266 (March 27, 2002) UN Doc A/RES/56/66.

[22] Anthony Gifford, "Pipe Dream or Necessary Atonement?" (2007) 36 Index on Censorship 89, 91. Similarly, Beckles also relies on the assertion that slavery was, at the time, a crime against humanity without interrogating the legal justification for this claim: Beckles (n 13). While Wittmann goes further in interrogating claims of the historic international legality of transatlantic enslavement, the relationship between contemporary formulations of "crimes against humanity" and historic international humanitarian and criminal law norms remains underdeveloped: Nora Wittmann, *Slavery Reparations Time Is Now: Exposing Lies, Claiming Justice for Global Survival, an International Legal Assessment* (Power of the TrInIty Publishers 2013).

[23] See, for instance, Jon M Van Dyke, "Reparations for the Descendants of American Slaves under International Law" in Raymond A Winbush (ed), *Should America Pay?: Slavery and the Raging Debate on Reparations* (Harper Collins 2003); Molefi Kete Asante, "The African American Warrant for Reparations: The Crime of European Enslavement of Africans and its Consequences" in Winbush, *Should America Pay*; Patricia M Muhammad, "The Trans-Atlantic Slave Trade: A Forgotten Crime Against Humanity as Defined by International Law" (2004) 19 Amherst University Law Review 883; Richard Croucher and Didier Michel, "'Legal at the Time'?: Companies, Governments and Reparations for Mauritian Slavery" (2014) 58(1) Journal of African Law 89. cf Andreas Büser, "Colonial Injustices and the Law of State Responsibility: The CARICOM Claim for Reparations," KFG Working Paper Series No. 4, Berlin Potsdam Research Group, "The International Rule of Law: Rise or Decline?" (August 2016); Jean Allain, *Slavery in International Law: Of Human*

On the other side of the debate, the presumption of the historical international legality of enslavement generally relies on contemporary positivistic approaches to international law and seldom interrogates beyond finding ubiquitous practice.[24] While there has been some problematization of the characterization of enslavement as legal based upon the practices of a European global minority, there has been little attempt to integrate the nuances of African complicity and its significance into this critical legal assessment.[25] Furthermore, the impact of the predominant natural law philosophies of the time on the conclusion of legality seldom features in considerations, despite explicit reference to law as understood at the time.[26] Thus, although the moral and philosophical cases for reparations have been extensively explored, the legal frameworks governing and informing redress, and the implications of these in practice, have not been established.[27]

In engaging the international legal frameworks, the following chapters occupy a site of tension—the nexus between recognition of the problematic imperial foundations of international law and their continuing legacies and the application of international law as a system through which universal justice is conceptualized and implemented. They simultaneously recognize the limits of the law and its power, presenting analysis acknowledging the flawed history of international legal frameworks, and account for the commitments made therein. In many ways, this is reflective of the discourse of reparations activists themselves, who call for promises of justice within the international legal order to be fulfilled in the case.[28] Moreover, it recognizes the boundaries of international legal mechanisms but does not treat these as a conceptual or moral bar to recovery. What is important in this regard are the spaces

Exploitation and Trafficking (Martinus Nijhoff 2013) 57–104; M Cherif Bassiouni, "Enslavement as an International Crime" (1991) 23 New York University Journal of International Law and Politics 45.

[24] See, for instance, Max du Plessis, "Historical Injustice and International Law: An Exploratory Discussion of Reparations for Slavery" (2003) 25 Human Rights Quarterly 624; Buser (n 23).

[25] See, for instance, Wittmann (n 22).

[26] See Buser (n 23).

[27] See, for instance, Kete Asante (n 23); Janna Thompson, *Taking Responsibility for the Past: Reparation and Historical Justice* (Polity 2002); Rhoda Howard-Hassmann and Anthony Lombardo, *Reparations to Africa* (University of Pennsylvania Press 2008).

[28] The Caribbean Community, for instance, has often referred to its intention to bring a claim before the International Court of Justice should European enslaver states refuse to engage in dialogue and negotiations on the question of reparations. See Samiha Shafy, "Caribbean States Call for Slavery Reparations" *Spiegel Online* (March 21, 2014) <www.spiegel.de/international/world/caribbean-states-want-reparations-for-western-europe-slave-trade-a-960109.html> accessed November 19, 2018; "14 Caribbean Nations Sue European Countries for Slavery Reparations" (*Aljazeera*, September 27, 2013) <america.aljazeera.com/articles/2013/9/27/14-caribbean-nationssueeuropeancountriesforreparationsoverslaver.html> accessed November 19, 2018.

and tensions existing within international law, which offer a foothold for the rejection of the monolithic understanding of legality and liability in favor of a more nuanced approach.

The history of international law has never been static. It has shifted and evolved to reflect changing ideologies, as well as global relations of power and influence.[29] This encompasses not only a changing understanding of the primary norms of the international legal system but also substantial shifts in its theoretical foundations. The claim for reparations for historical enslavement connects present legal frameworks to the centuries of development that produced them. It cannot be considered on the basis of contemporary assumptions alone, but likewise should not be assessed only against antecedent understandings. It relies on the premise that there is something more to international law than simply the oscillations of power; that there are embedded principles of justice that may be used as a lever to advance claims for justice beyond positivist limits and beyond the borders of technical legal mechanisms, particularly with consideration of historical jurisprudential thinking. Ultimately, this evaluation destabilizes the assertion that the corpus of international law through time precludes the reparations case and highlights the ways in which underlying legal principles in fact provide a framework for, and support, a moral or political case.

I.2. Framing the injustice

Reparations advocates highlight the importance of language and framing when discussing the wrong committed against African peoples.[30] In the reparatory context, defining the wrong is particularly significant, as framing can impact both the identification of parties to a case and whether social hierarchies perpetuating abuse are reinforced or resisted.[31] The language of

[29] See, for instance, Antony Anghie, *Imperialism, Sovereignty and the Making of International Law* (CUP 2007).

[30] See, for instance, International Network of Scholars and Activists for Afrikan Reparations, "Public Report: Launch of the International Network of Scholars and Activists for Afrikan Reparations (INOSAAR)" (London, October 2016) 6. <www.inosaar.llc.ed.ac.uk/sites/default/files/atoms/files/public_report_21_oct_2017.pdf> accessed May 23, 2018.

[31] On the impact of stereotypes of women in contemporary human trafficking discourse, see Ratna Kapur, "The Tragedy of Victimization Rhetoric: Resurrecting the 'Native' Subject in International/Postcolonial Feminist Legal Politics" in Ratna Kapur, *Erotic Justice: Law and the New Politics of Postcolonialism* (Glasshouse 2005) 129. For an assessment related to victims/survivors of sexual abuse with strong analogy to victims/survivors of enslavement, see Jericho Hockett and Donald Saucier, "A Systematic Literature Review of 'Rape Victims' versus 'Rape Survivors': Implications for Theory, Research, and Practice" (2015) 25 Aggression and Violent Behaviour 1. See also Wendy

oppression and survival serves an important function in the reformation of ravaged communities and identities.[32] Yet, until recently, much of the academic analysis of issues concerning enslavement failed to take account of the significance of the language employed in defining and discussing the topic or to respect the voices of people of African descent who continue to experience the legacies of racialized chattel enslavement today and who renounce these labels.[33]

This text seeks to not only be comprehensive and thorough in its coverage of the legal issues surrounding reparations but also internally consistent with the theories presented and developed.

The dominant narrative of transatlantic enslavement continues to be defined by the states that participated in it as a legal "trade." Thus, expressions of abhorrence for the horrors perpetrated against African peoples frequently frame these abuses as regrettable but only from the contemporary perspective. Tony Blair, then Prime Minister of the United Kingdom, in 2006 epitomized this account:

> The transatlantic slave trade stands as one of the most inhuman enterprises in history. At a time when the capitals of Europe and America championed the Enlightenment of man, their merchants were enslaving a continent. Racism, not the rights of man, drove the horrors of the triangular trade. . . . It is hard to believe that what would now be a crime against humanity was legal at the time.[34]

The prevailing presumption of legality and the insertion of moral relativism are characteristic of the contemporary approach of the European powers that perpetrated the abuses in question. While recognizing the brutality of enslavement, these descriptions reinforce public amnesia of the atrocities by framing them as a "trade" understood as morally acceptable at the time. Maulana Karenga describes this categorization of enslavement and

Brown, *States of Injury* (Princeton UP 1995); Rebecca Stringer, *Knowing Victims: Feminism and Victim Politics in Neoliberal Times* (Routledge 2014); Jan van Dijk, "Free the Victim: A Critique of the Western Conception of Victimhood" (2009) 16 International Review of Victimology 1.

[32] The symbolic and affective dimensions of injustice are considered in depth in chapters 4, 5, and 7.
[33] See INOSAAR (n 30).
[34] Tony Blair, "PM's Article for the New Nation Newspaper" (November 27, 2006) <webarchive.nationalarchives.gov.uk/20040105034004/http://number10.gov.uk/page10487> accessed November 1, 2016.

associated conduct as sanitizing the abuses committed against African people by making the violence commercial rather than moral; "mass murder or genocide" is presented as "simply collateral damage of a commercial venture gone bad."[35]

The commodification of African people and their descendants was driven, at least in large part, by economic motives and carried out as a global trade, leading some commentators to support the continued use of this label. On this account, it is only accurate to characterize the system of transatlantic chattel enslavement as "slave trade" and those persons held captive within it as "slaves"—this cannot therefore be a denial of historical experiences. Furthermore, slavery and the slave trade are the specific practices prohibited by international and domestic law, making them the appropriate terms for discussion of the relevant legal frameworks.[36] Why then problematize these terms in discussing historical enslavement?

First, the terms are problematized to recognize the placement of enslavement in a broader framework of violence committed against African and indigenous peoples. Transatlantic enslavement did not occur in a vacuum. It was one element of a global system of imperial domination of Africans and people of African descent. To recognize this framework of violence, the term "*maangamizi*" will be used throughout this text. This term places the specific injustices within their broader context, recognizing not only that individuals were victims of enslavement but also that this treatment was intentionally perpetrated, widespread, specifically targeted toward Africans and their descendants, and interwoven with a range of related abuses.[37]

Designations of the Shoah as the "crime of crimes" are well established. Since Hannah Arendt described the Nazi crimes as "exploding the limits of the law"—"guilt beyond crime"—the phrase has found increasing purchase in discourse surrounding mass atrocities.[38] Although the law has developed various mechanisms to secure its own seams in these contexts, the rhetorical

[35] Maulana Karenga, "The Ethics of Reparations: Engaging the Holocaust of Enslavement" (Coalition of Blacks for Reparations in America Conference, Baton Rouge, June 22–23, 2001).

[36] On the terms of international treaties, see section 2.3.

[37] See Anthony Gifford, "Pipe Dream or Necessary Atonement?" (2007) 36 Index on Censorship 89, 93; "Durban Declaration and Plan of Action, Adopted at the World Conference against Racism, Racial Discrimination, Xenophobia and Related Intolerance" (Durban, September 8, 2001). The Durban Declaration was endorsed by the United Nations General Assembly in UNGA Res 56/266 (March 27, 2002) UN Doc A/RES/56/66, art 158; Karenga (n 35).

[38] Lotte Kohler and Hans Saner (eds), *Hannah Arendt—Karl Jaspers Correspondence 1926–1969* (Robert Kimber and Rita Kimber trs, Harcourt Brace and Jovanovich 1992) 54. See also Austin Sarat, Lawrence Douglas, and Martha Merrill (eds), *The Limits of the Law* (Stanford UP 2005).

power of the terms holocaust and genocide have imprinted upon public consciousness—not just as legal phenomena but as social constructs. Yet, despite the sheer number of victims and the mass industrialization of murder and atrocity that constituted the system of transatlantic chattel enslavement, the inclusion of transatlantic enslavement within these categories of atrocity is relatively rare and struggles to find purchase in the rhetoric of those states that created and operated the system. "Slavery" and the "slave trade" remain the institutions of the dominant discourse, and it is against this language that reparations activists assert the term "*maangamizi*"—the African holocaust.[39]

Understanding the *maangamizi* as a continuum of harm against people of African descent and as a morally monstrous system of abuse, exploitation, and mass murder shifts the narrative to provide recognition of the nature of the wrong and the impact upon victims and victim populations. The term is advocated by people of African descent currently fighting within grassroots activist organizations for recognition of the injustices associated with the transatlantic system.[40] It therefore exists within a framework consistent with the aim of reparations to acknowledge agency, experience, and identity. Giving voice to those most affected by injustice in this context reflects the objectives and elements of reparatory justice explored in this text.

While *maangamizi* is well suited to capture atrocities associated with the system of transatlantic chattel enslavement and colonialism as a whole, this text is particularly focused on the place of "slavery" and the "slave trade" as defined concepts in international law. While not precluding consideration of other instances of widespread historical enslavement, the analysis is generally confined in scope to the consideration of enslavement taking place within the context of the transatlantic relationships and interactions between Western Europe, Africa, and the Americas. Thus, a variety of more specific terms are employed to discuss this extreme form of human exploitation and the specific instances of such that occurred during what is otherwise labeled as the "transatlantic slave trade."

[39] Karenga (n 35). See also Reparations Scholar, "What Is the International Social Movement for Afrikan Reparations (ISMAR)?" (February 20, 2015) <reparationsscholaractivist.wordpress.com/2015/02/20/what-is-the-ismar/> accessed October 21, 2016; Ludovica Laccino, "Stop the Maangamizi: Africans 'Never Received Even an Apology for Slavery'" (August 2, 2016) <www.ibtimes.co.uk/stop-maangamizi-africans-never-received-even-apology-slavery-1573817> accessed November 1, 2016.

[40] See, for instance, Esther Stanford-Xosei, "What is the *Maangamizi*" (From the Transatlantic Slave Trade to Engaging the Maangamizi: Historical Injustice and Reparations Conference, Belfast, June 29–30, 2016); International Steering Committee for Stop the Maangamizi: We Charge Genocide/Ecocide, "About" (*Stop the Maangamizi*) <stopthemaangamizi.com> accessed June 1, 2018.

The dominant language employed in the text is that of "the system of transatlantic enslavement," or "transatlantic enslavement" and the "transatlantic system" in brief. The terms "slavery" and "slave trade" are used only where required to indicate the specific terms of law, the regulated commerce in enslaved persons, or where they are drawn directly from references or introduced in relation to a particular discussion of the issues involved. The inclusion of these terms is not intended to serve as an affirmation of their uncritical use in discourse but rather as a critical acknowledgment of their prevalence.

The second reason the language of the "slave trade" and "slaves" is generally avoided is to acknowledge the humanity of the millions of people enslaved within the transatlantic system and define them by that humanity rather than by their enslavement. The term "enslavement" is therefore used over "slavery," and "enslaved person" over "slave," to recognize exploitation as a condition imposed upon a person by another, rather than as definitive of the individual.[41]

Third, the continuation and transmission of the legacies of enslavement and the *maangamizi* necessitate a nuanced understanding of the impact of these injustices on both collective memory and lived experience. This need is particularly acute in contexts where official narratives are constituted variously of sanitization and forgetting, and the converse: representations of "black history" as defined by the horrors, brutality, and humiliation of mass enslavement.[42] The tension of these two portrayals of history can reinforce the dehumanization of enslaved Africans and entrench the notions of moral relativism simultaneously. As Sepúlveda Dos Santos identifies, the suffering can become a "distant and objectivized image from the past" that appears as fate rather than culpable wrongdoing:

> there was nobody to be held responsible for their suffering. Slaves were victims of a mistaken regime from the past. The following generations have inherited the identification with the victims, but have found no way

[41] The term "enslavement" is used in its rhetorical, rather than legal sense throughout, as enslavement as a crime against humanity under the Rome Statute of the International Criminal Court, and associated legal frameworks, is not substantively considered in this text.

[42] See Mneesha Gellman, "Only Looking Forward: The Absence of War History in Sierra Leone" in Denise Bentrovato, Karina Korostelina, and Martina Schulze (eds), *History Can Bite: History Education in Divided and Postwar Societies* (V&R Unipres 2016) 143–52; Omar Encarnación, *Democracy without Justice in Spain: The Politics of Forgetting* (University of Pennsylvania Press 2014).

to escape this position, since there is no one to blame apart from the regime itself.[43]

When the nature and choices of the regime are conceived as symptoms of the time, seemingly conflicting narratives come together to "sanitize" the moral history of transatlantic enslavement. Moreover, they continue to neglect the significance of African people in shaping the future as actors and not merely bodies for exploitation.[44] Reparations claims generally seek to redress not only the material suffering identified as connected to enslavement and the *maangamizi* but also the extensive symbolic and cultural harms entrenched by the inculcation of racialization and othering of African people, reconstructing history to reflect the experiences and contributions of people of African descent.[45] Thus, language and framing are central to the project of reparatory justice discussed in the following chapters, providing an additional justification for conscious choices in this regard.

Fourth, terms used in discussing transatlantic enslavement are problematized to avoid the presumption of legality in the highly nuanced debate explored throughout this text. The recognition of enslaved persons as "slaves" and transatlantic enslavement as a "slave trade" implies uncritical acceptance of their legal status, running counter to the objectives of this evaluation, which aims to interrogate prevailing assumptions.

Finally, it is recognized that the discussion does not take place in the context of the nineteenth-century world, but in a twenty-first century that recognizes the atrocity regardless of its legal status. In accepting that legality and illegality do not always align with the interests of justice and equality, this text adopts an approach to framing that accepts possible disjunct between the two but recognizes injustice nonetheless.

With regard to the limits of the period of transatlantic enslavement, the exact timeframe discussed cannot be definitively fixed, and indeed the concept of *maangamizi* embraces the continuum of chattel, colonial, and neocolonial enslavement as three parts of a single whole. Moreover, the function

[43] Myrian Sepúlveda Dos Santos, "The Repressed Memory of Brazilian Slavery" (2008) 11(2) International Journal of Cultural Studies 157, 167.

[44] As Waterhouse, advocating for total recall of the systems of American slavery and the role of enslaved Africans on the development of the nation, notes: the "neglect, minimization, and denial of the indispensable role enslaved Africans played in the construction and development of America represent the norm." Carlton Waterhouse, "Total Recall: Restoring the Public Memory of Enslaved African-Americans and the American System of Slavery through Rectificatory Justice and Reparations" (2011) 14 The Journal of Gender, Race and Justice 703, 704.

[45] See, for instance, CARICOM Reparations Commission (n 10).

of this inquiry is not to formulate a particular legal claim, and thus the exact details in question need not be articulated with absolute certainty. Yet, some degree of clarity as to the relevant period being discussed is necessary in order to frame the historical legal analysis and the questions of attribution, succession, and causation.

The period of "historical" transatlantic enslavement is presented in this text as opening with colonial encounters at the conclusion of the fifteenth century. This is consistent with the United Nations General Assembly Resolution on the "commemoration of the two-hundredth anniversary of the abolition of the transatlantic slave trade" and Anthony Anghie's identification of Christopher Columbus' first voyage claiming sovereignty over the "Indies" as a "founding moment of modern international law."[46]

An exact end date for "historical" enslavement is difficult to set at the international level, for "the slave trade" and "slavery" were generally prohibited domestically at different times and followed by the continuation of legally coerced labor in various forms, as well as de facto enslavement. Furthermore, colonial domination as an element of the *maangamizi* continued through the twentieth century.

In considering state responsibility specifically for transatlantic enslavement, this text focuses on the period in which widespread state activities supported de jure enslavement. The termination date for consideration is therefore taken as 1956, marking the definite crystallization of the prohibition of "slavery" and the "slave trade" in international law, preceded by domestic abolition by European enslaver states in the nineteenth century.[47] Yet, the harms of enslavement are recognized as continuing, and thus there is no end date for the consideration of reparatory justice in international law or transitional justice.[48] The labeling of this phenomenon as "historical" enslavement is not intended to present it as completed and confined to the past but to recognize that the acts of direct enslavement occurred in relation to generations of persons no longer alive today.

[46] UNGA Res 61/19 (November 28, 2006) UN Doc A/RES/61/19 defining the period of the "transatlantic slave trade" as between the fifteenth and the late-nineteenth centuries; Antony Anghie, "International Law and the Pre-History of Globalisation" (2015) 33 Singapore Law Review 3, 10; Antony Anghie, "LatCrit and TWAIL" (2011–12) 42 California Western International Law Journal 311, 317.

[47] Supplementary Convention on the Abolition of Slavery, the Slave Trade, and Institutions and Practices Similar to Slavery (adopted September 7, 1956, entered into force April 30, 1957) 266 UNTS 3. This is a clear point in the historical record at which the prohibition was firmly established, although arguments for earlier crystallization are considered in chapter 2.

[48] Issues of historicity with regard to reparatory justice are further considered in chapters 3 and 6.

As this text does not seek to be prescriptive in relation to possible claims, the terms "enslaver states" and "European enslaver states" are used generally to refer to states who participated in, and perpetuated, the system of transatlantic enslavement. Exactly which states qualify within this category is outside the scope of this analysis, although necessary for the consideration of specific claims.

In general terms, the primary states under consideration in relation to international legal claims are France, the Netherlands, Portugal, Spain, and the United Kingdom, as the states with the most significant involvement in the transatlantic system.[49] However, Hilary Beckles, chair of the CARICOM Reparations Committee, also identifies Denmark, Germany, Norway, Russia, and Sweden as potentially bearing obligations with regard to Caribbean reparations claims, and cases within states that continued their involvement in enslavement after independence may also be formulated.[50] The following analysis relies only upon the presumption that the states falling within the category of "European enslaver states" were substantially involved in the system of transatlantic enslavement and relatedly in many cases in imperial domination in Africa and the Americas. Given the historical record, this prerequisite appears to be an acceptable leap for analysis of international obligations and frameworks in the general sense.

I.3. The case for reparations: contested legal terrain

International law did not simply support the conduct that made up the transatlantic system at its inception. The fundamental rules of the modern international legal system were constructed at the time by European states to justify and enable imperialism, incursions into African and American territories, and enslavement. Rules that had previously limited the conditions in which persons might be enslaved were overthrown. International norms that might have censured this conduct were adapted to enable it. Advanced by the founding fathers of (European) international law, permissions and regulations of transatlantic enslavement were built into the budding modern

[49] See Emory University, "Estimates Tables" (*The Transatlantic Slave Trade Voyages Database*, 2013) <slavevoyages.org/assessment/estimates> accessed October 27, 2018.
[50] Beckles (n 13) 164–65.

international legal order by European jurists to advance the interests of European actors.

The evolution of international law in this period reveals the intimate connection between the development of a Eurocentric international legal order and the dehumanization of the populations of three continents, racialized chattel enslavement, and exploitation. These legal frameworks did not exist independent of the interests of enslaver states but were a byproduct of them. While the shaky foundations of international law in this period may not provide a positive legal case for reparations today, they do destabilize the assertion that transatlantic enslavement was legal at the time as a denial of the moral case to answer. They change the framing of the wrong, not as a system that already existed with wide acceptance but as an international system deliberately constructed.

On recognizing a foundational wrong, the passage of time alone does not shake an international legal case. There is no set limitation period in international law. Where responsibility is attributed to the ongoing entity of the state rather than to individual enslavers, the obligation remains with the wrongdoer. This is not an abstraction of individual responsibility across generations but the continuation of responsibility of a distinct, continuous entity—the state. However, the recognition of international wrongdoing attributed to the state—even after a significant period of time has passed—is distinct from the question of whether this can be adjudicated by a particular legal body.

The specific construction of international legal mechanisms may prevent claimants from invoking the responsibility of enslaver states in international legal fora. Responsibility may exist without the possibility of a claimant invoking such in an international court. While each potential case must be considered on its own facts, significant barriers to accessing international justice mechanisms exist in addressing historic injustices. In these cases, international legal arguments and the recognition of wrongdoing attributed to the state may nonetheless support the moral and political case for reparations.

How then do the frameworks of international justice apply to the case of transatlantic enslavement? Whether pursued through legal or extralegal mechanisms, the framework of reparatory justice provides a foundation for considering redress in historic cases, including in addressing the history and legacies of transatlantic enslavement. Based on fundamental principles of justice, remedy is an inherent power in the law; *ubi jus, ibi remedium*—where there is a right, there is a remedy. Legal mechanisms have evolved to deliver justice through the reparatory obligation, returning parties to equality, deterring violations, and transforming societies. The new theory of reparatory justice developed in this text provides a framework for considering both whether, and how, historic injustices should be addressed, both within and outside the law.

Questions of whether and how reparations should be made are answered not only by the theory explaining what reparations are for but also by the form they take. Far from a myopic focus on compensation, international law envisages a range of modalities of redress that respond to the various dynamics of wrongdoing—both material and immaterial. The significance of this variety in delivering the objectives of reparatory justice in historic cases should not be overlooked.

Reparatory justice calls for redress proportionate to the nature and extent of the harms caused by the violation. At some point in the causal inquiry, harms become too remote to be the subject of a legal obligation. This test is a consideration of legal policy rather than objective fact; a question of what costs the wrongdoer ought to bear or which justice demands. By expanding the range of possible forms of redress—recognizing symbolic and responsive measures of satisfaction, cessation, and guarantees of non-repetition—the calculus on this fundamental question shifts. What costs a wrongdoer might bear becomes a question of form and not merely of quantum, opening possibilities for appropriate legal redress to be delivered in a wider variety of cases.

In some historic cases, appropriate redress may be limited to acknowledgment of a breach and recognition of responsibility. The norm-affirming nature of reparatory justice in international (and domestic) law supports such decisions, even if distinct, proximate, causally connected contemporary material harm cannot be established. In others, however, the ongoing legacies of the violations may be sufficient to warrant additional positive measures. The principles and practice of reparatory justice in international law—with the potential to deliver deeply responsive forms of redress—may therefore provide a meaningful framework for reparations for transatlantic enslavement.

These frameworks and principles of reparatory justice in international law are relevant both for legal resolution and extralegal processes. The rubric of transitional justice provides important lessons for these alternative solutions. It is in this context that many widespread reparatory justice programs have been adopted and implemented in practice, and thus these frameworks provide guidance to the consideration of transatlantic enslavement. Furthermore, the transitional imperative constructed within the paradigm of metamorphizing authoritarian regimes, moving from conflict to peace, stability, and democracy, offers new lessons for the consideration of the international legal system as a whole. Reconsidering the imperial foundations of the modern international legal system and the ways in which these developed to facilitate enslavement invites a reckoning—a demand for international law to reckon with its own history of violence, exploitation, and expropriation.

Injustice in the present does not occur in a vacuum. As Ana Lucia Araujo articulates:[51]

> In both Africa and the Americas, the Atlantic slave trade and slavery left behind a trail of blood, death, disease, sexual violence, and trauma, experiences that although hard to measure were unquestionably transmitted to later generations. Still today the legacies of these atrocities remain alive in the collective memory of the various populations who were victims of these extreme and complex forms of violence.

The immensity of the injustices associated with the system of transatlantic enslavement and the *maangamizi* could hardly do anything but leave a substantial mark on both world and legal history. The othering and dehumanization of African peoples and their descendants developed to justify enslavement paved the way for decades of racial discrimination up to the present. As Thomas Alenikoff summarizes: "plunder in the past made plunder in the present efficient."[52]

Whether a legal claim for reparations is viable or successful is not the determining factor in establishing the continued existence of legacies of the transatlantic system, nor is it determinative of the moral case. Yet, as a central feature of reparations discourse entailing symbolic signaling functions of its own, a coherent understanding of the law severed from allegiances is crucial to the advancement of the discourse.[53]

The seven chapters of this text cross-examine current legal conclusions and the assumptions on which they are based, work through the relevant international frameworks, and recognize their limitations, opening a space for

[51] Araujo, *Reparations* (n 4) 42–43.

[52] Nehisi-Coates (n 11).

[53] Wenger argues that "remedy and injury are mutually constitutive" and therefore that people do, to some extent, "define injury backward from the existence of a legal remedy." Kaimipono David Wenger, "'Too Big to Remedy?': Rethinking Mass Restitution for Slavery and Jim Crow" (2010) 44 Loyola Los Angeles Law Review 177.

deeper consideration of the demands of reparatory justice in relation to historical enslavement and the *maangamizi.* This does not represent a concluded legal case for or against reparatory justice but rather reconceptualizes the relevant justice frameworks to address reparations claims absent presumptions regarding reparability.

Reparations claims grapple with the history of atrocity permeating not only individual nations but also the international legal order as a whole, deny the attempt to minimize or legitimize brutality solely on the basis of its pervasiveness, and disrupt continuing injustices that find their roots in historical conduct but continue to grow and evolve. If race-neutral approaches "simply postpone our society's inevitable rendezvous with its history of racism," an open and meaningful discussion of historical injustices, their legacies, and the demand for repair serves the opposite purpose.[54] Thus, serious consideration and discussion of redress itself becomes reparatory.

[54] Thomas Alexander Aleinikoff, "A Case for Race-Consciousness" (1991) 91 Columbia Law Review 1060, 1122.

1
From the "Transatlantic Slave Trade" to the *Maangamizi*

Identifying the injustice to which reparations claims speak is necessary to understand their continued relevance in the contemporary world and consider their merits. The narrative of the *maangamizi*—a continuum encompassing chattel, colonial, and neocolonial enslavement—engages reparations activists by echoing their lived experience of the world and their heritage.[1] It speaks to a conceptualization of the wrongs beyond individual interactions between enslavers and enslaved persons, in order to recognize the systematic and structural violence committed against Africans and people of African descent.[2] Irrespective of the language employed to frame demands, the sense of wrongdoing, continuity, collective memory, and pervasive structural harms suffuse reparations discourse.[3]

Several key issues related to the history of enslavement emerge as points of contention in reparations debates. At times, these operate to close off serious consideration of the issue of reparations and overlook the nuances of the case. Comparisons between transatlantic and other historical forms of enslavement, the implications of African complicity, the dynamics of

[1] See Esther Stanford-Xosei, "'Stop the Maangamizi!' Campaign Message" (*Vimeo*, July 3, 2018) <vimeo.com/278175852> accessed October 29, 2018.

[2] Randall Robinson, for instance, speaks of the evisceration of culture, language, religion, and custom in addition to the plunder, rape, and commodification of African people and the destruction of African social and economic institutions—Randall Robinson, "African Americans Are Owed for Years of Bottomness" *LA Times* (Los Angeles, February 6, 2000) <articles.latimes.com/2000/feb/06/opinion/op-61518> accessed October 23, 2018. Maulana Karenga suggests that the Holocaust of transatlantic enslavement expresses itself through the destruction of human life, culture, and possibility—Maulana Karenga, "The Ethics of Reparations: Engaging the Holocaust of Enslavement" (The National Coalition of Blacks for Reparations in America Convention, Baton Rouge, June 2001) <www.ncobraonline.org/wp-content/uploads/2016/02/Karenga-THE-ETHICS-OF-REPARATIONS.pdf> accessed October 23, 2018.

[3] See Boris Bittker, *The Case for Black Reparations* (Beacon Press 2003); Charles P Henry, *Long Overdue: The Politics of Racial Reparations from Forty Acres to Atonement and Beyond* (New York UP 2009); Hilary Beckles, *Britain's Black Debt: Reparations for Caribbean Slavery and Native Genocide* (University of the West Indies Press 2013); J Angelo Corlett, *Heirs of Oppression* (Rowman & Littlefield 2010); Randall Robinson, *The Debt: What America Owes to Blacks* (Dutton 2000); William Kweku Asare, *Slavery Reparations in Perspective* (Trafford 2002).

Reparations for Slavery in International Law. Katarina Schwarz, Oxford University Press. © Oxford University Press 2022.
DOI: 10.1093/oso/9780197636398.003.0002

internationalization and racialization, and the evolution and legacies of transatlantic enslavement shape discussion of the wrong of transatlantic enslavement. These issues structure the foundational understandings of the wrong, thereby framing conclusions on the question of whether reparations are due.

Both reparations proponents and detractors often present these issues as binary phenomena. Either enslavement existed in Africa prior to European expansion, or it was introduced by European enslavers.[4] Either race-based enslavement was constructed by and for the transatlantic system, or it was simply a further example of the alienation that had been used to justify the treatment of human beings as property for millennia.[5] Either the legacies of transatlantic enslavement continue to manifest and impact the lives of contemporary citizens, or it is "in the past" and people should now "move on."[6] Yet, the historical record belies these clear dichotomies. Institutions of exploitation and dependency may be both different and alike in various ways. Africans both participated in and resisted enslavement. Experiences in the past may nonetheless echo in the present.

This chapter contextualizes contemporary reparations claims, working through the history of transatlantic enslavement, unpacking the *maangamizi*, and reconsidering the ways in which injustices were addressed, continued, and reiterated after the formal conclusion of European support for enslavement. It considers the transatlantic system within the long global history of enslavement, not simply as a translation of this record in a specific case but as a sui generis phenomenon characterized by the specific ways the commodification of human beings was accomplished. It explores the complexities of the transatlantic system rather than shying away from them, grappling with the *maangamizi* in its multiple dimensions and in context.

[4] See David Horowitz, "Ten Reasons Why Reparations for Slavery Is a Bad Idea—and Racist Too" (2001) 31(2) The Black Scholar 48. cf Walter Rodney, "African Slavery and Other Forms of Social Oppression on the Upper Guinea Coast in the Context of the Atlantic Slave-Trade" (1966) 2(3) Journal of African History 431.

[5] See, for instance, Nora Wittmann, *Slavery Reparations Time Is Now: Exposing Lies, Claiming Justice for Global Survival, an International Legal Assessment* (Power of the TrInIty Publishers 2013). cf Patterson's recognition of racial differences in systems of enslavement in a "significant number of other societies ranging from the Ethiopians, the Bemba, and even the Lozis of Africa, to the Gilyaks and Lolos of Eastern Asia"—Orlando Patterson, *Slavery and Social Death: A Comparative Study* (Harvard UP 1982) 58.

[6] See, for instance, Corlett (n 3). cf Lord Chesham's statements in the House of Lords debate on reparations in 1996 declaring that the problems of poverty and underdevelopment in Africa have "nothing to do with the slave trade" and that "Slavery has not had the enduring effect claimed for it"—HL Deb, March 14, 1996, vol 570, cols 1057–62.

Dealing with centuries of history, this chapter can present only a brief overview of the complexities of transatlantic enslavement in historical perspective. It provides context for the consideration of international legality and reparability, rather than a comprehensive survey of the history and legacies of transatlantic enslavement. It should therefore be taken as an introduction to the complexities and specificities of the *maangamizi*—the foundational wrongs on which claims to reparations are built. The threshold condition for reparatory justice—the injustice of transatlantic enslavement and the *maangamizi*—is thereby engaged.

1.1. The limits of the long record of enslavement

Enslavement infuses human history. From ancient Greece, Rome, and the Near East to the Sassanian, Abyssinian, and Akkadian Empires, from the first "global economies" in the Indian Ocean and Asian worlds to early Islamic law, Hindu Rajyas, medieval Korea, and early Christianity, systems of enslavement are well documented.[7] Systems of enslavement took root in Mesopotamia as early as the third millennia BCE.[8] In the ancient Near East, from a very early period, persons were, and could be, bought and sold within a framework fitting the "traditional definition of slavery," involving the imposition of social death and dishonor.[9] In ancient Rome, mass enslavement and the growth of the "slave society" took root in the third century BCE and escalated rapidly in the second to reach between 20 and 30 percent of the population by the late first century BCE.[10] In ancient Greece, the "slave trade was everywhere," both physically and ideologically, and enslavement,

[7] See Gad Heuman and Trevor Burnard (eds), *The Routledge History of Slavery* (Routledge 2011); Patterson (n 5). On slavery in ancient Greece, Rome, and the Near East see Keith Bradley (ed), *The Cambridge World History of Slavery: The Ancient Mediterranean World*, vol I (CUP 2011); Niall McKeown, "Greek and Roman Slavery" in Nicolas Ralph Edmund Fisher, *Slavery in Classical Greece* (Bristol Classical Press 1993); Nicolas Fisher, *Slavery in Classical Greece* (Bristol Classical Press 1993). On slavery in Asia, see Anthony Reid, *Slavery, Bondage and Dependency in Southeast Asia* (University of Queensland Press 1983); James Watson (ed), *Asian and African Systems of Slavery* (University of California Press 1980). On Islamic law of slavery, see Bernard Freamon, "Definitions and Conceptions of Slave Ownership in Islamic Law" in Jean Allain (ed), *The Legal Understanding of Slavery: From the Historical to the Contemporary* (OUP 2012). On slavery in early Christianity, see Jennifer Glancy, *Slavery in Early Christianity* (OUP 2002).

[8] Jack Goody, "Slavery in Time and Space" in Watson (n 7) 18.

[9] Daniel Snell, "Slavery in the Ancient Near East" in Bradley (n 7) 4–5.

[10] This equated to a figure of 1 to 1.5 million enslaved persons in a population of 5 to 6 million. Sandra Joshel, *Slavery in the Roman World* (CUP 2010) 55–56.

"slave-trading," and the commodification of human beings were normalized practices.[11]

Seldom does a text considering the history of enslavement conclude without reference to the prevalence of the institution of slavery at every stage of human history. It is this historical ubiquity that led David Eltis and Stanley Engerman to argue that it is the paradigm of free labor not enslavement that constitutes the historical exception, with institutionalized coercive relationships representing the norm until the twentieth century.[12]

The historical ubiquity of enslavement fuels challenges to reparations claims. If enslavement existed across the world as a widely accepted practice throughout history, then the assertion that this represented wrongdoing is undermined. From this argument arises the suggestion that reparations advocates are engaged in "presentism"—applying the moral standards of the present to a past that followed a different set of rules.[13] A second core criticism also flows from the historical comparison that recognizing a reparatory obligation for transatlantic enslavement would open the floodgates to an infinite stream of historical cases.[14]

In the first instance, it is important to recognize that comparison is not the test of justiciability. Analogy to other instances of enslavement in the historical record does not determine the reparatory obligation, which is to be assessed against legal frameworks in place at the time on the facts of the case at hand. While evidence of widespread practice may speak to the crystallization of international norms (addressed in chapter 2), it does not in itself determine the rightful or wrongful character of conduct in legal (or moral) terms.

"Floodgates" arguments are likewise not automatically determinative. Nonetheless, they may influence considerations of causation in law (addressed in chapter 6). Furthermore, other factors may operate to limit the flood of historical claims or reduce the cost of such—including specificities of the case, manifestation of contemporary harms, and potential for various

11 David Braund, "The Slave Supply in Classical Greece" in Bradley (n 7) 112–13.

12 David Eltis and Stanley Engerman, "Dependence, Servility, and Coerced Labour" in David Eltis and Stanley Engerman (eds), *The Cambridge World History of Slavery*, vol 3 (CUP 2011) 3.

13 See, for instance, Max du Plessis, "Historical Injustice and International Law: An Exploratory Discussion of Reparation for Slavery" (2003) 25(3) Human Rights Quarterly 624, 634–37; Peter Flaherty and John Carlisle, "United States' Payout for Slave Reparations Not Warranted" in Maria Tenaglia-Webster (ed), *Slavery* (Greenhaven Press 2009).

14 See, for instance, Flaherty and Carlisle (n 13); Gorman Beauchamp, "Apologies All Around: Today's Tendency to Make Amends for the Crimes of History Raises the Question: Where Do We Stop?" (2007) 76(4) The American Scholar 83.

modalities of redress that respond to ongoing harms. The positioning of these arguments as barriers to careful consideration of claims to reparations for transatlantic enslavement is therefore misplaced.

In assessing the case for reparations for transatlantic enslavement on its own facts and merits, it is necessary to consider the specificities of the case in historical perspective. In other words, the history of transatlantic enslavement must be examined with attention to the factors that differentiate it from other historical instances of enslavement as well as those that are shared. Enslavement's occupation of the historical record does not close off the possibility for different manifestations of the institution to exist in different cases.

Despite the apparent universality of enslavement as a "recurrent historical dialectic," different forms of exploitation have manifested in different contexts at different times.[15] As Pierre Dockès suggests,

> The nature of slavery changes from one period of history to another, and, within a given period, it varies from one region to the next. Even in one particular spot at one moment in time, quite different kinds of slaves are found.[16]

Equating all other institutions of enslavement with the system of transatlantic enslavement can be misleading, particularly where evidence suggests that other regimes of enslavement and servitude did not resemble the transatlantic system.[17] Thus, the long history of enslavement should not automatically be taken as an argument in favor of treating all historical systems as synonymous. The starting point for consideration should not be a presumption of analogy but an exploration of the nature of the system in question, albeit within the context of the longer history.

It is clear from the historical record that the commodification of human beings was not a new phenomenon in Africa when the Portuguese began their involvement in raids and kidnappings in Senegambia in the fifteenth

[15] Joseph Miller, "Slaving as an Historical Process: Examples from the Ancient Mediterranean and the Modern Atlantic" in Enrico Dal Lago and Constantina Katsari (eds), *Slave Systems: Ancient and Modern* (CUP 2008) 70.

[16] Pierre Dockès, *Medieval Slavery and Liberation* (Arthur Goldhammer tr, University of Chicago Press 1982) 49.

[17] Campbell and Alpers, for instance, argue that regimes of servitude and enslavement in Indian Ocean Africa and Asia "varied greatly both geographically and over time, rarely approximating to the image of New World plantation slavery except in a few sectors"—Gwyn Campbell and Edward Alpers, "Slavery, Forced Labour and Resistance in Indian Ocean Africa and Asia" (2004) 25(2) Slavery and Abolition ix, x.

century.[18] Paul Lovejoy suggests that enslavement within Africa, including indigenous practices enabling the buying and selling of human beings, predates documented history and was ubiquitous on the continent as it was elsewhere in the world.[19] JJ Crooks supports this characterization of African enslavement as an ancient institution without reference to the transatlantic system.[20] JD Fage notes that the earliest European accounts of the West African coast often mention enslaved persons being offered in trade, suggesting that African societies already included an enslaved population that could be subjected to transfer.[21]

In these contexts, Lovejoy asserts that enslaved persons were treated not only as economic assets but also as social and political capital.[22] Suzanne Miers and Igor Kopytoff characterize enslaved persons as the "currency of political transaction," used as tributes for chiefs, gifts between rulers, and rewards to subordinates.[23] This political positioning of servile laborers is reflected in early relations between African political leaders and Europeans, wherein enslaved persons were included in the gifts bestowed upon travelers and sent across the seas to European rulers.[24] Furthermore, legal or legitimate paths to enslavement were recognized—primarily for captives taken in war and those found to have committed grave crimes.[25] These persons might then be traded, bought, sold, and exploited as if they were property.

Yet, the degree to which international institutions of dependency and exploitation within the African continent could be classified as directly analogous to the form of chattel enslavement that characterized the transatlantic system is contested. Although various forms of servility, including

[18] Ana Lucia Araujo, *Reparations for Slavery and the Slave Trade: A Transnational and Comparative History* (Bloomsbury Academic 2017) 15.

[19] Paul Lovejoy, "Slavery in Africa" in Heuman and Burnard (n 7).

[20] JJ Crooks, *A History of the Colony of Sierra Leone, Western Africa* (reprint, Brown & Nolan 1903).

[21] JD Fage, "Slaves and Society in Western Africa, c. 1445–c. 1700" (1980) 21 Journal of African History 289, 297. Fage highlights the consistency of early European accounts identifying enslaved persons as a social category in Africa in support of the conclusion of enslavement's indigeneity, highlighting the lack of existing literature and related stereotypical associations of Africa with enslavement available to influence these writers' assessments. However, this fails to acknowledge the infusion of such ideas from the Muslim world that occurred during the medieval period considered further in section 1.5.

[22] Lovejoy highlights the fact that "slavery was integrated into the political economy and social structures of African society" prior to European expansion. Lovejoy, "Slavery in Africa" (n 19) 38.

[23] Suzanne Miers and Igor Kopytoff, *Slavery in Africa: Historical and Anthropological Perspectives* (University of Wisconsin Press 1977).

[24] See, for instance, Linda M Heywood, "Slavery and Its Transformation in the Kingdom of Kongo: 1491–1800" (2009) 50(1) The Journal of African History 1.

[25] See PEH Hair, "Sources on Early Sierra Leone: Barreira on Just Enslavement, 1606" (1975) 6 Africana Research Bulletin 52, 67. On legitimate pathways to enslavement, see further section 2.4.

enslavement, existed in West Africa prior to the arrival of Europeans in the region, their presence alone does not speak to its extent, character, or dynamics.[26] In particular, the reports of early European travelers should not be considered conclusive in determining the nature of indigenous institutions, for they often risked conflating other forms of servility, and relationships of dependency, with enslavement.[27]

Several commentators suggest that the nature of African relationships of dependency and forms of servile labor were fundamentally different from those that developed within the transatlantic system. Joseph Inikori asserts that the characterization of indigenous forms of dependency as enslavement mislabels these social relationships, which are better described using local language.[28] Hilary Beckles contends that indigenous forms of enslavement did not represent a legal categorization of a person as nonhuman, perpetual property, or reproductive chattel.[29] Nora Wittmann suggests that African forms of servile labor cannot be treated as synonymous with enslavement within the transatlantic system.[30] Ali Mazrui goes further to contend that the transatlantic system and enslavement in the Americas were comparable neither to domestic enslavement within Africa prior to European involvement nor to the trans-Saharan system and enslavement in the Muslim Arab world.[31] However, others see little to differentiate trans-Saharan from transatlantic enslavement and argue that any divergence in the degree of abuse does not erase the wrongs of Islamic enslavement of Africans.[32]

Distinctions between indigenous African forms of enslavement and the transatlantic system focus not only on the nature of exploitation in the individual case but also on the placement of the institution in the broader societal context. Paul Lovejoy suggests that although enslavement was one of the many forms of dependency that existed in precolonial Africa, this was essentially a social feature rather than a central economic institution.[33] That servile relationships were embedded in kinship-based societies, wherein

[26] G Ugo Nwokeji, "Slavery in Non-Islamic West Africa, 1420–1820" in Eltis and Engerman (n 12) 81.

[27] ibid 82–83.

[28] Joseph Inikori, "Slavery in Africa and the Transatlantic Slave Trade" in Alusine Jalloh and Stephen Maizlish (eds), *The African Diaspora* (Texas A&M UP 1996) 39–40.

[29] Beckles (n 3) 18.

[30] Wittmann (n 5).

[31] Ali Mazrui, *Black Reparations in the Era of Globalization* (Institute of Global Cultural Studies 2002).

[32] See Wole Soyinka, *The Burden of Memory, the Muse of Forgiveness* (OUP 1999) 53–55. The exact dynamics of the trans-Saharan system are beyond the scope of this text.

[33] Paul Lovejoy, *Transformations in Slavery: A History of Slavery in Africa* (CUP 2011) 13.

political influence was connected to the size of social groupings, is central to this positioning, with the "acquisition" of persons closely related to this demand.[34] Despite the potential for commodification of human beings in these contexts—enslaved persons could be, and in fact were, bought, sold, and otherwise treated as a form of property—the social structures in which these relationships were embedded are identified as increasing the likelihood of integration into the kinship unit over time.[35] Furthermore, commentators suggest that enslaved persons in these contexts were much more likely to be treated as a part of the family unit, their children were less likely to be automatically enslaved, and there were greater restrictions on the treatment of dependents than there were in the context of economically motivated transatlantic enslavement.[36]

Despite these professed distinctions, to deny the history of African forms of enslavement misrepresents the historical record. Although these relationships of dependency may, in general, have been less severe than the brutalities of the transatlantic system, they nonetheless involved the commodification of human beings, descent-based social stratification, othering and marginalization (including social death), and acquisition through violence in a range of instances.[37] However, the contextual investigation of these indigenous institutions reveals a further distinction with regard to their positioning in society and the way this changed as the transatlantic system took root.

Moses Finley frames this transformation as a fundamental shift in the way enslavement was embedded in social formations; a metamorphosis that may be characterized as the transformation of African states from societies in which enslavement existed to "genuine slave societies" wherein enslavement operated as the foundation of socioeconomic structures.[38] While there were some preexisting institutions in place enabling enslavement, it was the pull

[34] ibid.

[35] See ibid 12–13.

[36] Walter Rodney argues that these African forms of enslavement involved the inclusion of the enslaved person as a member of the master's household, protection from sale except in the case of serious offenses having been committed, rights to a proportion of their own labor and often their own plots of land, the ability to marry, rights of inheritance for their children, and a distinct status for children born of one free parent—Rodney (n 4) 431–32.

[37] Miller confirms that men, women, and children in West Central Africa were considered and treated as capital at least as early as the fifteenth century—Joseph Miller, *Way of Death: Merchant Capitalism and the Angolan Slave Trade, 1740–1830* (University of Wisconsin Press 1988) 42–43.

[38] Moses Finley, *Ancient Slavery and Modern Ideology* (expanded edn, Brent D Shaw ed, Markus Wiener Publishers 1998) 271–75. See also Noel Lemski and Catherine M Cameron (eds), *What Is a Slave Society? The Practice of Slavery in Global Perspective* (CUP 2018).

of the European market that drove this transformation, shifting indigenous practices premised on kinship relationships into institutions based on the role of enslavement in the larger economy.[39]

While other forms of enslavement may have predated the transatlantic system, other features of this system may speak to its unique character. In this view, it is not the discrete or individualized nature of the experience of enslavement that is brought to the fore, but the manifestation of transatlantic enslavement as a system. The European Union in 2007 separated transatlantic enslavement from the thousands of years of exploitation preceding it, recognizing it as distinguishable in scale, character, and context:

> The barbarism of the transatlantic slave trade stands out in the history of humanity in terms of its magnitude, organised nature and especially its negation of the human dignity of the victims. While Europe was pioneering the Age of Reason and Enlightenment, European merchants took off to enslave the African continent.[40]

This perspective promulgated by European states, including those most deeply implicated in the transatlantic system, is consistent with the characterization of transatlantic enslavement as a "dark chapter" in the historical record that stands out from those surrounding it; rhetoric echoed by political actors and scholars alike.[41] It therefore calls for examination of these features of transatlantic enslavement in considering the specific injustices of this

[39] Lovejoy, *Transformations* (n 33) 18. Likewise, Nora Wittmann concludes that it was European involvement in the continent that changed the nature of African systems of servile labor—Wittmann (n 5) 10–139. See also Inikori (n 28); Joseph Inikori (ed), *Forced Migration: The Impact of the Export Slave Trade on African Societies* (Hutchinson & Co 1982); ; Rodney (n 4).

[40] "Declaration by the Presidency on behalf of the EU on the commemoration of the 200th anniversary of the abolition of the transatlantic slave trade" (Brussels, March 26, 2007) P/07/23; 7735/1/07 Rev 1 (Presse 60) <europa.eu/rapid/press-release_PESC-07-23_en.htm> accessed October 25, 2018.

[41] The following paragraph of the Declaration specifically frames the period of transatlantic enslavement as a "dark chapter" in history—this is echoed throughout many public statements, academic commentaries, and political addressed on the topic. Baroness Amos, for instance, then Leader of the UK House of Lords, in 2007 labeled transatlantic enslavement "one of the darkest and most uncomfortable chapters in British history"—Alexis Akwagyiram, "Poignant Site to Remember Slave Trade" *BBC News* (March 26, 2007) <news.bbc.co.uk/1/hi/uk/6494097.stm> accessed October 25, 2018. The Mayor of Nantes, Jean-Marc Ayrault in 2012 echoed this language—Stefan Simons, "French City Confronts Its Brutal Past" *Spiegel Online* (Nantes, April 24, 2012) <www.spiegel.de/international/europe/nantes-opens-memorial-to-slave-trade-a-829447.html> accessed October 25, 2018. The Danish Foreign Minister also employed this language—Astrid Nonbo Andersen, "'We Have Reconquered the Islands': Figurations in Public Memories of Slavery and Colonialism in Denmark 1948–2012" (2013) 26(1) International Journal of Politics, Culture and Society 57.

case—looking beyond the comparison of the nature of enslavement at the individual level, to assess the system as a whole.

1.2. The internationalization of enslavement

Transatlantic enslavement has been described as the "largest forced migration in human history," with Europe charged with a key role in the intense growth in African enslavement during this period.[42] Scale itself is therefore presented as a fundamental characteristic of the transatlantic system. The extent to which people were enslaved, bought, sold, forcibly migrated, and exploited is substantially different in the comparative between precolonial Africa and the period of transatlantic enslavement. Prior to both Islamic and European expansion within the African continent, slavery was marginal.[43] At the beginning of the sixteenth century, Africans and people of African descent represented only a minority of the global enslaved population.[44] However, by the opening of eighteenth century, they constituted a substantial majority.[45]

In the early years of European exploration of West Africa, there was little demand within Europe for enslaved persons and trade with Africa was predominantly focused on gold and ivory.[46] Imperial expansion into the continent was limited, with the primary incursion into African territories being the establishment of trading stations along the coast.[47] Thus, prior to the fifteenth century, Europe exerted little influence over the nature and extent of African institutions of enslavement.[48] This changed dramatically with European "discovery" of the Americas, at which point the exploration of the African coastline and existing trade relationships opened the gateway

[42] See Johannes Postma, *The Atlantic Slave Trade* (ABC-CLIO Inc 2003); Jon F Sensbach, "Charting a Course in Early African-American History" (1993) 50(2) The William and Mary Quarterly 394, 399; Ronaldo Munck, "Slavery: Exception or Rule?" in Gillian Wylie and Penelope McRedmond (eds), *Human Trafficking in Europe: Character, Causes and Consequences* (Palgrave Macmillan 2010).

[43] Lovejoy, *Transformations* (n 33) 21; Nwokeji (n 26) 86. See also Manning, highlighting the limits of internal African markets and institutions on the numbers of persons internally enslaved—Patrick Manning, "Why Africans? The Rise of the Slave Trade to 1700" in Gad Heuman and James Walvin (eds), *The Slavery Reader* (Routledge 2003).

[44] Manning, "Why Africans?" (n 43) 32. See also Lovejoy, *Transformations* (n 33).

[45] ibid.

[46] JD Fage, *Introduction to the History of West Africa* (CUP 1955) 48.

[47] ibid.

[48] See Lovejoy, *Transformations* (n 33) 11; Fage, *Introduction* (n 46) 39.

for the establishment of commercial relations between West Africa and the Americas.[49]

European expansion into the Americas drove the demand for enslaved Africans.[50] Initially, processes of European colonial domination were imposed upon indigenous populations in the Americas, including the extraction of enslaved labor throughout the sixteenth century.[51] However, indigenous resistance, disease, and competition with the Jesuits seeking to convert local populations resulted in the depletion of local sources of coerced labor, creating a gap to be filled through the importation of an external labor force.[52] Thus, international demand fueled the rise in the enslavement and forced migration of Africans. The growth and evolution of African servile institutions correlated with European incursions into the African continent in conjunction with expansion in the Americas.

The number of enslaved persons forcibly migrated from West Africa to the Americas by European actors speaks to the exponential rise of enslavement alongside the development of the transatlantic system. In the first five years of the sixteenth century, only an estimated 950 enslaved persons were transported on voyages within the transatlantic system.[53] In just under three centuries, this number rose to over 500,000 enslaved persons transported from the African coast to the Americas on vessels flying European flags within a five-year period (see Figure 1.1).[54] While these numbers do not speak to the extent to which internal enslavement preceded the transatlantic system, they do indicate the degree of European involvement in enslavement and forced migration on a massive scale and significantly increasing over time.

Although it is impossible to accurately calculate the number of enslaved persons transported from Africa to the Americas, or the total number

[49] See Daniel Mannix, *Black Cargoes: A History of the Atlantic Slave Trade, 1518–1865* (Longmans, Green and Co 1962).

[50] JD Fage, "Slavery and the Slave Trade in the Context of West African History" (1969) 10(3) Journal of African History 393.

[51] Patrick Manning highlights the "first impulse" of Spanish in the Americas as the enslavement of Native Americans; however, high mortality rates and continuing "hope of escape made them unsatisfactory slaves." Manning, "Why Africans?" (n 43) 33.

[52] John Monteiro, "From Indian to Slave: Forced Native Labour and Colonial Society in São Paulo During the Seventeenth Century" in Patrick Manning (ed), *Slave Trades, 1500–1800: Globalization of Forced Labour* (Variorum 1996) 110–11.

[53] These 950 enslaved persons were transported from Senegambia and the off-shore Atlantic, although only 670 of those persons would arrive at their destinations in the Spanish Americas.

[54] From 1786 to 1790, an estimated 505,335 people were embarked upon transatlantic voyages, with an estimated 63,433 of those people never disembarking—these figures also include persons transported on ships under US flags, from 1641 onward.

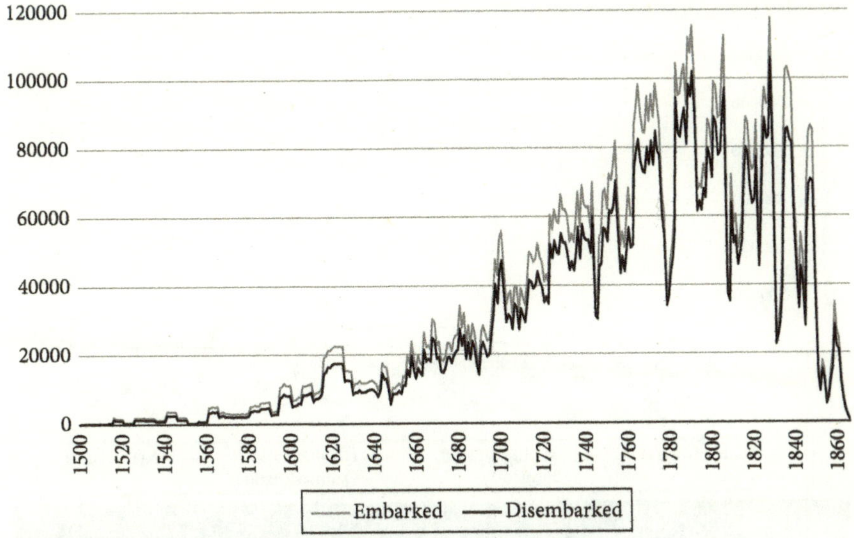

Figure 1.1 Number of captives embarked and disembarked per year

Figure created with data from Emory University, "Timeline: Number of Captives Embarked and Disembarked per Year" (*The Transatlantic Slave Trade Voyages Database*, 2013) <slavevoyages.org/assessment/estimates> accessed October 27, 2018.

enslaved within American colonies, the Transatlantic Slave Trade Database provides substantial insights into the flows of the transatlantic system and those states embedded within it.[55] These estimates reveal the scale of forced migration and the significance of European involvement in the enslavement of African people. Dutch ships participated in the forced transport and exploitation of over half-a-million African people. Spanish and French ships were responsible for over a million each, British for over three million, and Portuguese for almost six million (see Figure 1.2). Twelve million Africans were taken from their homeland to lives of grueling labor and brutality at the hands of predominantly European masters. Almost all of these individuals, and millions of their descendants, would die on foreign shores without ever experiencing freedom from their enslavement.

[55] David Eltis, David Richardson, Stephen Behrendt, and Manolo Garcia Florentino were the main contributors to the online database, which expands upon an earlier compilation. The database includes around 80 percent of all voyages occurring within the transatlantic system and thus produces robust estimates—David Richardson, "Involuntary Migration in the Early Modern World, 1500–1800" in Eltis and Engerman (n 12) 572.

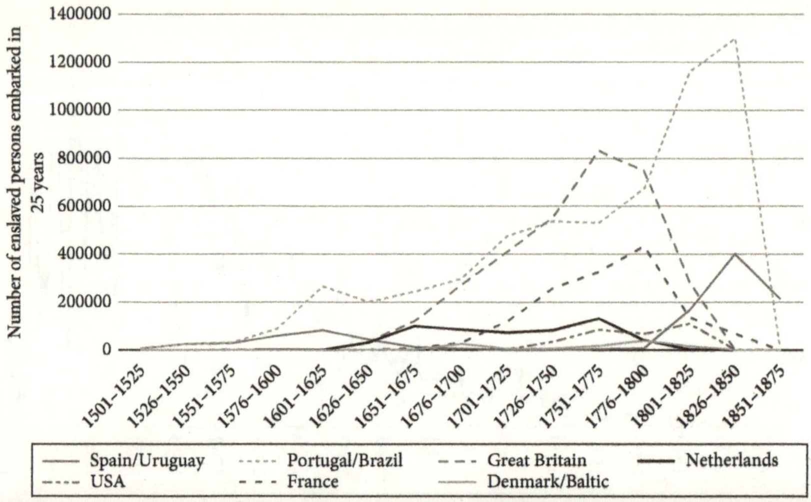

	Spain / Uruguay	Portugal / Brazil	Great Britain	Netherlands	USA	France	Denmark / Baltic	Totals
1501–1525	6363	7000	0	0	0	0	0	13363
1526–1550	25375	25387	0	0	0	0	0	50762
1551–1575	28167	31089	1685	0	0	66	0	61007
1576–1600	60056	90715	237	1365	0	0	0	152373
1601–1625	83496	267519	0	1829	0	0	0	352844
1626–1650	44313	201609	33695	31729	824	1827	1053	315050
1651–1675	12601	244793	122367	100526	0	7125	653	488065
1676–1700	5860	297272	272200	85847	3327	29484	25685	719675
1701–1725	0	474447	410597	73816	3277	120939	5833	1088909
1726–1750	0	536696	554042	83095	34004	259095	4793	1471725
1751–1775	4239	528693	832047	132330	84580	325918	17508	1925315
1776–1800	6415	673167	748612	40773	67443	433061	39199	2008670
1801–1825	168087	1160601	283959	2669	109545	135815	16316	1876992
1826–1850	400728	1299969	0	357	1850	68074	0	1770978
1851–1875	215824	9309	0	0	476	0	0	225609
Totals	1061524	5848266	3259441	554336	305326	1381404	111040	12521337

Figure 1.2 Embarkations by flag country of transporting ships

Figure created with data from Emory University, "Estimates Tables" (*The Transatlantic Slave Trade Voyages Database*, 2013) <slavevoyages.org/assessment/estimates> accessed October 27, 2018.

Not all of the twelve million Africans extracted from the continent would make it through the voyage itself. Almost two million African people forced onto European ships would never make it to the Americas. The marked difference between embarkation and disembarkation figures testifies to the conditions on board vessels traveling from Africa to the Americas (see Figure 1.1 and comparison between Figures 1.2 and 1.3), supported by firsthand accounts of the conditions in which enslaved persons were kept during these journeys. Olaudah Equiano, accounting his

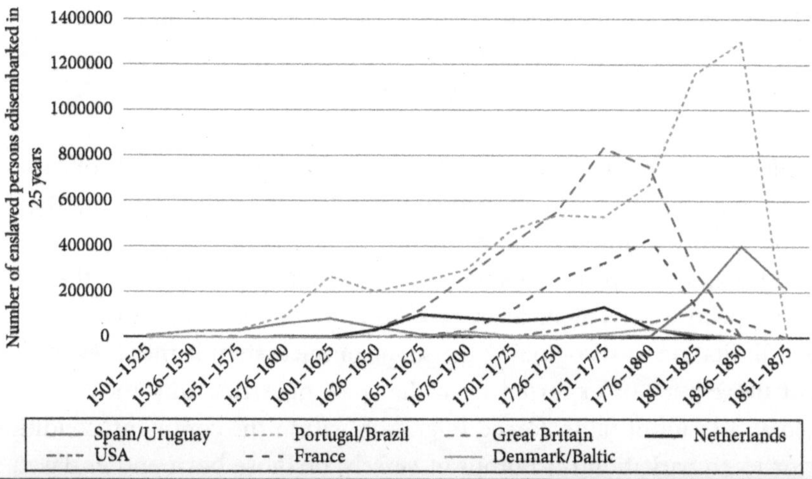

	Spain/ Uruguay	Portugal /Brazil	Great Britain	Netherlands	U.S.A.	France	Denmark /Baltic	Totals
1501–1525	4462	4914	0	0	0	0	0	9376
1526–1550	17763	17771	0	0	0	0	0	35534
1551–1575	19720	22174	1188	0	0	50	0	43132
1576–1600	42037	67879	168	1160	0	0	0	111244
1601–1625	58445	214808	0	1577	0	0	0	274830
1626–1650	31422	166017	26315	26106	702	1479	836	252877
1651–1675	9464	209690	93209	81918	0	5456	544	400281
1676–1700	4670	261523	208431	74878	2548	22265	20374	594689
1701–1725	0	421232	339007	62477	2612	95357	3882	924567
1726–1750	0	470236	455284	71268	27500	216213	3820	1244321
1751–1775	3634	476596	682454	117855	70624	278479	14711	1644353
1776–1800	5601	623298	673590	35202	56601	369121	33215	1796628
1801–1825	151367	1037342	253678	2475	89990	117969	14351	1667172
1826–1850	354813	1099018	0	324	1662	58579	0	1514396
1851–1875	181526	7318	0	0	413	0	0	189257
Totals	884924	5099816	2733324	475240	252652	1164968	91733	10702657

Figure 1.3 Disembarkations by flag country of transporting ships
Figure created with data from Emory University, "Estimates Tables" (*The Transatlantic Slave Trade Voyages Database*, 2013) <slavevoyages.org/assessment/estimates> accessed October 27, 2018.

own experience on board such a vessel, describes the conditions in the following passage:

> The closeness of the place, and the heat of the climate, added to the number in the ship, which was so crowded that each had scarcely room to turn himself, almost suffocated us. This produced copious perspirations, so that the air soon became unfit for respiration, from a variety of loathsome smells, and brought on a sickness among the slaves, of which many died—thus

> falling victims to the improvident avarice, as I may call it, of their purchasers . . . The shrieks of the women, and the groans of the dying, rendered the whole a scene of horror almost inconceivable.[56]

While some were driven to commit suicide rather than live a life of enslavement on a foreign continent, many more fell to the unsanitary, unsafe, and brutal conditions imposed upon them.[57]

These figures explain the scale of the transatlantic system and the extent of European involvement in the enslavement of millions of Africans. Yet, their limitation in recognizing the scope of the system is that they only report those persons exported from the coast of Africa and not those who died as a result of raids, forced migration within the continent, conditions prior to embarkation on European vessels, or those born and enslaved in the Americas.[58] Thus, they do not reveal in specific detail the ebbs and flows of the transatlantic system as a whole. However, they do speak to the widespread involvement of Britain, France, the Netherlands, Portugal, Denmark, and the newly independent United States in the dramatic expansion of enslavement of African people, the forced migration of twelve million Africans, and the deaths of two million through transportation alone. The scale of these voyages further signals the impact of transatlantic enslavement on the African continent.

1.3. The transformation of African "supply" to meet external demand

Significant structural changes occurred within African societies as a result of European demand for enslaved Africans to be imported to the Americas. Various forms of political, economic, and military manipulation were employed by European actors to facilitate these shifts. As the transatlantic system grew, enslavement and relationships with Europe became so central

[56] Olaudah Equiano, *The Interesting Narrative of the Life of Olaudah Equiano, or Gustavus Vassa, The African* (8th edn, Norwich 1794) 51–52.

[57] See Richard H Steckel and Richard A Jensen, "New Evidence on the Causes of Slave and Crew Mortality in the Atlantic Slave Trade" (1986) 46(1) Journal of Economic History 57.

[58] Lovejoy suggests that perhaps as many enslaved persons as were exported in the transatlantic and Muslim systems combined never left the continent, many of whom having died in the processes of enslavement, internal migration, and captivity that preceded export—Lovejoy, *Transformations* (n 33) 63.

to internal African politics that the emergence, rise, and decline of African states was closely associated with the transatlantic system. African societies that engaged in the external trade in enslaved persons with Europe achieved political ascendancy over time.[59] The superiority of arms gained by trading with Europeans enabled enslaver states to overwhelm their neighbors, with the result that participation in the transatlantic system soon became necessary for survival in the region.[60] Thus, the commercial organization of relationships between Europe, Africa, and the Americas drove military operations, which in turn fed the trade in enslaved persons.[61]

Conflict was the primary source of enslaved persons for export, creating direct and cyclical relationships between enslavement and warfare within Africa.[62] The increasing conflict in West and West Central Africa and growing demand for enslaved labor in the Americas created insecurity not only between African societies but also within them.[63] Where previously foreign prisoners of war satisfied the bulk of internal demand (protecting freeborn subjects), the transatlantic system created significant risks of internal capture and enslavement.[64] Instability within African societies was thus driven by the transatlantic system, and the cycle of violence paved the way for further European incursion, and sustained presence, in the region.[65]

Where the opening of the sixteenth century saw both African enslavement and European involvement in the continent as marginal, the end of the nineteenth marked the enslavement of over twelve million people and almost the entirety of West Africa ruled by European governments.[66] The path to colonial domination was paved by the system of transatlantic chattel enslavement and the substantial impact this had upon African societies and political

[59] Robin Law, *The Slave Coast of West Africa 1550–1750: The Impact of the Atlantic Slave Trade on an African Society* (Clarendon Press 1991); Lovejoy, *Transformations* (n 33) 22.

[60] The King of Kongo, Nzinga Nkuwu, for instance, accepted a Portuguese alliance involving supplying captive Africans in exchange for European military assistance to wage war against neighboring kingdoms, as well as conversion to Catholicism—John K Thornton, *A Cultural History of the Atlantic World, 1250–1820* (CUP 2010) 183. See also Toby Green, *The Rise of the Trans-Atlantic Slave Trade in Western Africa, 1300–1589* (CUP 2012).

[61] Linda Heywood and John Thornton, *Central Africans, Atlantic Creoles, and the Foundation of the Americas, 1585–1660: The First Generation of African Americans in North America and the Caribbean, 1619–1660* (CUP 2007). See also Jean Allain, *Slavery in International Law: Of Human Exploitation and Trafficking* (Martinus Nijhoff 2013) 63.

[62] See Toby Green, "Cycles of War and Trade in the African Atlantic, circa 1550–1580" in Green (n 60).

[63] Walter Hawthorne, *From Africa to Brazil: Culture, Identity, and an Atlantic Slave Trade, 1600–1830* (CUP 2010) 64.

[64] Araujo (n 18) 15.

[65] ibid 42.

[66] Fage, *Introduction* (n 46) 39.

structures.[67] The destabilization of West African political institutions in particular served as an entry point for colonial administration.[68] The significance of transatlantic enslavement on African politics culminated in the fact and ubiquity of enslavement within Africa being used as an indicator of a lack of civilization after European abolitionism had taken hold, justifying European division of African territories.[69]

During the period of transatlantic enslavement, indigenous and internal slaveries existed alongside the transatlantic and trans-Saharan systems and expanded as a result of the influence of these external markets.[70] The number of persons enslaved within the continent increased dramatically, driven in large part by the growth of the transatlantic system.[71] Enslaved persons not purchased by Europeans remained captive on the continent and in general were utilized for the economic gain of their (typically) African captors.[72] John Matthews' eighteenth-century account describes "slave towns" of up to 1,000 enslaved inhabitants ruled by Mandinga chiefs on the Upper Guinea Coast.[73] Other contemporary accounts suggest that these collectives of enslaved persons also existed in other West African areas.[74] Thus, the significance of enslavement within Africa changed dramatically from its prior marginal positioning, creating an internal population of millions of enslaved persons.[75]

[67] See Warren Whatley, "The Transatlantic Slave Trade and the Evolution of Political Authority in West Africa" (2012) IDEAS Working Paper Series from RePEc <ideas.repec.org/p/pra/mprapa/44932.html> accessed October 29, 2018. This is discussed further in section 1.4.

[68] ibid.

[69] JF Ade Ajayi, "The Policy of Reparation in the Context of Globalization" (2004) 173–74 African Studies Papers 41 <journals.openedition.org/etudesafricaines/4524> accessed October 31, 2018.

[70] Nwokeji (n 26). In relation to the scale of the trans-Saharan system of enslavement, Austen estimates that over five million enslaved Africans were transported to the Muslim world—Ralph Austen, "The Mediterranean Islamic Slave Trade out of Africa: A Tentative Census" in Elizabeth Savage (ed), *The Human Commodity: Perspectives on the Trans-Saharan Slave Trade* (Frank Cass 1992); Ralph Austen, "The Trans-Saharan Slave Trade: A Tentative Census" in Henry Gemery and Jan Hogendorn (eds), *The Uncommon Market: Essays in the Economic History of the Atlantic Slave Trade* (Academic Press 1979).

[71] Roquinaldo Ferreira, "Slaving and Resistance to Slaving in West Central Africa" in Eltis and Engerman (n 12).

[72] Rodney (n 4) 435.

[73] John Matthews, *A Voyage to the River Sierra Leone* (B White & Son 1788).

[74] See, for instance, AG Laing, *Travels in the Timammee, Kooranko and Soolima Countries* (William Clowes, Northumberland Court 1825) 221.; P Marty, "Islam in French Guinea" (1936) 29 Sierra Leone Studies 49.

[75] Patrick Manning suggests that this internal population rivaled or outstripped the Muslim system and "reached a volume of at least half" that of the transatlantic system—Patrick Manning, *Slavery and African Life* (CUP 1990) 41. This should be contrasted against the marginal position of slavery in African society identified in sections 1.2 and 1.3.

The boom in demand for enslaved persons also altered the initial processes of enslavement, through the extension of existing mechanisms and development of new methods to enslave free people.[76] This included the expansion of warfare as a key means of producing enslaved persons as well as decreasing the threshold for enslavement through other established pathways. As Francis Moore identified in the early eighteenth century, the development of external "trade" resulted in all punishments being changed to enslavement, where previously this would only have been attached to more serious offenses.[77]

Internal violence proliferated, and previously uncommon or unknown pathways to enslavement were developed to meet external demand.[78] Raids and razzias became substantially more common, involving subjecting those who could not be legally or legitimately enslaved to captivity.[79] Outside influences shaped this transformation, yet it was generally internal actors that rose to meet external demand. The role of these African participants in the enslavement of Africans should not be overlooked in considering the system of transatlantic enslavement from a holistic perspective.

1.4. The controversy of African complicity

African involvement in the capture, commodification, and forced migration of enslaved African people is one of the most fraught issues in the consideration of the historical record of transatlantic enslavement. It is often framed as crucial to the question of whether a contemporary reparatory obligation exists.[80] The very characterization of the system of transatlantic enslavement as "trade" relies on the premise that European involvement primarily featured the exchange of commodities for already internally enslaved

[76] José Curto, "Experiences of Enslavement in West Central Africa" (2008) 41(82) Histoire Sociale/Social History 381, 382.

[77] Francis Moore, *Travels into the Inland Parts of Africa* (London 1738) 42.

[78] Curto recognizes the proliferation of violence as an important feature of processes of enslavement; see Curto (n 76) 383. This is reflected in the broader literature concerning the impact of transatlantic and trans-Saharan demand on African societies—see Dennis D Cordell, "Warlords and Enslavement: A Sample of Slave-raiders from Eastern Ubangi-Shari, 1870–1920" in Paul Lovejoy (ed), *Africans in Bondage: Essays Presented to Philip D Curtin on the Occasion of the 25th Anniversary of the African Studies Program* (University of Wisconsin Press 1986); John K Thornton, *Africa and Africans in the Making of the Atlantic World, 1400–1800* (2nd edn, CUP 1998); Manning, *Slavery and African Life* (n 75).

[79] Curto (n 76).

[80] See, for instance, HL Deb (n 6).

people: that "Africa 'produced' slaves, traded them, and consumed its own people."[81] In other words, early Europeans traveling to the coast of Africa were not involved in the initial acts of enslavement but only in the "trade" of already internally enslaved persons.

Lang Fafa Dampha describes this position of dual responsibility: if "black people were bought by whites, they were sold by African leaders too."[82] This is further captured in Lord Chesham's speech to the UK House of Lords in 1996, in which he argued that the claimed imposition of the system of transatlantic enslavement by Western states on "powerless African communities" represents a denial of African political history.[83] His account further alienates responsibility from European nations by suggesting that individual traders and companies, and not the state, conducted these "trades."[84]

The expansion of enslavement within the African continent, and internal adaptations made to meet external demand, make it clear that the transatlantic system was built by African leaders as well as by forced African labor. Indigenous relationships of dependency and enslavement existed on the continent prior to European engagement, and early contact between European travelers and African political figures involved the transfer of internally enslaved persons.[85] African leaders and opportunistic individuals alike participated in the enslavement of African people to feed external markets. This contributes to a broader rhetorical strategy characterizing enslavement as both legal and globally accepted at the time.[86] Yet, an historical review of European involvement in the internal machinations of African politics, as well as physical incursions into the continent, requires a more nuanced perspective than the simple assertion of the indigeneity of enslavement as a basis for moral acceptability and the denial of European responsibility.

A significant history of African resistance to European enslavement at both the political and the individual level attests to the complexity of characterizing enslavement as either an established institution or an alien imposition. The ubiquity of resistance throughout the entire period of transatlantic enslavement, at every stage of the process from the African interior to the Americas, is addressed in a growing body of literature highlighting African

[81] Lovejoy, "Slavery in Africa" (n 19) 37.

[82] Lang Fafa Dampha, *Reparation for Slavery and Colonialism: The Teachings of Durban* (CreateSpace 2015) 50.

[83] HL Deb (n 6) cols 1057–62.

[84] ibid.

[85] See section 1.1.

[86] See, for instance, HL Deb (n 6) cols 1057–62.

agency and action in overthrowing systems of exploitation.[87] From the initial processes of enslavement, to internal migration, at "slave forts" on the coast, aboard canoes and transatlantic vessels, on plantations, and in the fields, the mills, and the houses of the "masters," Africans and their descendants resisted their denigration to the status of chattels. This long history of rebellions, large and small, led Herbert Aptheker to contend that it is resistance, rather than acquiescence, that is at the core of the history of transatlantic enslavement.[88]

Yet, resistance does not address the full story of African action within the transatlantic system. While many African political leaders opposed the European system of enslavement, this did not determine the status of enslavement in their geographies, for these rulers were often then destabilized and destroyed to enable the European-imposed system to take root in the continent.[89] As Patrick Manning observes, the resistance of African leaders, including kings in Jolof, Benin, and Kongo, could not protect against the lure of external markets:

> It only required a few greedy or opportunistic persons, who felt they should enrich themselves rather than resist the inexorable pressures of supply and demand, to keep the slave trade alive. Those suppliers, in turn, rapidly became wealthy enough to become a focus of power to whom others had to accommodate.[90]

The transatlantic system initially required only a limited number of African participants. These individuals derived significant economic gains and

[87] Herbert Aptheker, for instance, highlights the centrality of resistance in African responses to enslavement in the Americas—Herbert Aptheker, *American Negro Slave Revolts* (Columbia UP 1943). Roquinaldo Ferreira also emphasizes the significance of resistance in the history of transatlantic bondage, particularly in the internal African context (n 71). See also Michael Mullin, *Africa in America: Slave Acculturation and Resistance in the American South and the British Caribbean, 1736–1831* (University of Illinois Press 1992); Richard Hart, *Slaves Who Abolished Slavery: Blacks in Rebellion* (University of the West Indies Press 2002); on rebellions aboard vessels transporting enslaved persons, see David Richardson, "Shipboard Revolts, African Authority, and the Atlantic Slave Trade" (2001) 58(1) The William and Mary Quarterly 69; Eric Robert Taylor, *If We Must Die: Shipboard Insurrections in the Era of the Atlantic Slave Trade* (Louisiana State UP 2006); Maggie Montesinos Sale, *American Slave Ship Revolts and the Production of Rebellious Masculinity* (Duke UP 1997).

[88] In Michael Craton, *Testing the Chains: Resistance to Slavery in the British West Indies* (Cornell UP 2009) 11.

[89] Beckles argues that in fact the majority of African leaders adopted this stance of resistance: Beckles (n 3) 168.

[90] Manning, "Why Africans?" (n 43) 36.

political power from European support, enabling their gradual ascension and thus the continued expansion of the institution on the African continent.[91]

Characterizing the system of transatlantic enslavement as an entirely European endeavor erases significant African actors in the history of the institution's development. However, framing this complicity as concluding consideration of the nature of triangular transatlantic interactions also overlooks the nuances of the historical record. Hilary Beckles and Verene Shepherd identify a qualification on the significance of early African involvement, arguing that the fundamental distinction between enslavement in African communities and in European colonies changes the nature of African complicity in the early years.[92] The system in which Africans were complicit is characterized with regard to the extant understandings of African actors in the early years of engagement—framed as a different institution than that which was inflicted upon enslaved Africans in the Americas. In short, this perspective suggests that these African participants were not aware of the nature of the system in which they were involved.

While different understandings of the nature and conditions of enslaved labor do not obviate African participation, particularly once conditions in the Americas became evident, it does contextualize early participation of African actors in the transfer of enslaved persons to European masters. In later years, the military, economic, and political power secured by those who participated in the system enabled its continuation in the face of extensive resistance. In other words, the system once established was more easily maintained than overthrown. Moreover, it was not only these evolving internal asymmetries that characterized the transatlantic system, but also the substantial variance in the power dynamic between Africans and Europeans. Ajayi presents this disjunction as an issue of significant inequality that changed the nature of the relationship and thereby responsibility:

> The difference is that the Europeans controlled the capital in terms of transportation, ammunition and goods. Africans who participated in this trade were victims not only because they had no initiative, but also because they were participating, as traders, in an extremely unequal exchange that

[91] Araujo (n 18) 42.

[92] Beckles and Shepherd argue that, although Africans engaged in "slave raiding, wars, and other contests, in order to procure captives for sale to Europeans," the "racist colonial culture into which [Africans] were imported, that questioned their very humanity and sought to enforce their inferiority to whites, was entirely new to them." Hilary Beckles and Verene Shepherd, *Trading Souls: Europe's Transatlantic Trade in Africans* (Ian Randle 2007) 5.

impoverished them gradually so that he enriched their so-called business partners.[93]

Viewing the dynamics of transatlantic enslavement from the macro perspective, as well as on the basis of individual interactions, changes the way the institution as a whole is perceived. While not erasing African participation in the system, it highlights the degree to which this was manipulated or constrained by European action. The basic distinction between Europeans and Africans within the system ran deep, substantially impacting the way their relations played out in discrete instances and on the whole.

1.5. The racialization of transatlantic enslavement

Moses Finley, Orlando Patterson, and Paul Lovejoy argue that race is not central to enslavement; that throughout history it is marginality rather than race per se that enables and entrenches exploitation.[94] On this account, the racialization of transatlantic enslavement is not the defining feature of the system but simply the focal point for the process of othering in the specific case. Yet, the premise of these studies is the attempt to formulate a coherent conceptualization or definition of "slavery" that encompasses the institution as a singular phenomenon, in its various manifestations, throughout history. Thus, it is the broad commonalities that are highlighted rather than the distinctions. With this in mind, engaging with the particularities of transatlantic enslavement and the *maangamizi* enables a perspective that accounts not only for enslavement as an institution existing throughout history but also for the circumstances of this particular case.

The categorization of African people as "black" and negative associations with this description, were not created by or for the system of transatlantic enslavement but rather far predate it.[95] Yet, it was the transatlantic system that institutionalized and inculcated the negative characterization of

[93] Ajayi (n 69) 20.

[94] Finley speaks of the attribution of "outsider status," Patterson of "othering," and Lovejoy of alienation in justifying the differentiation between free persons and those enslaved. Moses Finley, "Slavery" in *Encyclopaedia of the Social Sciences*, vol 14 (Macmillan Co and Free Press 1968) 307–13; Patterson (n 5); Lovejoy, *Transformations* (n 33). Kopytoff and Miers also define slavery by the "institutions of marginality," while Meillassoux emphasizes alienation—Igor Kopytoff and Suzanne Miers, "African Slavery as an Institution of Marginality" in Miers and Kopytoff (n 23); Claude Meillassoux, *The Anthropology of Slavery: The Womb of Iron and Gold* (University of Chicago Press 1991).

[95] See Kwesi Tsri, *Africans Are Not Black: The Case for Conceptual Liberation* (Routledge 2016).

blackness, overriding or obviating positive representations that had existed alongside these symbolic devaluations of the color black and those people characterized as such.[96]

Given the active process of constructing "blackness" that occurred within the transatlantic system (as justification from inception and as a byproduct of the system of enslavement), it is racialization rather than race itself that is the fundamental concern of this section. "Race" is therefore not engaged as an objective reality, biological fact, manifestation of self-identification or community, or indication of "common history, traditions and impulses."[97] Rather, it is the external process of racialization of African people and people of African descent—both as "black" and as a singular population—that is engaged here.

Previous systems of enslavement were based upon patterns of marginalization and othering that denigrated outsider people on the basis of broad assertions of barbarism, animalistic qualities, or a lesser degree of civilization.[98] The transatlantic system adapted this practice to focus on a single indicium as determinative of this range of characteristics and the humanity of the population of almost an entire continent: race.[99] This externally imposed, morally arbitrary factor was not associated with "otherness" in general or with religious distinctions.[100] Rather than justifying enslavement on the basis of othering broadly, this approach narrowed down the enslavable "other" to those racialized as black. The conflation of blackness with the characteristics necessary for the justification of enslavement came to serve as the basis on which people were enslaved, independent of preexisting understandings of the legitimate conditions in which free people might be enslaved.[101]

This racialization of enslavement was not solely related to the transatlantic system but built upon the gradually developing association between

[96] See David Brion Davis, *Inhuman Bondage: The Rise and Fall of Slavery in the New World* (OUP 2006).

[97] WEB Du Bois, "The Conservation of Races" in Nahum Dimitri Chandler (ed), *The Problem of the Color Line at the Turn of the Twentieth Century: The Essential Early Essays* (reprint, Fordham UP 2015) 53.

[98] See Davis (n 97) 48–64. This is consistent with Finley and Patterson's assumptions about the nature of the institution of enslavement—Finley, *Ancient Slavery* (n38); Patterson (n 5).

[99] See James Sweet, "The Iberian Roots of American Racist Thought" (1997) 54 William and Mary Quarterly 159, 166.

[100] Race is here classified as an "externally imposed" factor because prior to the characterization of Africans as "black," and indeed of the homogeneity of "Africans" as a single group of people, there was no pan-African identity. See Law (n 59) 13–32. On differentials in the impacts of the transatlantic system on different African societies, see Inikori (n 39).

[101] The conditions are considered further in section 2.4.

blackness and the most degrading forms of unfree labor that gained traction in the medieval Muslim world.[102] The system of trans-Saharan enslavement associated with Islamic expansion into Africa fueled racial prejudices in Northern Africa, in turn developing racialized enslavement.[103] By the fifteenth century, and through to the nineteenth, there was a close association between "blackness and slavery" on the frontiers of North and sub-Saharan Africa.[104]

The interchange of stereotypes between the medieval Muslim and Christian worlds created an international stereotype of the "African," perceived as a single race rather than a multiplicity of different ethnic groups, which aligned with the characteristics required to justify their enslavement en masse.[105] Thus, by the beginning of the sixteenth century, the archetype was sufficiently cemented in the European consciousness to serve as a basis for Bartolomé de Las Casas' arguments for the protection of Native Americans through the mass exploitation and enslavement of Africans.[106] By the mid-sixteenth century, Iberians conceived of blackness and enslavement as synonymous, creating an almost exclusively racialized institution.[107]

At a time when the enslavement of other Europeans was considered contrary to international and domestic laws in the European states that engaged in transatlantic enslavement, the characterization of African societies as barbarous, savage, and uncivilized enabled the treatment and exploitation of Africans as if they were property.[108] In this period, being outside the religious order ceased serving as the primary justification for exploitation, replaced by racial hierarchies.[109] Thus, for Africans, conversion to Christianity would not serve as a defense against enslavement despite preexisting standards preventing the enslavement of fellow Christians. Many international legal

102 Davis (n 97) 60–64.

103 Chouki El Hamel, *Black Morocco: A History of Slavery, Race, and Islam* (CUP 2013).

104 Rudolph T Ware III, "Slavery in Islamic Africa, 1400–1800" in Eltis and Engerman (n 12) 48.

105 ibid 73.

106 Bartolomé de Las Casas, *A Short Account of the Destruction of the Indies* (Nigel Griffin tr, Penguin 1992). See also Lawrence Clayton, *Bartolomé de Las Casas and the Conquest of the Americas* (John Wiley & Sons 2010). At the end of his life, de Las Casas came to renounce his own position on the enslavement of Africans, then framing it as equally unjust as the enslavement of indigenous Americans—*History of the Indies* (Andrée Collard tr, Harper & Row 1971).

107 Araujo (n 18) 18.

108 The juridification of European racialized enslavement in the writings of international jurists is considered in section 2.4.

109 Jurists in the Muslim world had maintained the recognition that legitimate enslavement relied upon the enslavement of non-Muslims in the medieval period, despite practice to the contrary, while Christian jurists similarly maintained that only those outside the Christian world could be lawfully enslaved. See Davis (n 97).

scholars were comfortable accepting or justifying exceptions to the general prohibition of enslavement within the Christian world on the basis of stereotypes of race-based inferiority.[110]

Paraphrasing Sartre for the transatlantic context, it was not the experience of African peoples and civilizations that produced either the concept of blackness or the association of Africa with barbarism. Rather, it was the idea of the "savage negro" cemented to justify colonialism and enslavement that explained the experience (both intellectual and physical) of interactions between Europeans and Africans. If the "savage negro" did not exist, the white supremacist enslaver would invent him.[111]

This relationship between the construction of the African and the experience of enslavement is evident in David Goldenberg's reflections on the transformation of interpretations of the biblical story of the curse of Canaan, frequently used as a justification for racialized enslavement.[112] The enslavement of "Ham's black descendants" was not justified by an inherently racist biblical text, but rather that interpretation of the script was racialized by the inculcation of the enslavement of Africans.[113] Blackness was not merely correlated with the enslavement of Africans and their descendants, but in many ways causative, and likewise "whiteness" and white pathology were not only the cause of racialized enslavement but were also produced by it.[114]

The construction of blackness and its correlation with enslavement had far-reaching and multitudinous effects that grew beyond the institution of chattel enslavement alone. While racial distinctions were developed in relation to the expansion of enslavement, they were not restricted to it. As Locksley Edmondson emphasizes, transatlantic enslavement consolidated patterns of international, political, and economic race relations, resulting in the "triumph of white-world racism."[115] These racialized dynamics infused social and international interactions to a significant degree and are yet to be eradicated.[116]

[110] See section 2.4.

[111] Jean-Paul Sartre, *Anti-Semite and the Jew* (George J Becker tr, Schocken Books 1974) 13.

[112] David Goldenberg, *The Curse of Ham: Race and Slavery in Early Judaism, Christianity, and Islam* (Princeton UP 2005).

[113] ibid 175–76.

[114] Ronald Salzberger and Mary Turck, "Slavery's Insults: The Continuing Nonmaterial Injuries of Slavery" in Ronald Salzberger and Mary Turck (eds), *Reparations for Slavery: A Reader* (Rowman & Littlefield 2004) 48.

[115] Locksley Edmondson, "Trans-Atlantic Slavery and the Internationalization of Race" (1976) 22 Caribbean Quarterly 5.

[116] See Alexis de Tocqueville, *Democracy in America* (JP Mayer and Max Lerner eds, George Lawrence tr, Harper & Row 1966) 294.

While understandings of race were not static or monolithic during this period, demonstrating evolution and fluctuations, the trajectory of the dominant construction of the African was shaped by the transatlantic system. The racialized dynamics that developed in the medieval Muslim world and that took root, grew, and were tended by the racialization of transatlantic enslavement, continue to bear strange fruit decades after the system of legal enslavement itself was abolished.

1.6. The contemporary legacies of transatlantic enslavement

At the heart of reparations claims is an understanding of the system of transatlantic enslavement that did not end in the nineteenth century when major European powers abolished the institution within their territories.[117] Laura Hein articulates the relationship between past and present, suggesting that "demands for redress are really about claiming humanity in the present by demonstrating that this status was unjustly denied in the past."[118] Thus, calls for reparations are focused on reframing present structures and institutions so that historical victimization and its legacies are addressed.[119]

United Nations General Assembly (UNGA) Resolution 61/19 acknowledged that transatlantic enslavement is at the core of situations of "profound social and economic inequality, hatred, bigotry, racism and prejudice" existing today, echoing the Durban Declaration's recognition of the contemporary legacies of the transatlantic system.[120] Thus, the moral significance of reparations claims rests not only upon historical injustice but also upon the impact wrongdoings continue to have on the present.[121]

The legacies of the transatlantic system manifest in the social, economic, and political development of African and diasporic states as well as

[117] France, Great Britain, the Netherlands, Portugal, Spain, and the United States, all effected legal abolition in the forty-year period between 1834 and 1873.

[118] Laura Hein, "War Compensation: Claims against the Japanese Government and Japanese Corporations for War Crimes" in John Torpey (ed), *Politics and the Past: On Repairing Historical Injustices* (Rowman & Littlefield 2004).

[119] ibid. This characterization of reparations is further explored in chapters 4 to 7.

[120] UNGA Res 61/19 (November 28, 2006) UN Doc A/RES/61/19, preamble; "Durban Declaration and Plan of Action, Adopted at the World Conference against Racism, Racial Discrimination, Xenophobia and Related Intolerance" (Durban, September 8, 2001), art 158.

[121] Waldron argues that the moral significance of past events is tied up in the difference it makes in the present—Jeremy Waldron, "Superseding Historical Injustices" in Salzberger and Turck (n 115) 208.

in symbolic and immaterial harms to people of African descent. Lord Judd highlighted the impact of structures of plantation-based enslavement on African and Caribbean development, noting that "traditional, balanced self-sufficiency" with established coping mechanisms for systemic shocks were ousted during the centuries of colonial enslavement and replaced by "over-dependence on a single commodity," making these states extremely vulnerable to global market fluctuations.[122] Similarly, Sidney Mintz emphasized that the plantation system developed by colonial powers shaped the economic character of Caribbean states far beyond the abolition of enslavement, with elements of coercion and deception remaining central.[123] Similar economic repercussions can be identified in other European colonies.[124]

On the individual and community level, postemancipation conditions continued to subordinate people of African descent.[125] Disparities in intergenerational wealth transfers between people of African descent in the diaspora and other racial groups are highlighted as continuations of the dispossession of transatlantic enslavement.[126] Gregory Price estimates the life span of adverse effects of slavery on males in the United States with paternal slave descendants to last between approximately 128 and 175 years from 1930—already 65 years after emancipation—impacting economic status and mobility.[127] Without accounting for the ongoing impacts of other legacies of enslavement—including reformation of exploitative practices and racial discrimination—this finds the legacies of slavery to be persistent.

The failure to provide redress upon abolition is characterized as having cemented the gap between the descendants of enslaved persons and enslavers.[128] As Randall Robinson declared,

122 Lord Judd, HL Deb (n 6) col 1055.

123 Sidney Mintz, *Caribbean Transformations* (Aldine Publishing 1974) 31.

124 See Herbert Klein, *African Slavery in Latin America and the Caribbean* (2nd edn, OUP 2007); Jeremy Adelman, *Colonial Legacies: The Problem of Persistence in Latin American History* (Routledge 1999); John Coatsworth, "Inequality, Institutions and Economic Growth in Latin America" (2008) 40 Journal of Latin American Studies 545; Victor Bulmer-Thomas, *The Economic History of Latin America Since Independence* (2nd edn, CUP 2003).

125 Salzberger and Turck (n 115) 51.

126 See Darrell Gaskin, Alvin Headen, and Shelley White-Means, "Racial Disparities in Health and Wealth: The Effects of Slavery and Past Discrimination" (2005) 32 The Review of Black Political Economy 95; Palma Strand, "Inheriting Inequality: Wealth, Race, and the Laws of Succession" (2010–2011) 89 Oregon Law Review 453; William Collins and Marianne Wanamaker, "Up from Slavery? African American Intergenerational Economic Mobility since 1880" (2017) <www.nber.org/papers/w23395> accessed October 31, 2018.

127 Gregory N Price, "How Long Are the Chains of Slavery in the United States? Estimates of the Intergenerational Effects for Black Males between 1880–1930" (2019) 68 Social and Economic Studies 147.

128 See, for instance, Melinda Miller, "Land and Racial Wealth Equality" (2011) 101 American Economic Review 371; Rhonda Magee, "The Master's Tools from the Bottom Up: Responses to

> No nation can enslave a race of people for hundreds of years, set them free bedraggled and penniless, pit them, without assistance in a hostile environment, against privileged victimizers, and then reasonably expect the gap between the heirs of the two groups to narrow.[129]

Legal freedom did not constitute the realization of substantive freedom; nor could it serve as the foundation for equality without further measures.[130] Yet, adding to a pattern of exploitation and denial, the further measures actually adopted in the aftermath of abolition were not those that would support the recovery of previously enslaved persons, as demanded by the frameworks of reparatory justice.[131] Rather, structures put in place in the years following emancipation enabled the continued exploitation and marginalization of people of African descent.

Enslavement was not eradicated, but reformed. New forms of exploitation arose to enable the continued extraction of labor from people of African descent under coercive conditions—what Beckles labels the "continuation of most criminal violations against blacks."[132] Structures of embedded racism, collective memories of enslavement, and collective identities born from this system also continue to have direct impacts on the lives of Africans and people of African descent.[133] Persistent structures of white supremacy and the stigmatization of blackness that had evolved to support the institutions of racialized enslavement compounded economic deprivation, making recovery for freed persons and their descendants a much more difficult endeavor.[134]

African-American Reparations Theory in Mainstream and Outsider Remedies Discourse" (1993) 79 Virginal Law Review 863.

129 Robinson, *The Debt* (n 3) 74.

130 Watson Branch, "Reparations for Slavery: A Dream Deferred" (2002) 3 San Diego International Law Journal 177, 185.

131 The frameworks are considered in chapters 4 and 5.

132 Beckles (n 3) 169. See also Douglas Blackmon, *Slavery by Another Name: The Re-Enslavement of Black Americans from the Civil War to World War II* (Icon Books 2012).

133 Allen Jr and Chrisman suggest that the descendants of enslaved person are still subjected to social constructions of racial identity and thus continue to suffer the "institutional legacies of slavery"—Ernest Allen Jr and Robert Chrisman, "Ten Reasons: A Response to David Horowitz" in Salzberger and Turck (n 115) 134. Brophy argues that reparations aim to address these racial dynamics, by working to eradicate or reduce the "caste system established during slavery, which continues to the present"—Alfred Brophy, "The World of Reparations: Slavery Reparations in Historical Perspective" (2002) 3 Journal of Law in Society 105, 109.

134 Salzberger and Turck (n 115) 51. See also Robert Westley, "Many Billions Gone: Is It Time to Reconsider the Case for Black Reparation?" (1998) 40 Boston College Law Review 429.

Janna Thompson highlights the ways in which contemporary experiences are shaped by historical injustices on the collective level:

> Members of nations whose ancestors were the victims of unrequited historical wrongs often suffer from despair, depression and loss of both confidence and hope for the future. Even the material disadvantages that result from historical injustice are viewed by the people who suffer them from the perspective of their history.[135]

Reparations claims seek to address these structural and institutional failures created, supported, or compounded by the injustices in question, as well as responding to the connections between historical injustices and the lived experiences of people of African descent.

1.7. Considering transatlantic enslavement as a sui generis case

Severing enslavement from the broader context of injustices committed against African peoples and their descendants impoverishes understandings of the realities of the system of transatlantic chattel enslavement. Such artificial partition of the abuses committed against Africans—as peoples and as individuals—not only fails to capture the broader picture of European interactions with Africa but also creates a false equivalence between the *maangamizi* and other systems of enslavement operating throughout history. Such an approach fails to grapple with the continuities connecting contemporary experiences of people of African descent with the history of racialized chattel enslavement.

The historical record is littered with examples of systems of enslavement premised upon the alienation of particular peoples. Many of these have involved forced migration, they are often effected through violence, and some have demonstrated racial denigration. Nonetheless, the *maangamizi* has unique dimensions that should not be overlooked when considering the case for reparations, for it is these features to which calls for redress speak. It is the

[135] Janna Thompson, *Taking Responsibility for the Past: Reparation and Historical Injustice* (Polity 2002) 66.

system of transatlantic chattel enslavement, in its particularities and in context, that is the subject of these claims.

Echoing Rhonda Magee's characterization of the transatlantic system as a "super-wrong," and the notion of this as a "dark chapter" in history, Randall Robinson separates the enslavement of Africans and their descendants as its own chapter in the historical record and a sui generis injustice:[136]

> Like slavery, other human rights crimes have resulted in the loss of millions of lives. But only slavery, with its sadistic patience, asphyxiated memory, and smothered cultures, has hulled empty a whole race of people with inter-generational efficiency. Every artifact of the victims' past cultures, every custom, every ritual, every god, every language, every trace element of a people's whole hereditary identity, wrenched from them and ground into a sharp choking dust. It is a human rights crime without parallel in the modern world. For it produces victims ad infinitum, long after the active state of the crime has ended.[137]

It is this broad understanding of the system of transatlantic chattel enslavement that serves as the starting point for the consideration of reparations.

[136] Magee (n 129) 901.
[137] Robinson, *The Debt* (n 3) 216.

2

The *Maangamizi* and the Making of International Law

Considerations of legality are central in reparations discourse—not only in assessing the justiciability of legal claims but also the moral case. This is true for reparations proponents, who employ the language of criminality and justice to support their claims, as well as for reparations detractors exploiting the rhetoric of legality as a moral defense.[1] The claim to legality "at the time" can be as persuasive an argument as cries of injustice, and often proves to be more so in the consideration of claims to reparations for historical enslavement.[2] On both sides of the reparations debate, it is often to legal systems that those seeking to assert or deny wrongdoing and responsibility for historical injustices refer. Engaging with the ways transatlantic enslavement and the *maangamizi* interact with the international legal system is therefore vital to the development of an understanding of present duties of redress.

Although enslavement itself is often the primary point of reference for reparations movements, a range of injustices inextricably linked to processes of enslavement occurred within, or related to, the transatlantic system. Yet, discourse on postcolonial redress and the consideration of reparations for chattel enslavement remain largely disparate.[3] This separation may be explained by the disparities between the nineteenth-century movement for the abolition of slavery and the mid-twentieth-century push for decolonization. The legitimacy of the two institutions was not seen as fundamentally

[1] See, for instance, Hilary Beckles, *Britain's Black Debt: Reparations for Caribbean Slavery and Native Genocide* (University of the West Indies Press 2013); Nora Wittmann, *Slavery Reparations Time Is Now: Exposing Lies, Claiming Justice for Global Survival, an International Legal Assessment* (Power of the TrInIty Publishers 2013); Anthony Gifford, "Pipe Dream or Necessary Atonement?" (2007) 36 Index on Censorship 89. cf Lord Chesham, HL Deb March 14, 1996, vol 570, cols 1057–62; Tony Blair, "The Shame of Slavery" *New Nation* (November 27, 2006) 2 <www.ligali.org/truth2007/learning/tony_blair_statement_of_sorrow_new_nation_27_nov_06.pdf> accessed March 2, 2018.

[2] A number of commentators conclude that the legality of enslavement at the time renders reparations inappropriate. See, for instance, HL Deb (n 1); Blair (n 1).

[3] See John Torpey, *Making Whole What Has Been Smashed: On Reparations Politics* (Harvard UP 2006) 3.

Reparations for Slavery in International Law. Katarina Schwarz, Oxford University Press. © Oxford University Press 2022.
DOI: 10.1093/oso/9780197636398.003.0003

intertwined for the purposes of their elimination, and thus the movements gained traction in different time periods, with different actors, targeting distinct agendas, and utilizing different methods.[4] Yet, despite the differentiation in movements to eradicate or overcome these injustices, European colonial abuses were entangled at inception and during their respective periods of dominance. The following analysis will therefore address the injustice of chattel enslavement of African people and people of African descent both in isolation and in the broader context of the *maangamizi*—recognizing the imperial roots of international law.

In considering the crystallization of international law, understandings of enslavement within the systems of *jus naturale* and jus gentium, the existence of limitations on enslavement as a specific category of legal wrongdoing, and the development of abolition and prohibition are evaluated in this chapter. Tracing the roots of modern international law reveals that a singular, positive prohibition against enslavement in the general sense is only one part of a larger whole. This chapter therefore considers the centrality of the *maangamizi* and colonialism in the evolution of a global legal system, and questions whether the limits of legality and justice ought now to be assessed against this framework.

The abolition of slavery was shaped by the resistance of Africans and people of African descent in the diaspora.[5] The influence of these actors should not be overshadowed by a narrative prioritizing or aggrandizing the actions of European abolitionists. However, in the positive international law of the nineteenth and twentieth centuries, European states engaged in a conscious movement toward international abolition that speaks significantly to the development of international law. This represents the perspective of the central perpetrators from the sixteenth to the nineteenth centuries who had constructed international law in this period as an almost exclusively Western European ideological framework. Thus, any disproportionate focus on European state action in the following analysis should not be taken as disregard for the role of African people—both enslaved and free—in the process

[4] The international movement toward global abolition of the slave trade and slavery primarily took place during the nineteenth and early twentieth century, while decolonization was more highly concentrated in the latter half of the twentieth century when a plethora of "new" post-colonial states were incorporated into the international community.

[5] See, for instance, Douglas Egerton, "Slave Resistance" in Mark M Smith and Robert L Paquette, *The Oxford Handbook of Slavery in the Americas* (OUP 2010) 447; Howard Jones, *Mutiny on the Amistad: The Saga of a Slave Revolt and Its Impact on American Abolition, Law, and Diplomacy* (OUP 1987); Manisha Sinha, *The Slave's Cause: A History of Abolition* (Yale UP 2016).

of abolition. Rather, attention is turned toward European conduct precisely because these states were the primary perpetrators in the system of chattel enslavement. Simultaneously, it was these states that generated the international legal structures of the past five centuries, including those identified as having permitted the *maangamizi*.

2.1. International law's "other"

According to Hugo Grotius, the European jurist often labeled the "father of international law," jus gentium acquires obligatory force by virtue of the consent of all nations, or at least of several.[6] Thomas Lawrence similarly conceived of law as based upon interactions between states and the rules observed in this context, rather than the recognition, interpretation, and application of transcendental rules of right, although he allowed reference to the fundamental principles on which law was based.[7] In the age of expanding European "civilization," this consent-based theory developed to create a hierarchy in which the conduct of some states mattered, while others did not.[8] The doctrine of sovereignty was constructed from the perspective of European jurists to "account for relations between the European and non-European worlds" and, in particular, to justify colonial expansion and the exploitation of non-European lands and peoples.[9] European colonial states sought to control those outside Europe, stigmatizing, marginalizing, destroying, and dispossessing the "other" of all they had.[10]

With recognition of sovereignty employed by European states to exclude some peoples from Grotius' group of "all nations," the international character of this developing body of international law is brought into question. While it may be established that a European regional law of nations came to dominance prior to the institution of transatlantic enslavement, shaping the international legal landscape for the majority of this period, the conclusion

[6] In Henry Wheaton, *Elements of International Law* (Little, Brown and Co 1866) 10.

[7] Lawrence suggests that nineteenth-century jurists turned international law into a science based on the observation of rules actually followed by states, to be classified with reference to the "fundamental principles" on which they are based. Thomas Lawrence, *The Principles of International Law* (D C Heath 1895).

[8] Although Grotius did not make such a distinction between states, later jurists and the conduct of European colonial powers would entrench it. See, for instance, Wheaton (n 6).

[9] Antony Anghie, *Imperialism, Sovereignty and the Making of International Law* (CUP 2007) 3.

[10] Shelley Wright, *International Human Rights, Decolonisation and Globalisation: Becoming Human* (Routledge 2001) 57.

that this constitutes universal law is far from assured. Yet, it is the writings of European jurists that forged understandings of early-modern international law.[11] These foundational commentaries involved the global assertion of norms defined by a select group of states, directly and explicitly excluding others, both as creators and subjects of international law. Thus, the basis on which European Christian states purported to impose a legal framework of norms onto the "New World" must be interrogated.[12] Anghie frames this fundamental question: "How could it be claimed the European civilization, in all its avowed specificity, was somehow universal and binding on non-European States?"[13]

The lack of a conception of property, as understood in the European world, served as a central legal justification for dispossession of African, aboriginal, and indigenous lands and reinforced the associated treatment of these peoples.[14] Prominent jurists from the sixteenth to the eighteenth century came to define the very notion of sovereignty by the nature of the relationship between the people and the land, excluding the possibility of indigenous sovereignty in many cases because inhabitants were considered to "range over" rather than possess land.[15] The lack of sovereignty, in turn, legitimized a hierarchy of civilization that situated African, indigenous, and aboriginal people as less than their European counterparts not only in terms of statehood but also in a much broader sense.[16] This European-constructed inferiority was employed to legitimize chattel enslavement for centuries.[17]

Not only did the distinction between "civilized" and "uncivilized" peoples reinforce the racial dynamic of the transatlantic system, but it also permitted the waging of wars that would provide enslaved persons for European

[11] Contemporary historical reviews of international law generally highlight a selection of European jurists as the "classics" of international law. For the most part, these influential texts are found in the Carnegie Institute's *Classics of International Law* series of twenty-two volumes edited by James Brown Scott, published between 1911 and 1950.

[12] See Wittmann (n 1) 10–139.

[13] Anghie, *Imperialism* (n 9) 4.

[14] See, for instance, *Milirrpum v Nabalco Pty Ltd* (1971) 17 FLR 141 concerning the acquisition of land in Australia on the basis of lack of a concept of property amongst aboriginal people.

[15] See Emer de Vattel, *The Law of Nations* (Béla Kapossy and Richard Whatmore eds, Liberty Fund 2012) criticizing Spanish conquest of Mexico and Peru but approving dispossession of Native Americans because of their relationship with the land. See also Francisco de Vitoria, "The First Reflecto of the Reverend Father, Brother Franciscus de Victoria On the Indians Lately Discovered" in James Brown Scott (ed), *The Spanish Origins of International Law: Francisco de Vitoria and His Law of Nations* (Clarendon Press 1934).

[16] On the racialization and denigration of Africans and their descendants, see section 1.5. On aboriginal and indigenous people, see S James Anaya, *Indigenous Peoples in International Law* (2nd edn, OUP 2004) 15–48.

[17] See section 1.5.

exploitation. By justifying warfare and conquest through a self-defense argument premised on the fundamental, international legal right to engage in trade and commerce, jurists like Vitoria legitimized the enslavement of indigenous and African peoples on the basis of the classic jus gentium exceptional circumstance.[18] Provided jurists could find a justification for war, racialized natural law justifications for slavery were unnecessary. Thus, even without accepting a racial hierarchy of civilization, international law created the preconditions for mass enslavement and wars of conquest on the basis of an international right to commerce. However, it was the characterization of African and indigenous populations as economically backward, closed off to trade, and incapable of capitalizing on the asset of their own territory that provided the justification for the allowance of conquest and outright denial of sovereignty, and thereby enslavement.[19]

The marginalization of African peoples in the international legal order, and justifications for their enslavement, did not conclude with the legitimation of warfare. As a measure of human evolution, the claimed lack of political organization and economic development of non-European peoples, in conjunction with religious and sociocultural differences, fueled the repositioning of enslavement from its place in jus gentium into a system resembling or constituting *jus naturale*. This aligned with Aristotle's characterizations of the "natural slave."[20] Although international jurists continued to highlight necessary preconditions for lawful enslavement, the transatlantic system grew to accept and defend the enslavement of almost any person racialized as black, with few caveats.[21] Thus, the definition of civilization, and the denial of such in relation to non-European peoples, came to fundamentally alter the placement and parameters of enslavement in international law.[22]

The international legality of both colonialism and enslavement relied on the assumption that non-European states, and specifically societies in Africa and the Americas, did not have international legal personality—or at least not

[18] The positioning of enslavement as a jus gentium exception to the general *jus naturale* prohibiting enslavement is discussed further in section 2.4. Vitoria based the distinction on the refusal of the "Indians" to allow Spaniards to travel and trade within their territories, as the right to self-defense extended to international commerce. Vitoria (n 15).

[19] The characterization of legal forms of enslavement in the writings of international jurists is considered in section 2.4.

[20] On the significance of Aristotle's "natural slave" and its relationship with the racialization of enslavement from the medieval to the modern period, see David Brion Davis, *Inhuman Bondage: The Rise and Fall of Slavery in the New World* (OUP 2006) 48–76.

[21] See section 1.5.

[22] The specific developments in relation to enslavement's position in international law are considered further in section 2.4.

in the same way that European states did.[23] However, the characterization of these people as lacking political organization, "uncivilized," and "savage" has been revealed to have been inaccurate, self-serving, and unjust.[24] Accepting the developments of international law relating to enslavement and the *maangamizi* from this perspective alone is therefore problematic, for it relies on the recognition of these prejudicial conclusions as a legitimate foundation not only for European law but also for a universal legal framework applying equally to those peoples.

Acknowledging the political identity of non-European states denied statehood on the basis of a lack of civilization—and the humanity of non-European peoples—necessitates a reconsideration of the historical international legal status of transatlantic enslavement and the *maangamizi*. This is so as it was these presumptions on which the practices were legitimized. The starting point then is not the assumption of the universality of European international legal thought but the recognition that such may have represented only a regional system of international law. Nora Wittmann, advocating this approach, goes further to suggest that the capacity of European states to impose norms upon the "New World" was itself "a consequence of the crime of transatlantic slavery."[25]

Wittmann's conclusion, discussed in chapter 1, is that international restrictions on enslavement were established prior to the birth of the transatlantic system, involving a collection of rights for enslaved persons contravened by transatlantic enslavement.[26] However, this position does not account for the situations in which enslaved persons were not afforded significant rights of their own, including those indigenous African systems of dependency and servility considered in chapter 1, nor does it foresee the potential for international law to evolve and change for the worse.[27]

[23] See Anghie, *Imperialism* (n 9) 101.

[24] See, for instance, the rejection of the terra nullius claim to sovereignty where such relied on the classification of indigenous people as sub-human—*Mabo and Others v Queensland* (No 2) [1992] HCA 23.

[25] Wittmann (n 1) 11.

[26] ibid 138. Enslavement in just war was also a primary justification for enslavement in the transatlantic system. However, as discussed in chapter 1, this was so widely abused and manipulated by both Europeans and Africans involved in the system that it cannot stand scrutiny. Interrogation of the legitimacy of the conditions in which Africans were enslaved was nonexistent, the illegitimate circumstances of internal enslavement were widely known, Europeans themselves participated in raids and *razzias* outside the confines of "just war," and European actors manipulated and involved themselves in African politics to ensure the continuation of conflict thus securing the supply of captives.

[27] As discussed previously, limitations on masters in Roman law were not for the benefit of enslaved persons, and a master would suffer no consequence for killing an enslaved person over whom he exercised property rights. Moreover, in instances in which a master was killed by an enslaved person,

Nonetheless, the practice and opinions of African states and peoples in determining the reach or extent of European international law must be considered in framing universal norms. This approach is adopted in the consideration of developing customary international law discussed in section 2.4.

The conflicted history of enslavement also raises a fundamental question for the consideration of international law governing contemporary reparations for historical injustices committed against African, aboriginal, and indigenous people alike. Should the legal frameworks constructed by European states in order to justify dispossession and enslavement now be used to assess that same conduct? This concerns not only the consideration of subaltern perspectives in determining the development and existence of international norms but also the procedural elements of the legal system that impact the ways in which rules are established, recognized, and altered. The requirements of *opinio juris* and state practice in the formulation of customary international law, the doctrine of intertemporal law, the specifications of attribution, and the parameters of causation are all features of a system constructed by European states.[28]

Despite the inequalities embedded in their foundations, engaging with the structures of European international law contributes to the reparations debate in several ways. First, it is these frameworks to which reparations detractors refer in justifying the denial of a case to answer in the legal context but also with regard to the political and moral justifications for redress.[29] Destabilizing these international legal arguments therefore creates space in which reparations discourse can occur with full acknowledgment of the complex and problematic infrastructure of international law, without treating such as a complete bar to recovery. Second, the procedural frameworks provide a point of reference for the consideration of historical injustices that speaks in the language of detractors. Thus, this approach reconceptualizes accepted principles and approaches to account for the intricacies and nuances

Roman law condoned the killing of all slaves in the household, irrespective of their involvement. Slaves were also often precluded from legal personality, and denied the ability to testify in courts of law. See WW Buckland, *The Roman Law of Slavery: The Condition of the Slave in Private Law from Augustus to Justinian* (CUP 1908).

[28] See, for instance, George Rodrigo Bandeira Galindo and César Yip, "Customary International Law and the Third World: Do Not Step on the Grass" (2017) 16 Chinese Journal of International Law 251; Umut Özsu, "An Anti-Imperialist Universalism? Jus Cogens and the Politics of International Law" in Martti Koskenniemi, Walter Rech, and Manuel Jiménez Fonseca (eds), *International Law and Empire: Historical Explorations* (OUP 2017).

[29] See, for instance, Andreas Buser, "Colonial Injustices and the Law of State Responsibility: The CARICOM Claim for Reparations" (2017) 2 Heidelberg Journal of International Law 409.

of the historical record, carrying the weight of these frameworks without blindly accepting them.

The question of universality and legitimacy in the establishment and evolution of international law from the period of colonization, enslavement, and denial of statehood is further complicated by abolition, decolonization, and increasing recognition of postcolonial states and indigenous people. International law did not remain a static representation of European imperial domination, but rather evolved to recognize and integrate those states it had previously denied.[30] Postcolonial states did not simply remove themselves from the international legal order constructed through the colonial encounter but rather acceded to it in many instances, demanding its adaptation in a variety of ways but otherwise reinforcing its broader legitimacy.[31] Though this does not serve as the foundation for uncritical acceptance of the system as a whole, contemporary decolonial developments support its value in considering reparations claims.

Finally, in applying problematic international legal frameworks to claims demanding the redress of historical injustices that in part constitute this system, the underlying principles of international law serve as a point of reference. The promises of international law express a universal perspective; a system situated within broader understandings of justice, equality, and representation.[32] It is this aspiration to which reparations proponents speak when they call for international legal responses, and it is this ambition that frames the following consideration of the international legal dimensions of claims to reparations for transatlantic enslavement and the *maangamizi*, regardless of whether a legal claim is feasible in practice.

[30] See CG Weeramantry, *Universalising International Law* (Brill 2004); Matthew Craven, *The Decolonization of International Law: State Succession and the Law of Treaties* (OUP 2007); Rajat Rana, "Symphony of Decolonisation: Third World and Human Rights Discourse" (2007) 11(4) International Journal of Human Rights 367. On the tensions between emancipatory ideas and the current structure of the international order, see Dianne Otto, "Subalternity and International Law: The Problems of Global Community and the Incommensurability of Difference" (1996) 5 Social and Legal Studies 337; Nathaniel Berman, *Passion and Ambivalence: Nationalism, Colonialism, and International Law* (Brill 2011); Sundhya Pahuja, *Decolonising International Law: Development, Economic Growth and the Politics of Universality* (CUP 2011); Sundhya Pahuja, "The Postcoloniality of International Law" (2005) 46(2) Harvard Journal of International Law 459.

[31] Considering the tensions in postcolonial states' choice to join the existing international legal order, see Vasuki Nesiah, "Placing International Law: White Spaces on a Map" (2003) 16 Leiden Journal of International Law 1.

[32] See, for instance, Wright (n 10) and Pahuja's critique of this text—Sundhya Pahuja, "This Is the World: Have Faith" (2004) 15(2) European Journal of International Law 381.

2.2. Constructing responsibility in international law

Notions of state responsibility in the past and the present are central to the consideration of international legal obligations to provide redress. Without a doctrine of responsibility and an understanding of what constitutes wrongdoing, a case for reparations cannot be formulated in either the moral/political or the legal context. Current international law in this regard is articulated in the Articles on the Responsibility of States for Internationally Wrongful Acts, under which responsibility rests upon the twin pillars of attribution and breach.[33] This second element, satisfied where international law has crystallized at the time of the breach and frustrated where the relevant prohibition comes into force at a later date, is often at the very heart of reparations denials.[34] Wittmann asserts that the claim to contemporary legality—in conjunction with nonretroactivity—is the "basic argument that European and US ex-enslaver States always come up with first and last."[35] Similarly, Hilary Beckles suggests that European states have persistently premised denials of the reparations case on the basis of historical legality.[36]

The nature of denials demonstrates the interaction between the requirement of a breach of an international obligation and the doctrine of intertemporal law, demanding such obligation be in force at the time of the conduct in question.[37] As *The Island of Palmas Case* suggests: "Juridical fact must be appreciated in the light of the law contemporary with it, and not of the law in force at the time when a dispute in regard to it arises or falls to be settled."[38] Yet, despite persistent denials by those in positions of global power, the international law governing historical enslavement is not as clear

[33] International Law Commission, "Draft Articles on Responsibility of States for Internationally Wrongful Acts" (November 2001) UN Doc A/56/10 (Articles on State Responsibility), art 2. This approach is consistent with the approach taken by the International Court of Justice in *Case Concerning United States Diplomatic and Consular Staff in Tehran (United States of America v Iran)* [1980] ICJ Rep 64.

[34] The first element, attribution, will be considered in chapter 5, alongside an analysis of harm and causation. On the role of arguments concerning the historical legality of enslavement, see Blair (n 1); HL Deb (n 1).

[35] Wittmann (n 1) 2.

[36] Beckles (n 1) 167.

[37] Articles on State Responsibility (n 33) art 13. See also Vienna Convention on the Law of Treaties (adopted May 23, 1969, entered into force January 27, 1970) 1155 UNTS 331, art 28.

[38] *Island of Palmas Case (United States v the Netherlands)* (1928) 2 RIAA 829, 845. This case concerned a territorial dispute between the Netherlands and the United States. In light of the quoted passage, the court proceeded to assess the question of the effect of "discovery" of the island by Spain against the law in force in the first half of the sixteenth century. Ultimately, the Tribunal found in favor of the Netherlands by virtue of the continuous and peaceful display of sovereignty, as opposed to the US claim based on Spanish "discovery" that lacked the actual exercise of authority.

as reparations detractors suggest. Among activists, the claim that the institution was illegal during the period of transatlantic chattel enslavement is ubiquitous, supported by academics, and notably Justice Patrick Robinson—serving judge in the International Court of Justice from 2015.[39] Robinson concluded in response to Wittmann's monograph that a "*prima facie* case for the illegality of slavery" had been established, "notwithstanding the difference in the practice followed in the colonies."[40] The justification for these assertions in the legal frameworks is therefore interrogated in this chapter.

The doctrine of intertemporal law presents an additional challenge in the consideration of claims to reparations for historical enslavement beyond the crystallization and evolution of international norms and the problems of Eurocentrism addressed in section 2.1. In demanding that the case for reparations be considered in light of legal understandings in effect at the time, a return to the predominant modes of legal thinking is mandated. In the context of historical abuses dating beyond the nineteenth century, this entails a fundamental shift in the way international law is conceived. Though positivism is widely accepted in the present, international jurists from the fifteenth through the end of the eighteenth century premised their understandings on natural law philosophies.[41] Thus, although the starting point for the following analysis is the codification of international law governing enslavement, the consideration of customary international law integrates early-modern international jurisprudential thinking in engaging with the legal frameworks in place at the time.

2.3. Codifying abolition and prohibition

Attempting to backdate the abolition of enslavement in treaty law to precede the transatlantic system is a largely fruitless endeavor. Although enslavement had been abolished internally in a number of locations throughout history

[39] See also Richard Mitchell, "Compensate Us for Slavery—Robinson" *The Gleaner* (Kingston, March 3, 2015) <jamaica-gleaner.com/article/lead-stories/20150303/compensate-us-slavery-robinson> accessed March 2, 2018; Gifford (n 1); Wittmann (n 1); Beckles (n 1); Verene Shepherd, "Slavery, Shame and Pride: Debates over the Marking of the Bicentennial of the Abolition of the British Trans-Atlantic Trade in Africans in 2007" (2010) 56 Caribbean Quarterly 1.

[40] In Wittmann (n 1).

[41] Thomas Lawrence, for instance, despite a consent-based understanding of international law, suggested that the organization of international rules according to the "fundamental principles" that they realize is a part of the business of international law, implying that legal norms reference overarching principles (naturalist norms)—n 7.

prior to European expansion into the "New World," it was not until the twentieth century that a treaty of universal scope was adopted prohibiting "slavery" and the "slave trade."[42] The League of Nations Slavery Convention of 1926 was the first universal international instrument establishing specific rules requiring the abolition of the slave trade and the institution of slavery, albeit "progressively and as soon as possible" with regard to the latter.[43] The 1956 Supplementary Convention on the Abolition of Slavery, the Slave Trade, and Institutions and Practices Similar to Slavery closed this transitional period, affirming a fully crystallized international prohibition against both "slavery" and the "slave trade."[44] Ten years later, the International Covenant on Civil and Political Rights identified the prohibition of "slavery" and the "slave trade" in all their forms as nonderogable human rights.[45] Yet, enslavement was the subject matter of a multitude of treaty provisions prior to the drafting of the 1926 Slavery Convention and in many cases treaties conducted between dominant enslaver states.

The 1919 Treaty of Saint Germain-en-Laye marking the conclusion of the First World War, the 1890 Brussels Conference Act, the 1885 General Act of the Berlin Conference, Act 15 of the 1815 Congress of Vienna, and the related 1814 Treaty of Paris mark significant milestones in situating the "slave trade" in international law from the perspective of European enslaver states. Yet, these movements toward abolition do little for claims against these states, whose domestic law (for the most part) had already been brought into conformity with their terms.[46] Thus, at least in relation to codified international

[42] A small window of time in the early nineteenth century serves as a limited exception to this conclusion, wherein British courts came to accept a natural law justification for a jus gentium right to visit foreign ships in times of peace in order to suppress the "slave trade." Between the 1810 decision in *The Amedie* and the 1817 *Le Louis* case, however, this would shift to a strongly positivist perspective on international law requiring the consent of other states. See Jean Allain, *Slavery in International Law: Of Human Exploitation and Trafficking* (Martinus Nijhoff 2013) 65.

[43] Slavery Convention (adopted September 25, 1926, entered into force March 9, 1927) 60 LNTS 253.

[44] Supplementary Convention on the Abolition of Slavery, the Slave Trade, and Institutions and Practices Similar to Slavery (adopted September 7, 1956, entered into force April 30, 1957) 266 UNTS 3.

[45] Article 8 contains the prohibition against slavery, the slave trade, and servitude while Article 4 makes this nonderogable—International Covenant on Civil and Political Rights (adopted December 16, 1966, entered into force March 23, 1976) 999 UNTS 171.

[46] France abolished slavery in 1794 only for Napoleon to renege on this position and reinstate in 1802, to then prohibit slave trading in 1818 and slavery in 1848; Great Britain prohibited the slave trade in 1807 and slavery in all its territories in 1834; the Netherlands prohibited slave trading in 1814 and slavery in 1863; Portugal prohibited slave trading in 1836 and slavery in 1869; Spain prohibited slave trading in 1817 and slavery in 1837 in all colonies bar Cuba, Puerto Rico, and Santo Domingo not completing abolition in Puerto Rico until 1873. Denmark-Norway in 1792 declared the transatlantic slave trade illegal with effect from 1803, although it was not until 1848 that slavery in the colonies would be abolished.

norms, rules were cemented after the practices that might constitute a breach had already ceased. Moreover, the requirements for suppression were generally couched in language allowing for gradual, rather than immediate, abolition, and treaty relationships were primarily between European powers.[47]

The 1815 Act of the Congress of Vienna is labeled as the first international instrument dealing "specifically with the slave trade in general," although it is probably more appropriate to classify it as the first multilateral agreement dealing with the abolition of the "slave trade" in general.[48] The Declaration of the Powers, on the Abolition of the Slave Trade contained therein declared "slave trading" "repugnant to the principles of humanity and universal morality" as recognized by "just and enlightened men of all ages," suggested that the public voice in all "civilized" countries called for "prompt suppression," and concluded that all the powers had acknowledged the "duty and necessity of abolishing it."[49] The plenipotentiaries therefore committed themselves to securing the universal abolition of the "slave trade," however, allowing for an (undefined) transitional period in which suppression was scheduled to take place, to be determined by negotiation between the parties.[50]

Although the transitional period was limited by the requirement that parties not neglect proper means of securing the attainment of, and accelerating, complete abolition, the exact end date at which obligations became strictly binding is unclear. The 1885 Declaration Relative to the Slave Trade in the General Act of the Berlin Conference, on the other hand, declared "trading in slaves" to be "forbidden in conformity with the principles of international law as recognized by the Signatory Powers."[51] Thus, the

[47] With the result being that a claim for breach of obligations must be brought between parties, and those outside the treaty relationship would have no recourse for violations of its terms.

[48] Preceding treaties between European powers having regulated transatlantic enslavement as opposed to prohibiting it. Joaquín Alcáide Fernandez, "Hostes Humani Generis: Pirates, Slavers, and Other Criminals" in Bardo Fassbender and others (eds), *The Oxford Handbook of the History of International Law* (OUP 2012) 120, 131. See also Allain, *Slavery in International Law* (n 42) 58.

[49] Declaration of the Eight Courts Relative to the Universal Abolition of the Slave Trade (adopted February 8, 1815) 63 CTS 473 (annexed to the General Treaty of the Vienna Congress as Act 15).

[50] The specification in the Treaty of Paris between the United Kingdom and France of a five-year period for universal cessation of the slave trade, and definitive cessation under any circumstances on the part of the French government, may serve as an indicator of an appropriate timeframe for the transitional period in the Congress of Vienna Act, which makes explicit reference to this bilateral treaty. This, however, should not be treated as determinative given the specific reference to negotiation between parties to the 1815 Declaration. A Definitive Treaty of Peace between his Britannic Majesty and his most Christian Majesty Louis XVIII (UK-France) (adopted May 30, 1814).

[51] General Act of the Berlin Conference on West Africa (adopted February 26, 1885) art 9. Signatories to the treaty included the major enslaving states engaged in transatlantic chattel enslavement—Great Britain, Austria-Hungary, Belgium, Denmark, France, Germany, Italy, the Netherlands, Portugal, Russia, Spain, Sweden and Norway, Turkey, and the United States.

plenipotentiaries bound themselves to employ all means at their disposal to bring an end to the "trade" and to punish those involved. However, this provision specifically concerned the "territories forming the Conventional basin of the Congo," rather than claiming universal effect.[52] Moreover, the more extensive provisions concerning enslavement found in the 1890 Full Act of the Brussels Conference, which were not subject to the same geographic limitation, reiterated the transitional period in relation to the suppression of the "slave trade," with signatories consenting to proceed "gradually, as circumstances may permit . . . with the repression of the slave-trade" within their own territories.[53] Thus the differential mandatory weight represents a distinction between the specific multilateral regime governing a particular territory in Africa and universal international norms, rather than the universal crystallization in 1885.[54]

Until the adoption of the 1890 Final Act of the Brussels Conference, international agreements had maintained their focus on outlawing and repressing the "slave trade," as opposed to dealing with the institution of "slavery" more generally. Although evidence suggests that this approach was conceived as a window to complete abolition, the distinction between commerce and exploitation occurred both in international agreements and in domestic legislation, suggesting that the two prohibitions must be viewed separately for the purpose of establishing contemporary international rules.[55] The 1815 Final Act of the Congress of Vienna and the 1885 General Act of the Berlin Conference addressed the commerce in enslaved persons, but remained silent on enslavement itself, leaving the status of "slavery" ambiguous.[56]

[52] ibid.

[53] Convention Relative to the Slave Trade and Importation into Africa of Firearms, Ammunition, and Spiritous Liquors (adopted July 2, 1890, entered into force August 31, 1891) art 3 (Brussels Conference Act). Signatories included the major slaving powers of the sixteenth to nineteenth centuries: Austria-Hungary, Belgium, the Congo Free State, Denmark, France, the German Empire, Italy, the Netherlands, the Ottoman Empire, Persia, Portugal, the Russian Empire, Spain, Sweden-Norway, the United Kingdom, the United States of America, and Zanzibar.

[54] Although Geraldine van Bueren suggests that the terms of the Berlin Conference Act indicated that the slave trade was already considered illegal as contrary to the principles of international law, this does not account for the limited geographic scope of the regime or the distinction between states' internal laws and international legal opinions. Geraldine van Bueren, "Slavery as Piracy: The Legal Case for Reparations for the Slave Trade" in Christien van den Anker, *The Political Economy of New Slavery* (Palgrave Macmillan 2004) 239–40. On the flaws of this approach, see Allain, *Slavery in International Law* (n 42) 72.

[55] See, for instance, Holger Lutz Kern, "Strategies of Legal Change: Great Britain, International Law, and the Abolition of the Transatlantic Slave Trade" (2004) 6 Journal of the History of International Law 233. This, supported by the distinctions between the domain of international law and that of sovereign states that at the time, kept the internal affairs of states entirely removed from the international arena, except where states had consented to incursions.

[56] Declaration of the Eight Courts (n 49); General Act of the Berlin Conference (n 51).

Affirming the distinction, the 1890 Brussels Conference Act highlighted both the duty to suppress the "slave trade," and the responsibility of parties to liberate enslaved persons, and to protect them once liberated.[57]

Over time, "slavery" was increasingly recognized in international instruments, extending abolition from the "slave trade." However, the distinction between the two was continuously affirmed.[58] Like the "slave trade" before it, the prohibition against "slavery" in treaty law allowed for a transitional period between articulation and crystallization, with the 1926 Slavery Convention presenting the obligation to "prevent and suppress the slave trade" as immediate, while the abolition of slavery internally was allowed to occur "progressively and as soon as possible."[59] It was not until 1956 that the codified prohibition against "slavery" itself no longer permitted a transitional period.[60] Thus, at this point, obligations to criminalize domestically and obligations to penalize subsidiary or related acts attached to both the "slave trade" and "slavery." Thus, while an international prohibition against the "slave trade" can be identified as having crystallized with the 1926 Slavery Convention at the latest, recognition of an absolute prohibition against the institution of slavery itself would take longer, coming into effect in the thirty years between 1926 and 1956.

The inclusion of transitional periods in most multilateral treaties dealing with enslavement creates uncertainty over the definitive point at which the respective prohibitions crystallized. The codification in 1956 of the international prohibition of slavery does little for the claim to reparations for transatlantic chattel enslavement, for the domestic law of enslaver states had already broadly coalesced into prohibition in the nineteenth century.[61] While there may be limited instances in which states were involved in enslavement subsequent to domestic prohibition and international codification, this does not provide an avenue for considering the involvement of these states in the centuries of enslavement and brutality that constituted the transatlantic system.

[57] Article 7, for instance, allowed fugitive slaves to claim the protection of the signatory powers (and demanded that they provide it), Article 18 required contracting powers protect liberated slaves, Article 28 affirmed that taking refuge on a ship of the signatories would set an enslaved person free, and Article 29 gave enslaved people on certain native ships the right to demand their liberty. Brussels Conference Act (n 53).

[58] See Convention Revising the General Act of Berlin, February 26, 1885, and the General Act and Declaration of Brussels, July 2, 1890 (adopted September 10, 1919) 15(4) American Journal of International Law 314, Annex to Article 1, Article 11 (Treaty of Saint-Germain-en-Laye); 1926 Slavery Convention (n 43); Supplementary Slavery Convention (n 44)

[59] Slavery Convention (n 43) arts 1 and 2.

[60] Supplementary Slavery Convention (n 44) arts 3–7.

[61] On the dates of domestic prohibition, see (n 46).

Yet, 1956 does serve as a definitive starting point for consideration of the crystallization of international norms in customary, rather than codified, international law.

2.4. The expansion of enslavement in customary international law

For most proponents of reparations for transatlantic enslavement, it is not treaty law upon which the international prohibition against enslavement relies. Rather, the prohibition is located in customary international law, tracing beyond the period of positive prohibition of the nineteenth and twentieth centuries.[62] The orthodox account of the development of the prohibition against enslavement in customary international law dates crystallization some time in the last 150 to 200 years. Capturing this sentiment, Geoffrey Robertson suggests,

> there was no defining moment like the Nuremberg judgement, but rather an accumulation of treaties throughout the nineteenth century and a gradual abandonment by the Great Powers of their toleration of the practice, marked in turn by military offensives against traders . . . and by domestic court declarations that freed any slave brought within the jurisdiction.[63]

Robertson concludes that the exact period in which the prohibition came to have legal force was some time between the Treaty of Berlin in 1885 and the conclusion of the Slavery Convention in 1926. Although this period undoubtedly marks a shift toward the positive abolition by European powers of the institution of transatlantic chattel enslavement they themselves had established, it takes the unrestricted legality of transatlantic enslavement as its starting point. In other words, it operates on the uninterrogated premise that the pervasiveness of enslavement during this period marked its international legality. It does not question the international legal status of enslavement prior to European expansion into the "New World."

[62] See (n 1): Gifford 91; Beckles; Wittmann.

[63] Geoffrey Robertson, *Crimes against Humanity: The Struggle for Global Justice* (Penguin 1999) at 209.

Enslavement's occupation of the historical record—well beyond the transatlantic system—is pervasive and undeniable.[64] However, the question for legal scholarship turns not only upon the presence of enslavement but also upon the treatment of that situation in law through time. In an international legal assessment, historical ubiquity and domestic legality are not decisive, although they may provide evidence of state practice and *opinio juris* required for the formulation of customary international law.[65] Moreover, customary international rules permit modification over time.[66] It is therefore necessary to consider whether international custom oscillated so significantly on the issue of enslavement that prohibition or restriction was established, usurped, and later established again.

In Roman law—the foundation of much European and subsequently modern international law—enslavement was characterized as an aspect of jus gentium, despite its recognized contravention of natural law. Justinian's institutes permitted this conflict between *jus naturale* and jus gentium by allowing enslavement as an alternative to death.[67] Enslavement might therefore arise when a person was convicted of a crime subject to capital punishment, as an escape from poverty and starvation (for a person selling themselves or their dependents into enslavement), or as a substitute for death in war. This justification for human enslavement predominated legal reasoning for over a millennium, featuring in the *Islamic Law of Nations* (*Siyar*), internal laws of Africa, and in the writings of many of the foundational

[64] See Orlando Patterson, *Slavery and Social Death: A Comparative Study* (Harvard UP 1982) vii. This is further considered in chapter 1.

[65] See *North Sea Continental Shelf Cases (Federal Republic of Germany v Denmark; Federal Republic of Germany v Netherlands)* (Judgment) [1969] ICJ Rep 3, 44; *Case Concerning the Continental Shelf (Libyan Arab Jamahiriya v Malta)* (Judgment) [1985] ICJ Rep 13, 29. See also generally Malcolm Shaw, *International Law* (8th edn, CUP 2017) 53–69; Hugh Thirlway, "The Sources of International Law" in Malcolm Evans, *International Law* (4th edn, OUP 2014) 97–105.

[66] On the status of internal law in considerations of international law, and the potential for the two regimes to exist in conflict rather than complementarity, see Articles on State Responsibility (n 33) arts 3, 31; Vienna Convention on the Law of Treaties (n 37) art 27; *Treatment of Polish Nationals and Other Persons of Polish Origin or Speech in the Danzig Territory* (Advisory Opinion) [1932] PCIJ Rep Series A/B No 44 [62]–[63]. See also *Case of the Free Zones of Upper Savoy and the District of Gex (France v Switzerland)* (Order of December 6) [1930] PCIJ Rep Series A No 24, 12; *Case of the SS "Wimbledon" (United Kingdom, France, Italy, Japan v Germany)* [1923] PCIJ Rep Series A/B No 74, 29; *The Greco-Bulgarian "Communities"* (Advisory Opinion) [1930] PCIJ Rep Series B No 17, 32.

[67] As Girard suggests: "The victor, having the right to kill the vanquished has *a fortiori* the right to make him his property." Paul Frédéric Girard, *Manuel Élémentaire de Droit Romain* (A Rousseau 1929) 102–03. This reasoning also applies in instances of slavery as a punishment for a capital crime, and, with some alteration, to children sold into slavery as a result of poverty where death by starvation could be considered the natural course of events. On these two alternative situations in which slavery was considered permissible, see WW Buckland, *A Text-Book of Roman Law: From Augustus to Justinian* (Peter Stein ed, 3rd edn, CUP 1963) 69–71.

authors of (Western) international law.[68] Rather than simply operating as a justification for the existence of enslavement in a system closely connected to natural law philosophy, this allowance of enslavement can be described as an exception to a general rule prohibiting it. In other words, enslavement in a general sense was prohibited as a contravention of *jus naturale*, while enslavement in defined circumstances (as an alternative to death) was permitted as a matter of jus gentium.[69]

In this understanding of the legal justification for enslavement, the collection of rights a person might claim is seen as subsidiary to, or derivative of, the fundamental right to life. At the point at which a person may lawfully be killed, or in some circumstances when they otherwise would have died, they lose their claim to the range of other legal rights normal citizens possess—in particular the natural law right to liberty.[70] Thus, enslavement in such a case may be viewed not only as a social death but also as a legal death—the loss of legal personality in favor of chattel status.[71] In Gentili's words, "Slavery is all but death."[72] Yet, for the general population not placed in a situation in which they would otherwise die, or might lawfully be killed, the prohibition against enslavement and the protection of their right to life, liberty, and property remained in effect. This formulation is not limited to Roman and European

[68] In *Sharia* law, the only two situations which permitted enslavement were the (relatively rare) slavery by birth and capture of non-Muslims in war. See Majid Kaddhouri, *The Islamic Law of Nations: Shaybani's Siyar* (Johns Hopkins UP 1966); Joseph Schacht, *An Introduction to Islamic Law* (Clarendon Press 1982) 127–30. On early African law, see Wittmann (n 1) 34–85. In Western European international law, Vitoria's *On the Indians Lately Discovered*, Suárez's *De Legibus, Ac Deo Legislatore*, and Belli's *De Re Militari et Bello Tractatus, 1563*, all conceive of slavery as a permissible deviation from the laws of nature on the basis of such situations. Vitoria (n 15); Pierino Belli, *De Re Militari et Bello Tractatus* (Clarendon Press 1936); Francisco Suárez, "*De Legibus, Ac Deo Legislatore, 1612*" in *Selection from Three Works of Francisco Suárez*, vol 2 (William S Hein & Co 1995).

[69] Note that this is a justification predominating the identified domestic legal systems, and not purely (or even primarily) an argument concerning international law.

[70] This formulation of the nature of slavery is consistent with Buckland's characterization of slavery as the manifestation of *dominum*—"the ultimate right, that which has no right behind it"—over a person. Buckland, *A Text-Book* (n 67) 54. See also Orlando Patterson's assertion that "dominium constituted absolute power" including the right to "derive the full economic value of a thing, to use (usus) and enjoy its fruits (fructus), as well as to use it up (*ab-usus*), to alienate it, but perhaps most significantly . . . [to have] inner power over a thing beyond mere control." Patterson argues that the very concept of *dominium* arose in relation to slavery—n 64, 31. With regard to the right to life, masters retained the right to kill enslaved persons, and increasing restrictions on masters had nothing to do with the well-being of the persons enslaved. See Alan Watson, *Roman Slave Law* (Johns Hopkins UP 1987) 120.

[71] At the point in which a person was captured in war, they were deemed to have died, suffering "*capitus deminutio maxima*—the 'greatest change of status'—involving the loss of freedom, citizenship and family." Paul du Plessis, *Borkowski's Textbook on Roman Law* (4th edn, OUP 2010) 91.

[72] Alberico Gentili, *De Iure Belli Libri Tres, 1612* (Clarendon Press 1933) 325.

legal reasoning, but is consistent with African laws permitting certain forms of enslavement prior to European involvement in the continent.[73]

Later, both Christian and Islamic jurists would begin to qualify their acceptance of this restricted practice of enslavement by limiting it to people outside their own religious communities.[74] This religious international law created distinctions between people within the faith and those outside it, drawing borders not only on the boundaries of statehood but also along theological lines. This was true of the major evangelizing religions predominating the period leading up to the institution of transatlantic chattel enslavement—Christendom and Islam.[75]

In Christendom, Gentili, Belli, Ayala, Legnano, and Grotius (among others) concluded that enslavement was impermissible in wars between Christian nations, but in wars with "infidels" and "pagans," the enemy could be lawfully enslaved.[76] In the Islamic law of nations, a similar understanding came to dominate, with a central distinction drawn between Muslims and non-Muslims in the "Abode of War."[77] Although this blurs the boundaries between the jus gentium justification for enslavement as an alternative to death and a *jus naturale* understanding of some people as suited for a life of servitude, this understanding nonetheless maintained the classic caveats. Enslavement remained prima facie prohibited—even in relation to "pagan," "barbaric," or "backward" peoples—with an exception carved out for situations in which death could lawfully be meted out.[78]

Because the preconditions for lawful enslavement still applied in the context of religious distinction, increasing restrictions within religious communities on the treatment of captives of war can be characterized as the rise

[73] See (n 1).

[74] In Islamic law, this qualification was incorporated already into the *Siyar*, wherein only non-Muslims were to be subjects of enslavement. See Schacht (n 68) 127–30.

[75] On the significance of the Islamic law of nations in this period of international legal development see Jean Allain, "Acculturation through the Middle Ages: the Islamic Law of Nations and Its Place in the History of International Law" in Alexander Orakhelashvili (ed), *Research Handbook on the Theory and History of International Law* (Edward Elgar Publishing 2011) 394.

[76] See Allain, *Slavery in International Law* (n 42) 9–56.

[77] Although non-Muslims were not necessarily to be subjected to a life of servitude—they would be released when the "Abode of Peace" was achieved. Despite the Quran's instruction that prisoners of war be freed at the conclusion of hostilities, Clarence-Smith notes that people increasingly found excuses to avoid this dictate, including through "public interest" arguments based on other mandates of the Quran. William Gervase Clarence-Smith, *Islam and the Abolition of Slavery* (OUP 2006) 25. On the distinction between Muslims and non-Muslims, see Kaddhouri (n 68); Schacht (n 68) 127–30; Allain, *Slavery in International Law* (n 42) 17–20.

[78] Legnano maintained the jus gentium foundations of enslavement, but only permitted such in relation to "enemy" states—Giovanni da Legnano, Tractatus *De Bello, De Represaliis et De Duello, 1390* (Thomas Erskine Holland ed, OUP 1917).

of a regional international law restricting enslavement within its borders. European jurists affirmed this development by continuing to frame enslaved persons as an exception to the rules of postliminy—"the right to recovery of something in the possession of the enemy"—but exempting Christians who, as brothers, could not be enslaved by their captors.[79] The right to recovery of Christian prisoners therefore remained, and the rise of ransom payments provided an alternative for post-war treatment of these captives.[80]

Although the justification of enslavement within limited circumstances predominated the historical record prior to and even during much of the period of transatlantic chattel enslavement, an alternative justification became increasingly significant with the growing racialization of enslavement. This understanding of the institution considered in chapter 1, which would legitimize treating the color of a person's skin as reason for their servitude, rested not upon slavery as a feature of jus gentium but on an understanding of enslavement nestled in *jus naturale*. Yet, despite its meteoric rise in the latter half of the last millennium, characterizing enslavement as an aspect of the natural order features in the subtext of many of the opinions regarding the institution throughout history, simply experiencing rises and falls in how transparent commentators were in their reliance.

The belief in a natural law justification for enslavement is often traced to Aristotle, who suggested that some humans were, by nature, not their own but "of someone else."[81] Although not stripping such humans of their status as humans entirely, Aristotle contended that they would be "a piece of property . . . a tool for action separate from its owner."[82] Reiterating this fourth century BCE opinion, Sepúlveda in the sixteenth century suggested that "Indians were slaves by nature," and Pufendorf supported such in his seventeenth-century descriptions of those people he considered to be naturally suited for a life of servitude.[83] This discourse centered the natural or biological predilection of certain persons toward servitude, encompassing

[79] Belli (n 68) 104, 242.

[80] See Balthazar Ayala, *De Jure et Oficiis Bellicis et Disciplina Militari, 1582* (Carnegie Institution of Washington 1912) 40; Gentili (n 72) 328–33; Legnano (n 78).

[81] On the increasing significance of Aristotle's understanding of the "natural slave," see Brion Davis (n 20).

[82] Aristotle, "Politics" in John Gillies (ed), *Aristotle's Ethics and Politics*, vol 2 (A Strahan, T Cadell and W Davies 1797) 1–52 (bk 1).

[83] On Sepúlveda, see Allain, *Slavery in International Law* (n 42) 28. Pufendorf describes such people as inherently stupid and lazy, lacking capacity to observe their own needs and conduct which would benefit them. Samuel Pufendorf, *De Jure Naturae et Gentium Libri Octo, 1672* (Clarendon Press 1934) 934.

the growth of "scientific slavery," and rose to international prominence in discussions of European enslavement of African people as well justifications of colonialism more generally.[84]

Alongside growing social and cultural understanding of blackness, legal frameworks evidenced increasing racialization, disseminating the idea that Africans were best suited for lives of enslavement.[85] Thus, the social consciousness of the white masses, cultivated by enslavers, came to associate "blackness" with enslavement and to accept race as a basis for legal discrimination.[86] So-called black codes proliferated, persons of color were subjected to legal presumptions of enslaved status, and "negro" became a legal, as well as a social, classification.[87] No longer was enslavement primarily justified as an alternative to death but now as a byproduct of natural differences between men—a difference primarily defined by the color of a person's skin.[88] Thus, the denial of the two basic and foundational human rights (freedom from enslavement and racial discrimination) identified in *Barcelona Traction* as jus cogens norms with obligations *erga omnes* coalesced.[89]

This shift in the justification for enslaving Africans and people of African descent was central to the system of racialized chattel enslavement, for it allowed the enslavement of Africans and people of African descent who had been converted to Christianity, baptized, given Christian names, and born and raised in Christian states. Africans who converted to Christianity either by choice, coercion, or force were not thereby ensured a life free from enslavement as prior restrictions on enslavement provided. Rather, there were many instances in which forcible conversions and baptisms were conducted in slave forts prior to forced emigration.[90] Thus, the "law of nations" could

[84] On biological determinism, or scientific racism, see Stephen Gould, *The Mismeasure of Man* (2nd edn, WW Norton & Co 1996).

[85] On social and cultural depictions of race, see Dana Van Kooy and Jeffrey N Cox, "Melodramatic Slaves" (2012) 55(4) Modern Drama 459; Eric Lott, *Love and Theft: Blackface Minstrelsy and the American Working Class* (OUP 2013); Katrina Dyonne Thompson, *Ring Shout, Wheel About* (University of Illinois Publishing 2014).

[86] See generally Andrew S Curran, *The Anatomy of Blackness: Science and Slavery in an Age of Enlightenment* (Johns Hopkins UP 2011).

[87] The US Constitution, for instance, famously counted "negroes" as only three-fifths of a person for the purpose of apportioning representatives. Regardless of the reasoning behind this compromise, the legal category of "negro" was thereby affirmed. Constitution of the United States (1787). See also Annette Gordon-Reed, "America's Original Sin: Slavery and the Legacy of White Supremacy" (2018) 97(1) Foreign Affairs 2.

[88] See section 1.5.

[89] *Barcelona Traction* singles out slavery and racial discrimination in its discussion of *erga omnes* obligations. *Case concerning the Barcelona Traction, Light and Power Company Ltd (Belgium v Spain)* [1970] ICJ Rep 3, 32 at [34].

[90] See John W Catron, "Evangelical Networks in the Greater Caribbean and the Origins of the Black Church" (2010) 79(1) Church History 77; Dominic Erdozain, "The Secularisation of Sin in the

no longer be seen as creating a system of international law with one system of treatment for those inside the regional or religious order and another for those outside. The increasing secularization of international law in the late nineteenth century saw religious boundaries deteriorating, but not in favor of a universal system. Instead, new boundaries were erected justifying the othering of African peoples, borders enforced by the concept of "civilization."[91]

2.5. African voices on transatlantic enslavement

Given the bias of European institutions when it came to assessing and asserting the legality of enslavement, it is important to note the way that enslaved Africans and people of African descent spoke of their own situation. For many enslaved persons, the status of the institution was not perceived as a question of law but of power.[92] Although enslaved people may have had to adapt to the system of brutality and perpetual servitude, acclimatization is not necessarily an indicator of acquiescence. Rebellions within the system were common from the outset, in source countries, on board slave ships, and on plantations.[93] Thus, the characterization of enslaved Africans as "docile" and "acquiescent" enslavers sought to project to reinforce race-based enslavement was refuted by enslaved people themselves, even in conditions where punishments for resistance were horrific.[94] Even beyond violent rebellion, enslaved persons found ways to indicate resistance against the assumption that their enslavement was lawful and legitimate, when they had a voice and the ability to consider enslavement beyond their own situation.

Nineteenth Century" (2011) 62(1) The Journal of Ecclesiastical History 59; Ty Reese, "'Sheep in the Jaws of So Many Ravenous Wolves': The Slave Trade and Anglican Missionary Activity at Cape Coast Castle, 1752–1816" (2004) 34(3) Journal of Religion in Africa 348.

[91] Se generally Gerrit Gong, *The Standard of "Civilization" in International Society* (OUP 1984).

[92] See, for instance, Gad Heuman and James Walvin, *The Slavery Reader* (Routledge 2003) 546–634.

[93] On resistance, see section 1.4. See also Egerton (n 5); Michael Craton, *Testing the Chains: Resistance to Slavery in the British West Indies* (Cornell UP 2009); Eugene Genovese, *From Rebellion to Revolution: Afro-American Slave Revolts in the Making of the Modern World* (Louisiana State UP 1979); David Richardson, "Shipboard Revolts, African Authority, and the Atlantic Slave Trade" (2001) 58(1) The William and Mary Quarterly 69, 72. Richardson identifies 485 shipboard rebellions on French, Dutch, and British ships between 1650 and 1860, although sources from which these were drawn were understandably limited, and thus the number should not be taken as indicative of the total number of shipboard rebellions that in fact occurred on ships belonging to these states.

[94] Genovese refers to this as the "myth of slave docility and quiescence" in Genovese (n 93).

Historical reports explained revolts as demonstrations of Africans' belief that Europeans had no right to enslave them and carry them away from their home countries. For instance, James Towne in recounting a slave rebellion on board a ship he had served indicated that Africans "rejected the right of Europeans to enslave them and to carry them away 'from their own country' and their 'wives and children.'"[95] Enslaved people on plantations in the Americas often spoke of themselves and their kin as having been "stolen" from Africa or from some other location to which they attached themselves when slavery had become intergenerational.[96] Many accounts of the history of transatlantic enslavement include such identifications by enslaved persons. Edward E Baptist highlights the significance of this narrative framing, arguing that enslaved persons' frequent use of the word "stole" indicated their understandings of illegality: "They made it clear that this common story was a crime story. Buying and selling people was a crime. Buyers and sellers were criminals."[97]

Not only was the presumption of lawfulness resisted through this language, but also the provenance of enslaved persons having been forcibly migrated from Africa to the Americas was challenged. Thus, even in a world in which slavery was considered consistent with European international law in defined circumstances, enslaved people spoke of their own dubious origins.[98] The characterization of enslavement as legitimate international trade captured neither the violent and unlawful ways in which people were captured for enslavement nor the role of European people and powers in this process.

While enslaved persons demonstrated opposition to their own enslavement and spoke in the language of criminality in so doing, in the eyes of international law as formulated by European colonial powers, these voices could not be persuasive. International law during this period was concerned with the "opinions" of states deemed sufficiently civilized so as to qualify for the recognition of sovereignty over their own territories.[99] This account suggests that individuals were only conceived as the subject matter of international

[95] In Richardson (n 93) 71.

[96] See Edward E Baptist, "'Stol' and Fetched Here": Enslaved Migration, Ex-Slave Narratives, and Vernacular History' in Edward E Baptist and Stephanie MH Camp (eds), *New Studies in the History of American Slavery* (University of Georgia Press 2006).

[97] Edward E Baptist, *The Half Has Never Been Told: Slavery and the Making of American Capitalism* (Basic Books 2014) 187–89.

[98] See ibid 191.

[99] See Thirlway (n 65) 100; Gong (n 91).

law indirectly, through the representation of their state of nationality.[100] For Africans and their descendants, as well as indigenous people in colonial territories, this rendered their voices invisible to the international legal system, for they possessed neither international rights of their own nor citizenship in a recognized state through which to claim protection.

To establish African opposition within the international legal system, the political leaders of African states would need to have presented the uniform and consistent opposition required for the formation of international custom.[101] While resistance in this context need not be universal or absolute in its uniformity, inconsistent practice must be treated as a breach in order for a prohibitive norm to prevail.[102] Problematically, not only was opposition to slavery variable, with many African leaders engaging in enslavement, but also in some cases the very terms of resistance indicated against a universal prohibition based on morality, custom, or consent. In the early sixteenth century, the King of Kongo entreated Portugal's John III to cease engaging in enslavement and trade in enslaved persons in the territory:

> The merchants abduct our subjects, children of this country, sons of nobles and vassals, even people of our family.... This corruption and this deprivation are so common that our land is entirely depopulated.... It is our volition that this kingdom shall not be a territory neither of the trade nor of the transit of slaves.[103]

Framed in the language of pragmatism favoring internal interests, rather than moral condemnation, this letter highlights diplomatic necessity and the "depopulation" problem as the basis for a request for the cessation of enslavement and trade in enslaved persons in and from the Kongo. Moreover, the specific geographic focus of the letter—a request for discontinuance only within the boundaries of the "kingdom"—limits its significance as evidence of a belief in international prohibition. Such expressions indicate that the practice of non-European states was far from the threshold

[100] See Shaw (n 65) 204; Robert McCorquodale, "The Individual and the International Legal System" in Evans (n 65) 280; JG Starke, *Starke's International Law* (IA Shearer ed, 11th edn, Butterworths 1994) 51.

[101] Requiring "constant and uniform usage practised by States" for the formation of customary norms, see *Asylum Case (Colombia v Peru)* (Judgment) [1950] ICJ Rep 266, 276.

[102] *Case Concerning Military and Paramilitary Activities in and against Nicaragua (Nicaragua v United States of America)* (Merits) [1986] ICJ Rep 14, 98.

[103] In Nora Wittmann, "Slavery Reparations Are a Must" (2009) 488 New African 24, 26.

expected in the formation of international custom or in persistent objection to a growing permissive rule as formulated within the embryonic European system.[104]

Reference to African "complicity" alone is insufficient to found an African *opinio juris* of the legality of enslavement in international law. However, the involvement of political figures and rulers speaks in support of the evolving international law allowing transatlantic enslavement. The relevance of the historical evidence of participation of African political entities in global enslavement is not in the conclusion that Africans occupied the same boat as European slave traders but rather in reflecting the inchoate character of universal opinion at the time. It is not the practices of individual African enslavers that are relevant to this dialogue—African enslavers would be just as capable of contravening international law as individual Europeans—but the actions of official entities who could reinforce a conception of international law involving the *opinio juris* of states.

Even if, prior to the institution of transatlantic enslavement, international law evidenced a universal prohibition against enslavement with only limited permissive exceptions, the development of the transatlantic system in cooperation with African political leaders would likely constitute the changing of international custom, as opposed to nearly four centuries of near-constant breaches. It is the treatment of the conduct as normative, rather than as persistent violation, that contributes to the evolution of custom—in this case, the usurpation of existing restrictions on enslavement by racialized exploitation.[105] African leaders' interactions with Europeans are far from decisive in decrying the system of transatlantic enslavement and farther from a clear and consistent opposition in either positive conduct or abstention.[106] Thus, although European states' assertion of a lack of civilization in the "New World" cannot be decisive, fluctuating levels of participation and resistance

[104] Thirlway suggests that in order to establish persistent objection to a developing rule of customary international law, state opposition must be "established, widespread and consistent": Thirlway (n 65) 98.

[105] On the role of breaches on customary international law, see *Military and Paramilitary Activities in Nicaragua* (n 102); Antony Anghie, *Imperialism, Sovereignty, and the Making of International Law* (CUP 2007) 44; Shaw (n 65) 68.

[106] The *Lotus Case* indicates that abstention is only likely to involve the recognition of a custom if based upon a conscious duty (of international law) to abstain—a standard which is unlikely to be reached in the case of those states not involved in transatlantic enslavement. *Case of the SS Lotus (France v Turkey)* [1927] PCIJ Series A No 10, 28. On African interactions with Europe, see Heuman and Walvin (n 92) 30–102, 701–63.

presented by African political leaders make the claim to universal prohibition for the period of transatlantic enslavement similarly inadequate.[107]

2.6. The implications of oscillation and lacunae in international law

Perhaps the most persuasive message advanced by the oscillating practice of justifying and restricting enslavement is the lack of a clear and consistent narrative in the history of international law. This is true not only of international law regarding enslavement but also for the development of the international legal system as a reflection of European interests more generally. The changing international legal conclusions drawn by jurists throughout the period of transatlantic chattel enslavement speak to their own institutional, national, and economic biases more than indicating a coherent international legal order. As Jean Allain highlights,

> there is no true sense of evolution in international law where slavery is concerned. Instead, the texts speak to the specific interests of the authors, whether these are the meta-narrative of Grotius or the practical military manual of Ayala. In so doing, various justifications are marshalled over time to either expand or contract the space opened for slavery as constituting part of the contemporaneous international law.[108]

What evolution can be gleaned from the changing landscape of international legal thought concerning enslavement fails to provide a stable foundation for a declaration of outright prohibition prior to the institution of the transatlantic system.

One of the greatest weaknesses in historical assessment of international law concerning enslavement is the high degree of ambiguity present in the practice and pronouncements of states in both the national and international spheres. When ambiguity suffuses treaty law as well as the practice and

[107] At the time of abolition by European states, the practice of enslavement was still present within the African continent, and the US Supreme Court then expressed the inappropriateness of extending its own laws on enslavement to Africa. In *The Antelope*, the court stated (perhaps ironically at this point): "The parties to the modern law of nations do not propagate their principles by force; and Africa has not yet adopted them. Throughout the world of that immense continent, so far as we know its history, it is still the law of nations that prisoners are slaves." *The Antelope* [1825] 23 US 66.

[108] Allain, *Slavery in International Law* (n 42) 12.

commentaries that might serve as evidence of the formulation of customary international law, it becomes difficult to draw a definitive conclusion on the status of international law at the time. Moreover, when a persuasive case rooted in appropriate sources of evidence can be made to justify either position, historical international law presents an inquirer with more questions than answers. Yet, in finding argumentation in the midst of a sea of uncertainty, the reality of the international legal order during and directly following the period of transatlantic enslavement becomes clearer.

The oscillations, the opacities, the vagaries, and the contradictions of international law on the issue of enslavement and the *maangamizi* reveal the intimate connection between the development of a Eurocentric international legal order and the dehumanization of the native populations of three continents, racialized chattel enslavement, and exploitation.[109] The international legal texts themselves reveal this tension. These contradictions indicate that the reliance on the international legal order of the time, as the basis of obligations, may not be a reliable or desirable approach. However, they also suggest that advertence to present international law as the basis for a denial of obligations is a similarly problematic endeavor. An international legal order constructed by European enslaver states to further their own economic interests is a questionable source from which to derive an understanding of universal obligations.

Recognition of the oscillations of international norms concerning enslavement does not provide a positive argument for a fully crystallized prohibition against enslavement in global international law, breached by imperial European "Powers." Rather, it is the denial of a denial. The deprivation of a common basis on which discussion of international obligations is rejected provides the opening of a space where meaningful moral and political discourse on the question can take place.[110] Perhaps ironically, the positivist doctrine of intertemporal law provides an entry point for naturalist legal frameworks to influence this discourse, for it was these philosophies that predominated international jurisprudential thinking at the time.[111]

Enslavement has been recognized throughout history, albeit inconsistently, as contrary to fundamental rights and the laws of nature, with related assertions that contrary jus gentium may only be enacted through clear and

[109] See Anghie, *Imperialism* (n 9).

[110] This may then serve as the foundation for morally and politically motivated reparatory justice, as considered in relation to transitional justice in chapter 7.

[111] See Shaw (n 65) 36–39.

deliberate positive law.[112] During the period of transatlantic enslavement, the language of antislavery campaigners and previously enslaved persons demonstrated this naturalist understanding of the criminality of enslavement, irrespective of its positive legal status. Thomas Clarkson, for instance, questioned enslavement's legality:

> Is there no crime in adopting a system which keeps down all the noble faculties of their souls, and which positively debases and corrupts their nature? Is there no crime in perpetuating these evils among their innocent offspring?[113]

Even in the early twentieth century, with positivism having taken a firm hold of international jurisprudential thought, the notion of enslavement as a contravention of fundamental values remained.[114]

The growth of positivist thought in the international legal order did violence to non-European peoples by enabling their denigration and conquest, and legitimizing extreme violence, in the name of the civilizing mission.[115] This capacity of international norms to support imperial expansion and dominance derived from the usurpation of fundamental norms premised on moral dictates through positive law.[116] Thus, developments in international law permitting and regulating enslavement and the *maangamizi* enabled the establishment and inculcation of European hegemony. Yet, in looking back to the root these injustices from an historical perspective consistent with positivist doctrine, naturalist norms reaffirm their relevance.

[112] See, for instance, *Somersett v Stewart* [1772] 98 ER 499, 510, asserting that "the state of slavery" is "so odious, that nothing can be suffered to support it, but positive law."

[113] Thomas Clarkson, *The History of the Rise, Progress, and Accomplishment of the Abolition of the African Slave-Trade by the British Parliament* (New impression, Frank Cass & Co Ltd 1968) 20–21.

[114] The British government in negotiating the Slavery Convention advocated a notion of enslavement as a "crimes against the human race" according to the international consensus of "civilised" nations. League of Nations, "Draft Convention on Slavery Recommended by the Sixth Assembly: Reply from the British Government" (1926) A.10.1926.VI; 8 League of Nations Official Journal 1031, 1032. However, other parties to the negotiations, though supporting the moral sentiment, expressed a distinction between the legal frameworks and moral principles in this regard. League of Nations, "Draft Convention on Slavery Recommended by the Sixth Assembly" (1926) A.10(a).1926.VI, 9 League of Nations Official Journal 1140. See Allain, *Slavery in International Law* (n 42) 81.

[115] Antony Anghie, "Finding the Peripheries: Sovereignty and Colonialism in Nineteenth-Century International Law" (1999) 40 Harvard International Law Journal 1, 17.

[116] Detley F Vagts, "Hegemonic International Law" (2001) 95 Amherst Journal of International Law 843, 845.

The recognition of oscillations or lacunae in the history of international law governing enslavement may open the door to a naturalist presumption in favor of illegitimacy that may not have been overcome by the inconsistent, self-interested, and prejudicial practice of European states from the fifteenth to nineteenth centuries. This argument may not find voice in the positive legal mechanisms of the contemporary international legal system but may nonetheless inform the moral and political case for reparations for historical enslavement and the *maangamizi*.

To claim enslavement was "legal at the time," and therefore that it is inappropriate to condemn the conduct of European enslaver states, is to overlook the ways in which the racialized system of chattel enslavement of African, indigenous, and aboriginal peoples was constructed, altered, and perpetuated by European powers to advance their own interests. Even if the practice of enslavement was permitted in international law prior to European expansion into the "New World," the foundations on which this was justified, and the conditions under which it could be conducted, were substantially modified. Therefore, it is important to separate the investigation of slavery from its widespread practice throughout history to interrogate the terms and conditions of its permissibility.

Beyond questions of the terms on which slavery might have been permitted, it is necessary to consider the ways in which the growth and evolution of the institution of slavery from an exception to a racialized rule was the byproduct not of universal consensus but of the interests of a few. Not because this might help to conclude on the existence of universal prohibition, for *The Legality of the Threat and Use of Nuclear Weapons* speaks against such.[117] Rather, because this may assist in deconstructing the prevailing opinion that enslavement was positively legalized in universal international law—the belief not only that there was no prohibition against slavery but that participating in enslavement and trading in human lives as if they were property was a centrally protected property right in a global legal system.

[117] In requiring those states with the most significant interest to be involved in the formulation of prohibitive universal custom, the International Court of Justice barred the formulation of norms without the support of those states most implicated in breaching an allegedly crystallizing norm (in this case, nuclear states)—*Legality of the Threat or Use of Nuclear Weapons* (Advisory Opinion) [1996] ICJ Rep 226, 255.

Finding a lacuna in international legal regulation should not be equated with a permissive rule. Not because it may result in legal consequences, for this requires a breach of a binding international rule; rather, because it serves an important signaling function in the way that redress is approached in the contemporary age. Legality cannot be employed as a defense to a moral or political claim to reparations if there is no governing law.

3

Adjudicating the "Past"

The Impact of Time on Reparability

Substantial ambiguities in the governing international legal frameworks create uncertainty as to the value international law provides in the consideration of reparations for transatlantic enslavement and the *maangamizi*. From the purely positivist perspective, the result may be that they offer very little; absence of law creates a space entirely governed by other frameworks, involving a shift from legal mechanisms to moral and political processes.[1] Yet, the contested legal territory leaves open the possibility of judicial mechanisms operating to provide redress in historical cases, making assessment of the other requirements of these legal frameworks valuable. Furthermore, legal conclusions continue to influence the discussion of moral and political obligations in reparations discourse; European international law is the legitimizing framework for the *maangamizi* and contemporary refusals to seriously consider reparations claims. Thus, recognizing the limits of the law does not automatically necessitate the disengagement of legal frameworks and reasoning, although it may require a reconsideration of their positioning.

Many commentators addressing the issue of reparations for transatlantic enslavement suggest that historicity alone presents a legal bar to recovery. Often armed with nothing more than intuition and influenced by a public discourse informing people of African descent that it is now time to "move on" from the past, authors from a range of disciplines assert that the legal claim to redress has been frustrated by the passage of time.[2] This is echoed by

[1] This is a position supported by Hart's conclusions on what should happen in the event of lacuna in the law—namely that these should be resolved through reform of the law or extralegal mechanisms, and not through the inclusion of moral arguments in legal reasoning. See HLA Hart, *The Concept of Law* (2nd edn, OUP 1994).

[2] See The Rt Hon David Cameron, "PM's Speech to the Jamaican Parliament" (*UK Government*, September 30, 2015) <www.gov.uk/government/speeches/pms-speech-to-the-jamaican-parliam ent> accessed March 14, 2018; HL Deb March 14, 1996, vol 570, col 1042. Vincene Verdun identifies that opponents tend to present the reparations claim as "absurd, frivolous, or unworthy of serious consideration": Vincene Verdun, "If the Shoe Fits, Wear It: An Analysis of Reparations to African Americans" (1993) 67 Tulane Law Review 597, 625. Hilary Beckles also discusses this as a strategy

Reparations for Slavery in International Law. Katarina Schwarz, Oxford University Press. © Oxford University Press 2022.
DOI: 10.1093/oso/9780197636398.003.0004

politicians and other actors addressing the issue. Setting aside the question of whether an international norm can be said to have crystallized at the relevant time (considered in chapter 2), issues of acquiescence, attribution, and succession are central to the justiciability of claims in the international legal arena. Although not embedded in the political frameworks, these considerations have bearing on extralegal processes, where the deconstruction of legal barriers has rhetorical and persuasive power.

This chapter considers the implications of the passage of time upon claims to reparations and examines whether related issues pose an absolute bar to recovery. Tracing the history of state responsibility and the construction of attribution, it contemplates different ways in which challenges to contemporary responsibility for historical injustice may be addressed, and ultimately questions whether history has closed the door on redress.

Comprehensive review of the range of possible claims that might be brought into legal fora in relation to the *maangamizi* is beyond the scope of this analysis, which adopts a general, global perspective on the issues. Independent assessments of the continuity of all possible defendant states and the succession of possible claimant states—necessary to establish justiciability of a particular case—are therefore not the focus of the analysis. Although specific rules of standing and jurisdiction might impact the applicability of international legal frameworks in particular formulations of prospective cases, these are likewise not systematically addressed. It therefore cannot be considered conclusive on whether these potential cases have merit or on the likelihood of their success. Instead, what follows is a holistic discussion of the disputes concerning redress for historical abuses and potential solutions to blanket oppositional arguments. This is in recognition of the contested legal ground of reparations claims, and thus the likely engagement of political mechanisms. Thus, while this chapter does not provide a complete or solid foundation for legal argumentation in a case, it does provide a framework against which these cases may be considered.

In light of the critique of international legal frameworks considered in chapters 1 and 2, the following examination does not consider the application of procedural rules developed within this system to be determinative of broader moral and political claims. However, it does address many of the foundational challenges identified by reparations detractors as precluding

of the British government in denying reparations claims in *Britain's Black Debt: Reparations for Caribbean Slavery and Native Genocide* (University of West Indies Press 2013) 19.

the possibility of legal arguments for reparations. By opening a space in which these bars to recovery are identified as contested and contestable, this chapter highlights the ways dominant discourse sidelines legal frameworks and simultaneously how legal frameworks are influenced by the dominant discourse. Thus, even absent a finding of prohibition in international law during the relevant period, this chapter contributes to the debates concerning reparations in both legal and extralegal arenas.

3.1. Attenuation, limitation, and acquiescence

Reparations detractors often frame the passage of time itself—disconnected from any other element of legal responsibility—as frustrating claims for remedy. Beyond the predominance of these arguments in public and political discussion, many academics advance arguments placing the passage of time at the center of reparations denials.[3] Burt Neuborne suggests that historicity distinguishes the case for reparations for slavery from litigation over the Jewish holocaust, with the result that a legal approach is no longer appropriate.[4] Vincene Verdun argues that historical claims are problematic, for many of those who would be required to bear the cost have no connection to the perpetrators of the injustices.[5] Jeremy Waldron asserts that the capacity of rights to "fade" over time simply by virtue of their persistence is a widely recognized phenomenon.[6] Yet, the justifications for these rules of attrition are far from overriding and their decisiveness is far from predetermined.

The central justification for Waldron's acceptance of the supersession of historical injustices is not in the impact of time itself but in the attenuation of causal relationships between wrongdoing and suffering and the entrenchment of certain protected expectations.[7] Verdun's assertion that contemporary defendants are not perpetrators engages with the reality of a new

[3] See for instance Cameron (n 2); HL Deb (n 2) col 1042; WF Tyman, "We Must Let Go of Grudges from Slavery" *Chicago Tribune* (November 6, 2017) <www.chicagotribune.com/news/opinion/commentary/ct-perspec-slavery-reparations-white-supremacy-1107-20171106-story.html> accessed April 23, 2018.
[4] Burt Neuborne, "Holocaust Reparations Litigation: Lessons for the Slavery Reparations Movement" (2003) 58(4) NYU Annual Survey of American Law 615.
[5] Although not entirely dismissing reparations claims, Verdun argues that post-slavery immigrants (for instance) cannot be connected to a wrong associated with slavery and thus cannot be made to bear a part of the costs of a present claim for reparations in relation to it. Verdun (n 2) 630.
[6] Jeremy Waldron, "Superseding Historic Injustice" (1992) 103(1) Ethics 4, 15.
[7] ibid.

generation of citizens but fails to acknowledge the continuity of the state as a single legal and political entity. Neuborne is correct that distinctions must be drawn between claims concerning the Shoah—and likewise Japanese American internment, the "Mau Mau" rebellion, the Rawagede massacre, and most other instances of successful reparations awarded to living direct victims—and claims for historical injustice crossing generations. Yet, this does not account for those instances in which transgenerational claims are recognized.[8] Moreover, lack of analogy, in itself, does not constitute an argument against reparations. Such suggestions concerning the impact of time should therefore be taken on the basis of their internal reasoning, suggesting attenuation on the basis of particular factors identified. They do not justify the conclusion that time alone overrides the requirements of justice.

The attenuation of causal relationships and the attribution of historical conduct to a contemporary state are assessed on the facts, rather than on the basis of a general rule drawing a line after a specific period of time.[9] The question that remains in considering the impact of time upon the claim for redress is: Does a general rule of limitation operate to frustrate liability after a specified period of time? In general international law, historicity does not constitute a circumstance precluding wrongfulness, nor is there a general limitation period in public international law.[10] This differentiates the international legal system from domestic law, where limitation periods may frustrate claims to redress.[11] Some international rules go so far as to preclude the domestic application of limitation periods in relation to certain crimes.[12]

[8] For intergenerational claims, see for instance reparations by the Chilean National Corporation of Reparation and Reconciliation under Law 20.405, December 10, 2009. See also Ernesto Verdeja, "A Normative Theory of Reparations in Transitional Democracies" (2006) 37 Metaphilosophy 449, 459. See also the Peruvian Comprehensive Reparations Plan—Reglamento de la Ley N° 28592, *Ley Que Crea El Plan Integral de Reparaciones* (Pir), Decreto Supremo N° 015-2006-JUS, art 7(c); the practice of the Waitangi Tribunal—Janine Hayward and Nicola Wheen (eds), *Treaty of Waitangi Settlements* (Bridget Williams Books 2015).

[9] Attribution is addressed in section 3.3, while causation is discussed in chapter 6.

[10] Chapter V of the Articles on State Responsibility identifies the six "circumstances precluding wrongfulness" in the law of state responsibility as consent, self-defense, countermeasures in respect of an internationally wrongful act, force majeure, distress, and necessity. Chapter V, International Law Commission, "Draft Articles on the Responsibility of States for Internationally Wrongful Acts" (November 2001) UN Doc A/56/10 (Articles on State Responsibility).

[11] See for instance, *Kimathi & Ors v The Foreign and Commonwealth Office* [2018] EWHC 2066 (QB) where the court dismissed claims against the UK Foreign and Commonwealth Office on the basis of the statutory limitation period in section 33 of the Limitation Act 1980. However, it should be noted that discretion may still permit the waiving of limitation period in cases of historical injustices, as was the case in the related case of *Mutua & Ors v The Foreign and Commonwealth Office* [2012] EWHC 2678 (QB).

[12] The recognition of the inapplicability of limitation periods in relation to crimes against humanity and war crimes, for instance, is recognized as a norm of customary international law in relation to international and non-international armed conflicts. See ICRC, "Rule 160/ Statutes of

Where time may impact the operation of the rules of state responsibility is in the entitlement of states to invoke the responsibility of the state allegedly in breach of its obligations, if the claimant state has validly waived the claim or, by its conduct, acquiesced in the lapse of the claim.[13] In this context, these rules of attrition operate not as a defense to a claim of wrongful conduct but as a barrier to the claim for reparations.

Waivers must be explicit, clear, and unequivocal—conduct that is unlikely to arise in most cases of significant historical injustice.[14] Acquiescence, on the other hand, may result from the failure of the state to take action against the breach and may be satisfied by unreasonable delay but is not achieved by the passage of time alone.[15] The International Court of Justice explicitly recognized in *Certain Phosphate Lands in Nauru* that there was no specific time limit in international law that would amount to acquiescence, instead favoring a determination on the circumstances of the case.[16] The question of whether the claimant state has acquiesced in the lapse of the claim must therefore be determined on the facts at hand considered in light of the

Limitation" *Customary IHL Database* <ihl-databases.icrc.org/customary-ihl/eng/docs/v1_rul_rule160> accessed April 23, 2018. This is supported by the Convention on the Non-Applicability of Statutory Limitations to War Crimes and Crimes against Humanity (adopted November 26, 1968, entered into force November 11, 1970) A/RES/2391(XXIII). The Statute of the ICC also denies the application of statutes of limitation to the crimes under its jurisdiction—Statute of the International Criminal Court (adopted July 17, 1998, entered into force July 1, 2002) 2187 UNTS 90/37, art 29. See also Bogdan Bîrzu, "Considerations Regarding the Non-Applicability of Statutory Limitations to Genocide, Crimes against Humanity and War Crimes" (2015) 11 Acta Universitatis Danubius Juridica 96.

[13] Articles on State Responsibility (n 10) art 45. This article reflects the text of Article 45 of the 1969 Vienna Convention dealing with the loss of the right to invoke a ground for invalidating, terminating, withdrawing from, or suspending a treaty—Vienna Convention on the Law of Treaties (adopted May 23, 1969, entered into force January 27, 1980) 1155 UNTS 331. It also echoes a history of jurisprudence recognizing estoppel and acquiescence as principles which might preclude the invocation of responsibility on the facts of the case.

[14] See *Certain Phosphate Lands in Nauru (Nauru v Australia)* (Preliminary Objections) (1992) ICJ Rep 240, 247. The threshold for estoppel, however, may not be so clear cut. In the *Chagos Marine Protected Area Arbitration*, the Tribunal recognized that representations serving as the basis of estoppel may be through words, conduct, or silence—*Chagos Marine Protected Area Arbitration (Mauritius v United Kingdom)*, PCA (2015) 174 [438]. Thus the boundaries between waivers, estoppel, and acquiescence cannot be characterized as clear or distinct. In the *Gulf of Maine Case* the court explicitly recognized the close relation between estoppel and acquiescence, suggesting that the same facts are likely to serve as evidence for both—*Gulf of Maine Case (Canada v United States of America)* (Merits) [1984] ICJ Rep 303.

[15] International Law Commission, "Draft Articles on the Responsibility of States for Internationally Wrongful Acts, with commentaries" (2001) 2(2) Yearbook of the International Law Commission 31, 121–23 (Commentaries to the Articles on State Responsibility).

[16] This in relation the obligation to rehabilitate lands which served as phosphate mines under Australian administration of Nauru prior to its independence—*Certain Phosphate Lands in Nauru* (n 14) 253–54.

relevant legal rules, rather than on the basis of the passage of a specific period of time.

According to the principle *qui tacet consentire videtur si loqui debuisset ac potuisset* (he who keeps silent is held to consent if he must and can speak) that served as the basis of the International Court of Justice's determination in *Temple of Preah Vihear*:

> It is an established rule of law that the plea of error cannot be allowed as an element vitiating consent if the party advancing it contributed by its own conduct to the error, or could have avoided it, or if the circumstances were such as to put that party on notice of a possible error.[17]

Thus, what is required to establish acquiescence is knowledge of the relevant facts, failure to act when there is an expectation on the claimant state to do so, or conduct of the claimant state affirming the state of affairs constituting the breach (including prolonged abstention).[18]

Further articulating the requirements of acquiescence, Nuno Sérgio Marques Antunes identifies five features characterizing a situation in which a state may be considered to have acquiesced in the lapsing of a claim:

> Acquiescence only emerges where it refers to facts that are (or ought to be) known by the acquiescing State (*notoriety*), where such facts are of direct interest for the acquiescing State (*interest*), when these facts have existed for a significant period (*lapse of time*) without significant change of context and

[17] *Case Concerning the Temple of Preah Vihear (Cambodia v Thailand)* (Judgment) [1962] ICJ Rep 6, 26. In this case, Thailand disputed an inaccurate rendering of the boundary line between Thailand and Cambodia contained in a treaty of 1904, but was found to have acquiesced to this error because it had knowledge of the inconsistency and opportunity to object but failed to do so. The court therefore concluded that Thailand had aroused expectations by its own conduct on which Cambodia ought to be able to rely, with the additional suggestion that no interested person could have failed to see what the map was purporting to do, and any failure to independently investigate the map was the fault of the Siamese authorities. See also Sven Mißling, "A Legal View of the Case of the Temple Preah Vihear" in Brigitta Hauser-Schäublin (ed), *World Heritage Angkor and Beyond: Circumstances and Implications of UNESCO Listings in Cambodia* (Göttingen UP 2011) 61.

[18] For additional support for this proposition, see *Fisheries Case (United Kingdom v Norway)* (Judgment) [1951] ICJ Rep 116, 139; *Arbitral Sentence of the King of Spain Case (Honduras v Nicaragua)* (Merits) [1960] ICJ Rep 192, 213; *Island of Palmas Case (Netherlands v United States of America)* [1928] 2 RIAA 829, 868–69; *The Grisbådarna Case (Norway v Sweden)* (Award of the Tribunal) (1909) XI RIAA 155.

> the meaning conveyed (*consistency*), and in cases in which the conduct is attributable to a relevant representative of the State (*provenance*).[19]

Conversely, a lack of knowledge of relevant facts and continuing (though not necessarily constant) affirmations of breach by relevant parties mitigate against a finding of acquiescence.

The "complex background circumstances" of the case may be accounted for in determining whether acquiescence occurred, including external factors limiting the capacity of a state to assert its rights.[20] For instance, in the *Case Concerning Sovereignty over Certain Frontier Lands*, the court considered the intervention of World War I to be relevant to the question of whether Belgium had acquiesced to the loss of its sovereignty over the land in question by the nonassertion of rights.[21] Thus, in considering whether states have validly acquiesced in the lapse of a right to bring a reparations claim for historical enslavement, the history and continuity of reparations claims from the time of purportedly "legal" enslavement to today must be acknowledged.

Far from being something new that states have only recently begun undertaking, calls for redress for the enslavement of African people and their descendants have an historical pedigree.[22] Although reparations efforts over time may not have been continuous or systematic, the denial of acquiescence does not necessarily require constant sustained effort on the part of the claimant state. What is required is some display by the claimant state to "counterbalance or annihilate" the conduct constituting the breach.[23] Repeated assertions of the right to reparation for the injustices committed within the system of transatlantic chattel enslavement from the period of purported legality to today may be seen as a refusal to accept the lapsing of the claim, thus keeping the right to invoke responsibility alive.[24] The particulars of this question must be assessed in light of the specific claimant state in question, and no universal conclusion can be reached as to whether

[19] Nuno Sérgio Marques Antunes, "Acquiescence" *Max Planck Encyclopedia of Public International Law* (2006) < opil.ouplaw.com/view/10.1093/law:epil/9780199231690/law-9780199231690-e1373> accessed April 18, 2018 [21], emphasis in original.

[20] See *Case Concerning Sovereignty over Certain Frontier Lands (Belgium v Netherlands)* [1959] ICJ Rep 209.

[21] The court ultimately concluded that the circumstances of the case indicated against acquiescence by Belgium, and thus that the Netherlands had not obtained sovereignty over the land in question, ibid.

[22] See Ana Lucia Araujo, *Reparations for Slavery and the Slave Trade: A Transnational and Comparative History* (Bloomsbury Academic 2017).

[23] *Island of Palmas Case* (n 18) 868.

[24] On the history of reparations claims, see Araujo (n 22).

any or all potential claimant states did, or did not, acquiesce in the lapse of their claim to reparations. However, some general observations against acquiescence may be formulated.

The question of acquiescence is assessed against the complex milieu of circumstances that coalesce to deprive claimants of the capacity to assert their rights through official channels. The caveat contained in the principle of *qui tacet consentire videtur si loqui debuisset ac potuisset*—if they must and can speak—should not be overlooked or presumed simply by virtue of the passage of time.[25] When viewed in conjunction with the body of international jurisprudence concerning acquiescence, the determination of obligations on the claimant state to speak or protest derives from the specific convergence of facts and not from a general rule.[26] Thus, although acquiescence may affirm substantial incursions on international legal arrangements, including going so far as to override preexisting territorial boundaries of states, it is not a foregone conclusion simply by virtue of a substantial period of time.[27]

The capacity of potential claimant states to bring a claim for redress in practice is a relevant consideration in determining whether failure to do so could constitute acquiescence. Colonized states continuing under the rule of European enslaver states, those going through the processes of freeing themselves from colonial rule, and newly independent states were unlikely to be in a position to contest the history of enslavement in international legal fora. Moreover, for many states, the possibility of claiming redress was not actualized until the twentieth century, when they gained legal recognition in international law.[28] Even then, the lack of clarity in international legal thought

[25] In the *Fisheries Case*, for instance, it was the requirement of a history of protest that had not been met in the case that served as the basis for acquiescence, and not the period of time that had elapsed itself. *Fisheries Case* (n 18).

[26] A direct comparison between the *Fisheries Case* and *Case Concerning Sovereignty over Certain Frontier Lands* reveals this distinction. *Fisheries Case*, ibid. cf *Case Concerning Sovereignty over Certain Frontier Lands* (n 20).

[27] In the *Temple of Preah Vihear*, the court acknowledged the error in the demarcation but nonetheless found acquiescence, the result being that in the case Thailand's territorial integrity could be superseded by silence. *Case Concerning the Temple of Preah Vihear* (n 17). The same conclusion (on different facts) was reached in *Island of Palmas Case* (n 18).

[28] The growing body of literature discussing the role of colonialism in developing modern international law provides support for the suggestion that post-colonial states would not have been in a position to resist or oppose the hegemonic international legal system crafted to protect the interests of enslaver states. See for instance Antony Anghie, *Imperialism, Sovereignty, and the Making of International Law* (CUP 2007); Sundhya Pahuja, *Decolonising International Law* (CUP 2011); Antony Anghie and others (eds), *The Third World and International Order: Law, Politics, and Globalization* (Kluwer Law International 2003). Haiti's independence debt may serve as testimony of the post-emancipation realities facing potential claimant states. See generally Charles Forsdick, "Haiti and France: Settling the Debts of the Past" in Kate Quinn and Paul Sutton (eds), *Politics and Power in Haiti: Studies of the Americas* (Palgrave Macmillan 2013) 141; Paul Farmer, *The Uses of Haiti* (3rd edn,

concerning the status of enslavement, and a dominant discourse precluding such claims, ought to be considered as a factor contributing to any identified failure to consistently assert the rights in question.

Acquiescence derives from a principled conception of the requirements of certainty and justice in the legal system—good faith and equity.[29] When accounting for the complex history and continuing hegemony of European enslaver states in international law, it may be more difficult to conclude that claimant states accepted the lapse of potential claims on the basis of equity and good faith. This is because the international legal system to which they would have to avert was constructed by European states to enable the very exploitation and marginalization about which claims relate.[30]

3.2. Tracing the history of state responsibility

Limitation and acquiescence are not the only problems historicity poses to contemporary calls for reparations, as the history of the secondary rules of international law does not present a single set of constant norms. The modern framework of state responsibility—predominantly set out in the International Law Commission's Articles on State Responsibility—cannot be juxtaposed throughout the history of international law without consideration of the rules and legal understandings of relevant time periods. While some provisions of the Articles on State Responsibility may constitute the "progressive development" of international law, on the whole, the Articles set out existing rules as accepted by the international community.[31] However, tracing the claim for reparations for transatlantic enslavement requires consideration of centuries of international legal thought and practice,

Common Courage Press 2005); Robert Debs Heinl and Nancy Gordon Heinl, *Written in Blood: The Story of the Haitian People 1492–1995* (rev edn, UP of America 2005).

[29] Antunes (n 19) [27].

[30] See chapters 1 and 2.

[31] The opening paragraph of the commentaries to the Articles indicates the dual focus of codifying and progressively developing the basic rules of international law concerning state responsibility. Commentaries to the Articles on State Responsibility (n 15) 31. Their adoption in General Assembly Resolution 56/83 of December 12, 2001 evidences widespread state support for their general terms. For the acceptance of the Articles on State Responsibility as reflective of customary international law, see for instance *Noble Ventures, Inc. v Romania* (Award) (2005) ICSID Case No ARB/01/11; *LG&E Energy Corp and Ors v Argentina* (Decision on Liability) (2006) ICSID Case No ARB 02/1 [31]; *CMS Gas Transmission Company v Argentina* (Award) (2005) ICSID Case No ARB/01/8 [315].

which cannot be presumed to be encompassed by the International Law Commission's twenty-first century text.

Within the European tradition, it is often suggested that the roots of public international law are to be traced to Roman law.[32] Therefore, the principles of responsibility and reparation in this context serve as a suitable starting point in tracing the concepts, even if this account is not entirely satisfactory. In Roman law, the now established principle of restitutio in integrum arose as a development from earlier retaliatory and self-help remedies. This shift is seen to have taken place with the enactment of *Lex Aquila* in the late second century BCE.[33] This principle found its way into the reasoning of international tribunals in the twentieth century—notably the *Chorzów Factory Case* highlighting restitutio in integrum as the fundamental reparatory obligation in international law.[34] Likewise, the introduction of *culpa* as an element of wrongfulness in Roman law some 150 years after the enactment of *Lex Aquila* continues to echo through the history of international law, demonstrating an actor-centered understanding of legal responsibility consistent with the placement of attribution in determining wrongfulness and the separation of assessment of harms to the determination of damages.[35] Thus, both concerns with attribution (defining wrongfulness) and causation can be located in Roman law.[36] Yet, these principles were not directly transplanted from Roman to international law.

The doctrine of state responsibility derives from the adaptation and amalgamation in Europe over time of private law concepts (from Roman law and elsewhere) as well as early international law for the protection of foreign nationals, reprisals, denial of justice, and the practice of international protection.[37] Much like the shift in Roman law from retaliatory and self-help

[32] Arthur Nussbaum, "The Significance of Roman Law in the History of International Law" (1951–52) 100 University of Pennsylvania Law Review 678, 681. See also Hannis Tylor, *A Treatise on International Public Law* (Calaghan & Company 1901).

[33] The orthodox account suggests that 287 BCE was the date of enactment—see Reinhard Zimmermann, *The Law of Obligations: Roman Foundations of the Civilian Tradition* (Juta 1990). Honoré, however, argues the timeline for enactment lies between 195 and 209 BCE—Anthony Honoré, "Linguistic and Social Context of the *Lex Aquilia*" (1972) 7 Irish Jurist 138, 150.

[34] *Case Concerning the Factory at Chorzów (Germany v Poland)* (Merits) [1928] PCIJ Rep Series A No 17 [47]. The place of restitutio in integrum in international law can also be traced through the peace treaties of Westphalia including provisions for the restoration of lands—see Randall Lesaffer, *Peace Treaties and International Law in European History* (CUP 2004). This principle is considered in greater depth in chapter 6.

[35] See David Ibbetson, "How the Romans Did for Us: Ancient Roots of the Tort of Negligence" (2003) 26 University of New South Wales Law Journal 475.

[36] Causation is further considered in chapter 6.

[37] Borzu Sabahi, "A Concise History of the Law of State Responsibility and Reparation in International Law" in Borzu Sabahi, *Compensation and Restitution in Investor-State Arbitration: Principles and Practice* (OUP 2011) 7, 7–9.

remedies to the incorporation of reparations as an alternative, advertence to reparations in early European public law serves, in part, as a substitute for reprisals.[38] Where reprisals might predominate in systems lacking strong, centralized power, the growing significance of alternative mechanisms intertwined with the development of international law as a system of governance.[39] Furthermore, the entitlement to engage in reprisals presumes the existence of a system of international wrongdoing that can be ascribed to states. Grotius, Gentili, and Legnano's recognition of *déni de justice* and *défi de justice* as conditions allowing reprisals presumed the existence of international wrongdoing (international delict) and thus attribution in some form.[40] Despite the changing dominance of self-help mechanisms, the obligation to make reparation for breaches was one of the few constants of differing theorizations of international responsibility.[41] Aquinas, for instance, highlighted the obligation to make *restitutio* and seek *satisfactio* in the event of wrongdoing, based on *culpa*.[42] This in turn influenced the School of Salamanca and later Grotius.[43]

The shift from theorizing responsibility in the context of specific causes of action to formulating a general theory of liability occurred in Christian canon law (often adapting Roman law) and subsequently the work of theologians incorporating principles of Roman and canon law, including Aquinas in the thirteenth century.[44] Grotius in *Rights of War and Peace* made substantial progress in formulating a general theory of international responsibility, advancing a general doctrine of liability based on fault and concluding that

[38] See ibid 34–38.

[39] In discussing the significance of reprisals in Roman law, Bartolus suggested that their importance rose and fell in an inverse relationship with the strength of central authority. See Hans Spiegel, "Origin and Development of Denial of Justice" (1938) 32 American Journal of International Law 63, 70.

[40] See Hans Spiegel, "Origin and Development of Denial of Justice" (1938) 32 American Journal of International Law 63, 70–73.

[41] Although the exact nature of the reparatory obligation differed somewhat between theorists, the obligation to provide redress in the instance of wrongdoing was a feature of both canonist thinking (prioritizing *damnum injuria datum*) and the work of theologians (focusing on penance and restitution). Sabahi (n 37) 7, 25.

[42] In this context, *restitutio* constituted the restoration of that which the victim had been deprived of (whether material or immaterial), while *satisfactio* was concerned with the wrongdoer seeking forgiveness for their wrongdoing. See Harry Dondorp, "Crime and Punishment: Negligentia for the Canonists and Moral Theologians" in Eltjo Schrage (ed), *Negligence: The Comparative History of the Law of Torts* (Duncker & Humblot 2001) 101, 117.

[43] See Gero Dolezalek, "The Moral Theologian's Doctrine of Restitution and Its Juridification in the Sixteenth and Seventeenth Centuries" [1992] Acta Juridica 104.

[44] See Eltjo Schrage (ed), *Negligence: The Comparative History of the Law of Torts* (Duncker & Humblot 2001); Arthur von Mehren and James Gordley, *The Civil Law System: An Introduction to the Comparative Study of Law* (2nd edn, Little, Brown and Co 1977) 569.

wrongful conduct (whether by positive act or omission) gives rise, by the law of nature, to an obligation to "make good" the damage caused.[45]

Perhaps ironically, according to Francesco Parisi, this shift in focus from the fault of the wrongdoer to the "need to compensate the innocent victim" severs the consequences of wrongdoing from the formulation of fault that was the central function of this part of Grotius' treatise.[46] That is to say, that *culpa* becomes an element of determining wrongfulness and not a consideration embedded in the causal analysis of damage, detracting from the effort to formulate a general theory of liability based on fault. However, rather than undercutting a general theory of liability, this may be seen as an early example of the approach taken in the 2001 Articles on State Responsibility wherein the question of fault (*culpa*), or the finding of internationally wrongful conduct, is severed from the determination of its consequences.[47] Thus, the causal analysis of injuries resulting from the breach occurs subsequent to the determination of the breach itself.[48]

Although not an exact facsimile, the parity between Grotius' approach to state responsibility and that formulated in the Articles on State Responsibility supports the application of this framework in assessing responsibility for transatlantic enslavement. Despite oscillations in the exact formulation of responsibility from the fifteenth through the twenty-first century, attribution of wrongful conduct to a state (in addition to the existence of an international norm) and causal connection between the wrong and reparable harms remained features of international legal theorizations. Therefore, it is not necessary to find the entirety of the terms of the Articles on State Responsibility to have been constant throughout history to apply their core approach to responsibility to the history of international law from the inception of the transatlantic system. In relation to the norms engaged in the question of responsibility for transatlantic enslavement, and notably questions concerning attribution and causation, international law has evidenced sufficient constancy (or rather sufficiently limited oscillation) to assess the historical claims within its rubric.[49]

45 Hugo Grotius, *The Rights of War and Peace*, vol 2 (Richard Tuck tr, Liberty Fund 2005) ch 17.

46 Francesco Parisi, "Alterum non Laedere: An Intellectual History of Civil Liability" (1994) 39 American Journal of Jurisprudence 317, 341.

47 Sabahi argues that the focus on the need to compensate the innocent victim "seems to undercut the fault-based liability theory itself, as it does not allocate a sufficient role to fault in determining *consequences*." Sabahi (n 37) 7, 29, emphasis in original.

48 The question of causation consistent with this approach is considered in chapter 6.

49 Recognizing these continuities, Daillier and Bories' observations concerning the changing landscape of international responsibility need not be seen as extending to the particular norms in question. Patrick Daillier, "The Development of the Law of Responsibility through the Case Law" in James

3.3. Attribution of internationally wrongful conduct

International and domestic law are not equivalent for the purpose of establishing the existence of a justiciable breach of law, for injury and fault are not elements of state responsibility under international law.[50] The Articles on State Responsibility conclude that wrongful conduct and the attribution of such to a state are the only necessary components of an internationally wrongful act, which necessarily entails international responsibility.[51] In the Western tradition, Grotius' inclusion of *culpa* as an element determining wrongfulness rather than an aspect of the question of causation of damages likewise severs the question of damage and injury from the determination of wrongfulness.[52] Thus, harm and associated questions of causation need not be established in order to reach a finding of internationally wrongful conduct.[53]

The "antilegal nature" of the conduct in question—the violation of law—is, in itself, a form of damage on the international plane.[54] In formulating responsibility in this way, Roberto Ago (an early architect of the Articles on State Responsibility) affirmed the role of international law in upholding the international legal order.[55] In other words, legal redress is conceived not merely as a response to injuries flowing from wrongdoing but as a means of rectifying the moral injury of the wrongdoing itself—what Brigitte Stern labels the "objective control of legality."[56] The jurisprudence of international tribunals throughout their respective histories concluding with declarations

Crawford, Alain Pellet, and Simon Olleson (eds), *The Law of International Responsibility* (OUP 2010) 37, 37; Clémentine Bories, "The Hague Conference of 1930" in ibid 61, 62.

[50] León Castellanos-Jankiewicz, "Causation and International State Responsibility" (2012) SHARES Research Paper 07, ACIL 2012-07, 4 <papers.ssrn.com/sol3/papers.cfm?abstract_id=2419913> accessed April 10, 2018.

[51] Articles on State Responsibility (n 10) arts 1 and 2.

[52] Grotius (n 45).

[53] Such elements are rather considered in determining those injuries that must be repaired, and are considered in chapter 6.

[54] See Dionisio Anzilotti, "La responsabilité internationale des Etats à raison des dommages soufferts par des étrangers" (1906) 8 Revue Générale de Droit International Public 5, 13. Ian Brownlie likewise argued that "The duty to pay compensation is a normal consequence of responsibility, but is not conterminous with it." Ian Brownlie, *Principles of Public international Law* (6th edn, OUP 2003) 421.

[55] UNGA, "Report by Mr R Ago, Chairman of the Sub-Committee on State Responsibility" (1963) UN Doc A/CN.4/152, 250.

[56] Brigitte Stern, "The Elements of an Internationally Wrongful Act" in Crawford, Pellet, and Olleson (n 49) 193, 194.

of a breach absent any other form of reparations are a testament to this understanding of international wrongdoing.[57]

Arguments over the harms suffered by potential contemporary beneficiaries of reparations for historical injustices and the causal links between wrongdoing and injury (discussed in chapter 6) are relevant only to the question of the necessary consequences of wrongdoing and not to the establishment of wrongdoing in the first instance. Thus, the question that must be considered in determining the existence of internationally wrongful conduct is: Is conduct amounting to a breach of international law attributable to the State?[58]

Conduct of state organs, persons, and entities exercising governmental authority; conduct directed or controlled by the state; and conduct acknowledged and adopted by the state as its own are all attributable to the state as an entity in international law.[59] Conduct in this context may refer to actions or omissions by the state, or a combination of the two.[60] Although borderline cases of attribution might be susceptible to variations in understandings of its parameters, cases concerning direct conduct of state organs in their official functions have always fallen directly within the ambit of international legal attribution—"from the perspective of the outside, all organs and servants of the State are 'the State.'"[61]

[57] See for instance *Phosphates in Morocco (Italy v France)* (Preliminary Objections) [1938] PCIJ Rep Series A/B No 74 [28] wherein the court noted that international responsibility was established "immediately as between the two States" upon commission of an internationally wrongful act by one state against another. This is further considered in section 5.1.

[58] For support of the status of the requirement of attribution prior to the development of the articles, see *Phosphates in Morocco (Italy v France)* (Judgment) [1938] PCIJ Rep Series A/B No 74; *Case Concerning United States Diplomatic and Consular Staff in Tehran (United States of America v Iran)* [1980] ICJ Rep 64; *Case Concerning Military and Paramilitary Activities in and against Nicaragua (Nicaragua v United States)* (Merits) [1986] ICJ Rep 14; *Gabčíkovo-Nagymaros Project (Hungary/Slovakia)* (Merits) [1997] ICJ Rep 7; *Application of the Convention on the Prevention and Punishment of the Crime of Genocide (Bosnia and Herzegovina v Serbia and Montenegro)* (Merits) [2007] ICJ Rep 43.

[59] Articles on State Responsibility (n 10) arts 4, 5, 8, and 11.

[60] ibid, art 2. International jurisprudence also supports the contention that attribution of responsibility is possible without direct state participation where the state fails to take measures to address acts which are being committed when there is an obligation to do so. See *Corfu Channel (United Kingdom of Great Britain and Northern Ireland) (Merits)* [1949] ICJ Rep 1, 22–23 where the court found Albanian responsibility in the fact that it knew, or must have known, of the presence of the mines in its territorial waters but failed to take action to make third states aware of them. See also *Case Concerning United States Diplomatic and Consular Staff in Tehran (United States of America v Iran)* [1980] ICJ Rep 64, 3 where Iranian responsibility was premised upon the inaction of authorities who failed to take appropriate steps when such were called for.

[61] Rosalyn Higgins, *Problems and Process: International Law and How We Use It* (Clarendon Press 1994) 151.

Targeted attempts to build a case for reparations against particular states for defined activities would require a thorough accounting of the conduct attributable to that state and on what basis it was to be imputed. However, analysis of the general viability of claims need not be so methodical. Many of the actions and omissions involved in the system of transatlantic system were not marginal cases. European enslaver states created entire regulatory regimes to enable enslavement. States instituted licensing and permit systems within which enslavement was required to take place, imposed taxes and levies upon traders in enslaved persons, granted private contracts to businessmen to facilitate the system, and set up public corporations engaging directly in enslavement.[62] On the international level, European states regulated the transatlantic system between them, constructing a regional-international framework for the enslavement and forced migration of Africans.[63] Consistent with the ruling of the Permanent Court of International Justice in *Certain German Interests in Polish Upper Silesia*, determining that legal decisions and administrative measures "express the will and constitute the activities of the State," this tableau of official conduct constituting the transatlantic system is attributable to the state in the most direct sense.[64]

Even without the deep and multifaceted engagement of European enslaver states themselves with the transatlantic system, their liability might be founded upon their allowance of enslavement and related practices.[65] If enslavement was contemporaneously prohibited as a contravention of the most basic and fundamental norms of naturalist international law, the failure of states to take action against widespread enslavement and brutality committed by their own nationals and within their territories could be framed as a breach by omission.[66]

[62] See generally Moses Finley, *Classical Slavery* (Taylor & Francis 2014); Justin Roberts, *Slavery and Enlightenment in the British Atlantic* (CUP 2013); Gad Heuman and James Walvin, *The Slavery Reader* (Routledge 2003); James Walvin, *Atlas of Slavery* (Taylor & Francis 2014).

[63] See Jean Allain, *Slavery in International Law: Of Human Exploitation and Trafficking* (Martinus Nijhoff 2013) 20–56; Jean Allain, "What We Know Today: A Contemporary Understanding of the Atlantic Slave Trade" in Jean Allain, *The Law and Slavery: Prohibiting Human Exploitation* (Brill Nijhoff 2015) 37.

[64] This with regard to the Polish government's intention to liquidate certain estates in Poland owned by German companies—*Certain German Interests in Polish Upper Silesia (Germany v Poland)* (Merits) [1926] PCIJ Series A No 7, 19.

[65] International law allows liability for omissions in circumstances where states have a duty to act which they fail to fulfill. See for instance *Corfu Channel Case (United Kingdom v Albania)* (Merits) [1949] ICJ Rep 4; *Case Concerning United States Diplomatic and Consular Staff in Tehran (United States of America v Iran)* [1980] ICJ Rep 64.

[66] Failure to prevent or punish private acts might constitute a breach of international law. See for instance *Laura M B Janes et al (United States of America v United Mexican States)* [1925] 4 RIAA 82.

The attempt to locate conduct amounting to breaches of an international prohibition against slavery in the annals of history, and attribution of such involvement to relevant enslaver states, are likely satisfied by the thoroughly documented history of European involvement in the system of transatlantic chattel enslavement. A legal case would require an accounting of injustices and the relevant states' relationships to those abuses—both for the determination of attribution and for the assessment of necessary reparations. However, in general, the nature of state participation in the atrocities committed within the transatlantic system leaves little question as to the attributability of relevant conduct to the state. Furthermore, the evidential barriers that may present substantial challenges to other cases of historical injustice are not overwhelming in the case of transatlantic enslavement because of the degree to which the conduct occurred within the public arena, with international treaties, domestic legislation, and historical records reflecting the role of states in the system. Where claims are formulated within political mechanisms, evidentiary burdens may be further decreased.

3.4. Continuity and succession

Attribution and the impact of time coalesce in the consideration of the transmission of state responsibility through time, regulated by the rules of continuity and succession. On the issue of continuity, critics of reparations suggest a dissociation between historical and contemporary states as legal entities to support their conclusion of a break in responsibility.[67] However, this perspective wrongly conflates the nature of individual liability with state responsibility. The liability of nations is neither premised upon the individual conduct of those operating as part of its mechanisms, nor does it cease when those individuals occupying official positions within the regime change. The very structure of state responsibility requires the abstraction of liability. As León Castellanos-Jankiewicz recognizes: "There are no activities of the State which can be called 'its own' from the point of view of natural causality" and thus responsibility must be translated from natural person to the legal person of the state.[68] In other words, the state as an entity is necessarily held

[67] See, for instance, Verdun (n 2) 630.

[68] Castellanos-Jankiewicz (n 50) 16. As the commentary to the Articles on State Responsibility highlights, the state is treated as a unity, consistent with its recognition as a single legal person in international law. Commentaries to the Articles on State Responsibility (n 15) 35.

responsible for the actions of particular individuals operating as agents of the state. Thus, from the perspective of international law, the status of international legal personality is to be assessed within the frameworks of continuity of states and state succession, and not merely on the basis of time having passed and different individuals having filled positions within the machinery of the state.

The significance of a finding of continuity or succession in the context of responsibility for historical injustice lies in the general principle that continuing states remain responsible for unlawful acts, while successor states are not generally liable for the international wrongdoing of their predecessor.[69] Although there are no concrete rules of international law operating to determine the application of continuity or succession, governing principles are applied on a case-by-case basis in light of the circumstances.[70] The rule precluding liability of successor states is not absolute, as states may adopt the breaches of their predecessors and thus bear responsibility.[71] Succession may therefore be considered either partial or total, and the facts of the case determine the degree to which responsibility is transmitted.[72]

The range of situations involving political turmoil in which the identity of the state is nonetheless considered to continue in international law supports the argument for continuity in considering the responsibility of enslaver states for their role in transatlantic enslavement. Over time, state practice affirmed the irrelevance of internal political changes (including coups d'état and other situations of revolutionary activity) and military occupations by third states in determining membership in treaties and liability for international debts.[73] Likewise, state identity can survive significant territorial changes, although, at some point along the spectrum, the rules of succession as opposed to continuity will be triggered.[74] In general terms, in cases of loss of part of a state's territory (through independence or merger with a third state), responsibility continues unless a "clear, direct and intrinsic link

[69] Malcolm N Shaw, "State Succession" in Malcolm N Shaw, *International Law* (8th edn, CUP 2017) 725, 762.

[70] ibid 727.

[71] See for instance the *Lighthouses Arbitration (France v Greece)* (1956) 12 RIAA 155; 23 ILR 659 in which Greece was found to have adopted the wrongful conduct of Turkey and Crete.

[72] See Patrick Dumberry, *State Succession to International Responsibility* (Martinus Nijhoff 2007) 17.

[73] Andreas Zimmermann, "Continuity of States" *Max Planck Encyclopedia of Public International Law* (2006) <opil.ouplaw.com/view/10.1093/law:epil/9780199231690/law-9780199231690-e1389> accessed May 2, 2018 [9–10].

[74] See DP O'Connell, *State Succession in Municipal Law and International Law*, vol 2 (CUP 1967).

between the consequences of the act and the territory and population of the part of the State" severed exists.[75] Even "failed states" lacking central governmental authority for a prolonged period of time, and characterized by extensive civil conflict between groups absent legitimate government, retain international legal personality unless the state of affairs has become "permanent and decisive."[76]

In the context of European enslaver states, the continuity of states is, for the most part, straightforward. Despite the loss of significant amounts of colonial territory, and some internal political reconfigurations, the states in question have persisted in their international identity, retaining historically determinative territory and self-identity. Zimmermann argues that the "self-proclaimed will of a State to continue the international legal personality of a given State and the acceptance of such claim by third States (both within and outside international organizations) play a decisive role."[77] European enslaver nations, including Denmark, France, the Netherlands, Portugal, Spain, and the United Kingdom, may therefore be appropriately characterized as continuing states, resulting in an unbroken chain of responsibility.[78]

3.5. Invoking international responsibility

The attribution of responsibility to a continuing state does not necessarily entail the jurisdiction of any international court to adjudicate on a matter. European states identified as potential defendants in a case for reparations for transatlantic enslavement may not accept the compulsory jurisdiction of the International Court of Justice or have reservations in relation to justiciable time periods. For instance, the United Kingdom's acceptance of the compulsory jurisdiction of the International Court of Justice is limited to disputes arising after January 1, 1987 in relation to situations or facts subsequent to this date and excludes disputes with Commonwealth states (present or past).[79] Reciprocity requirements are also common under the optional

[75] Shaw (n 69) 725, 762.

[76] Zimmermann, "Continuity of States" (n 73) [11].

[77] ibid [15].

[78] Of course, this assessment must also be tempered by the recognition that the continuity of each potential defendant state in a formulated claim must be considered on the basis of its own history, and no general conclusion may be drawn concerning all relevant slaver states.

[79] United Kingdom of Great Britain and Northern Ireland, "Declaration recognizing the jurisdiction of the Court as compulsory" (February 22, 2017). Likewise, Spain's reservation bars jurisdiction for events before 1990, Portugal's before 1974, and Belgium's before 1948. The Netherlands,

clause system, with many European states permitting jurisdiction only in cases where the claimant state also accepts the same obligation, which may be the case for some potential reparations claims, but not all.[80]

The successful formulation of liable perpetrators in the present legal landscape is only half of the battle in leveling the playing field for a meaningful reparations debate to occur. A legal claim necessarily has two sides, relating not only to the breach but also to the identification of those entitled to bring a claim, the beneficiaries of potential reparatory measures, and reparable harms. Although individuals now receive some degree of recognition as subjects in international law, particularly within international human rights law, the classical formulation of the international legal framework permits only interstate claims.[81] Thus, injuries to individuals are only amenable to an international legal claim where the injury to that individual is adjudicated via state-state mechanisms. This is reflected in Part Three of the Articles on State Responsibility, concerning the implementation of the international responsibility of a state, recognizing only the right of states to invoke responsibility.[82]

for its part, prevents claims relating to conduct occurring over one hundred years before the dispute is brought, while Denmark, Austria, Norway, and Sweden express no such reservations. Spain, "Declaration Recognizing the Jurisdiction of the Court as Compulsory" (October 29, 1990); Portugal, "Declaration Recognizing the Jurisdiction of the Court as Compulsory" (February 25, 2005); The Netherlands, "Declaration Recognizing the Jurisdiction of the Court as Compulsory" (February 21, 2017); Belgium, "Declaration Recognizing the Jurisdiction of the Court as Compulsory" (June 17, 1958); Denmark, "Declaration Recognizing the Jurisdiction of the Court as Compulsory" (December 10, 1956); Austria, "Declaration Recognizing the Jurisdiction of the Court as Compulsory" (May 19, 1971); Norway, "Declaration Recognizing the Jurisdiction of the Court as Compulsory" (June 24, 1996); Sweden, "Declaration Recognizing the Jurisdiction of the Court as Compulsory" (April 6, 1957).

[80] Notably, Jamaica has not deposited a declaration recognizing the jurisdiction of the court as compulsory pursuant to Article 36(2). See International Court of Justice, "Declarations Recognizing the Jurisdiction of the Court as Compulsory" (International Court of Justice 2018) <www.icj-cij.org/en/declarations> accessed March 14, 2018.

[81] Vattel, for instance, asserted the basis of international responsibility for harm to individuals by declaring that harm to individuals constituted an injury of their home state. Hans Spiegel, "Origin and Development of Denial of Justice" (1938) 32 American Journal of International Law 63, 74–75. Individuals or private actors might now also achieve subjecthood in international law through international investment law where treaties might grant standing to investors to bring a claim. See generally Christoph Schreuer, "Consent to Arbitration" in Peter Muchlinski, Federico Ortino, and Christoph Schreuer (eds), *The Oxford Handbook of International Investment Law* (OUP 2008) 830; Christopher Dugan and others, *Investor State Arbitration* (OUP 2008) 27–28. The absence of a treaty providing standing, however, may result in the denial of the right to bring a claim, and the recognition of private claimants in this context ought not to be considered to be reflective of general international law on the issue—see for instance *Case Concerning Elettronica Sicula S.p.A. (ELSI) (United States v Italy)* [1989] ICJ Rep 15.

[82] The primary formulation is for the invocation of responsibility by an injured state itself, although art 48 permits the invocation of responsibility of a state other than the injured state when the obligation in question involves a collective interest which the invoking state is a part of. Articles on State Responsibility (n 10).

The determination of internationally wrongful conduct and identification of a state (or states) entitled to invoke responsibility in international law, are separate issues from the question of the legal consequences of the breach. The division of these questions is significant not only because it allows for a finding of wrongfulness without specific harm, but also because it allows for the responsibility of a wrongdoing state absent a right to invoke such responsibility. In other words, the finding of wrongdoing, determination of the content of the international responsibility of the state, and the right to invoke responsibility are distinct legal issues. The formulation of these dimensions of state responsibility are reflected in the Articles on State Responsibility, Part One of which addresses international wrongdoing, Part Two the content of responsibility, and Part Three the invocation of responsibility.[83] Although contingent upon a finding of internationally wrongful conduct, the right to invoke responsibility is not, therefore, a prerequisite of international responsibility itself, and the consequences of a breach may be considered independently of questions of standing and jurisdiction.

Presumptions about justiciability often lead to historical injustices being framed as entirely unlike typical successful reparations claims. Consideration of these cases is frequently premised on this presumed distinction, framed in terms of analogy with existing successful reparations awards. In other words, the starting point for analysis is the presumption that the passage of time alone detracts from claims to reparations for historical injustices. This, in turn, influences the analysis of procedural rules, supporting conclusions on limitation, acquiescence, attribution, and continuity based on presumptions as to justiciability, rather than the legal frameworks themselves. This approach presents these requirements as both legal and political barriers to reparations claims, for settled legal bars mitigate against political claims. This circular reasoning alone ought not to be taken as determinative of the legal position. Yet, it often serves as the basis for refusal to engage in serious consideration of the reparations question.

Shifting from the deductive to an inductive approach displaces many of the presumed bars to recovery posed by the procedural rules of international law. The passage of time itself is no longer characterized as sufficient grounds for a conclusion on responsibility for conduct within the transatlantic system, and the governing rules of the international system are engaged. Although this does not provide a foundation for the justiciability of

[83] ibid.

historical cases in any particular legal forum, it does destabilize reparations denials based on these legal barriers. Thus, space is created in which specific reparations cases may be considered within the legal frameworks. This contributes to the broader discourse on reparations in extralegal processes, wherein legal structures have rhetorical and persuasive impact.

4

Toward a Theory of Reparatory Justice

In the event of wrongdoing, reparations are the means by which international law effects justice, both in individual cases and holistically. While establishing attributable wrongful conduct is a prerequisite to the engagement of reparations, the jurisprudence of redress provides an independent, substantive framework for the consideration of the consequences of responsibility. This interrogation shifts the focus from the violation itself to its victims—those harmed by the wrongdoing—whether states, individuals, or collectives. This chapter explores reparations theory and practice in international law to develop an understanding of the nature and scope of reparatory justice, which may then be applied in cases of both historical and contemporary injustice.

The theory formulated in this chapter is built upon the legal frameworks governing redress, but also transcends them. It speaks to the contours of reparations in international law to identify the underlying philosophy explaining their operation, a framework that contributes not only to legal claims but also to the moral and political cases. Acknowledging potential gaps in positive international legal frameworks, reparations as a legal mechanism may be insufficient to address calls for redress. However, a deeper understanding of the nature and scope of reparations in international law, and the positioning of different understandings of justice within reparations theory, enables a more nuanced consideration of claims to redress for historical injustices irrespective of their justiciability in legal fora. Understanding reparatory justice in international law may therefore contribute meaningfully to consideration of reparations pursued through other avenues.

4.1. Remedy as an inherent power

Reparation is not a new concept but the product of centuries of jurisprudence obliging wrongdoers to redress the damages caused by their actions. In this broad sense, reparations are not concerned automatically with severe

Reparations for Slavery in International Law. Katarina Schwarz, Oxford University Press. © Oxford University Press 2022.
DOI: 10.1093/oso/9780197636398.003.0005

injustices, atrocities, and human rights abuses but with the simple proposition of law that a "breach of an engagement involves an obligation to make reparation in an adequate form."[1] The very legitimacy of the law is often characterized as contingent on the ability of judicial tribunals to provide a remedy in the instance of a breach, and the validity of law is seen to be undermined where breaches entail no legal consequences.[2] *Ubi jus, ibi remedium*—where there is a right, there is a remedy, and a correlative right to have the infringement addressed in the courts. Thus, both domestic and international courts have consistently recognized their inherent power to grant remedies in the instance of a breach of law within their jurisdiction.[3]

In the fifteenth century, Grotius recognized the need for international legal rights to be enforceable in courts of law, noting that self-help ought only to occur in exceptional circumstances and that wrongdoing states must be "compelled to make restitution."[4] Grotius thus made clear the synchronicity between domestic and international practice in enforcing an obligation to remedy, dedicating a whole chapter of his treatise to the reparatory obligation.[5] Austin, for his part, placed legal consequences at the very heart of law's definition, shaping the recognition of law by reference to the presence of sanctions in the instance of a breach.[6] Ancient legal sources similarly paired the promulgation of rights with the need to provide remedies upon their breach. Rome's *Twelve Tables*, Justinian's *Digest*, and the *Code of Hammurabi* all contemplate various remedies, both explicit in relation to particular offenses and at the discretion of the court.[7] Through the consistent

[1] *Case Concerning the Factory at Chorzów (Germany v Poland)* (Merits) [1928] PCIJ Rep Series A No 17, 29.

[2] See, *Lusitania Cases (United States v Germany)* (1923) 7 RIAA 32, 36. Stern makes this point by arguing that the obligation to make reparation is not the consequence of international responsibility, but rather that international responsibility is the obligation to make reparation—Brigitte Stern, "The Elements of an Internationally Wrongful Act" in James Crawford, Alain Pellet, and Simon Olleson (eds), *The Law of International Responsibility* (OUP 2010) 194.

[3] See for instance *Case Concerning the Factory at Chorzów (Germany v Poland)* (Jurisdiction) [1927] PCIJ Rep Series A No 9; *Corfu Channel Case (United Kingdom v Albania)* (Merits) [1949] ICJ Rep 4; *Ahmadou Adio Diallo (Republic of Guinea v Democratic Republic of the Congo)* (Compensation) [2012] ICJ Rep 103. See also in English law, *Ashby v White* (1703) 92 ER 126 (KB) 135–37 (Holt CJ dissenting); and in US jurisprudence, *Paxton's Case* 1 Quincy 51 (Mass 1761) 57.

[4] Hugo Grotius, *The Freedom of the Seas or the Right Which Belongs to the Dutch to Take Part in the East Indian Trade* (Batoche Books 1999) 19.

[5] Hugo Grotius, *The Rights of War and Peace, in three books. Wherein are explained, the law of nature and nations, and The Principal Points relating to Government. Written in Latin by the learned Hugo Grotius, and translated into English. To which are added, all the large notes of Mr. J. Barbeyrac, Professor of Law at Groningen, and Member of the Royal Academy of Sciences at Berlin* (London 1738) bk 2, ch 17 (*The Rights of War and Peace*).

[6] John Austin, *The Province of Jurisprudence Determined* (2nd edn, J Murray 1861).

[7] Allan Chester Johnson, Paul Robinson Coleman-Norton, and Frank Card Bourne, *Ancient Roman Statutes: Translation with Introduction, Commentary, Glossary and Index* (Clyde Pharr ed,

requirement of remedy for breaches of law, regardless of whether such is explicated in the foundational legal texts, the futility of laws without redress has been reaffirmed across jurisdictions for millennia.[8]

Much like domestic law, international law intertwines legal rights with remedies, having recognized throughout its history that breaches of international law require sanctions of some kind to maintain the international legal system.[9] Like in national systems, reparation is recognized in the law applied by international courts and tribunals as a "logical consequence flowing from the very nature of law and is an integral part of every legal order."[10] This fundamental quality of the reparatory obligation in international law was pronounced by the Permanent Court of International Justice in *Factory at Chorzów*:

> It is a principle of international law that the breach of an engagement involves an obligation to make reparation in an adequate form. Reparation therefore is the indispensable complement of a failure to apply a convention and there is no necessity for this to be stated in the convention itself.[11]

Thus, the court framed the obligation as not merely a means of resolving disputes confined to the texts of positive legal instruments but as an essential counterpart of primary rules, existing regardless of whether it was explicitly provided for in the relevant treaty. The reparatory obligation is recognized as more fundamental to the international legal order than protecting the state from legal consequences, overriding "undue invocation" of state sovereignty and immunity.[12]

Codifying this existing principle of international law, the International Law Commission's Articles on State Responsibility recognize that the international responsibility of a state, entailed by an internationally wrongful act,

University of Texas Press 1961); Alan Watson ed, *The Digest of Justinian* (University of Pennsylvania Press 2011); Chilperic Edwards, *The Hammurabi Code, and the Sinaitic Legislation; with a Complete Translation of the Great Babylonian Inscription Discovered at Susa* (Kennikat Press 1971).

[8] Shelton affirms the existence of this inherent right of courts to remedy breaches of law, with no further restrictions than that the case is within their jurisdiction. Dinah Shelton, *Remedies in International Human Rights Law* (3rd edn, OUP 2015) 238.

[9] See (n 3).

[10] Bin Cheng, *General Principles of Law as Applied by International Courts and Tribunals* (Cambridge 1953) 170.

[11] *Factory at Chorzów* (Jurisdiction) (n 3) 21.

[12] See *Ahmadou Adio Diallo* (n 3), Separate Opinion of Judge Cançado Trindade, 40.

necessarily involves legal consequences.[13] The central obligations deriving from such responsibility are threefold: cessation of continuing breaches; provision of assurances and guarantees of non-repetition; and full reparation for injury caused by the wrongful act, as appropriate in the case.[14] While this formulation prima facie draws clean lines between the three identified secondary obligations, the boundaries between these consequences in practice blur, overlap, and disappear.[15] Measures ordered as guarantees of non-repetition and satisfaction as a form of reparations in particular evidence substantial intersection in both form and justification.[16]

The automatic character of the obligation to make reparations pursuant to an internationally wrongful act reinforces its primacy and the difficulty of completely severing it from the primary rule.[17] Although the principle does not require explicit pronouncement in international instruments to operate, it is nonetheless a central feature of a large number of international human rights law treaties and international declarations.[18] Notably, in 2006 the United Nations adopted the Basic Principles and Guidelines on the Right

[13] International Law Commission, "Draft Articles on the Responsibility of States for Internationally Wrongful Acts" (November 2001) UN Doc A/56/10, art 28 (Articles on State Responsibility).

[14] ibid, arts 30 and 31.

[15] Reparations, cessation, and guarantees of non-repetition are considered secondary legal obligations, for they arise only in the instance of a breach of a primary norm.

[16] On overlapping modalities, see chapter 5.

[17] The reparatory obligations are characterized as automatic because it is not contingent upon specific treaty provisions stating the obligation or upon a demand for redress by another state. International Law Commission, "Report of the International Law Commission on the Work of its Fifty-Third Session" (2001) 2(2) Yearbook of the International Law Commission 31, 91. See also *Corfu Channel* (n 3).

[18] See Universal Declaration of Human Rights (adopted December 10, 1948) UNGA Res 217 A(III), art 8; International Covenant on Civil and Political Rights (adopted December 16, 1966, entered into force March 23, 1976) 999 UNTS 171, art 2; International Convention on the Elimination of All Forms of Racial Discrimination (adopted December 21, 1965, entered into force January 4, 1969) 660 UNTS 195, art 6; Convention against Torture and Other Cruel, Inhuman or Degrading Treatment or Punishment (adopted December 10, 1984, entered into force June 26, 1987) 1465 UNTS 85, art 14. On regional instruments, see European Convention for the Protection of Fundamental Rights and Freedoms (adopted November 4, 1950, entered into force September 3, 1953) ETS 5, art 12; Charter of Fundamental Rights of the European Union (December 7, 2000) OJ C 83/02, art 47; American Convention on Human Rights (adopted November 22, 1969, entered into force July 18, 1978) OAS Treaty Series No 36, 9 ILM 99 (1969), art 25; African Charter on Human and Peoples' Rights (adopted June 27, 1981, entered into force October 21, 1986) CAB/LEG/67/3 rev 5, 21 ILM 58 (1982), art 7; Arab Charter on Human Rights (adopted September 15, 1994, entered into force October 21, 1986) OAU Doc CAB/LEG/67/3 rev 5, 21 ILM 58 (1982), art 9. In international declarations, see UNGA "Basic Principles and Guidelines on the Right to a Remedy and Reparation for Victims of Gross Violations of International Human Rights Law and Serious Violations of International Humanitarian Law" (March 21, 2006) UN Doc A/RES/60/147 (UNBPG); UNGA "Declaration of Basic Principles of Justice for Victims of Crime and Abuse of Power" (November 29, 1985) UN Doc A/Res/40/34; UNGA "Declaration on the Protection of all Persons from Enforced Disappearance" (December 18, 1992) UN Doc A/Res/47/133, art 19.

to a Remedy for Gross Violations of International Human Rights Law and Serious Violations of International Humanitarian Law (UNBPG), which, after a long period of development and negotiation, codified existing principles on redress in these fields of international law.[19] The UNBPG give shape to customary norms with regard to reparations, making them a useful reference point in considering the contours of the obligation.[20]

The status of the reparatory obligation as a customary international norm is supported both by its ubiquity in treaties and by the approach of international courts and tribunals to situations where it is not explicated.[21] As well as highlighting the inherency of the reparatory obligation in primary rules, authoritative international bodies have sustained their capacity to order remedies and determine the appropriate measures of redress where they have jurisdiction over the merits of the case. This is true irrespective of whether states have specifically agreed to the court's jurisdiction over the determination of redress.[22] As the International Court of Justice determined in *Corfu Channel*, "it follows from the establishment of responsibility that compensation is due," and it would be a vain exercise if the court were empowered to make a determination of the status of the law and find a breach, without the power to order remedy.[23]

In *Blake v Guatemala*, the Inter-American Court of Human Rights recognized the right to remedy as one of the basic pillars not only of the American Convention but also of the rule of law and democracy.[24] The Articles on State Responsibility and the UNBPG affirm the status of the reparatory obligation as a norm of customary international law, which they merely codify.[25] The

[19] UNBPG, ibid, preamble.

[20] See Theo Van Boven, "Victims' Right to a Remedy and Reparation: The New United Nations Principles and Guidelines" in Carla Ferstman, Mariana Goetz, and Alan Stephens (eds), *Reparations for Victims of Genocide, War Crimes and Crimes against Humanity: Systems in Place and Systems in the Making* (Brill 2009).

[21] The repetition of a norm in treaty law serves as evidence of state practice and *opinio juris* in the formulation of customary international law, and thus the consistent repetition in treaty law supports the finding of customary status. See, for instance, *North Sea Continental Shelf Cases (Federal Republic of Germany v Denmark; Federal Republic of Germany v the Netherlands)* (1969) ICJ Rep 3, 38–42; *Case Concerning Continental Shelf (Libyan Arab Jamahiriya v Malta)* (1985) ICJ Rep 13, 29–30. See also Mark Villiger, *Customary International Law and Treaties: A Study of Their Interactions and Interrelations* (Brill 1985); RR Baxter, "Multilateral Treaties as Evidence of Customary International Law" (1965–1966) 41 British Yearbook of International Law 275.

[22] See *Corfu Channel* (n 3).

[23] ibid 23–24.

[24] *Blake v Guatemala* (Merits) IACHR Series C No 36 (January 24, 1998); *Blake v Guatemala* (Reparations and Costs) IACHR Series C No 48 (January 22, 1999). The case concerned the abduction, murder, and forced disappearance of a US journalist in Guatemala.

[25] Articles on State Responsibility (n 13) preamble; UNBPG (n 18) preamble.

Permanent Court of International Justice and International Court of Justice both consistently rely on the inherent power to grant remedies for violations of international legal rights, irrespective of whether such is explicated in the text of the relevant treaty, affirming Dionisio Anzilotti's observations at the turn of the century that the obligation to provide a remedy in the instance of a breach (and the correlative right) is a norm of customary international law.[26] Thus the foundation for legal redress is defined as an implicit reality of the legal system; rights without remedies are futile, demanding reparatory obligations. However, without the strict bounds of written provisions and codified terms, the defining features of redress and reparations are open to interpretation—the boundaries are amorphous, objectives not explicated, and potential forms of redress not prescribed, although existing frameworks governing forms of redress can provide guidance. Thus, an interrogation of the theoretical foundations of redress can support a clearer understanding of its objectives and parameters.

4.2. Conceptions of (reparatory) justice and the basis of redress

In reparations discourse, all meanings depend on the key of interpretation; exactly what is meant by reparation differs significantly depending on the context in which it is discussed, and the underlying objectives and desires of the speaker. Although often publicly conceived of as synonymous with compensation, reparations encompass a broader range of measures designed to redress wrongdoing, both within the legal process and beyond.[27] The exact scope and boundaries of reparations remain fluid, and the extent to which nonmonetary forms of redress are recognized varies depending on the context. The interplay between reparations and other justice mechanisms continues to fuel these uncertainties, posing challenges to a fully coherent understanding of the concept and its place in a broader scheme of justice. Moreover, it is not only the nature and scope of reparations as a justice mechanism that remains contentious but also the very conception of justice against which they must be assessed. Therefore, it is necessary to consider the

[26] Dionisio Anzilotti, *General Theory of State Responsibility in International Law* (Firenze 1902).
[27] Modalities of redress are considered in chapter 5.

interplay between reparations and established conceptions of justice to determine the boundaries of reparatory justice.

Principle 15 of the UNBPG affirm that the notion of justice is central to the formulation of reparations, characterizing reparations as measures intended to promote justice through redress.[28] Exactly what differentiates effective judicial remedy (justice) from insufficient redress, however, is not addressed in the text. Richard Falk similarly notes that reparations in international law are a part of an overall commitment to "global justice."[29] Beyond the centrality of redress and restitution to this "global justice" agenda and the fact that it is carried out in "global arenas" with reference to "global standards and procedures," what characterizes "justice" in this context is again unclear.[30] Theo van Boven in his final report submitted to the UN Economic and Social Council remarks that redress, by definition, entails "full justice" being done vis-à-vis society as a whole, the persons responsible, and the victims.[31] However, other than declaring compensatory measures an element of a "policy of justice," how justice is to be measured in relation to these three parties again remains unarticulated. While justice has repeatedly been recognized as the foundation of reparations, the philosophical underpinnings and boundaries of justice in this context have not yet been fully articulated.

To formulate a coherent understanding of the purpose of reparatory justice, and what this entails, it is therefore necessary to probe these conclusions and the underlying assumptions on which they rest. The foundations and objectives of redress, assessed against established theories of justice—namely corrective justice, economic analysis of law, transformative justice, and distributive justice—help uncover a more comprehensive conception of the purpose and scope of justice in the context of reparations and reparations in the context of justice. When considering marginal cases such as historical enslavement, existing within ambiguous legal frameworks themselves implicated in injustice, where natural law principles may be engaged, this theory of reparatory justice becomes central to the consideration of the case.[32]

[28] UNBPG (n 18).

[29] Richard Falk, "Reparations, International Law, and Global Justice: A New Frontier" in Pablo de Greiff (ed), *The Handbook of Reparations* (OUP 2008) 478, 497.

[30] ibid.

[31] UN Sub-Commission on the Promotion and Protection of Human Rights, "Study Concerning the Right to Restitution, Compensation and Rehabilitation for Victims of Gross Violations of Fundamental Rights and Freedoms: Final Report Submitted by Theo van Boven, Special Rapporteur" (July 2, 1993) E/CN.4/Sub.2/1993/8 [188].

[32] On the legal frameworks and relevance of natural law theories, see chapter 2.

4.2.1. Reparations and corrective justice

The primary objective of reparations and the determination of judicial awards is frequently framed as restitutio in integrum—measures ordered ought to be designed to restore the victim to the position they were in prior to the breach, the status quo ante. As identified by the Permanent Court of International Justice in its famous ruling in *Factory at Chorzów*:

> The essential principle contained in the actual notion of an illegal act—a principle which seems to be established by international practice and in particular by the decisions of arbitral tribunals—is that reparation must, as far as possible, wipe out all the consequences of the illegal act and reestablish the situation which would, in all probability, have existed if that act had not been committed.[33]

The dominance of this idea in reparations discourse and judicial decisions reveals the centrality of corrective justice thinking in defining redress.

Corrective justice suggests that a wrong alters the relationship between parties and aims to return them to equality—equality in this case being relative to the wrongdoing. As Aristotle framed the issue in *Ethics*: judges aim to do justice by returning parties to a situation of equality through the imposition of penalties on the perpetrator proportionate to the illegitimate gains and the provision of redress to victims proportionate to their loss.[34] Equality in this context is not the absolute equality that might be advocated by distributive justice ideals but a return to the prior status of the parties vis-à-vis one another. In short, corrective justice aims to restore relationships between victims and perpetrators by redressing the wrong. Thus, in the context of reparations, the corrective approach has three dimensions, affecting which circumstances give rise to reparatory rights and duties, who can be required to pay reparations, and who is entitled to receive them.

Corrective restoration of equality relies on specific wrongful acts or omissions. This notion of a violation creating a legal entitlement is connected to ideas of injury or harm but not premised upon physical or quantifiable damage. Moral and symbolic harm may create an (intangible) imbalance between the parties that demands redress in the same manner as

[33] *Factory at Chorzów* (Merits) (n 1) [124].

[34] Aristotle, *The Ethics* (JAKThompson tr, Penguin Books 1955) 148–49.

material injury.[35] The nature of the wrong, rather than the injury, is determinative of the nature of reparations required; a legal wrong creates a concomitant legal reparatory right/duty, while a moral wrong may only give rise to a moral reparatory right/duty (albeit a moral duty which might in some circumstances be satisfied through the creation of law). As Naomi Roht-Arriaza and Katharine Orlovsky note, "reparations are distinguished first by their roots as a legal entitlement based on an obligation to repair harm, and second by an element of recognition of wrongdoing as well as harm, atonement, or making good."[36] Reparations under a corrective justice framework thus operate within the bilateral (or multilateral) relationships created by wrongdoing.

The context of the perpetrator-victim relationship defines who can be party to reparations on both sides. Whether injustice is attributable to a state, private actors, or a combination of the two, the reparatory obligation rests with the perpetrator of abuses (although the justiciability of claims against that perpetrator in any given court or tribunal is an entirely separate matter).[37] Conversely, the recipient of reparations must be a victim of the wrongful conduct with sufficient proximity to the violation to justify redress. In the Articles on State Responsibility, injury caused by an internationally wrongful act, whether material or immaterial, is subject to an obligation to make full reparations without further qualification, framing victims as any actors suffering harm.[38]

The approach of international tribunals in assessing damages is consistent with the corrective justice approach, with the objective being to match remedies to injuries and provide proportionate redress. As the tribunal in the *Lusitania* arbitration noted, "remedy must be commensurate with the injury

[35] See Shelton, *Remedies in International Human Rights Law* (n 8) 39. See further section 5.1 on symbolic redress.

[36] Naomi Roht-Arriaza and Katharine Orlovsky, "A Complementary Relationship: Reparations and Development" in Pablo de Greiff and Roger Duthie (eds), *Transitional Justice and Development: Making Connections* (Social Science Research Council 2009) 172.

[37] Principle 15 of the UNBPG (n 18) makes this clear in specifying that the legal duty attaches to the state only when the actions in question are attributable to that state, and the duty resides with a private legal person where they are found liable of the abuses. On invocation of responsibility, see section 3.5.

[38] See (n 13) art 31. See also reparations practice under the mandate of the International Criminal Court, contingent on a perpetrator being convicted, victim eligibility, and on harm "personal to the victim"—*The Prosecutor v Thomas Lubanga Dyilo* (Decision establishing the principles and procedures to be applied to reparations) ICC-01/04-01/06-2904 (August 7, 2012) (*Lubanga Principles*), Principles 1–3. Likewise, the UNBPG frame parties to reparations within the victim-perpetrator paradigm, with victims being individuals or collectives suffering direct or indirect harm as a result of violations—n 18, Principle 8.

received. . . . The compensation must be adequate and balance as near as may be the injury suffered."[39] The idea of proportionality is intimately connected to the idea of balancing the wrong and returning parties to equality. In the context of international criminal law, the *Lubanga Principles* developed by the International Criminal Court in the case of *Lubanga Dyilo* echo this requirement, asserting:

> a convicted person's liability must be proportionate to the harm caused and, inter alia, his or her participation in the commission of the crimes for which he or she was found guilty, in the specific circumstances of the case.[40]

The *Lubanga* formulation evidences dual considerations in determining the extent of liability for reparations, considering not only the injury received but also the extent of participation in the relevant international crimes of the perpetrator before the International Criminal Court. This displays a more nuanced approach to the perpetrator-victim relationship, which in fact may involve multiple perpetrators and/or multiple victims, as well as a spectrum of culpability and connected harm.

The requirement of proportionality connected to the notion of restitutio in integrum provided in *Factory at Chorzów* maintains the objective of redress as the re-establishment of the situation that would, in all probability, have existed if that act had not been committed.[41] This approach anticipates the construction of a fictional world absent the wrongdoing, and the direct comparison of such against actual outcomes, to determine the consequences of the wrongdoing that must be redressed.[42] In this vein, Nozick assumes that the purpose of reparations is to create in the present, the closest possible situation to that which would have occurred without the injustice, advocating a "best estimate" approach to the determination of redress based upon available information and probability distribution.[43] While this method of

[39] *Lusitania Cases* (n 2) 36.
[40] Principle 5, *Lubanga Principles* (n 38).
[41] *Factory at Chorzów* (Merits) (n 1) [47].
[42] This approach is adopted by a number of commentators considering reparations for historical injustice, and often seen as a barrier to claims relating to abuses that alter the counterfactual to such a degree that claimants no longer exist, making it impossible to consider their relative positions in the two worlds. On counterfactual reasoning, see Jeremy Waldron, "Redressing Historic Injustices" (2002) 52 University of Toronto Law Journal 135; Stephen Kershnar, "Are the Descendants of Slaves Owed Compensation for Slavery?" (1999) 16(1) Journal of Applied Philosophy 95; David Lambert, "Black-Atlantic Counterfactualism: Speculating about Slavery and Its Aftermath" (2010) 36 Journal of Historical Geography 286.
[43] Robert Nozick, *Anarchy, State and Utopia* (Basic Books 2013).

assessing damage and determining redress is apt to ensure the objectives of corrective justice are met in theory, in practice the attempt at return can be problematic or incomplete. Where measures aim to condemn unlawful behavior or vindicate victims, and where violations are recognized as being beyond any attempt at return, the counterfactual approach becomes unfit to describe the objective of reparations, even within the bounds of corrective justice theory.

Many authors addressing the subject of reparations for historical injustices have become embroiled in the difficulties of establishing a counterfactual, particularly where the abuse serves as the foundation of the current social order.[44] In such cases, the magnitude of uncertainty as to the position plaintiffs would be in lacking the injustice precludes the quantification of damages, thus presenting a barrier to reparatory awards.[45] However, while the counterfactual approach to the objective of restitutio in integrum can be parceled into the corrective justice framework, it should not be characterized as the outer limit of measures designed to restore parties to equality. Equality may be re-established by returning parties to the position they would have been in but for the violation—the counterfactual—but may also be achieved by redressing the consequences of wrongdoing.[46] In fact, this approach may more appropriately address victims' suffering by recognizing the lived experience of violations, and more adequately dealing with continuing consequences, particularly in the context of severe abuses. As Kelsen opined in 1938, the significance of redress:

> does not lie with the fact that through such reparation—as its name implies—a wrong that has already happened will be repaired, as this is impossible. The wrongful behaviour cannot be made to disappear from the

[44] Jeremy Waldron recognizes the difficulty of dealing with the counterfactual approach in "Redressing Historic Injustices" (2002) 52 University of Toronto Law Journal 135. Kershnar also highlights the significant challenges posed by counterfactual reasoning, sidestepping the problem entirely in formulating his case for reparations by developing an inheritance-based claim—Stephen Kershnar, "Are the Descendants of Slaves Owed Compensation for Slavery?" (1999) 16(1) Journal of Applied Philosophy 95.

[45] See David Lambert, "Black-Atlantic Counterfactualism: Speculating about Slavery and its Aftermath" (2010) 36 Journal of Historical Geography 286. See also David Horowitz, *Uncivil Wars: The Controversy Over Reparations for Slavery* (Encounter Books 2002).

[46] Consistent with this approach, Waldron suggests that even where the wrongdoing itself cannot be altered, it may be possible to interfere with the normal course of its consequences. Jeremy Waldron, "Superseding Historic Injustice" in Ronald Salzberger and Mary Turck (eds), *Reparations for Slavery: A Reader* (Rowman & Littlefield 2004) 208.

world. Its significance lies with the fact that through it, pursuant to a rule, the onset of the consequences of the wrong is made impossible.[47]

Evaluating a completed set of events is often more efficient and likely to yield results than engaging with a "controversy about future probabilities," particularly when considering nonmonetary remedies.[48] This recognizes harm as a continuous and contextually specific experience, which, in many cases, cannot be effaced, only mitigated or mediated.

The threshold for difficulties with the counterfactual approach is not necessarily high. Abuses of a range of human rights and humanitarian laws are broadly understood to defy total restitution.[49] In this context, the lack of equivalence between monetary compensation and the lives of victims makes it an imperfect substitute incapable of even approximating the status quo ante. If victims are deprived of a chosen, specific pursuit in their lives, receiving money to pursue an alternative is not a true substitute. "Where the choices and values are incommensurable," Dinah Shelton explains, "a loss is sustained for which full compensation is impossible."[50] This is particularly true in relation to violations resulting in the death of victims, for some rights and experiences cannot be bought out or exchanged through compensation or other reparatory measures with anything resembling equality. As Posner highlights, "most people would not exchange their lives for anything less than an infinite sum of money if the exchange were to take place immediately."[51]

Shifting away from a purely restitutionary framework built upon the desire to return victims to the status quo ante does not entail a slippery slope into an abyss of responsibility as many reparations detractors suggest. Rather, a distinct set of limits curtail liability. The Inter-American Court of Human Rights, the international tribunal evidencing the greatest willingness to be expansive in its reparations awards, notes that the duty to provide redress is not infinite.[52] This despite the fact that the court is explicit in stating that compensation must be sufficient to remedy all the consequences of the

[47] Hans Kelsen, cited in *Ahmadou Adio Diallo* (Separate Opinion of Judge Cançado Trindade) (n 3) 37.
[48] Shelton, *Remedies in International Human Rights Law* (n 8) 304.
[49] See section 4.3.
[50] Shelton, *Remedies in International Human Rights Law* (n 8) 43.
[51] Richard Posner, *Economic Analysis of Law* (2nd edn, Little, Brown and Co 1977) 197.
[52] *Aloeboetoe and Ors v Suriname* (Reparations and costs) IACHR Series C no 15 [1993] IACHR 2, [47]–[48].

violations that took place without reference to the position that the victims would otherwise have been in.[53]

Returning victims to the status quo ante is only one potential way in which the corrective dimension of the reparatory obligation manifests in international law, although it is the most proliferate in judicial and academic commentaries. Measures of satisfaction, moral damages, and awards designed to indicate the court's condemnation of wrongdoing open avenues for redress not premised upon the possibility of describing a plausible counterfactual or achieving a return to the status quo ante.[54] Official apologies, expressions of regret, and acknowledgments of responsibility are premised not upon return but on recognition of the injustices and reaffirmation of the status of the victims.[55] Measures may be targeted toward damage suffered as a consequence of a violation irrespective of alternative scenarios in order to avoid the counterfactual quagmire, but may also be based upon efforts to recognize wrongdoing, vindicate victims, and transform society to better achieve absolute equality—objectives which fall outside of the corrective paradigm. The corrective framework for redress is therefore insufficient to describe the role, purpose, and function of reparations.

4.2.2. The economic approach to redress

Reparations in many circumstances evidence dual aims—to repair and restore damaged relationships and to address the wrongs themselves.[56] Proportionality requirements in public international law, international human rights law, and international criminal law all consider the nature and gravity of the violations as a factor in determining redress. This differentiates the notion of "addressing the wrongdoing" from the restitutionary objectives of corrective justice.[57] A purely corrective approach would require the restoration of equality through redress and encapsulate dealing with the violation as an aspect of that discrete relationship between victim and perpetrator. The economic approach, on the other hand, differentiates between

[53] ibid [47]. See further sections 6.3–6.5 on the role of role of remoteness and foreseeability in reparations.

[54] See section 5.1.

[55] See Articles on State Responsibility (n 13) art 37.

[56] Lorie Graham, "Reparations, Self-Determination, and the Seventh Generation" (2008) 21 Harvard Human Rights Journal 47, 77.

[57] UNBPG (n 18) Principle 15.

discrete instances of wrongdoing and the relationships they create and the wider function of reparations in dealing with wrongdoing more generally.[58] According to the economic approach, redress must serve a deterrent function in order to be effective, and thus goes beyond the aim of returning parties to equality.[59]

Economic analysis (relying on the presumption that people on the whole act rationally) concludes that properly quantified reparations will impact an individual's cost-benefit analysis with regard to violation, thereby deterring wrongdoing.[60] This attaches both to the individual defendant in the case and to other potential perpetrators. If the conditions are right—namely the cost of violations is set high enough, damage awards adequately replicate the true cost of violations, and sanctions are certain—the presumed result is the "product" (wrongdoing) being priced out of the market.[61] Given that sanctions cannot be made certain, inflating the cost of violations is necessary to create an effective market deterrent. Thus, economic analysis of redress may demand that reparations exceed compensatory or corrective measures to ensure potential violators are deterred by potential costs.[62] Consideration of the wealth of the perpetrator and the existence of patterns of violation in determining exemplary damages display the concern with making violations too costly to repeat, both for the perpetrator at hand and potential future wrongdoers.[63]

The suggestion that legal penalties ought to serve a deterrent function (as well as set to rights the relationship between the discrete perpetrators and victims) takes redress beyond the objective of returning the victim to the position they were in prior to the wrongdoing.[64] For instance, cases involving the disgorgement of profits wrongfully gained may in fact leave the plaintiff better off than they would have been but for the breach, yet may be necessary

[58] The English Court in *Wilkes v Wood*, for instance, noted that damages "are designed not only as satisfaction to the injured person, but likewise as a punishment to the guilty, to deter from any such proceeding for the future, and as a proof of the detestation of the jury to the action itself" and could therefore be greater than the injury received. *Wilkes v Wood* [1763] 98 Eng Rep 489.

[59] See Shelton, *Remedies in International Human Rights Law* (n 8) 28.

[60] ibid.

[61] ibid 42.

[62] See Louis Kaplow and Steven Shavell, "Accuracy in the Assessment of Damages" (1996) 39 Journal of Law and Economics 191.

[63] See Linda Schlueter and Kenneth Redden, *Punitive Damages* (3rd edn, Butterworth Legal Publishers 1995). In practice, see, for instance, *TXO Production Corp. v Alliance Resources Corp.* 113 S.Ct. 2711 (1993).

[64] See generally Michael Rustad and Thomas Koenig, "The Historical Continuity of Punitive Damages Awards: Reforming the Tort Reformers" (1993) 42 American University Law Review 1269.

to condemn wrongful conduct and deter similar violations.[65] Thus, deterrence measures can be seen not only as nonreparatory elements of judicial remedies but also as reparatory elements of the attempt to do justice for victims operating in the same way as guarantees of non-repetition and satisfaction.

Like corrective justice paradigms, punitive damages consistent with the economic approach have an historical pedigree and continuity. Justinian's Digest declares that the law aims to make men good through fear of penalties.[66] Anzilotti differentiated between satisfaction and reparation as elements of redress: satisfaction in this context involving punishing the violation while reparation made good damage sustained.[67] Both elements, he declared, would be present in any judicial award, although the relative proportions might vary. Similarly, Vattel affirmed that redress, appropriately set, ought to both punish and deter:

> the offended party have a right to provide for their future security, and to chastise the offender, by inflicting upon him a punishment capable of deterring him thenceforward from similar aggressions and of intimidating those who might be tempted to imitate him.[68]

In international law, remedies are aimed both at repairing injury resulting from violations and with sanctioning violations of law as distinct objectives, supporting the relevance of the economic approach in defining the aims of reparations.[69] This approach places reparations measures in the broader context of international law as a system, upholding the validity of norms through punishment and deterrence at the same time as having reparatory significance for victims, accounting for the status of states themselves (as well as individuals) as victims of the breach. That these functions need to be satisfied

[65] See generally Peter Jaffrey, *The Nature and Scope of Restitution: Vitiated Transfers, Imputed Contracts and Disgorgement* (Hart 2000).

[66] Alan Watson, *The Digest of Justinian*, vol 1 (University of Pennsylvania Press 2011) 72.

[67] Anzilotti (n 26) 425.

[68] Emer de Vattel, *The Law of Nations* (Béla Kapossy and Richard Whatmore eds, Liberty Fund 2012) bk 2, s 52.

[69] See the Commentary to the Articles on State Responsibility (n 17) 32 (commentary to Article 1) which notes the prevailing view as to the nature of state responsibility is that "consequences of an internationally wrongful act cannot be limited either to reparation or to a 'sanction.'" See also L Oppenheim, *International Law: A Treatise*, vol 1: *Peace* (H Lauterpacht ed, 8th edn, Longmans, Green and Co 1955) 352–54.

concomitantly, rather than alternatively, indicates that both corrective justice and economic approaches contribute to the notion of reparatory justice.

4.2.3. Reparations and transformative justice

In some situations, an over-focus on corrective or economic punitive justice can entrench rather than redress marginalization. In response, Pablo de Greiff recognized the centrality of social transformation in justice procedures, foregrounding the need to interrupt cycles of violence that entrench existing structures of marginalization.[70] Such transformation can be particularly important in transitional contexts following significant societal upheaval. However, it can also be vital to attempts to deal with injustices in nontransitional contexts where violations are connected to entrenched social, cultural, and political norms.[71] In these cases, restitution may hinder, rather than advance, the objectives of justice.

The notion that reparations ought to address not only the symptoms of unjust social relations (specific abuses of people's rights) but also the underlying causes of injustice is connected to ideas of equality, as well as preventing future violations and guaranteeing non-repetition.[72] For instance, the United Nations Truth Commission Report on El Salvador explicitly highlighted the need to "avoid any risk of reverting to the *status quo ante*" to support transition to democracy with respect for human rights and the rule of law.[73] Transformative measures explicitly reject restitutio in integrum (return to the status quo ante) and thus represent a significant break from the traditionally recognized objectives of corrective justice and the economic approach to judicial redress.

Where transformative measures aim toward the improvement of society and are not tied to remedying specific violations or preventing those breaches

[70] Pablo de Greiff, "Articulating the Links between Transitional Justice and Development: Justice and Social Integration" in de Greiff and Duthie (n 36) 29.

[71] This has been particularly noted in relation to the situation facing women and girls following violations of their rights. See International Meeting on Women's and Girls' Right to a Remedy and Reparation, "Nairobi Declaration on Women's and Girls' Right to a Remedy and Reparation" (Nairobi, March 21, 2007), Principles 1(D), 3.

[72] See, for instance, Principle 4 of the ICC's *Lubanga Principles* (n 38), which highlights that reparations "need to address any underlying injustices and in their implementation the Court should avoid replicating discriminatory practices or structures that predated the commission of the crimes."

[73] UNSC, Annex, "From Madness to Hope: The 12-Year War in El Salvador: Report of the United Nations Commission on the Truth for El Salvador" (April 1, 1993) UN Doc S/25500.

in the future, they fall outside the purview of reparatory justice.[74] However, where reform is connected to preventing the repetition of violations and guaranteeing non-recurrence, it may constitute an element of reparations. Satisfaction, cessation, and guarantees and assurances of non-repetition may cross the borders between transformative and reparatory justice, connecting to specific instances of wrongdoing existing in the past and committing to a future absent such violations.

For victims, transformative reparations can be the most significant form of reparations available. Particularly in situations of instability involving official violations, the future conduct of the state can be more important to victims than any other form of redress—particularly nominal awards of compensation.[75] Such measures represent the affirmation and restoration of the victims' status as rights bearers, as well as a significant transformation where the status quo was a situation of marginalization or oppression enabling the offenses in the first instance.[76] Such awards may also be more appropriate in relation to historical violations with continuing structural harms, because they directly target the ongoing damage rather than the original violations. Thus, transformation may, in some circumstances, fall within the scope of reparatory justice, but only insofar as it eschews notions of absolute equality in favor of the restoration and enforcement of legal rights of victims of specific wrongdoing.

4.2.4. Reparations and distributive justice

The removal of the foundations of redress from the distributive fields of aid and assistance is regularly viewed as a prerequisite for classification as reparatory measures. Transformative justice is only characterized as reparatory where it deals with specific instances of wrongdoing and not with achieving equality more generally. Aristotle made the distinction between restorative justice—which related to legal rights and entailed entitlements to justice in the instance of a breach—and distributive justice involving discretionary moral rather than legal claims.[77] Grotius reframed these concerns

[74] This is considered further in section 7.3.
[75] Christine Gray, *Judicial Remedies in International Law* (Clarendon Press 1987) 217.
[76] See Christian J Tams, "Recognizing Guarantees of Non-Repetition: LaGrand and the Law of State Responsibility" (2002) 27 Yale Journal of International Law 441.
[77] Aristotle, *The Nicomachean Ethics* (David Ross tr, OUP 2009).

as expletive and attributive justice but maintained the fundamental distinction: the former was the subject of legal rights and entitlements while the latter concerned "those virtues which have as their purpose to do good to others, as generosity, compassion, and foresight in matters of government" and entailed only moral rights and duties.[78] Measures undertaken within these divergent categories of justice may take similar or identical forms but are distinguished by the basis upon which they are assumed.

That reparations are targeted toward specific instances of wrongdoing (requiring unlawful conduct in the context of legal reparations) means that they should not be conflated with distributive justice measures, despite the fact that they may possess distributive qualities. Roht-Ariazza and Orlovsky highlight this distinction:

> What distinguishes reparations from assistance is the moral and political content of the former, positing that victims are entitled to reparations because their rights have been violated by the state (through acts or omissions).[79]

Even in the context of nonlegal reparations programs instituted by political or other nonjudicial mechanisms, measures labeled reparations are segregated from distributive justice initiatives. Notions of wrongdoing, obligation, and entitlement still permeate political reparations packages, differentiating between the general population and those entitled to redress by reference to these indicators.[80]

In international human rights law, reparations play an important role and may be combined with assistance and development measures. However, they are not conflated with such processes.[81] General social programs aimed toward the development of all citizens, or not targeted specifically toward the victim population in question, are not considered to be reparations.[82] General duties of states to provide for citizens and alleviate suffering are distinguished from the obligation of a wrongdoer, having committed atrocities,

[78] Stephen Neff (ed), *Hugo Grotius on the Law of War and Peace* (CUP 2012) 27.

[79] Naomi Roht-Arriaza and Katharine Orlovsky, "A Complementary Relationship: Reparations and Development" in de Greiff and Duthie (n 36) 179.

[80] See section 7.3.1.

[81] Peter Dixon, "Reparations, Assistance and the Experience of Justice: Lessons from Colombia and the Democratic Republic of the Congo" (2016) 10 International Journal of Transitional Justice 88.

[82] See Brandon Hamber "Narrowing the Micro and the Macro: A Psychological Perspective on Reparations in Societies in Transition" in de Greiff, *The Handbook of Reparations* (n 29) 560, at 575.

to provide a remedy to victims for the harms associated with that conduct. This is true in public international law, wherein foreign aid is distinguished from the reparatory obligation. Where aid is given and taken on the basis of political and diplomatic relations, reparations are a legal obligation incumbent upon wrongdoing states. Similarly, in international criminal law, the practice of the International Criminal Court's Trust Fund for Victims is characteristic of this differentiation, separating assistance from the judicial process and reparations obligations.[83] Furthermore, the distinction has symbolic and psychological dimensions, with aid and distributive justice measures reinforcing relationships of dominance and dependency, while reparations turn the "plea for aid into a demand for justice."[84]

While differentiation between assistance and reparations—distributive and reparatory justice—remains steady, the nuances of this divergence are not often methodically addressed. Peter Dixon identified five intersecting frameworks distinguishing between reparations and assistance measures: (1) ascription of responsibility; (2) recognition of victims and their status as rights bearers; (3) nature of processes dealing with eligibility and receipt of benefits; (4) form of support addressing harms or needs; and (5) goals and impact.[85] In all these elements, reparations bear some degree of differentiation from distributive justice, although not all bear equal significance. It is therefore necessary to carry these distinctions forward in consideration of the elements of reparatory justice, interweaving features of corrective and transformative justice with the economic approach.

4.3. The elements of reparatory justice

Moving beyond the general theoretical basis of reparatory justice to identify specific features of reparations assists in formulating a more comprehensive and workable understanding of redress. While notions such as full

[83] The TFV was established by Article 79 of the Rome Statute of the International Criminal Court (adopted July 17, 1998, entered into force July 1, 2002) 2187 UNTS 90/37 (Rome Statute). Rule 98 of the Rules of Procedure and Evidence and the Trust Fund's own Rules and Regulations separate assistance—which may include material, psychological, or physical aid—from the judicial process, whereas reparations (material and symbolic) are ordered against a perpetrator found guilty by the court to individuals or collectives recognized as victims of the crime by the court. ICC "Rules of Procedure and Evidence of the International Criminal Court" (September 9, 2002) ICC-ASP/1/3 10; and ICC "Regulations of the Trust Fund for Victims" (December 3, 2005) ICC-ASP/4/Res.3.

[84] Anthony Gifford "Pipe Dream or Necessary Atonement" (2007) 36 Index on Censorship 89, 94.

[85] Dixon (n 81) 95.

reparation, *restitutio in integrum*, and deterrence may guide a general theory of remedies, they fail to provide practical guidance on the elements that should guide determination in cases or the development of claims practice.[86] The following analysis therefore highlights the key elements of reparatory justice that distinguish it from other conceptions of justice, recognizing the locations of intersection and defining its scope.

The elements of reparatory justice might be realized through a range of modalities of redress, both legal and extralegal.[87] However, the forms reparations might take are likely to be influenced by the different elements of reparatory justice identified. Thus, understanding these elements at the theoretical level enables the consideration of novel or atypical cases and the determination of appropriate modalities of redress to meet the objectives of reparatory justice. Where established jurisprudence fails to provide clear answers and where legal reasoning is employed in an extralegal context, this holistic understanding of what constitutes reparatory justice is vital for nuanced consideration of claims that builds upon the existing frameworks.

4.3.1. Responsibility and violation

Violation, or wrongdoing, represents the threshold of reparations, below which lies distributive justice and above which sits corrective and reparatory justice. Responsibility, as a feature of reparatory justice, relates to the perpetrator's share in the relationship of wrongdoing, recognizing culpability for wrongful acts (or omissions), and the consequences thereof. Thus, the element of responsibility has three dimensions. Firstly, it requires that there be a violation for which an identifiable perpetrator is responsible, fortifying the corrective paradigm. Secondly, it involves liability and the ascription of responsibility to the wrongdoer, enforcing accountability and distancing reparations from distributive justice.[88] Thirdly, where wrongdoing has resulted in little or no material damage, responsibility may demonstrate the operation of the economic approach to redress in fulfilling punitive or deterrence-based objectives. By demanding redress on the basis of responsibility for wrongful conduct alone, moral and symbolic rights are redressed,

[86] Dinah Shelton, "Righting Wrongs: Reparations in the Articles on State Responsibility" (2002) 96 American Journal of International Law 833, 845.
[87] Modalities of redress are considered further in chapter 5.
[88] See Luke Moffet, *Justice for Victims before the International Criminal Court* (Routledge 2014) 147.

and deterrence relates not to the extent of the injury but to the severity of the wrongdoing itself.

The distinction between duties of perpetrators and duties of states more generally identified in the UNBPG highlights the importance of responsibility in the reparations framework. While upholding the importance of ensuring harms to victims are sufficiently dealt with to provide for recovery, the UNBPG maintain a distinction between the general obligations of a state toward vulnerable groups within society and the obligations of a perpetrator to redress the suffering they caused by their actions. This division is highlighted by the different burdens imposed by Principles 15 and 16, making reparations a mandatory legal duty for perpetrators and an aspirational obligation for states without direct liability.[89] State programs are clearly identified as distinct and secondary to the obligations of perpetrators through this language, as well as through the maintenance of perpetrator liability where state initiatives have been undertaken—the perpetrator's duty to provide reparations is not extinguished simply because the needs of victims are met by the state.[90]

Where there is a lacuna in attribution of responsibility for wrongdoing unfilled by impartial mechanisms to deal with injustices, alternative narratives may creep in. These alternatives may reinforce the abdication of responsibility for wrongs committed, thereby entrenching hierarchies of power and the marginalization of victimized populations that served as the preconditions for the violations.[91] Such counternarratives enable "scapegoating"—the avoidance of responsibility by the real perpetrators—and thereby the continuation of structures of marginalization and violence. The assertion that the "Vietnamese" were the architects of the Khmer Rouge regime, for instance, is identified as a pervasive narrative within Cambodian society that continues to legitimize the structures of power that facilitated the atrocities committed.[92] Clear identification of wrongdoers and attribution of responsibility in the public domain can prevent this evasion of culpability. Moreover, such responsibility ought to be situated within the complex

[89] The language of Principle 16 requires that states "endeavour" to establish programs where the perpetrator does not, or cannot, meet the obligation, UNBPG (n 18).

[90] In such a case, the perpetrator becomes liable to the state to compensate for reparations paid by that state to victims. UNBPG (n 18).

[91] See, for instance, Inter-American Commission of Human Rights, "Uruguay Report" (1992) 13 Human Rights Law Journal 340.

[92] Aafke Sanders, *The Evil Within: Genocide, Memory and Mythmaking in Cambodia* (Radboud University 2006) 89.

social hierarchies and cultural norms of the environment in which atrocities occurred in order to ensure they respond both to the violence itself and to its causes.[93]

The notion of responsibility is inextricably connected to recognition of the victims. As Yael Danieli notes, acknowledgment and culpability in the reparatory context possess a symbolic power engaged in vindicating the victims and their experiences:

> It's not the money but what the money signifies—vindication. It signifies the governments' own admission of guilt, and an apology. . . . The money concretises for the victim the confirmation of responsibility, wrongfulness, he is not guilty, and somebody cares about it. It is at least a token. It does have a meaning.[94]

The foregrounding of responsibility and recognition as central to the reparations claim reflects the idea of harm to the moral character and dignity of the victims—the idea that injustice has an "affective dimension" that demands a remedy just as material harms do.[95] This affective dimension varies depending on the context. Where the state in international law is the primary victim, injuries are predominantly pecuniary, or damages are limited, the most notable impact of the breach may be in undermining the primary rules and the legal system itself.[96] Redress in such a case aims toward re-establishing and affirming the integrity of the primary rules.[97] However, where citizens have suffered severe violations, the symbolic dimensions of the wrongdoing attach not only to the legal system as a whole but also to the integrity and dignity of people. As elements of reparations, both responsibility and recognition respond to these affective dimensions of injustice.

By recognizing the possibility for damages not connected to direct physical or economic harms, courts throughout history have given weight to the idea of human dignity as having value in practice; the contravention of a person's rights, integrity, and autonomy is recognized as necessitating some

93 On the need for responsiveness, see section 7.4.4.

94 Yael Danieli, "Massive Trauma and the Healing Role of Reparative Justice" in Ferstman, Goetz, and Stephens (n 20) 59–60.

95 See Frank Haldemann, "Another Kind of Justice: Transitional Justice as Recognition" (2008) 41(2) Cornell International Law Journal 678.

96 See for instance *Campbell Case* 2 RIAA 1158 (June 10, 1931); *Maal Case* 10 RIAA (June 1, 1903) 732–33; *Rainbow Warrior II (New Zealand v France)* (1990) 20 UNRIAA 215; *Treaty of Neuilly, Article 179, Annex, Paragraph 4 (Interpretation, Judgment No 3)* PCIJ Series A No 3 (1924) 9.

97 See section 5.1.

form of redress, while the culpability of the perpetrator is confirmed.[98] The legal wrong for which an award is granted in the context of moral damages is not a tangible injury, and the reparation granted is not directly connected to a particular worldly harm. Harm is presumed from the wrongdoing itself and must be premised on the assumption that individuals have a right to a remedy for wrongs committed against them without any further qualification.[99] This represents an acknowledgment, throughout history, of the affective dimension of injustices and the need for responsibility and recognition irrespective of material damage. This is particularly acute in the context of gross and serious violations of human rights and humanitarian law where the UNBPG recognize violations that, by virtue of their gravity, constitute an affront to human dignity—acknowledging that the severity of the abuses necessarily entails a degradation of dignity.[100]

The centrality of human dignity and the symbolic face of wrongdoing have been recognized through time within human rights and humanitarian law.[101] The notion of dignity has a long history in philosophy and law, appearing in various forms through time.[102] Hugo Grotius in the seventeenth century indicated the universality and inalienability of human dignity within the laws of war in discussing the importance of funeral rites. Grotius connected the right of burial (which could not be denied "even to enemies") to the "dignity of man"—an inalienable right of nature and of men.[103] Although early ideas of human dignity were primarily connected to religion, the development of thought over time has established that the concept can be supported outside the religious paradigm, and therefore need not be severed at the root.[104]

[98] The UNGA "Declaration of Basic Principles of Justice for Victims of Crime and Abuse of Power" (n 18), for instance, affirmed universal and effective recognition of, and respect for, the rights of victims as a standalone, necessary, and important function of justice processes post-abuse.

[99] See Jason Taliadoros, "The Roots of Punitive Damages at Common Law: A Longer History" (2016) 64 Cleveland State Law Review 251.

[100] Preamble to the UNBPG (n 18).

[101] See Christopher McCrudden (ed), *Understanding Human Dignity* (OUP 2013).

[102] See Christopher McCrudden, "Human Dignity and the Interpretation of Human Rights" (2008) 19 European Journal of International Law 655.

[103] Grotius, *The Rights of War and Peace* (n 5) bk II, ch 19.

[104] Pico della Mirandola in 1486 suggested that the root of dignity arose from the ability to choose what he wants to be. Although he connected this to religion in labeling it a gift from God, the notion remains stable absent religious influence. See Pico della Mirandola, *On the Dignity of Man* (C Glenn Wallis tr, Hackett Publishing Company 1965) 5. Immanuel Kant developed notions of dignity that, though contested by Kantian scholars, clearly were not reliant on religion, and are premised on the idea of dignity as autonomy demanding that individuals be treated as ends in and of themselves and not merely as means to an end. See Giovanni Bognetti, "The Concept of Human Dignity in European and U.S. Constitutionalism" in Georg Nolte (ed), *European and US Constitutionalism* (Council of Europe 2005) 75.

The growth in universal conceptions of human rights saw an associated rise in the explication of the concept of dignity as central to humanity. In Europe and Latin America, dignity was deeply rooted in discourse surrounding the abolition of slavery and played a significant role in the civil rights movement in the United States.[105] The Universal Declaration of Human Rights was central to the popularization of the notion of dignity within the human rights frame, a concept which was also central to the Charter of the United Nations.[106] Human dignity now plays a significant role in human rights discourse, and both the International Covenant on Civil and Political Rights and the International Covenant on Economic, Social and Cultural Rights identify the inherent dignity of the person as the basis of all human rights.[107] As the mechanism through which rights are vindicated in the instance of a breach, reparations are a vehicle for the ascription of responsibility for violations of human dignity, as well as ways in which such is recognized in the face of injustice.

4.3.2. Recognition

The identification of the symbolic or affective dimensions of injustice and recognition of dignity as an element of justice impact both sides of the relationship of wrongdoing. Responsibility focuses upon the perpetrator, ensuring justice is done against wrongdoers. On the other hand, the nucleus of recognition as an element of reparatory justice is the victims and the moral injuries they suffer as a result of violations. Particularly in the context of international law, where failure to respect the honor and dignity of a state can be just as significant in international relations as financial injury, injury caused by a violation is often of a moral rather than material character.[108]

[105] Simón Bolivar in Bolivia, for instance, identified slavery as a "shameless violation of human dignity" and called for the abolition of the sacrilegious laws which perpetuated it. See Simón Bolivar, "Message to the Congress of Bolivia (Lima, 25 May 1826)," quoted in Paolo Carozza, "From Conquest to Constitutions: Retrieving a Latin American Tradition of the Idea of Human Rights " (2003) 25 Human Rights Quarterly 281, 301.

[106] UDHR (n 18); Charter of the United Nations (June 26, 1945) 59 Stat 1031, UNTS 993. The first sentence of the UDHR's preamble notes that "recognition of the inherent dignity and of the equal and inalienable rights of all members of the human family is the foundation of freedom, justice and peace in the world"; Article 1 recognizes that all human beings are "born free and equal in dignity and rights" and Article 22 goes on to note that each citizen is entitled to the realization of the economic, social, and cultural rights "indispensable for his dignity and the free development of his personality."

[107] ICCPR (n 18); International Covenant on Economic, Social and Cultural Rights (adopted December 16, 1966, entered into force January 3, 1976) 993 UNTS 3.

[108] Anzilotti (n 26) 13–14.

Anzilotti therefore suggests that "violation of a rule always constitutes trespass upon the interest which the rule protects and, consequently, upon the subjective right of the person whose interest is affected."[109]

The right to a remedy in international law is not contingent upon a state having suffered actual or material damage as a result of a violation. Rather, an internationally wrongful act of a state automatically gives rise to a concomitant obligation to remedy on the part of the wronged state, because any breach of international law causes moral injury to the state whose interests have been infringed.[110] This is equally true of individual victims of violations who may also suffer similar symbolic harms irrespective of material loss.

Frank Haldemann frames violations as acts of "misrecognition," through which victims of wrongdoing are differentiated from the corpus of humanity by the denial of their rights.[111] Violations degrade the identity of the victims as individuals, rights bearers, agents, and citizens, particularly where abuses are widespread or target particular communities. This constitutes a specific moral wrong with symbolic dimensions that states, as artificial legal persons, might also suffer. It is for this reason that the symbolic value of reparations is often considered particularly important and, in some instances, of greater significance than material redress.[112] Pablo de Greiff highlights the significance of recognition within the context of grave and widespread abuses in particular:

> The type of recognition that is relevant is one that acknowledges the victims' status as victims and the abuses to which they were subject, gives public space to their stories, and tries to reverse the marginalization which they typically suffer. But this is not all. In fact, it is even more important to recognize their status as *rights bearers*, ultimately, as co-participants in a common political project, that is, as *citizens*.[113]

[109] ibid.

[110] The automatic character of the obligation to remedy was affirmed in *Phosphates in Morocco (Italy v France)* (Preliminary Objections) [1938] PCIJ Rep Series A/B No 74 [28] wherein the court noted that international responsibility was established "immediately as between the two States" upon commission of an internationally wrongful act by one state against another. On moral injury, see FV Garcia Amador, *The Changing Law of International Claims*, vol 2 (Oceana Publications 1984) 567.

[111] Haldeman (n 95).

[112] The focus on truth-telling in post-conflict or post-atrocity settings displays such preference for the recognition of victims' experiences, even at the expense of accountability.

[113] Pablo de Greiff, "Transitional Justice and Development" in Bruce Currie-Alder and others (eds), *International Development: Ideas, Experience, and Prospects* (OUP 2014) 420, emphasis in original.

Recognition is a notably victim-centric aspect of reparations, shifting focus from the wrongdoing, the perpetrator, and punishment to the impact violations have upon victims. The concern with providing awards, whether designed to address material or immaterial harms, to victims of wrongdoing necessarily brings them to the fore, reinforcing the underlying objective of redressing injustice for victims and not for society at large. Reparations are, by their nature, victim-centered forms of redress. The centrality of the victim in reparations both defines and derives from their nature and form.[114] In the context of mass atrocity, this victim-centric approach moves reparations away from traditional criminal objectives of punishment and deterrence, recognizing that the injustices in question explode the limits of such goals and therefore demand a different, multifaceted approach.[115] This makes reparatory justice more relevant to historical cases, for it broadens the understanding of injustice beyond the individual victim-perpetrator relationship.

Recognition serves a corrective function in ensuring that parties are returned to equality and victims' status as rights bearers is affirmed, thus returning them to the legal status quo. Furthermore, it engages with the realities of wrongdoing and atrocity in a more nuanced way, recognizing injustice as well as striving toward justice. Preoccupation with the accountability of perpetrators and the attempt to impose punitive measures that reflect the gravity of the offending can prioritize justice to such an extent that it risks overshadowing the contours of injustice.[116] Injustice in this context stands for the lived experiences of the victims, which cannot be recanted or effaced. When the irreparability of some forms of wrongdoing is recognized, traditional measures of redress focused on return to the status quo ante become inadequate. Recognition and measures designed to ensure it fill this lacuna in redress by grappling with injustice without presuming the possibility of correction. Recognizing the experiences and suffering of victims and reaffirming their dignity and equal status as citizens are vital to recovery from atrocities and treat victimization as temporary rather than permanent.[117]

Acknowledgment of responsibility is an aspect of recognition distinct from the principle of responsibility and can also be a form of reparations in

[114] See Luke Moffett, *Justice for Victims before the International Criminal Court* (Routledge 2014) 43.

[115] Austin Sarat, Lawrence Douglas, and Martha Merrill (eds), *The Limits of the Law* (Stanford UP 2005).

[116] Judith Shklar, "Giving Injustice Its Due" (1989) 98 Yale Law Journal 1135.

[117] See Rachel López, "The (Re)collection of Memory after Mass Atrocity and the Dilemma for Transitional Justice" (2015) 47 New York University Journal of International Affairs and Politics 799.

and of itself.[118] While acknowledgment by the perpetrator is not a prerequisite for reparations or reparatory justice, it can contribute to the recognition of victims as rights bearers and do so with symbolic significance. Particularly where the perpetrators hold and maintain social, cultural, or political power, a lack of acknowledgment by the wrongdoer can undermine the efficacy of reparations measures. For instance, Vann Nath, a former S-21 detainee of the Khmer Rouge regime in Cambodia and complainant in Extraordinary Chambers in the Courts of Cambodia Case 001, highlighted the limitations of such failures:

> It is hard for reconciliation [sic] because there are no admissions from the perpetrators that they committed wrongdoings, and that they can face what they have done . . . they never say they were wrong.[119]

In the Cambodian context, the urge for broader acknowledgment of the wrongs committed under the Khmer Rouge is widely documented and connected to a culture of secrecy that defined the regime.[120]

Recognition of victims may be stymied by dominant social narratives sanitizing or euphemizing wrongdoing. Acknowledgment may become increasingly important the more influence the perpetrator holds over society.[121] State acknowledgment in particular can act as an "official sanction" of knowledge and truth about the violations, helping the recognition of victims to enter the public realm and aiding in rehabilitation of victims in society.[122] Recognition cannot be achieved internally by the victims, for it requires that the perpetrator or institutions that enabled the injustices recognize the wrongdoing and thereby the humanity and dignity of the victims.[123] Thus, reparatory measures are critical in achieving recognition, which may be

[118] UNBPG (n 18) Principle 22(e) identifies public apologies, including acknowledgment of the facts and acceptance of responsibility as a form of satisfaction within the reparations framework.

[119] Chheng Niem, Duong Keo, and Sin Putheary, *Behind the Darkness: Taking Responsibility or Acting under Orders?* (Youth for Peace 2011) 3–4.

[120] See Phuong Pham and others, *So We Will Never Forget: A Population-Based Survey on Attitudes about Social Reconstruction and the Extraordinary Chambers in the Courts of Cambodia* (Human Rights Centre, University of California 2009); Jaya Ramji, "Reclaiming Cambodian History: The Case for a Truth Commission" (2000) 24(1) Fletcher Forum of World Affairs 137.

[121] Official narratives downplaying abuses committed by the Japanese State, including the continued language labeling victims of sexual enslavement "comfort women," led to survivors' rejection of compensation. See Nishino Rumiko, Kim Puja, and Onozawa Akane, *Denying the Comfort Women: The Japanese State's Assault on Historical Truth* (Routledge 2018).

[122] IACHR (n 91).

[123] See Thema Bryant-Davis, "Healing Requires Recognition: the case for Race-Based Traumatic Stress" (2007) 35 The Counselling Psychologist 135.

supported through meaningful engagement with victims as rights bearers and decision makers.

4.3.3. Procedural justice

While Dixon identifies procedural justice as a central feature of reparations distinguishing it from assistance measures, the importance of this feature is not confined to reparatory justice. Participation in processes designed to bring about societal and distributive change are often vital in combating marginalization of excluded and disadvantaged communities. Connections between social and cultural exclusion and economic deprivation make involving the voices of targeted communities in measures designed to address such issues imperative—whether those measures take place within the realm of distributive or reparatory justice.[124] Thus the importance of procedural justice should be viewed not as a distinguishing feature of reparatory justice but as an important element of effective justice measures in both contexts.

Procedural justice aims to improve victims' satisfaction with measures undertaken by treating them with respect, ensuring fairness, and valuing their input.[125] While procedural justice concerns may arise in various contexts, they are particularly acute in reparations discourse where participation of victims is central to the fulfillment of reparatory objectives. The definition of reparations provided by REDRESS, a prominent nongovernmental organization focused on seeking reparations for survivors of torture, explicitly acknowledges the importance of process. REDRESS defines reparations as "the range of measures that may be taken in response to an actual or threatened violation; embracing both the substance of relief as well as the procedure through which it may be obtained."[126] With regard to historical enslavement, this would require meaningful engagement with affected communities and reparations activists at all stages of reparatory processes.

Consultation with victims in formulating reparations is an integral part of ensuring procedural justice and—in conjunction with their influence in

[124] See Kjell Törnblom and Riël Vermunt, *Distributive and Procedural Justice* (Taylor & Francis 2007).

[125] Jo-Anne Wemmers, "Victims' Need for Justice" in R Letschert and others (eds), *Victimological Approaches to International Crimes: Africa* (Intersentia 2011) 145–52.

[126] REDRESS, *Reparation: A Sourcebook for Victims of Torture and Other Violations of Human Rights and International Humanitarian Law* (REDRESS 2003) 8.

the design and implementation of awards and procedures—can be decisive of the overall success of reparations from the perspective of victims.[127] The additional care paid to victims within this context, and the focus on ensuring victims are recognized and empowered as agents and rights bearers, raise the threshold for consultation and participation beyond that traditionally provided by judicial proceedings. As noted by REDRESS:[128]

> for victims, justice is an experience. It is as much about the way that they are treated, consulted and respected procedurally throughout the reparation process, as it is about the substantive remedy, material or otherwise, they may be granted as part of the end result.

In international as well as domestic proceedings, fairness and justice often require that victims are empowered to request reparations for violations on their own behalf and supported throughout the relevant processes.[129]

The *Lubanga Principles* highlight the importance of victim participation in reparations procedures at the International Criminal Court, recognizing that victims, their families, and communities that meet the eligibility requirement for reparations should be able to participate in the process.[130] The Principles assert that victims should receive adequate support to make this participation "substantive and effective," and the court should consult with victims on issues concerning identification of beneficiaries and priorities.[131] At minimum, the right of victims to information concerning violations and reparations mechanisms is generally recognized and upheld. Principles 11 and 24 of the UNBPG affirm the entitlement of the victims to information and the duty of the state to ensure that the public is informed of available rights and remedies.[132] International human rights treaties likewise contain a number of guarantees for victims to ensure they are provided the necessary avenues of redress.[133]

[127] Brianne McGonigle Leyh, *Procedural Justice? Victim Participation in International Criminal Proceedings* (Intersentia 2011).

[128] REDRESS, "Collective Reparations: Concepts and Principles" (The REDRESS Trust 2015), 1.

[129] Richard Falk (n 29) 497. Further, the case of *Ahmadou Adio Siallo* (n 3), guarantees the right to remedy in international law for individual harms arising from breaches of human rights law.

[130] *Lubanga Principles* (n 38) Principle 8.

[131] ibid.

[132] UNBPG (n 18).

[133] See, for instance (n 18): ICCPR, art 2; American Convention, art 25; European Convention, art 12; African Charter, art 7; and Arab Charter, art 9.

Although procedural justice and participation remain somewhat amorphous in their mechanisms and exact requirements, their centrality in the construction of effective reparatory justice is frequently reaffirmed by commentators.[134] This may be viewed as an extension of the element of recognition as constructed in section 4.3.2, targeting the misrecognition of victims and denial of their status as rights bearers and prioritizing their agency to ensure effective recovery from violations. Official acknowledgment of victims' narratives and perspectives on their victimization affirms their dignity and the wrongfulness of the harm they suffered.[135] This may be particularly important in the context of gross violations of human rights where victims are denied basic humanity through the abuses and where impunity often attaches to wrongdoing.[136] Procedural justice can therefore be viewed not only as an element of reparatory justice but also as a form of reparation in its own right and a means of achieving the recognition of victims as rights bearers.[137]

Given that the focus of public international law remains claims between states, it is unsurprising that standards of procedural justice for individual victims are not as thoroughly articulated in this context as they are in international criminal, human rights, and humanitarian law. Yet, the principle of full and effective reparations remains central to awards in this arena; an objective that, in many instances, cannot be satisfied in terms of recognition, responsibility, and responsiveness without some degree of procedural justice.[138] The harms to be redressed in international law are not only those directly incurred by states party to the proceedings but also all injuries caused

134 The then Special Rapporteur of the United Nations Sub-Commission on Prevention of Discrimination and Protection of Minorities, Theo van Boven, for instance, highlights the importance of victims' perspectives in reparations discussions and asserts that their needs and wishes should be central in reparatory processes. UNCHR, "Study Concerning the Right to Restitution, Compensation and Rehabilitation for Victims of Gross Violations of Human Rights and Fundamental Freedoms, Final Report Submitted by Mr Theo van Boven, Special Rapporteur" (1993) UN Doc E/CN.4/Sub.2/1993/8 [133], [137]. See also Edgar Lind and Tom R Tyler, *The Social Psychology of Procedural Justice* (Springer 1988) 31–34; Margaret Urban Walker, *Moral Repair: Reconstructing Moral Relations after Wrongdoing* (CUP 2006); Yael Danieli, "Massive Trauma and the Healing Role of Reparative Justice" in Ferstman, Goetz, and Stephens (n 20) 66.

135 Yael Danieli, "Massive Trauma and the Healing Role of Reparative Justice" in Ferstman, Goetz, and Stephens (n 20) 41–78, 47.

136 Luke Moffett, "Transitional Justice and Reparations: Remedying the Past?" in Cheryl Lawther, Luke Moffett, and Dov Jacobs (eds), *Research Handbook on Transitional Justice* (Elgar 2017).

137 Danieli frames inclusion of victims in justice processes as "an opportunity for redress and healing" in itself (n 135) 66.

138 The obligation to make full reparation for injury caused by an internationally wrongful act is contained in Article 31 of the Articles on State Responsibility (n 13), affirming the determination of the Permanent Court of International Justice in *Factory at Chorzów* (Jurisdiction) and (Merits) (n 3) 21 and (n 1) 47.

by the internationally wrongful act, including moral injury to individuals.[139] Thus, developments concerning the construction of effective remedies for individual harms, and particularly those of a symbolic nature, in other international legal contexts, may appropriately infuse approaches to reparations in public international law.

4.3.4. Form

Dixon's fourth principle, the principle of form, often degrades in practice as reparations and assistance measures are frequently alike—even indistinguishable. This is particularly true where the modalities of reparations are recognized as encompassing a wide range of different possibilities.[140] The distinction is based on the conclusion that reparations target harms, while assistance measures target needs.[141] Harms to victims are converted to rights within the reparatory framework by virtue of the wrongdoing and often represent the needs of victims following injury. Yet, the nature of needs within distributive justice frameworks may bleed into concepts of rights, particularly where the state has obligations to protect citizens from certain forms of deprivation and ill treatment.[142] Thus, the theoretical differences between the two are not necessarily evident in the measures ultimately adopted, and even this theoretical distinction degrades at its borders. Dixon's principle of form may therefore be more accurately conceived as concerned not with the modalities of redress, for these may be the same in both the reparatory and the distributive context, but with the injuries to be redressed and the way in which remedies are crafted. It is this basis for shaping reparations that separates them from distributive measures and not whether the response takes a particular form.[143]

The distinction between forms is connected to the idea that reparations must fully return the victim to the status quo ante—wiping out all consequences of the illegal act—while assistance measures are intimately

[139] Articles on State Responsibility (n 13) art 31.
[140] See chapter 5.
[141] Dixon (n 81) 100.
[142] The protection of socioeconomic rights in particular may have a distinct distributive character, yet the deprivation of such may also be described as a breach of rights requiring state action to remedy.
[143] For further consideration of the need for responsiveness, see section 7.4.4.

tied to the availability of resources.[144] That reparations must be "more significant" than assistance measures belies the reality of situations in which such measures are adopted. In practice, assistance measures may be just as extensive as reparations.[145] While judicial practice tends toward ordering damages proportionate to the injury irrespective of the perpetrator's ability to pay, reparations programs in which the state is the perpetrator of abuses often account for resource limitations.[146] García Amador, the then Special Rapporteur on State Responsibility, emphasized the potential subsidiarity of the proportionality requirement in assessing remedies in the context of state responsibility in international law. Amador noted that "cases and situations in which compensation does not cover the full value of the expropriated property must be regarded as valid and effective."[147]

In many situations, full reparation for injuries caused is impossible for reasons of both moral irreparability and practicality. Igor Lukashuk argued that not only was it generally impossible to provide full compensation for major disasters such as the Second World War and aggression by Iraq against Kuwait, in many instances it would be undesirable to order such.[148] The memory of the Treaty of Versailles and its consequences weighing heavy on his mind, Lukashuk declared that partial rather than full restitution ought to be the model in such situations, giving primacy to guarantees of non-repetition and democratic development. Indeed, the Iraqi reparations to Kuwait ordered by the UN Security Council involved consideration of "the requirement of the people of Iraq, Iraq's payment capacity . . . and the needs of the Iraqi economy" and therefore limited compensation to the value of 30 percent of annual petroleum exports.[149] Even given this restriction, the reparations ordered by the UN Security Council were criticized as overly

144 This distinction degrades in the context of transitional justice, where political and practical compromises may be required. See sections 7.4.5 and 7.4.6.

145 Under the mandate of the ECCC, for instance, the court was only empowered to award moral and collective reparations to victims and could not award individual compensation or redress. See Extraordinary Chambers in the Courts of Cambodia, "Internal Rules (Rev 9)" January 16, 2015.

146 See, for instance, litigation under the Alien Tort Claims Act in the United States wherein the courts have consistently ordered large sums to be paid. It is worth noting, however, that awards under the legislation are rarely ever paid out.

147 FV García Amador, "Fourth Report on State Responsibility" (1959) UN Doc A/CN.4/119, 2 Yearbook of the International Law Commission 1 [89].

148 International Law Commission, "Summary Record of the 2392nd Meeting" (1995) 1 Yearbook of the International Law Commission 88 [31]–[37].

149 UNSC, "Report of the Secretary-General Pursuant to Paragraph 19 of Security Council Resolution 687" (April 3, 1991) UN Doc S/Res/687 [7]; and UNSC Res 705 (August 15, 1991) UN Doc S/Res/705 [2].

harsh, breaking from established doctrine concerning war reparations developed out of the ashes of the Treaty of Versailles.[150]

While full reparations ought to be the starting point and the presumptive objective of judicial redress in line with the legal obligations to provide redress proportionate to the harm, legal mechanisms should not be taken completely in isolation from their context. First, legal violations for which full redress is impossible nonetheless demand judicial remedies. The range of forms of reparation available within the legal framework offers an opportunity to ensure appropriate redress in such cases, responding to the specific wrongdoing and injuries evidenced in the case and dealing with these insofar as is possible.[151] Yet, these represent instances in which the law cannot provide full redress and must accept some degradation of the principle of proportionality. Second, where external considerations intersect with legal frameworks, including in the consideration of moral and political claims guided by legal principles, other factors may necessitate some sacrifices to be made with regard to the extent of reparations awards. As in the case of Kuwait, other factors outside legal considerations may impact the form and extent of redress. However, this relates to extralegal mechanisms and not to the form of reparations in legal proceedings.[152]

4.3.5. Impact

The principle of impact, as an element of reparatory justice, is an observation of a feature of reparations distinguishing them from other forms of justice rather than a consideration for courts crafting reparatory measures. According to Dixon, the symbolic value of reparations sets them apart from other forms of justice—at least changing their impact compared to assistance measures and potentially elevating reparations in their transformative capacity.[153] It is difficult to confirm the contention that reparations have a greater symbolic impact upon victims than do measures of assistance, particularly given that programs are often imperfect in practice. Yael Danieli's interviews with survivors of the Shoah indicate that reparations processes

[150] See, for instance, Andrea Gattini, "The UN Compensation Commission: Old Rules, New Procedures on War Reparations" (2002) 13 European Journal of International Law 161.
[151] Different modalities of redress available are discussed in chapter 5.
[152] This is considered further in section 7.4.6.
[153] Dixon (n 81) 101.

inefficiently conducted can make victims feel more frustrated than vindicated.[154] Despite this finding, there is a large body of literature upholding the idea that reparations properly administered have a unique moral and affective dimension which separates them from measures of assistance.[155]

In both domestic and international contexts, the distinction between assistance and reparations can be incredibly important to victims. Calls for reparations by communities of injured people often draw a stark distinction between reparations and aid, highlighting the claim to justice inherent in demands for reparations that affirms the status of victims rather than entrenching existing power dynamics. Rodney Coates, framing the calls for reparations for transatlantic chattel enslavement, centered this distinction:

> It is in the spirit of justice that I write—not for a hand-out but a pay check, not for welfare but our fair share, not for crumbs that fall from the massa's table—but for the wealth represented by the houses built by Africans. No, in the spirit of liberty we make our just demands.[156]

Thus, the importance of responsibility and recognition also manifest in the impact of reparations on victims, perpetrators, and their societies. Reparations and aid both impact relations between parties, public perceptions, and the material lives of victims. However, the implications of such transfers flow in different directions.[157] Where reparations acknowledge the recipient, aid uplifts the donor. In the international arena, the weight given to declaratory judgments as a form of reparation speaks to the significance of the symbolic dimensions of redress.[158]

[154] Yael Danieli, "Massive Trauma and the Healing Role of Reparative Justice" in Ferstman, Goetz, and Stephens (n 20).

[155] See for instance: Yael Danieli, "Preliminary Reflections from a Psychological Perspective" in Neil Kritz (ed), *Transitional Justice: How Emerging Democracies Reckon with Former Regimes*, vol 1: *General Considerations* (US Institute of Peace Press 1995); Brandon Hamber, "Narrowing the Micro and Macro: A Psychological Perspective on Reparations in Societies in Transition" in de Greiff, *The Handbook of Reparations* (n 29).

[156] Rodney Coates, "If a Tree Falls in the Wilderness: Reparations, Academic Silences, and Social Justice" 83 Social Forces 841, 842.

[157] Gifford notes that when European governments respond to injustices by way of development aid, it often carries an "overtone of condescension: the Africans are suffering because their leaders have messed things up, but we still help." This relationship is upset when measures are framed as an entitlement rather than a gift. Anthony Gifford, "Pipe Dream or Necessary Atonement?" (2007) 36 Index on Censorship 89, 94.

[158] See for instance *Corfu Channel* (n 3); *Case of the French Postal Vessel "Manouba" (France v Italy)* (1913) PCA Case No 1912-01; *Case of Suárez Rosero v Ecuador* (Merits) IACHR Series C No 35 (November 12, 1997).

Re-establishing respect for legal norms is a central function of reparations both in international and in domestic contexts, and an impact distinct from that which might be provided by other forms of justice. The restoration of the status quo ante, paying of damages, and awards of other forms of redress, combined with the deterrent function associated with these measures, are formulated not only to vindicate the rights of the victim but also to serve a signaling function to the legal community, reinforcing and maintaining primary rules. The political community, as well as communities of victims, are reconstructed through reparatory justice and formal legal responses, recognizing the status of victims as rights bearers.[159] This further distinguishes reparations from assistance.

Cessation, guarantees and assurances of non-repetition, and the measures undertaken therein to ensure non-recurrence are central to the fortification of the legal system and can thus take primacy in judicial considerations. For instance, in the case of *El Amparo* before the Inter-American Court of Human Rights, the Inter-American Commission of Human Rights emphasized the importance of re-establishing respect for international norms and focused upon reform of the Code of Military Justice as the primary form of redress required.[160] Although the court did not make orders relating to the Code as its provisions had not been applied in the case, it did recognize the acceptance of responsibility by Venezuela as the primary form of reparations for violations of the rights for which the reform was advocated.[161] While measures of assistance may improve the material conditions of recipients, they do not uphold legal norms. Thus, the impact of reparations on this level cannot be equated with distributive justice.

4.4. The value of a theory of reparatory justice

Understanding the theoretical foundations of reparatory justice, and the elements constituting such, is fundamental to the consideration of atypical claims. Widespread historical injustices built upon contested legal grounds, characterized by lacunae in positive norms, and evidencing conflicting principles are such cases. The lack of clarity on the applicable law, or indeed the very existence of relevant international norms, creates a space in which

159 Ruti G Teitel, *Transitional Justice* (OUP 2002) 127.
160 *Case of El Amparo v Venezuela* (Reparations) IACHR Series C No 28 (September 14, 1996).
161 ibid.

answers cannot be derived simply from positive legal frameworks and determinate rulings of authoritative international bodies. A coherent theory of reparatory justice, based upon centuries of jurisprudential development, provides a lens through which these cases can be considered.

While the decisions concerning the relevant fora for determination rest upon consideration of the development of legal prohibition, attribution, standing, rules of competence, and other technical legal questions, a theory of reparations based upon international legal frameworks can be applied irrespective of the arena. This approach is therefore relevant in moral and political cases as well as in legal proceedings, encouraging the application of principles of justice and established elements of reparations in the case for redress for transatlantic enslavement and the *maangamizi*.

This theory also provides guidance in relation to the question of whether reparatory justice ought to be considered in relation to specific wrongdoing by explaining its theoretical legal foundations and its constituent features. Reparations are conceived as both corrective and transformative. They are premised on the attempt to return parties to equality vis-à-vis one another and by the need to prevent future wrongdoing against victims. Fundamental to this formulation is the notion of responsibility and violation—that victims were "wronged and not merely harmed."[162] This is both the prerequisite condition for the engagement of reparatory justice and a key feature of its operation through the assertion of responsibility against perpetrators. This is particularly relevant in considering the influence of naturalist principles in constructing responsibility.

Acknowledgment of injustice and responsibility by perpetrators themselves is an important step in the long-term impact of reparatory justice with regard to satisfaction and guarantees of non-repetition.[163] Yet, the imposition of reparatory justice through legal mechanisms, and assertions of social and political pressure on the basis of legal frameworks, can also serve in recognizing the status of victims as agents and rights bearers undeserving of violations committed against them.[164] Thus, recognition of victims and

[162] Bernard Boxill, "Black Reparations" *Stanford Encyclopaedia of Philosophy* (Winter edn, 2011) <stanford.library.sydney.edu.au/archives/win2011/entries/black-reparations/> accessed November 13, 2018.

[163] Thompson suggests that reparatory justice always requires acknowledgment by the perpetrators, in order for those wronged to believe that they are "confronting their history and will henceforth treat them with respect." Janna Thompson, *Taking Responsibility for the Past: Reparation and Historical Justice* (Polity 2002) 96.

[164] See de Greiff, "Transitional Justice and Development" (n 70).

responsibility of perpetrators are not only elements of redress but also definitive of reparatory justice, carrying value themselves. As Alan Cairns highlights:

> recognition in itself is a component of justice. And furthermore, if we can explain why they were deprived of human dignity, their culture viewed as a dead end, or their lives treated as expendable, we will have provided a modicum of retrospective dignity to their lives and fates.[165]

Procedural justice is a mechanism through which this recognition of agency and dignity is realized; through meaningful participation in the processes concerning their own rights, victims are able to reform their own identity and voice. No legal mechanism can translate the suffering of millions of people into a package of reparatory measures and thereby efface those violations. The theory of reparatory justice nonetheless gives voice to the question of what these mechanisms ought to do in the face of such injustices.

[165] Alan Cairns, "Coming to Terms with the Past" in John Torpey (ed), *Politics and the Past: On Repairing Historical Injustices* (Rowman & Littlefield 2003) 84.

5

Expanding Understandings of Reparatory Justice through Multiple Modalities of Redress

The objectives and elements of reparatory justice have shaped the modalities of redress available, informing both judicial and political practice in constructing and delivering reparations. While compensation tends to dominate understandings of what constitutes reparation, options are far more extensive than monetary redress. International law has recognized multiple modalities of redress both in the broad category of obligations arising from internationally wrongful conduct (including cessation and guarantees of non-repetition) and the narrower formulation of reparations as understood in the Articles on State Responsibility (restitution, compensation, and satisfaction).[1] These frameworks are not simply discrete formulations of modalities tethered to their specific context but manifestations of the underpinning theory of reparatory justice and the elements of such. They build upon centuries of reparatory justice in practice and the jurisprudence of authoritative international bodies.

In examining the impact of underpinning theories and objectives of reparatory justice on the forms of redress available, a reciprocal relationship between the two begins to emerge. It is not only theory that informs practice; the manifestation of reparatory justice in specific cases of injustice also influences the development of the underlying theories. Considering the modalities of redress available within the context of reparatory justice is not

[1] International Law Commission, "Draft Articles on the Responsibility of States for Internationally Wrongful Acts" (November 2001) UN Doc A/56/10, arts 28–37. The ICC reparations principles and UNBPG replicate the recognition of these various forms of reparations, additionally separating rehabilitation as a distinct modality rather than as an aspect of other forms—*The Prosecutor v Thomas Lubanga Dyilo* (Decision establishing the principles and procedures to be applied to reparations) ICC-01/04-01/06-2904 (August 7, 2012) (*Lubanga Principles*) Principle 9(c); UNGA "Basic Principles and Guidelines on the Right to a Remedy and Reparation for Victims of Gross Violations of International Human Rights Law and Serious Violations of International Humanitarian Law" (March 21, 2006) UN Doc A/RES/60/147 (UNBPG) Principle 18.

Reparations for Slavery in International Law. Katarina Schwarz, Oxford University Press. © Oxford University Press 2022.
DOI: 10.1093/oso/9780197636398.003.0006

simply a matter of assessing what measures might be adopted in the construction of reparations for historical enslavement. Rather, this process invites a reconsideration of the limitations imposed upon reparatory justice, particularly with regard to causation and the questions of legal policy involved in this interrogation.[2] It opens the door for a different understanding of appropriate redress in historical cases based on the possibility of constructing responsive, multimodal reparations packages targeting different kinds of injury. Thus, the modalities of redress—crafted to meet the needs of reparatory justice—speak to the threshold questions of reparability and those injustices that ought to be redressed within the framework of primary rules.

This chapter considers the various forms of redress available within international legal frameworks, their historical roots, and developments in reparations practice to reconceptualize the presumptive boundaries of reparability. This is not a new legal framework, for these forms of redress are embedded in the relevant legal mechanisms. Rather, it is a new way of assessing the influence of these frameworks on approaches to the question of reparations for historical injustice. This interrogation speaks to the boundaries of decisions of legal policy and the scope of primary rules made by judges in specific cases. However, it also informs broader moral and political reparations discourse, expanding the spaces in which reparatory justice might occur and moving the conversation beyond the boundaries of compensation.

5.1. Satisfaction

Accounting for the centrality of recognition and accountability in reparatory justice, it is not only the material impact of injustice that matters but also what this signals about victims' relation to perpetrators and society and the way this echoes through their communities.[3] For widespread abuses in particular, it is often the affective dimensions of injustice that continue to impact the lives of descendants, including in their structural dimensions.[4] In such instances—where restoration is often impossible—satisfaction enables

[2] This is considered in further detail in chapter 6.

[3] See section 4.3.2.

[4] Shelton notes that compensation is "especially inadequate" where the violation causes irreparable injury, and where violations are ongoing or likely to be repeated. Dinah Shelton, *Remedies in International Human Rights Law* (3rd edn, OUP 2015) 379.

measures targeted toward irreparable and moral injuries.[5] Accounting for the indirect and structural nature of harms in historical cases, the capacity to award purely symbolic measures may have significant implications for the consideration of whether reparations ought to be awarded, and not only what shape they might take.[6] In this regard, the interplay between recognition of immaterial harms and responsive measures of satisfaction is crucial.

International judicial bodies recognize the affective dimensions of injustice by affirming the possibility of awards in the instance of a breach with no material consequences. In international law, there is no requirement of material or economic damage to find a violation of law. All that is required for an internationally wrongful act of a state is conduct attributable to a state, which constitutes a breach of an international obligation.[7] Damage is only a prerequisite of international responsibility when it forms a constituent part of the primary obligation—when it is an element of the primary rule—and thus cannot be considered a prerequisite of international responsibility for a wrongful act generally.[8] The corollary of this is that it is similarly unnecessary for a state to have suffered damage in order to claim reparations for a breach of international law. International tribunals reflect this approach to damages by including moral damages in awards of compensation and recognizing symbolic injuries to states.[9]

Irrespective of other harms suffered as a consequence of a breach, the violation itself can be recognized as a symbolic harm requiring reparations. For instance, in the *Rainbow Warrior II* arbitration, France contended that a central element of international responsibility was damage and that New Zealand's claims therefore did not show a basis for liability as they had not indicated "the slightest damage had been suffered, even moral damage."[10] However, the tribunal affirmed the possibility of moral and legal damage in international law, determining that:

[5] Jean Personnaz, *La Reparation du Prejudice en Droit International Public* (Librairie du Recueil Sirey 1939) 298.

[6] This contributes substantially to the consideration of the question of the appropriate scope of reparatory obligations in historical cases, considered in sections 6.3–6.5.

[7] Articles on State Responsibility (n 1) art 2.

[8] International Law Commission, "Report of the International Law Commission on the Work of its Fifty-Third Session" (2001) 2(2) Yearbook of the International Law Commission 31, 36.

[9] On moral damages in compensation awards, see *Treaty of Neuilly, Article 179, Annex, Paragraph 4 (Interpretation, Judgment No 3)* (1924) PCIJ Series A No 3, 9. The arbitral tribunals made similar rulings in *Maal Case* (1903) 10 RIAA 730, 732–33; and *Campbell Case* (1931) 2 RIAA 1158. Cases recognizing symbolic injuries to states include violations of sovereignty or territorial integrity as in *Rainbow Warrior II (New Zealand v France)* (1990) 20 UNRIAA 215. See also *Corfu Channel* (n 22).

[10] *Rainbow Warrior* (n 9) [107].

> in inter-State relations, the concept of damage does not possess an exclusive material or patrimonial character. Unlawful action against non-material interests, such as acts affecting the honor, dignity or prestige of a State, entitle the victim State to receive adequate reparation, even if those acts have not resulted in a pecuniary or material loss for the claimant State.[11]

This conclusion is consistent with corrective justice aims of returning the parties to equality, recognizing that violations can create moral or legal inequalities and produce material harm. This provides the entry point for measures of satisfaction.

Despite the recognition of moral and symbolic harms, and thus the aptitude of equivalent measures to redress such, many commentators confine their understanding of satisfaction to the forward-facing deterrent function inherent in the economic approach to redress. Bernhard Graefrath describes satisfaction as all "measures taken by the author State of an internationally wrongful act to affirm the existence of the affected obligation and to prevent continuation or repetition of the wrongful act."[12] Similarly, Edwin Borchard identifies the function of satisfaction as inducing the delinquent government to improve its behavior and assuring the claimant government that such violations will be prevented in the future if possible.[13] These definitions highlight the overlap between satisfaction and guarantees of non-repetition by focusing on the preventive dimension of such orders. However, they fail to account for the corrective dimensions of satisfaction. Satisfaction measures are not only forward facing and socially oriented but also backward facing and victim centric. This alternate function is confirmed by their existence as a secondary obligation connected to a violation and awarded specifically to the victims of such. Thus, satisfaction not only provides assurances for the future but also provides specific redress for wrongdoing, which may take a forward-facing form.

The lines between measures of satisfaction and cessation are often blurred, although the limits of cessation are much clearer. Measures of cessation are restricted to continuing violations of obligations still in force.[14] Satisfaction, on the other hand, is not bound by these preconditions and may be required

[11] ibid [109].

[12] Bernhard Graefrath, *Responsibility and Damages Caused: Relationship between Responsibility and Damages* (Nijhoff 1985) 17.

[13] Edwin Borchard, "Important Decisions of the Mixed Claims Commission, United States and Mexico" (1927) 21 American Journal of International Law 516, 518.

[14] On cessation specifically, see section 5.4.

where a breach has concluded and the obligation is no longer in force. Where a violation is continuing, the alteration of that situation—including the denial of rights and the application of legislation contravening international law—could equally be framed as a measure of cessation or as a guarantee of non-repetition.[15] Where an obligation is no longer in force, precluding measures of cessation, the completed performance of the original obligations may be characterized as a form of satisfaction. Thus, New Zealand's request for the return of French agents to detention in *Rainbow Warrior II* might more effectively have been framed as a measure of satisfaction, given that the detention period required by the agreement breached had expired. The tribunal determined that the return of the agents to detention was not an appropriate measure of cessation in the case because the obligation was no longer in force. However, it left open the possibility that such might have been considered within the boundaries of satisfaction had the parties made arguments to this effect.[16]

The focus on immaterial harms is not a qualifier on the forms of redress that might be constructed in relation to immaterial injury, for monetary redress can signal recognition and accountability in important ways.[17] As in many other situations concerning the taxonomy of redress, the boundaries between differently classified modalities are fluid and occasionally permeable. However, given the inclusion of moral damages in the categorization of compensation discussed in section 5.3, this section considers satisfaction as those measures beyond monetary awards transferred from the perpetrator to the victim.[18]

The Articles on State Responsibility define satisfaction nonexhaustively, with potential forms listed including acknowledgment of breach, expressions of regret, and formal apologies.[19] The UNBPG are more comprehensive in listing potential forms of satisfaction, including:

[15] Special Rapporteur Arangia-Ruiz, for instance, identified potential forms of satisfaction as including "demands of abrogation of discriminatory, racial or segregational legislation, popular consultations such as free elections or plebiscites, restoration of fundamental rights and freedoms, etc."—all of which could equally be framed as forms of cessation. UNGA, "Seventh Report on State Responsibility, by Mr. Gaetano Arangio-Ruiz, Special Rapporteur" (1995) UN Doc A/CN.4/469.

[16] *Rainbow Warrior II* (n 9).

[17] Personnaz, for instance, includes monetary redress targeted toward moral injuries in his description of satisfaction (n 5).

[18] This approach is also consistent with the formulation of satisfaction in the Articles on State Responsibility, art 37, and UNBPG, Principle 22 (n 1).

[19] See (n 1).

(a) measures aimed at the cessation of continuing violations;
(b) verification of the facts and full and public disclosure of the truth;
(c) searches for disappeared persons, bodies of those killed, and the identities of abducted children;
(d) official declarations and judicial decisions restoring the dignity, reputation, and rights of the victim and of persons closely connected with the victim;
(e) public apologies, acknowledgment of facts, and acceptance of responsibility;
(f) sanctions against perpetrators;
(g) commemorations and tributes to victims; and
(h) the inclusion of an accurate account of the violations that occurred in training and in educational material at all levels.[20]

These different constructions of the forms satisfaction may take are not in conflict, but rather indicate the divergent scope of the two instruments. The Articles on State Responsibility focus on measures of satisfaction for violations committed by states, briefly and within a more general text. The UNBPG focus specifically on the issue of remedy and reparation in the context of severe human rights and humanitarian law violations. Thus, the UNBPG can be viewed as supplemental to the nonexhaustive list provided in the Articles on State Responsibility rather than as separate regimes.

The most widely awarded and universally recognized measure of satisfaction in judicial practice is an authoritative pronouncement by the courts. In many cases involving moral or legal injury, authoritative international bodies have declared the judgment alone sufficient redress for the breach of law. Edwin Borchard declares:

> The adjudication, not the command, is the essence of judicial power, and in our civilized communities, it is the adjudication, and not the command, which evokes respect and official sanction, because it is a determination by the societal agent appointed to perform that function, and thus irrevocably fix legal relations.[21]

[20] UNPBG (n 1) Principle 22.
[21] Edwin Borchard, *Declaratory Judgments* (reprint, W S Hein 1941) 10.

Authoritative international bodies have affirmed the appropriateness and sufficiency of declaratory judgments as a form of satisfaction, including where parties sought additional measures such as official apologies by state perpetrators and nonpecuniary damages for political and moral prejudice.[22] In *The "Carthage,"* the tribunal went further, judging that there existed a general rule in international law that damages proportional to material loss in conjunction with the declaration itself constituted sufficient redress in most cases.[23] Thus, the Permanent Court of Arbitration declared a presumption against other forms of satisfaction beyond the declaration of the authoritative body. However, the decision also recognized the potential for special circumstances justifying additional awards recognizing the offense and providing satisfaction for moral and political injury.[24] This may bear particular relevance in the consideration of injustices entailing significant symbolic harms that manifest in material consequences but with significant intervening contributory causes or some attenuation in causation.[25] Declaratory judgments, as a form of satisfaction, are a means of restoring dignity, reputation, and rights, whether the victim is a state or an individual.[26]

Measures of satisfaction manifest the two primary elements defining reparatory justice considered in chapter 4—responsibility and recognition. These forms of redress are fundamentally concerned with the affective dimensions of injustice over material and economic consequences that are the subject of restitution and compensation. Despite its relative scarcity in reparations discourse and practice, satisfaction may be prioritized over material and economic redress. For instance, the Extraordinary Chambers in

[22] See *Corfu Channel Case (United Kingdom v Albania)* (Merits) [1949] ICJ Rep 4 *Corfu Channel* [23]; *Case of the French Postal Vessel "Manouba" (France v Italy)* (1913) PCA Case No 1912-01; *The "Carthage" (France v Italy)* ICGJ 398 (PCA 1913). In *Corfu Channel*, the International Court of Justice judged that the declaration of a violation of Albanian Sovereignty by the United Kingdom was in itself appropriate satisfaction, despite the fact that Albania contended that it was entitled to an apology. Albania also requested the court to consider whether monetary satisfaction was due despite the fact that there was no material damage caused. In the *Case of the French Postal Vessel "Manouba"* the tribunal rejected the French government's demand for damages for nonpecuniary damage to the French flag and political and moral prejudice resulting from the violation of international law, considering that the arbitral award itself constituted a serious sanction which was adequate in the circumstances. In *The "Carthage,"* the tribunal declared that "in case a Power should fail to fulfil its obligations, whether general or special, to another Power, the statement of this fact, especially in an arbitral award, constitutes in itself a serious penalty" made heavier by the requirement to pay for material losses.

[23] *The "Carthage"*.

[24] ibid.

[25] For further consideration of causation and attenuation, see chapter 6.

[26] *Case of Suárez Rosero v Ecuador* (Merits) IACHR Series C No 35 (November 12, 1997). The applicant in the case foregrounded the need for an official judgment or exculpatory declaration in fulfilling these objectives.

the Courts of Cambodia was only empowered to award collective and moral reparations to civil parties and not monetary payments.[27] This despite the fact that admission of civil parties was contingent upon the individual having suffered physical, material, or psychological injury as a direct consequence of a crime alleged against the charged person.[28] Likewise, during the transition from apartheid in South Africa, truth telling, transition, and indemnities were prioritized over the provision of actual awards for individuals suffering violations, although this was in the context of transitional justice mechanisms.[29] In such cases, remedying the affective dimensions of injustice, ensuring responsibility and recognition, and accounting for the scale of abuses are acknowledged as bearing greater importance than material redress. This may further extend to cases of historical injustice, in which material injuries have substantially attenuated, but significant moral and symbolic harms persist.

5.2. Restitution

Traditionally, restitution is the starting point for considering reparations, as famously declared by the Permanent Court of International Justice in *Factory at Chorzów*. Giving primacy to the principle of restitution after confirming the essential principle that reparation must, insofar as possible, wipe out all the consequences of wrongdoing and return parties to the position that would have existed absent the breach, the court concluded that restitution in kind, or the value equivalent to such, determines the amount of compensation due for internationally wrongful conduct.[30] Thus, the court framed restitution in kind as the primary remedy in international law, with proportionate compensation as the secondary remedy in such a case. This formulation of the nature of obligations has been consistently reiterated in international judicial decisions, reports, and declaratory documents.[31]

[27] Extraordinary Chambers in the Courts of Cambodia, "Internal Rules (Rev 9)" January 16, 2015, rule 23 *quinquies*.

[28] ibid, rule 23 *bis*.

[29] Christopher Colvin, "Overview of the Reparations Program in South Africa" in Pablo de Greiff (ed), *The Handbook of Reparations* (OUP 2006).

[30] *Case Concerning the Factory at Chorzów (Germany v Poland)* (Merits) [1928] PCIJ Rep Series A No 17 [47].

[31] On judicial decisions, see the more recent international arbitral decision in *Texaco Overseas Petroleum Co v Libya* (1977) International Arbitral Tribunal 17 ILM 3. On reports, see UNGA, "Second Report on the Content, Forms and Degrees of International Responsibility (Part 2 of the Draft Articles), by Mr Willem Riphagen, Special Rapporteur" (1981) UN Doc A/CN.4/344, 2(1)

Although the restitutionary framework is often conflated with measures of monetary compensation, it is important to maintain a distinction. Restitution and compensation constitute distinct measures of redress—restitution involving in kind restoration, while compensation awards an equivalent monetary value. On the other hand, the restitutionary framework, defined by the principle of restitutio in integrum, is concerned with returning victims to the status quo ante—the position they would have been in but for the violation of their rights—and can consists of a wide range of different measures. Thus, measures effectively designed to compensate for material damage and those aimed at re-establishing a situation of legality are separate concerns.[32]

To resolve this difficulty, Pierre-Marie Dupuy characterizes the restitutionary framework as the notion of "restoration," separating it from discussion of forms of redress, including restitution. In this context, restoration demands both the reinstatement of the initial material position of victims and the legal situation that existed prior to the violation.[33] This notion of restitution as restoration is affirmed by the UNBPG, noting that restitution should restore the victim to the original situation before the violations occurred.[34] The Articles on State Responsibility similarly note that restitution aims to re-establish the situation that existed before the wrongful act was committed.[35] Thus, while restitution is guided by restorative objectives, it may more simply be conceived of as in-kind reparation.

Restitution can take a number of different forms relating directly to the situation the victim would have been in had the violation never occurred. For instance, the UNBPG recognize that restitution can include restoration of liberty, enjoyment of human rights, identity, family life and citizenship, return to one's place of residence, restoration of employment, and return of property.[36] The *Lubanga Principles* note that restitution may include returning

Yearbook of the International Law Commission 79, 81–101. In declaratory documents, see Articles on State Responsibility (n 1) arts 35, 37, recognizing restitution as the primary remedy, providing for the avoidance of such obligation only where restitution is materially impossible or involves a burden out of all proportion to the benefit deriving from restitution instead of compensation.

[32] Pierre-Marie Dupuy, "The International Law of State Responsibility: Revolution or Evolution?" (1989) 11(1) Michigan Journal of International Law 105, 120.
[33] ibid 120–21.
[34] UNBPG (n 1) Principle 19.
[35] Articles on State Responsibility (n 1) art 35.
[36] UNBPG (n 1) Principle 19.

a victim to their family, home, and previous employment, providing continuing education and returning lost or stolen property.[37]

As a form of restitution in the *Loayza Tamayo v Peru* case, the Inter-American Court of Human Rights ordered that Peru take the necessary measures to reinstate the victim in her public sector teaching position with equivalent salary and benefits to that which she had received prior to her detention.[38] The court also required that she be ensured full retirement benefits accounting for the period of detention. This made it clear that the court aimed not merely to put the victim into the position that she was in prior to the breach, but to account for the position that she would have been in but for the violation.[39] These manifestations of restitution evidence the potential of such measures to cross into territory also occupied by satisfaction, cessation, and guarantees of non-repetition, further highlighting the fluidity of categories of redress and the difficulty of severing cessation and non-repetition from the reparatory framework.

Restitution, shepherded as it is by ideas of restoration, does not constitute a punitive remedy despite the fact that the quantum of the award may be shaped by the nature of the act creating the need for restitution. The essential function of restitution is simply to return to the victim something to which they are entitled and of which the wrongdoer deprived them.[40] Restitution thus adheres to the corrective conception of justice, focusing on re-establishing the prior situation of the victim and returning the relationship between victim and perpetrator to equality.[41] By affirming the status of restitution as the primary remedy—with equivalent compensation as an appropriate substitute when restoration is impossible or would be disproportionate to the breach—courts reinforce the corrective paradigm and the objective of restoration. Moreover, this represents a recognition of the fact that money is not automatically equivalent to a victim's legal entitlements, and that primary obligations ought to be upheld where practicable.

Despite the presumption in favor of restitution, in many instances historical injustices are likely to fail to meet the threshold condition for the award of such measures: that restitution should be awarded where appropriate. The impossibility of returning victims to the status quo ante in cases of widespread

[37] *Lubanga Principles* (n 1).
[38] *Loayza Tamayo v Peru* (Merits) IACHR Series C No 33 (September 17, 1997).
[39] ibid.
[40] Shelton (n 4) 298–314.
[41] The corrective justice paradigm is considered in section 4.2.

historical injustices, engaging the counterfactual quagmire, makes designing measures of restitution difficult, if not impossible.[42] However, restitution may be constructed with consideration for the consequences of wrongdoing, rather than those outcomes which otherwise would have arisen. In practice, this requires a consideration of specific opportunities denied, and harms imposed, as occurred in *Loayza Tamayo v Peru*, and the construction of in-kind restitution to fill these gaps. This avoids being tied to the impossibility of constructing a counterfactual, focusing on the consequences accruing from the wrongdoing, rather than the world that would have existed absent the injustice.

5.3. Compensation

Despite the judicially affirmed primacy of restitution in international law, compensation is often considered the dominant remedy available to courts and tribunals and predominates actual awards granted. The assumption articulated by Grotius in the seventeenth century that "money is the common measure of valuable things"—including intangibles such as legal rights—infuses international and domestic law, as well as reparations discourse.[43] Awards of damages are built upon both the corrective and the economic approaches to justice, transferring benefits from the perpetrator to the victim in an amount purportedly equivalent to the injuries suffered to return the parties to equality, and occasionally requiring additional sums to ensure deterrence at an effective level. Monetary awards, in general, maintain the focus on providing the closest possible alternative to restitutio in integrum, thus reinforcing the restorative paradigm, and may also respond to the affective dimensions of injustice through moral and punitive awards.

The role of compensation in redressing violations is well established in international law, with the starting point for considering compensation

[42] See David Lambert, "Black-Atlantic Counterfactualism: Speculating about Slavery and its Aftermath" (2010) 36 Journal of Historical Geography 286. For further consideration of the limits of counterfactual reasoning, see section 4.2.1.

[43] Hugo Grotius, *The Rights of War and Peace, in three books. Wherein are explained, the law of nature and nations, and The Principal Points relating to Government. Written in Latin by the learned Hugo Grotius, and translated into English. To which are added, all the large notes of Mr. J. Barbeyrac, Professor of Law at Groningen, and Member of the Royal Academy of Sciences at Berlin* (London 1738) bk 2, ch 17, 437.

being financially or economically assessable damages.[44] As an example, the International Criminal Court recognizes that compensation should be considered when economic harm is sufficiently quantifiable, it would be appropriate and proportionate in the circumstances and is feasible.[45] Qualifying material damage may include loss or damage to property, lost earnings, lost opportunity to work, unpaid wages or salaries, and loss of savings.[46] Legal services, medical expenses, and psychological assistance are similarly uncontentious in their amenability to economic quantification.[47] Thus, the costs of rehabilitation may be built into compensatory measures.

Although material damages—both direct and consequential—are the most amenable to determination and quantification by a judicial body, legal analysis does not stall at this point. Courts have a long history of awarding multiple forms of damages in situations requiring varying degrees of arbitrariness in determining the quantum of an award.[48] Awards for physical harm beyond medical expenses require an arbitrary determination of appropriate quantum of compensation but are internationally accepted as an appropriate remedy.[49] Similarly mental and emotional suffering are recognized as compensable harms, despite their failure to meet the requirement that harm be financially or economically assessable.[50] Lost opportunities in employment, education and social benefits, loss of status and harm to

[44] Articles on State Responsibility (n 1) art 36, notes that compensation should cover all financially assessable damage including lost profits. See also UNBPG (n 1) Principle 20; and the *Lubanga Principles* (n 1) Principle 9.

[45] *Lubanga Principles* (n 1) Principle 9(a).

[46] See, for instance, *Ayder and Others v Turkey* (Merits and Just Satisfaction) App No 23656/94 (ECtHR, January 8, 2004) [141]–[152]; *Case of El Amparo v Venezuela* (Reparations) IACHR Series C No 28 (September 14, 1996) [28]–[30].

[47] See for instance *Loayza Tamayo v Peru* (n 38) [129]; *Case of Barrios Altos v Peru* (Reparations and Costs) IACHR Series C No 87 (November 30, 2001) [42].

[48] Judicial awards redressing multiple forms of damages are documented as early as 2000 BCE. See James Sales and Kenneth Cole, "Punitive Damages: A Relic That Outlived Its Origins" (1984) 37 Vanderbilt Law Review 1117, 1119. See also Linda Schlueter and Kenneth Redden, *Punitive Damages 3* (3rd edn, Butterworth Legal Publishers 1995).

[49] See, for instance, *Velásquez Rodríguez v Honduras* (Merits) IACHR Series C No 4 (July 29, 1988) [156], [175], [187]; *X and Y v the Netherlands* (Merits and Just Satisfaction) App No 8978/80 (ECtHR, March 26, 1985) [22].

[50] See, for instance, *Garrido and Baigorria v Argentina* (Reparations and Costs) IACHR Series C No 39 (August 27, 1998) [49]; *Case of the Plan de Sánchez Massacre v Guatemala* (Reparations) IACHR Series C No 116 (November 19, 2004) [80]–[89]; *Case of the "Juvenile Reeducation Institute" v Paraguay* (Judgment) IACHR Series C No 112 (September 2, 2004) [295]. For ECtHR decisions on the same issue see *Selmouni v France* (Merits and Just Satisfaction) App No 25803/94 (ECtHR, July 28, 1999) [92], [98], [105]; *Aksoy v Turkey* (Merits and Just Satisfaction) App No 21987/93 (ECtHR, December 18, 1996) [113].

reputation, and interference with legal rights can also serve as the basis of compensatory awards.[51]

The widely recognized availability of compensation for a range of material and immaterial harms upholds the capacity of courts to attach a monetary value to nonmonetary harms.[52] Moreover, the recognition of immaterial harms is consistent with the forms of restitution available, whereby redress relates not only to tangible or quantifiable property (such as places of residence, employment, property) but also to immaterial rights, including restitution of liberty, enjoyment of human rights, identity, family life, and citizenship.[53] The award of moral damages is symbolic, designed to deal with harm presumed from the breach of the rights of the victim.[54] It need not be quantifiable or economically assessable for the court or tribunal to nominate an award.[55] Pecuniary damages may therefore address the affective dimensions of injustice, ensuring the recognition of victims as rights bearers and supporting notions of human dignity.[56]

Despite the primary recognition of states as the subjects of international law, in the consideration of reparations due, damage caused to private parties may equally be the foundation of compensation awards. This is true at all levels of international law and is not limited to the corpus of human rights law, which specifically recognizes the individual as a legal subject. For instance, in the case of the *French Postal Vessel "Manouba"* in 1913, the tribunal found that damages were due to private parties for the delay caused to

[51] See, for instance, in the jurisprudence of the European Court: *Campbell and Cosans v the United Kingdom* (Merits) App No 7511/76; 7743/76 (ECtHR, February 25, 1982) [26]; *T P and K M v the United Kingdom* (Merits and Just Satisfaction) App No 28945/95(ECtHR, May 10, 2001) [115]; and *Thlimmenos v Greece* (Preliminary Objection, Merits and Just Satisfaction) App No 34369/97 (ECtHR, April 6, 2000) [70].

[52] Compensable injury contains the same basic elements in virtually all legal systems: (1) medical and other expenses; (2) loss of past and future earnings; (3) loss of or injury to property, including lost profits; (4) pain and suffering and injury to health; (5) funeral expenses in wrongful death cases; and (6) loss of the services of the deceased. Moral damages are also widely recognized, including claims for "non-pecuniary injury such as harm to reputation, dignity, and other wrongs for which monetary value must be presumed as it cannot be assessed." Shelton (n 4) 317–18.

[53] See, for instance, UNBPG (n 1) Principle 19.

[54] See generally Dennis Klimchuk, "Unjust Enrichment and Reparations for Slavery" (2004) 84 Boston University Law Review 1257, recognizing that the core of the disgorgement claim is the indictment of the defendant's misconduct, thereby making the claim for restitution morally expressive.

[55] The court in *Rainbow Warrior II*, for instance, declared that monetary compensation for serious moral and legal damage was possible, but concluded that no award of compensation could be made in the case because New Zealand had not requested such and France had not had the opportunity to address this in its written pleadings or oral arguments. See (n 9) [118].

[56] Yudoff notes that "society's interest in human dignity is so great that the recovery may exceed any plausible estimate of economic injury." Mark Yudoff, "Liability for Constitutional Torts and the Risk-Averse Public School Official" (1976) 49 Southern California Law Review 1322, 1379–80.

the "*Manouba*" by its wrongful capture and rerouting to Cagliari, awarding damages of 4,000 francs to the interested parties represented by the French government.[57] Likewise, in *The "Carthage,"* the tribunal fixed indemnities due to two private companies—the Compagnie Générale Transatlantique and the aviator DUVAL—as well as the passengers and shippers, which were to be paid by the Italian government to the French government (then be dispensed to the private parties).[58] Compensation in international law therefore covers substantial ground, capable of providing redress for both private and public injuries for harms of a material or immaterial nature.

The focus of courts on awarding compensation proportionate to the injury suffered, even where that injury is only moral or legal, reinforces the corrective justice underpinnings of compensation and its deterrent functions. The award is tailored to equal the harms and, thus, in some equivalent way to return the parties to the status quo ante. If damages were limited to such injury (whether moral or material) it would be possible to consider corrective justice to be the defining feature of monetary awards. There is, however, an additional dimension, both to moral damages and to the recognition of punitive damages, which indicates an explanation beyond the correction of relationships.

Exemplary or punitive damages are designed not to repair any particular element of harm or suffering but to indicate the condemnation of the court for the perpetrator's behavior and deter similar conduct in the future. Exemplary damages provide a clear example of a court's deviation from the idea that awards may only be granted with the corrective justice objective of returning the defendant to the position they were in prior to the wrongdoing.[59] The recognition of multiple forms of redress going beyond actual damage suffered have historical continuity, tracing far beyond the period of transatlantic enslavement.[60] In relation to fundamental international wrongs in particular, the protection of norms may require the imposition of punitive damages to signal moral opprobrium and deter future violations.[61] In instances in which damages to victims may be difficult to establish or quantify, including in historical cases, the capacity of authoritative bodies to

[57] *Case of the French Postal Vessel "Manouba"* (n 22).

[58] *The "Carthage"* (n 22).

[59] See Michael Rustad and Thomas Koenig, "The Historical Continuity of Punitive Damages Awards: Reforming the Tort Reformers" (1993) 42 American University Law Review 1269.

[60] See Sales and Cole (n 48) 1119.

[61] See, for instance, the consideration of torture in *Filartiga v Pena-Irala* 577 F Supp 860 (1980) 863.

award punitive damages against perpetrators may provide an avenue for redress.[62]

5.4. Cessation

The obligation to cease wrongful conduct and the capacity of tribunals to order such in the event of a positive finding are vital in responding to violations of law. In many situations, particularly in relation to gross, serious, or widespread violations, the primacy of cessation over any other measures is highlighted.[63] In cases of mass atrocities condemned by the United Nations General Assembly or Security Council, the pragmatic emphasis in the immediate situation is often on "cessation and guarantees of non-repetition over reparation."[64] In part, this reflects the reality of such atrocities—that it is impossible to return the victims to the position that they would have been in absent the violations because of the very nature of those breaches. However, emphasis on cessation also recognizes the fundamental interest of victims in recognition and the affirmation of their status as citizens and rights bearers—if the violations do not cease, the denial of victims' status cannot be remedied.

Competent tribunals have the inherent power to issue an order for cessation or discontinuance of a wrongful act or omission when such relates to a continuous breach of an international obligation that continues to be in force.[65] The requirement of a continuing violation distinguishes cessation from the paradigm reparations order, leading some commentators to consider cessation an element of the primary rule, disconnected from secondary rules concerning redress in the instance of a breach. For instance, Christian Dominicé asserts that the duty of perpetrators to cease continuing wrongful conduct does not constitute a form of reparation but only "a return to the initial obligation."[66] Thus, Dominicé concludes that the obligation to provide

[62] On the positioning of punitive and exemplary damages in the theory of reparatory justice, see section 4.2.2.

[63] The ICJ has recognized that cessation can be more important than reparation. See for instance *Fisheries Jurisdiction (Federal Republic of Germany v Iceland)* (Merits) [1974] ICJ Rep 175, 201–05.

[64] Christine Gray, *Judicial Remedies in International Law* (Clarendon Press 1987) 216–17.

[65] *Rainbow Warrior II* (n 9) 270. See also *United States Diplomatic and Consular Staff in Tehran (United States v Iran)* [1980] ICJ Rep 3 [38–41]; *Case Concerning Military and Paramilitary Activities in and against Nicaragua (Nicaragua v United States)* (Merits) [1986] ICJ Rep 14 [292].

[66] Christian Dominicé, "Observations on the Rights of a State that is the Victim of an Internationally Wrongful Act" in Christian Dominicé and Milan Šahović (eds), *Droit International 2* (Pedone 1982) 15, 27.

restitutio in integrum in the general sense "does not actually mean reparation." Likewise, in the *United States Diplomatic and Consular Staff in Tehran*, the International Court of Justice characterized the call to ensure the release of consular staff as a measure of cessation of a continuing violation rather than as a form of restitution—assuming a distinction between the two.[67]

Despite efforts to entirely sever cessation from other measures of redress following wrongful conduct—to frame it exclusively as an element of the primary obligation and not as a secondary obligation—measures of cessation continue to straddle the divide between primary rule and secondary obligation. Like the obligation to provide a remedy, which is both accepted as a secondary obligation and recognized as indispensable to the primary rules, cessation only arises subsequent to a breach of law. Thus, cessation is always incidental to the principal duty—to comply with the rule in the first instance—and only arises in the event that the main obligation is not fulfilled. Yet, cessation cannot be fully characterized as a remedy given that the only secondary obligation created is the fulfillment of a primary duty and this only when that obligation continues in force.

What the formulation of cessation as entirely distinct from reparatory justice does not account for are the symbolic dimensions of injustice that may be remedied by measures such as judgments on the merits, official declarations of wrongdoing and responsibility, apologies, memorials, and reforms to ensure rights are respected. Such measures consistently fall within the category of satisfaction (discussed in section 5.1) and, like these measures, the cessation of violations focuses on ensuring the status of victims within society and their right to be free from violations.[68] Therefore, for victims, measures of cessation can have a crucial reparatory function and serve as a precondition for the efficacy of all other reparatory measures.

Injuries to victims continue to accrue where violations are ongoing and cannot be displaced by measures of restitution, compensation, or satisfaction when the wrongful conduct itself has not ceased. Failures in cessation preclude the realization of recognition and responsibility—rendering reparations mechanisms incapable of meeting the fundamental elements of redress. Moreover, specific compliance (or a return to compliance through

[67] *United States Diplomatic and Consular Staff in Tehran* (n 65) 44–45. The court found the actions of Iran to be a breach of international law, and called upon Iran to put a stop to the continuing detention of embassy staff and declared the obligation of Iran to compensate the United States.

[68] See Christian J Tams, "Recognizing Guarantees of Non-Repetition: LaGrand and the Law of State Responsibility" (2002) 27 Yale Journal of International Law 441.

the cessation of continuing violations) is a restorative act, which ensures a return to a situation of legality much like restitution. Thus, measures of cessation may be considered as a form of reparatory justice and should be considered as central to efforts to redress historical injustice.

5.5. Guarantees of non-repetition

The Articles on State Responsibility tie guarantees of non-repetition to the cessation of ongoing violations through Article 30, wherein wrongdoing states are under dual obligations to cease continuing acts or omissions and to offer appropriate assurances and guarantees of non-repetition if circumstances so require.[69] Both requirements aim to restrain a state from continuing to violate legal rights and safeguard the underlying legal rule still in force. However, cessation focuses on the "negative aspect of future performance" while assurances and guarantees fulfill a "preventive function and may be described as a positive reinforcement of future performance."[70] Thus, guarantees and assurances are not premised upon the requirement of continuing obligation as is the case for measures of cessation. This places guarantees more comfortably within the dominant reparatory paradigm, although the distinctions should not be regarded as rigid.

In some contexts, violations continue and repetition is likely for various reasons—including the continuation of structural underlying causes of victimization. While it is possible to simply support compensation in every situation of breach, the economic deterrent function can be imperfect and insufficient to prevent future violations, particularly where these result from social, cultural, and political systems that defy rational cost-benefit calculations.[71] Yet, in some situations, the nature of violations can make repetition unacceptable. Dinah Shelton identifies the weakness of purely compensatory measures in such an environment:

[69] The commentary to Article 30 of the Articles on State Responsibility notes that the obligations are "separate but linked issues"—International Law Commission, "Report of the International Law Commission on the Work of its Fifty-Third Session" (2001) 2(2) Yearbook of the International Law Commission 31, 88–91.

[70] ibid 88.

[71] As Alexander Pires succinctly frames this argument, money is necessary but not enough. "Making the Case for Racial Reparations: Does America Owe a Debt to the Descendants of its Slaves?—A Forum" in Ronald P Salzberger and Mary C Turck (eds), *Reparations for Slavery: A Reader* (Rowman & Littlefield 2004) 275.

> With damage awards, the government can continue to violate rights as long as it is willing to pay.... While money is an acceptable substitute for many recognized interests, it is not adequate to allow the wrongdoer simply to pay for the injury if the claim is of great importance.[72]

Where states only need to pay monetary compensation, they may in effect be able to buy the privilege of breaching rules, and the norm *pacta sunt servanda* would cease to have any real meaning.[73] Thus, measures of specific performance may be necessary to prevent continued or repeated violations against existing victims and the victimization of others. This reinforces the recognition of victims as rights bearers, acknowledging that rights may not be simply "bought out" but must be respected.

The possibility of assurances and guarantees of non-repetition as legal remedies consequential upon an internationally wrongful act was affirmed in *LaGrand*, regarding the failure to provide notice of the right to consular assistance to death row inmates.[74] This formulation makes it clear that such measures constitute a form of redress for violations—a response to a breach—and not merely a requirement in fulfillment of the primary obligations. In *LaGrand*, the court noted that there were a number of ways in which the United States could fulfill the obligations outlined by the court in the instance of a future breach and refused to be prescriptive in its orders.[75] The UNBPG, however, provide significant guidance as to potential measures associated with guarantees of non-repetition, noting that such should include, where applicable, any or all of the following:

(a) Ensuring effective civilian control of military and security forces;
(b) Ensuring that all civilian and military proceedings abide by international standards of due process, fairness, and impartiality;
(c) Strengthening the independence of the judiciary;
(d) Protecting persons in the legal, medical and healthcare professions, the media and other related professions, and human rights defenders;
(e) Providing, on a priority and continued basis, human rights and international humanitarian law education to all sectors of society and

[72] Shelton (n 4) 379.
[73] *Rainbow Warrior II* (n 9) [111].
[74] *LaGrand (Germany v United States of America)* (Judgment) [2001] ICJ Rep 466.
[75] ibid 513 [125].

training for law enforcement officials as well as military and security forces;

(f) Promoting the observance of codes of conduct and ethical norms, in particular international standards, by public servants, including law enforcement, correctional, media, medical, psychological, social service and military personnel, as well as by economic enterprises;

(g) Promoting mechanisms for preventing and monitoring social conflicts and their resolution;

(h) Reviewing and reforming laws contributing to or allowing gross violations of international human rights law and serious violations of international humanitarian law.[76]

These measures highlight the broad scope of potential mechanisms for satisfying the obligations associated with guaranteeing non-repetition and place prevention at the center of efforts to redress wrongdoing. Moreover, the approach taken by the International Court of Justice, alongside the Articles on State Responsibility and the UNBPG, makes it clear that guarantees and assurances are not limited to mere promises but involve practical measures designed to ensure the promise is fulfilled. In relation to multifaceted, historical injustices involving the continued marginalization of victims, significant structural reforms to ensure non-repetition may be crucial to the reparatory project. This reflects the focus on structural and institutional measures evidenced in calls for redress for historical enslavement,[77] and may be captured within the framework of non-repetition.

5.6. Toward a progressive approach to reparatory justice

The power to award a remedy in the instance of a breach, as an inherent power of international judicial bodies, may be exercised in a variety of ways. Reparations are not prescribed or curtailed by specific rules. Rather, international jurisprudence establishes the freedom of judges and arbitrators to determine appropriate redress.[78] Courts consistently seek to avoid condoning

[76] UNBPG (n 1) Principle 23.

[77] See, for instance, CARICOM, "CARICOM Ten Point Plan for Reparatory Justice" (*CARICOM*, March 2014) <www.caricom.org/caricom-ten-point-plan-for-reparatory-justice/> accessed June 1, 2018.

[78] Ladislas Reitzer, *La Reparation Comme Consequence De L'Acte Illicite en Droit International* (Librairie du Recueil Sirey 1938).

or upholding a situation in which rights do not possess corresponding remedies and may do so irrespective of whether specific empowering provisions enabling and shaping the reparation they may order exist. While some courts have demonstrated a reluctance to issue orders beyond declarations of illegality and monetary compensation, others have recognized multiple forms of redress, and the necessity of outlining the requirements of compliance with international obligations, in their decisions.[79] In relation to systemic or widespread violations in particular, expecting the state to enact the necessary reforms without further direction can be overly optimistic. Shelton notes that general international practice concerning remedies has been "partial and unimaginative," typically failing to resolve the problems that led to the victim bringing the case.[80] Yet, in many instances, states require "guidance and direction on the measures necessary to afford redress."[81]

The idea that reparations ought to be in an adequate form, enunciated by the Permanent Court of International Justice in *Factory at Chorzów*, provides support for judges to order responsive reparations.[82] In many instances, this ought to include consideration of the affective dimensions of injustice and the insufficiency of purely pecuniary damages in redressing grave violations. Kaimipono David Wenger notes that monetary awards may imply the reduction of grave violations to a commodity that may be purchased by perpetrators, and where awards are nominal, purchased at a low cost.[83] The nature of the harms of transatlantic enslavement and the *maangamizi*—centered on the commodification of human beings—exacerbates the problems associated with trading money for violations. Therefore, recognition that some forms of wrongdoing entail consequences beyond the material ought to open the door to correlative forms of redress that more adequately match the wrongdoing and the injuries suffered.

As research into the area of reparatory justice grows, international courts have increasingly permitted different forms of redress to achieve their objectives more adequately. The Articles on State Responsibility and UNBPG

[79] The jurisprudence of the European Court of Human Rights discussed earlier demonstrates this reluctance, while the jurisprudence of the International Criminal Court (particularly the *Lubanga Principles* (n 1)) and the Inter-American Court of Human Rights evidence a more responsive and multifaceted approach.

[80] Dinah Shelton, *Remedies in International Human Rights Law* (1st edn, OUP 1999) 37.

[81] Shelton (n 4) 238.

[82] *Case Concerning the Factory at Chorzów (Germany v Poland)* (Jurisdiction) PCIJ Rep Series A No 9, 21.

[83] Kaimipono David Wenger, "'Too Big to Remedy?': Rethinking Mass Restitution for Slavery and Jim Crow" (2010) 44 Loyola Los Angeles Law Review 177.

recognize multiple avenues of redress, including collective and symbolic measures.[84] The International Criminal Court's reparations principles permit the ordering of payments to legal entities that benefit members of the victim community and allow for symbolic, preventative, or transformative reparations.[85] The measures that ought to be adopted necessarily depend on the nature of the situation at hand, and the prevalence of the general caveat "when appropriate" reinforces the idea that awards ought to be responsive rather than formulaic. Guidance on appropriate modalities tends to be indicative rather than prescriptive—with open-ended lists of potential measures to be undertaken—supporting a flexible approach that adapts to new circumstances and new understandings.[86]

No court has engaged so thoroughly with the possibilities for adaptive, responsive redress, utilizing the multiple modalities discussed in this chapter, as the Inter-American Court of Human Rights. The court has contributed significantly to reparations jurisprudence through its interpretation of the remedy provision of the American Convention on Human Rights, as well as being receptive to expanding research. Article 63 of the American Convention declares that in the instance of finding a violation, the court shall rule that the injured party be ensured the enjoyment of his right or freedom that was violated and, where appropriate, that the consequences of the measure or situation that constituted the breach be remedied and fair compensation paid to the injured party.[87]

Prima facie, Article 63 resembles the plethora of other remedy provisions found in international law and could have been applied to provide only awards of monetary compensation, consistent with the approach of the European Court of Human Rights.[88] However, the Inter-American Court has

[84] UNBPG (n 1) Principle 18; Articles on State Responsibility (n 1) arts 30, 31.

[85] Principle 1(8) of the *Lubanga Principles* (n 1) permits payments to legal entities, including micro-financing organizations, cooperative and building societies, NGOs, charities, public schools, and hospitals, while Principle 9 recognizes the legitimacy of forms of reparation beyond restitution, rehabilitation and compensation, including those with a symbolic, preventative, or transformative value.

[86] The Articles on State Responsibility (n 1), UNBPG (n 1), and *Lubanga Principles* (n 1) all contain nonexhaustive lists of potential measures.

[87] American Convention on Human Rights (adopted November 22, 1969, entered into force July 18, 1978) OAS Treaty Series No 36, 9 ILM 99 (1969).

[88] On the approach of the European Court to "just satisfaction," see *Zanghi v Italy* (Merits and Just Satisfaction) App No 11491/85 (ECtHR, February 19, 1991) 48, wherein the court noted that "it is for the State to choose the means to be used in its domestic legal system to redress the situation that has given rise to the violation of the Convention." See also *Aksoy v Turkey* [1996] ECHR 68 [98]; *Case of McCann and Others v the United Kingdom* (Merits and Just Satisfaction) App No 18984/91 (ECtHR, September 27, 1995); *Kaya v Turkey* (Merits and Just Satisfaction) App No 22729/93

recognized the need to go beyond pecuniary awards in redressing violations, particularly in relation to grave violations of human rights. As the court declared in the *Case of the Plan de Sánchez Massacre*, "reparations are not exhausted by compensation for pecuniary and nonpecuniary damage; other forms of reparation must be added."[89]

The Inter-American Court's approach to reparations situates restitutio in integrum, or equivalent alternative measures, as central to re-establishing respect for international norms.[90] The focus on "setting things straight" in communities and restoring the dignity of victims highlights the corrective nature of redress within this system and acknowledges the significance of responsibility and recognition in recovery from violations.[91] Symbolic reparations, in particular, are "intended to repair the shame and humiliation previously inflicted on victims and to restore their reputation and equal status in the public eye."[92]

The notion of life projects in assessing restitution emphasizes the importance of agency and recognizes the difficulties of re-establishing the status quo ante in what has become a radically different context for victims. Assessing the role of life projects in shaping redress involves valuing the future plans, potential, goals, and desires of victims, as well as their capacity to choose their own path. In the *Case of the "Las Dos Erres" Massacre v Guatemala*, concerning the execution of 251 members of the "Las Dos Erres" community, and acts of rape, forced abortion, and violence by Guatemalan armed forces, the court declared:

> it is evident that the victims of prolonged impunity suffer different infringements in their search for justice, not only materially, but also other suffering and damages of a psychological and physical nature and in their life projects, as well as other potential alterations of their social relations and to the dynamics of their families and communities.[93]

(ECtHR, February 19, 1998); *Selçuk and Asker v Turkey* (Merits and Just Satisfaction) App No 23184/94 (ECtHR, April 24, 1998).

[89] *Case of the Plan de Sánchez Massacre* (Reparations) (n 50) [93].

[90] *Case of El Amparo v Venezuela* (n 46).

[91] See Lisa Magarrell, "Reparations for Massive or Widespread Human Rights Violations: Sorting Out Claims for Reparations and Social Justice" (2003) 22 Windsor Yearbook of Access to Justice 85, 91.

[92] Ruti G Teitel, *Transitional Justice* (OUP 2002) 126–27.

[93] *Case of the "Las Dos Erres" Massacre v Guatemala* (Preliminary Objection, Merits, Reparations and Costs) IACHR Series C No 211 (November 24, 2009) [226].

Thus, the court recognizes that wrongdoing impacts not only upon the material conditions of victims, but also on their freedom to pursue their own goals, achieve their desires, and design their lives.[94]

The willingness of the Inter-American Court to order reparations spanning all recognized modalities sets it far beyond other international tribunals, including regional equivalents elsewhere in the world. Like the European Court of Human Rights, the Inter-American Court recognizes the procedural dimensions of effective protection of enunciated fundamental rights.[95] However, unlike the European Court, the Inter-American Court has not only recognized this effectiveness criterion as an element of the primary rule but also as a secondary obligation that may be the subject of a judicial order.

In *Velásquez-Rodríquez*, the court suggested that the failure to investigate wrongdoing and compensate victims may constitute continuing violations in themselves, for which the state and its successors are liable.[96] In *Neira Alegría et al.*, the court declared that the government had an obligation to "do all in its power to locate and identify the remains of the victims and deliver them to their next of kin" as a form of moral reparations.[97] In *Caballero-Delgado and Santana v Colombia*, the court recognized the continuation of judicial proceedings inquiring into the violation and punishment of those responsible as a form of reparations and demonstrated its willingness to order states to adopt such measures.[98] Furthermore, the court has not shied away from declaring that a state must reform its domestic laws to conform to the American Convention as a measure of reparation for violation, as well as a guarantee of non-recurrence.[99]

[94] *Case of Loayza Tamayo v Peru* (Reparations and Costs) IACHR Series C No 42 (November 27, 1998) [147].

[95] Pasqualucci suggests that reparations in international law were not developed to deal with "large-scale violations of human rights or situations in which the government refuses to investigate the abuse or punish the violators," creating a distinction between the European and Inter-American systems on the basis that the former engages isolated instances of abuse, while the latter is confronted with gross and systematic abuses. Jo Pasqualucci, "Victim Reparations in the Inter-American Human Rights System: A Critical Assessment of Current Practice and Procedure" (1996) 18 Michigan Journal of International Law 1, 6. This is then employed in explaining the difference in the reparations practice of the two systems. Yet, this does not necessarily explain the distinction where violations within the European system have many of the symbolic and affective dimensions of the widespread or systematic cases.

[96] *Velásquez Rodríguez* (Merits) (n 49).

[97] *Neira Alegría et al.* (Reparations and Costs), IACHR Series C No 23 (September 19, 1996) [69].

[98] *Case of Caballero-Delgado and Santana v Colombia* (Merits) IACHR Series C No 22 (December 8, 1995).

[99] See *Case of Loayza Tamayo v Peru* (Merits) (n 38).

The Inter-American Court has consistently supported its statements as to the requirements of the law with concomitant orders as to what remedies must be provided. This decreases the implementation gap (wherein victims must rely on state action to deliver the procedural requirements of their rights or simply accept compensation as an alternative), reinforcing the inherent power of the court to award appropriate redress.

The orders made in the *Case of the Moiwana Community v Suriname* are characteristic of the breadth of remedies awarded by the court.[100] In a case concerning the razing of the village of Moiwana, the massacre of forty men, women, and children, and the exile and forced displacement of the remaining members of the community, the Inter-American Court ordered a range of measures against Suriname to vindicate the rights of the victims and recognize the wrongdoing. These included the construction of a memorial in a suitable public location, the investigation of the facts of the case and prosecution of responsible parties, the adoption of legislative and administrative measures to protect the property rights of the community, guarantees of safety for community members choosing to return to the village, and a public ceremony in which Suriname would recognize its international responsibility and issue an apology for the violations.[101] This case demonstrates how responsive reparations awards may be developed to target multiple dimensions of injustice, including material, immaterial, individual, and collective harms.[102]

This multilayered and multimodal approach to redressing violations begins to acknowledge, and seeks to grapple with, the multidimensional impact of injustices, particularly in the context of mass atrocity. In international law, the potential for reparations practice that responds to the specific circumstances of a case, adapts to new realities with equivalent forms of redress, and engages with affective as well as material consequences, is built into the system. Not only does this approach enable responsive justice in the case of widespread injustice but may also extend to engage the complexities of such cases after the passage of a significant period of time.

[100] *Case of the Moiwana Community v Suriname* (Preliminary Objections, Merits, Reparations and Costs) IACHR Series C No 124 (June 15, 2005).

[101] ibid 66–87.

[102] On the court's increasing engagement with collective remedies in the context of indigenous communities, see Diana Contreras-Garduño and Sebastiaan Rombouts, "Collective Reparations for Indigenous Communities Before the Inter-American Court of Human Rights" (2011) 27 Utrecht Journal of International and European Law 4.

The shape of remedies and the capacity of judicial tribunals to order such is not based purely on prescriptive instruments but on the inherent power of the court to give efficacy to primary obligations. Thus, it is not attached to any particular treaties or the time periods associated with these. Compensation and decisions on the merits need not be all that there is—international law recognizes more. The Inter-American Court may be blazing a trail, but it is a trail that employs the tools already built into international jurisprudence. Tools that more adequately respond to the understanding of injustice that permeates the international system and which achieve a more complete version of reparatory justice.

5.7. Reparations in the context of transatlantic enslavement

While the modalities considered in this chapter may guide the construction of reparations for historical enslavement and the *maangamizi*, and the approach taken to the question of reparability itself, it would be inappropriate here to provide concrete suggestions as to the measures which ought to be adopted. The centrality of procedural justice and victim participation in shaping such mechanisms, discussed in chapter 4, requires meaningful engagement with victim communities in the consideration and construction of reparatory programs.[103] The design of reparations ought to be a reciprocal process in which affected communities have their voices heard and accounted for, recognizing and reaffirming their agency, as well as ensuring measures adopted respond to their suffering and meet their needs.[104] Additionally, these frameworks should be applied in context, in response to the specific circumstances of victims and the case formulated. This makes broad, universal conclusions concerning suitable measures inappropriate.[105]

[103] See, for instance, UN Commission on Human Rights, "Study Concerning the Right to Restitution, Compensation and Rehabilitation for Victims of Gross Violations of Human Rights and Fundamental Freedoms: Final Report Submitted by Mr Theo van Boven, Special Rapporteur" (1993) UN Doc E/CN.4/Sub.2/1993/8 [133], [137].

[104] Muraszkiewicz notes that the inclusion of victims in proceedings responds directly to the loss of dignity inherent in the violations, contributing to the restoration of agency and indicating that their concerns are as important as those of the state—Julia Muraszkiewicz, "Article 12 of the EU Human Trafficking Directive: Fulfilling Aspirations for Victim Participation in Criminal Trials?" (2016) 7(3) New Journal of European Criminal Law 331, 341. McKay further considers the potential impact of procedural justice on the effectiveness and efficiency of measures adopted, ensuring that reparations take the right form for the victims—Fiona McKay, "What Outcomes for Victims?" in Dinah Shelton (ed), *The Oxford Handbook of International Human Rights Law* (OUP 2013) 922.

[105] On responsiveness, see section 7.4.4.

It is for these reasons that specific consideration of transatlantic enslavement and the *maangamizi* in the preceding analysis is limited.

This chapter does not seek to prescribe what might constitute appropriate modalities of redress in response to the case of historical enslavement. Rather, it provides an outline of the forms reparations might take and the international legal foundations underpinning the various modalities of redress, with emphasis on the importance of symbolic as well as material measures.

In the context of widespread historical injustices with continuing legacies, developing multifaceted, responsive reparations programs is particularly important. As Rhonda Magee notes, the pervasive and insidious nature of the problems in contemporary society built upon transatlantic enslavement demand "no less than a panoply of remedial solutions."[106] Whether reparations are ultimately formulated within legal mechanisms, or in extralegal fora, the legal foundations of reparations practice can substantially inform the choices made in designing redress. These frameworks provide guidance as to potential formulations of reparations programs, assist in justifying the utilization of a range of responsive measures beyond monetary awards, and support the realization of the underlying philosophy, objectives, and elements of reparatory justice considered in chapter 4.

The multiple modalities of redress provided in international law speak to the claim for redress for historical injustices not only at the point of designing reparations programs but also at the outset when considering whether reparations are mandated, necessary, or appropriate. Recognition of the full range of options in the form such redress may take assists in responding to questions concerning the relationships between antecedent abuses and contemporary suffering, the threshold for sufficiently proximate harm, and the degree to which recognition opens the "floodgates" to a near-infinite stream of historical injustices.[107] If material suffering has attenuated, moral injuries might nonetheless be sustained and recognized. If residual harms related to the original wrongdoing are symbolic only, the availability of purely symbolic forms of redress speaks to the appropriateness of reparatory justice in this context. If the burden of reparatory awards shifts from the economic to the moral in the context of historical injustices lacking material contemporary harms, the burden of a flood of such claims is substantially lessened.

[106] Rhonda Magee, "The Master's Tools, from the Bottom Up: Responses to African-American Reparations Theory in Mainstream and Outsider Remedies Discourse" (1993) 79 Virginia Law Review 863, 882.

[107] These elements of the reparations claims are considered in greater depth in chapter 6.

The multiple modalities of redress considered in this chapter provide the entry point for the fulfillment of the objectives of reparatory justice in complex historical cases. Moving beyond individualistic understandings of redress focused only on monetary awards emphasizes the damaged relationships arising from wrongdoing that endure when there is no attempt to reckon with the past or to address its persistence in the present. This is not necessarily a zero-sum game or a confrontation but rather a quest for justice, the pursuit of equality, and even a "search for unity."[108]

108 Hilary Beckles, *Britain's Black Debt: Reparations for Caribbean Slavery and Native Genocide* (University of the West Indies Press 2013) 17.

6

The Causal Chains Connecting Historical Enslavement and Contemporary Redress

In 1847, Frederick Douglass—an abolitionist leader who escaped enslavement in the American South—advocated that "the man who has suffered the wrong is the man to demand redress."[1] While in general international law, the invocation of responsibility must be mediated by the state, the formulation of both the persons suffering the wrongs and the injuries themselves necessarily brings victims into these proceedings.[2] This does not occur at the inception of cases, nor in establishing wrongful conduct and attributing this to the state. Rather, the suffering of those harmed falls to the consideration of what remedies are due, subsequent to the establishment of responsibility for internationally wrongful conduct. This is fundamentally a question of the relationship between wrongful conduct and its consequences. It is this interaction between breaches of law and their effects that determines what reparations are due within the frameworks considered in chapters 4 and 5 and to whom they must be directed.

What must be assessed to determine the reparatory obligations in the specific case of historical enslavement are those injuries that can be characterized as having been caused by the internationally wrongful acts in question.[3] Thus, this chapter engages with the issue of causation in international law, examining the boundaries of the causal inquiry and the relationships between historical enslavement, the *maangamizi*, and contemporary harms. The presumption of attenuation in the case of widespread historical injustices is problematized and the role of collective harms and remedies is considered.

The question of the relationship between transatlantic enslavement and the contemporary experiences of people of African descent is critical in

[1] Frederick Douglass, "To Eric Clay, The North Star, December 3, 1847" in Philip S Foner (ed), *Frederick Douglass: Selected Speeches and Writings* (Chicago Review Press 2000) 91.

[2] Procedural justice, as considered in section 4.3.3, is also an entry point for victims in reparations proceedings at all stages.

[3] International Law Commission, "Draft Articles on the Responsibility of States for Internationally Wrongful Acts" (November 2001) UN Doc A/56/10 (Articles on State Responsibility), art 31.

Reparations for Slavery in International Law. Katarina Schwarz, Oxford University Press. © Oxford University Press 2022.
DOI: 10.1093/oso/9780197636398.003.0007

reparations discourse. As in the consideration of rules of attrition and attribution (considered in chapter 3), the passage of time is often conceived as fatal in the construction of the causal relationship between historical injustice and contemporary suffering. George Sher suggests that the passage of time attenuates the connection between present harms and historical injustices, with the result that it becomes "increasingly implausible" to frame conditions in the present as consequences of the wrongdoing.[4] The presumption that this mitigation occurs automatically lacks theoretical grounding in the legal frameworks. Yet, it continues to influence the causal investigation in both legal and extralegal considerations of the reparations case. This chapter therefore recognizes the limitations of legal frameworks and judicial reasoning in constructing and interpreting the requirements of causation, conscious of the adaptive possibilities of reparations construed with reference to chapters 4 and 5.

6.1. Causation in international law

Reparations detractors often employ a perceived lack of causal connection between contemporary harms and historical injustices as a bar to assertions of justiciable wrongdoing. The question of causation is thereby engaged at the initial stage of the reparations claim, when commentators consider the existence of internationally wrongful conduct that might be the subject of a judicial (or political) decision. However, the law of state responsibility does not include harm in the elements of internationally wrongful conduct.[5] Wrongfulness itself is not qualified through a requirement of damage or causation, although these may constitute elements of the primary rule.[6] Although criticized by some, this approach engages the distinction between international and domestic law, for the rules of attribution and requirements of the primary obligations themselves serve as a replacement for causation in determining the existence of internationally wrongful conduct.[7] This system

[4] George Sher, "Ancient Wrongs and Modern Rights" (1981) 10 Philosophy and Public Affairs 3, 10–12.

[5] See Articles on State Responsibility (n 3) art 2, which requires only attribution and breach.

[6] International Law Commission, "Draft Articles Proposed by the Drafting Committee on Second Reading" (2000) 1 Yearbook of the International Law Commission 386, 388 (Proposed Draft Articles).

[7] For critique, see Brigitte Stern, "The Obligation to Make Reparation" in James Crawford, Alain Pellet, and Simon Olleson (eds), *The Law of International Responsibility* (OUP 2010) 563, 570. León Castellanos-Jankiewicz, "Causation and International State Responsibility" (2012) SHARES

of pseudo-strict liability reinforces the role of international law as a normative order, as opposed to being solely concerned with remedying wrongs.[8]

While causation of damage in international law is not a prerequisite for establishing wrongful conduct, it does enter the law of state responsibility at the stage of determining the legal consequences of international responsibility—consequences that arise in the instance of internationally wrongful conduct but are not determinative of the status of the breach itself.[9] Thus, the relevance of harm and causation lies in the determination of what reparatory measures are due in international law and to whom these should be directed by the Claimant State. This, as the requirement to provide reparations relates only to those injuries "caused by the internationally wrongful act" and not to the preliminary investigation of whether there was internationally wrongful conduct in the first instance.[10] Causation should not, therefore, be considered at the stage of determining whether an international violation has occurred. It only enters the conversation at the point of determining what reparations are to be awarded. Nonetheless, causation relies on the determination of wrongful conduct in accordance with chapters 2 and 3. Only acts constituting wrongful conduct can serve as the basis of a causal chain connecting abuses with contemporary effects.[11]

In relation to transatlantic enslavement, determinations on the lawfulness of the multiplicity of acts constituting the *maangamizi* might impact not only the determination of justiciable breaches of law but also the determination of reparable consequences. To the extent that conduct of European enslaver states cannot be categorized as a breach of international law in place at the time, the harms related to that conduct cannot form the basis of legal responsibility. Although conduct might form part of a general pattern of conduct of a state committing breaches, it is only the actions constituting the breach

Research Paper 07, ACIL 2012-07, 4 <papers.ssrn.com/sol3/papers.cfm?abstract_id=2419913> accessed April 10, 2018, 5.

[8] Supporting the understanding of international law as a normative order, see Brigitte Stern, "The Elements of an Internationally Wrongful Act" in Crawford, Pellet, and Olleson (n 7) 193, 194; Dionisio Anzilotti, *General Theory of State Responsibility in International Law* (Firenze 1902); UNGA, "Report by Mr R Ago, Chairman of the Sub-Committee on State Responsibility" (1963) UN Doc A/CN.4/152, 250.

[9] Articles on State Responsibility (n 3). Responsibility under Article 2 requires only attribution and breach, as considered in chapters 2 and 3. Article 31 requires states make full reparation for injury caused by their internationally wrongful acts, a requirement given further elaboration in Articles 36 and 37 in relation to compensation and satisfaction respectively.

[10] ibid, art 31.

[11] Fleming James and Roger Perry, "Legal Cause" (1951) 60 Yale Law Journal 761, 789.

themselves that serve as the basis of a finding of causation in law. Thus, connecting the harms associated with the legacies of transatlantic enslavement requires an assessment of the international legality of not only enslavement itself but also of the myriad of other abuses committed by states during the colonial encounter.[12] Despite reliance on specifically formulated legal wrongdoing, the nature of the causal inquiry can be interrogated to assess the frameworks governing the relationship between historical wrongdoing and contemporary consequences. The stringency of these frameworks may, however, be relaxed in the context of moral and political claims.

Causation remains an element of the assessment of remediable harms throughout the history of modern international law, from its Roman roots to the present.[13] In Roman law, awards of damages evolved from formulaic approaches to the calculation of damages to account for the circumstances of the case, including damaged expectations.[14] Causation also featured in Aquinas' *Summa Theologica*, wherein the obligation to make *restitutio* contained an inherent causal requirement to identify what had been "taken" (whether material or immaterial) and thereby what required restoration.[15] The requirements of *restitutio* and *satisfactio*, supported by moral theologians in the fifteenth and sixteenth centuries, necessarily involved consideration of what damages must be redressed.[16] By the seventeenth century, Grotius cemented the integral role of causation in the determination of damages by framing obligations in relation to damage caused by legal fault.[17] Thus, the evolution of international law affirms the requirement of causation in the assessment of reparations throughout the period of transatlantic enslavement.[18]

Despite the central role of causation in determining reparations for a breach, the causal inquiry in international law has not been thoroughly

[12] This project is beyond the scope of this text, requiring determination on the specific facts of the case under consideration, and not general rules.

[13] On the relevance of Roman law, see section 3.2.

[14] See William Burdick, *Principles of Roman Law* (Lawyers Cooperative Publishing Co 1938) 637–75; Reinhard Zimmermann, *The Law of Obligations: Roan Foundations of the Civilian Tradition* (Juta 1990) 771–825; Rudolph Sohm, *The Institutes: A Textbook of the History and System of Roman Private Law* (James Crawford Ledlie tr, Clearendon Press 1907) 369; JAC Thomas, "Review" (1964) 54 Journal of Roman Studies 211.

[15] See Harry Dondorp, "Crime and Punishment: *Negligentia* for the Canonists and Moral Theologians" in Eltjo Schrage (ed), *Negligence: The Comparative History of the Law of Torts* (Duncker & Humblot 2001) 101, 126.

[16] See EL Kendall, *A Living Sacrifice: A Study of Reparation* (Westminster Press 1960).

[17] Hugo Grotius, *The Rights of War and Peace*, vol 2 (Richard Tuck tr, Liberty Fund 2005) ch 17, [1].

[18] On the continuity of relevant rules of state responsibility more generally, see section 3.2.

developed as it has in relation to domestic law, and international adjudication has been neither comprehensive nor consistent in this regard.[19] Authoritative international bodies have demonstrated an ad hoc approach to the question of causation, failing to formulate a clear, principled understanding of causation that could give meaning to the terms of international norms requiring it. Ilias Plakokefolos labels the approach of international adjudicatory bodies "rudimentary," "haphazard and unprincipled."[20] Michael Straus suggests that "common-sense, rough-hewn, and sometimes vague doctrines" are used to cut off liability, as opposed to a clear conception of causation.[21] The International Law Commission, for its part, explicitly refused to elaborate on the content of causation beyond distinguishing between factual and legal causation, suggesting rather that the requirement would differ depending on the international obligation in question.[22] Notions of "directness," "proximity," "foreseeability," and "remoteness" are employed in international legal decisions to explain causation.[23] Furthermore, the International Law Commission suggests that the harm having been deliberately caused or being "within the ambit of the rule being breached" might also have bearing.[24] The lack of attention to the specificities of causation beyond these observations provides little solid ground for the assertions of attenuation in cases of historical injustice.

The limited guidance on causation provided by the Articles on State Responsibility outlines a distinction between "causality in fact" and the

[19] See Ilias Plakokefalos, "Causation in the Law of State Responsibility and the Problem of Overdetermination: In Search of Clarity" (2015) 26(2) European Journal of International Law 471, 473. See also Michael Straus, "Causation as an Element of State Responsibility" (1984) 16 Law and Policy in International Business 893.

[20] Plakokefalos, ibid 473.

[21] Straus (n 19) 894.

[22] International Law Commission, "Draft Articles on Responsibility of States for Internationally Wrongful Acts, with Commentaries" (2001) 2(2) Yearbook of the International Law Commission 31, 93 (Commentaries to the Articles on State Responsibility). This decision to leave causation largely unexplained was justified on the following basis: "The Drafting Committee had considered a number of suggestions for qualifying that causal link, but, in the end, it had taken the view that, since the requirements of a causal link were not necessarily the same in relation to every breach of an international obligation, it would not be prudent or even accurate to use a qualifier. The need for a causal link was usually stated in primary rules. It sufficed to state that the injury should be the consequence of the wrongful act." Proposed Draft Articles (n 6) 388.

[23] On "directness," see for instance UNSC Res 687 (April 3, 1991) UN Doc S/RES/687 [16]; on foreseeability, see *Portuguese Colonies (Naulilaa incident)* (1928) 2 RIAA 1011; *Naulilaa Case (Portugal v Germany)* (1949) 2 RIAA 1011, 1031; on "proximity," see *Administrative Decision No. II* (1923) 7 RIAA 23, 30; on "remoteness," see *Trail Smelter* (1938, 1941) 3 RIAA 1905, 1931. See also Commentaries to the Articles on State Responsibility, ibid 93.

[24] Commentaries to the Articles on State Responsibility, ibid 93. See *The Islamic Republic of Iran v The United States of America* (1998) 34 Iran-USCTR 105.

question of scope of responsibility limiting causation, mirroring the orthodox explanation of causation in domestic law.[25] This differentiates between causation as a question of fact and as a question of law: the former involves a factual investigation into the relationship between wrongdoing and harm, and the latter a policy decision as to the appropriate scope of the obligations in question. Hart and Honoré describe this bifurcation of causation:

> The single question typically confronted by the courts: "Was this harm (*Y*) the consequence of this act or omission (*X*)?" is divided into two questions. *First*: "Would *Y* have occurred if *X* had not occurred?" *Second*: "Is there any principle which precludes the treatment of *Y* as a consequence of *X* for legal purposes?"[26]

Although Hart and Honoré discuss causation in the context of domestic law, their theoretical approach to the question of causal connection is relevant to an international discourse that consistently refers to domestic approaches. International tribunals have frequently used the language of tort law in discussing the chain of circumstances connecting actions with consequences.[27] The International Law Commission's commentaries to the Articles on State Responsibility make several references to domestic and comparative law on the issue of causation.[28] Furthermore, commentators often draw from the well-developed jurisprudence in national courts in discussing causation in the determination of international damages.[29] Therefore, it is appropriate to include commentaries and decisions concerning causation in domestic law in the analysis of its place in international law and its application to the case of historical enslavement.

The division of factual and legal causation explains the approach of judicial bodies to the causal inquiry with greater clarity but does not represent a paradigm shift from approaches blurring the boundaries between the two questions. Throughout the history of both domestic and international

[25] On causation in domestic law, see HLA Hart and Tony Honoré, *Causation in the Law* (2nd edn, OUP 1985).

[26] ibid 110.

[27] The reference to *aquilan* liability in *Chorzów Factory*, for instance, is a direct link to Roman domestic law deriving from the Roman *Lex Aquila—Case concerning the Factory at Chorzów (Germany v Poland)* (Decision on Indemnity) [1928] PCIJ Series A No 17. See also *Naulilaa Case* (n 23).

[28] Commentaries to the Articles on State Responsibility (n 22) 92–93.

[29] See, for instance, Plakokefalos (n 19); Stern, "The Obligation to Make Reparation" (n 7) 563; Straus (n 19).

decisions, the question of causation has been approached both as a bipartite test (involving the separation of factual and legal causation) and as a single interrogation. Roman law, for instance, treated causation not by the duality of separate factual and legal tests but took a more holistic, common sense based approach.[30] Despite the recognition of the dual test in international law, international jurisprudence often approaches causation as a single question or undertakes the same considerations under both headings.[31] Thus, under either approach, the investigation involves consideration of both factual and legal causation, as questions of policy are always engaged in the determination of what relationships are to be considered sufficiently related to the wrongdoing to justify an obligation to remedy.

6.2. Causation in fact

Consideration of causation in fact entails judgments as to the necessity and/or sufficiency of the action in bringing about the relevant consequences. This inquiry distinguishes causes from conditions, attaching additional value to certain conditions contributing to an outcome to characterize them as causative factors.[32] Causal relationships can be complex regardless of the length of time that has passed since the identified act of wrongdoing. The actions of the perpetrator interact with a milieu of other circumstances and often the conduct of third parties; multiple factors combine to produce particular outcomes.[33] Judges in a range of cases, both domestic and international, are nonetheless required to make sense of these intricate questions of fact. Although the passage of time might enable the contribution or intervention of other factors, these ought to be considered on their terms rather than presuming that time alone has frustrated claims.[34]

30 Zimmermann (n 14) 991. Although initially considered only circumstances in which the damage was a direct result of the wrongful act with no intervening events, causal relationships in Roman law developed to encompass situations in which damage was indirectly caused by the conduct in question—Barry Nicholas, *An Introduction to Roman Law* (OUP 1962) 219.

31 Plakakefalos highlights the tendency of international adjudicatory bodies to conflate the two tests despite the theoretical recognition of bifurcation in international law (n 19) 475.

32 Castellanos-Jankiewicz (n 7) 4. See also Hart and Honoré's summary of Birkmeyer's efficiency theory—n 25, 438–42.

33 See, for instance, *Case Concerning United States Diplomatic and Consular Staff in Tehran (United States of America v Iran)* [1980] ICJ Rep 64; *Corfu Channel Case (United Kingdom v Albania)* (Merits) [1949] ICJ Rep 244; *The Zafiro Case* (1925) 6 RIAA 160.

34 The impact of time on reparations claims is further considered in chapter 3.

Although the question of causation in fact is often articulated as the "but for" test or as a question of conditions sine qua non, this approach is not sufficient to capture the full spectrum of causal relationships relevant to international law. The equivocal sentiment expressed by the International Law Commission in relation to the explanation of causal relationships—that it is inappropriate or impossible to provide a single formula to describe causation in all cases—reflects the division of theories of causation into multiple forms.[35]

The equivalence theory of causation queries whether the conduct amounting to the breach was necessary for the production of the damage in question, while the adequacy theory questions whether the probability of the damage sustained was increased by the breach.[36] Even within the equivalence theory, multiple forms of causation can be found, forming three primary subsets:

(a) The conduct amounting to the breach is necessary for the production of the outcomes in question (condition sine qua non or "but-for" causation);
(b) The conduct amounting to the breach forms a necessary element of a set of conditions sufficient to bring about the outcomes in question (necessary element of a sufficient set); or
(c) The conduct amounting to the breach forms a substantial factor in, or contributes to, the production of the outcomes in question—this approach may be more relevant in situations of interventions and contributions by third-parties or in cases in which multiple factors related to different parties cause the relevant damage.[37]

In considering the role of historical enslavement in contributing to harms suffered by contemporary claimants, it is necessary in each proposed case to assess the specific harms identified as causally connected to the wrongdoing. Different combinations of preexisting circumstances and intervening factors are likely to exist in the different contexts in which a claim might be formulated. For the purposes of the present evaluation,

[35] Proposed Draft Articles (n 6) 388.
[36] See Castellanos-Jankiewicz (n 7) 4.
[37] ibid; Hart and Honoré (n 25) 26–129; Antony M Honoré, "Causation and Remoteness of Damage" in A Tunc (ed), *International Encyclopedia of Comparative Law* (Mohr 1983); JL Mackie, *The Cement of the Universe: A Study of Causation* (Clarendon Press 1980).

it is sufficient to note that many of the legacies of enslavement that continue to impact upon the lives of people of African descent, considered in chapter 1, satisfy the three tests of causation. Although susceptible to the quagmire of counterfactual reasoning, the conditions of people in the African diaspora fully meet the requirements of "but for" causation—mass forced migration of people from the African continent to the Americas is a conditio sine qua non of the suffering of their diasporic descendants.[38]

Because transatlantic enslavement did not occur in a vacuum but in an environment of extensive abuses committed against African and indigenous peoples, it may be impossible to classify it as the singular cause of identified suffering. Harms resulted both from enslavement and from other abuses with the result that they may not satisfy the "but for" test. Yet, independently, both of these forms of abuse would constitute sufficient causes of the identified harms. Therefore, enslavement may be considered to satisfy the "necessary element of a sufficient set" test, wherein wrongdoing is identified as sufficient to result in the identified harms alone, although alternate actions committed by third parties also occurred and may themselves have been sufficient to cause the identified damage or which otherwise contributed to the harms.[39] The characterization of factual causation as manifesting in different ways accounts for additional causes beyond the wrongdoing in question, allowing wrongdoing be a necessary element of a jointly sufficient set rather than independently sufficient.[40] To some degree, this blurs the line between the second and third identified forms of causation.[41]

Transatlantic chattel enslavement played a significant role in the inculcation of white supremacy globally and within the boundaries of nation states through their various iterations.[42] The racialization and subsequent denigration of people of African descent justified, and was justified by, chattel enslavement in a self-affirming cycle. Although early accounts of the African continent and African peoples (predating mass enslavement) already

[38] The exception to this conclusion being those people of African descent whose ancestors voluntarily migrated to the diaspora.

[39] RW Wright, "Causation, Responsibility, Risk, Probability, Naked Statistics, and Proof: Pruning the Bramble Bush by Clarifying the Concepts" (1987–1988) 73 Iowa Law Review 1001, 1018.

[40] Intervening causes, which may interfere with this causal relationship, are considered further in section 6.4.

[41] Hart and Honoré, for instance, prioritize sufficiency over necessity—n 25.

[42] See section 1.5.

engaged in the rhetoric of racialization, the mechanisms of mass transatlantic enslavement were a substantial factor in the globalization and entrenchment of racial discrimination as it manifests today, likely meeting the requirements of the third causal test.[43] Because the systematic enslavement and dehumanization of African people and people of African descent constituted a substantial factor in the development and inculcation of racism, which continues to manifest in contemporary harms to new generations, the transatlantic system could be characterized as a factual cause of these harms in line with the third form of causation.[44]

These examples are illustrative rather than prescriptive, indicating the plausibility of factual causal connections being established between historical enslavement and contemporary harms. For the purposes of the present analysis, considering reparations claims on the whole and not in their specificities, it is sufficient to identify the plausibility of the recognition of an identifiable, extant causal chain from historical enslavement to contemporary suffering of the descendants of enslaved persons and people of African descent. However, this does not necessarily support a finding of causation in law, which operates to narrow the scope of liability through the application of limiting principles.

[43] For a discussion of racialization in early travel narratives of Africa see Katrina Dyonne Thompson, "The Script: 'Africa Was But a Blank Canvas for Europe's Imagination'" in Katrina Dyonne Thompson, *Ring Shout, Wheel About* (University of Illinois Publishing 2014) 13. See also Peter Mancall (ed), *Travel Narratives from the Age of Discovery* (OUP 2006). Although it is not within the ambit of his chapter to explore the expansive literature discussing the contributions of the system of transatlantic chattel enslavement to present racial discrimination, the continuity of racism in different environments ought to be acknowledged. See generally Douglas Blackmon, *Slavery by Another Name: The Re-Enslavement of Black Americans from the Civil War to World War II* (Icon Books 2012); Hilary Beckles, *Britain's Black Debt: Reparations for Caribbean Slavery and Native Genocide* (University of West Indies Press 2013); Maria Suzette Fernandes Dias, *Legacies of Slavery: Comparative Perspectives* (Cambridge Scholars Publishing 2007); Maurits S Hassankhan and others (eds), *Legacy of Slavery and Indentured Labour: Historical and Contemporary Issues in Suriname and the Caribbean* (Routledge 2016); Rebecca Shumway and Trevor Getz (eds), *Slavery and Its Legacy in Ghana and the Diaspora* (Bloomsbury Academic 2017); William Link and James Broomall (eds), *Rethinking American Emancipation: Legacies of Slavery and the Quest for Black Freedom* (CUP 2015).

[44] This formulation is based on adequacy theory, and may be constructed in a variety of ways. Von Kries required that the contingency in question be a sine qua non of the harm and have increased the probability of the harm by a significant amount; Traeger required an increase in objective probability of harm accounting for circumstances that a perceptive observer would have noticed at the time and those that the wrongdoer actually did know; and Tarnowski focused on consequences the probability of which was knowingly increased by the wrongdoer (thus differentiating between causes and conditions). See Hart and Honoré (n 25) 469–73.

6.3. Causation in law

Having distinguished between conditions and causes through necessity, sufficiency, or contribution, the potential consequences that may be causally connected to a particular act may still be immense. In *Aloeboetoe v Suriname*, the Inter-American Court of Human Rights articulated the problem of scope in determining legal redress, noting that every human act produces diverse and ever more imperceptible consequences.[45] Thus, the court determined:

> To compel the perpetrator of an illicit act to erase all the consequences produced by his action is completely impossible, since that action caused effects that multiplied to a degree that cannot be measured.[46]

Hart and Honoré go so far as to frame potential consequences of wrongdoing as an "*embarrass de choix* of literally cosmic proportions" to which law must apply limiting principles, entailing some degree of arbitrariness in distinguishing between reparable and nonreparable consequences.[47] International law therefore recognizes that the duty to provide redress for wrongful conduct is not infinite but limited by the consideration of factors such as proximity, foreseeability, and remoteness.[48] This limitation is based on a fundamental concern of legal equity: a distinction between those consequences a wrongdoer ought to bear the burden of and those they should not.[49]

Rules are not only formulated in an abstract, normative setting but often comprehend the kinds of harm they are designed to protect against and remedy.[50] Conversely, the purpose and terms of the rule in question might also indicate the harms intended to be outside the scope of the obligation. The nature of the breach itself, including the level of intentionality, may also

[45] *Aloeboetoe and Ors v Suriname* (Reparations and costs) Inter-American Court of Human Rights Series C No 15 (September 10, 1993) [48].

[46] ibid.

[47] Hart and Honoré (n 25) 110.

[48] Sabahi narrows the issue of legal causation down to foreseeability or remoteness (with proximity being identified as the inverse of the latter). Borzu Sabahi, "A Concise History of the Law of State Responsibility and Reparation in International Law" in Borzu Sabahi, *Compensation and Restitution in Investor-State Arbitration: Principles and Practice* (OUP 2011) 7, 19.

[49] Honoré suggests that all theories concerning causation incorporate consideration of equity as well as necessity, explanation, probability, and the norm in question (n 37).

[50] Hart and Honoré favor consideration of the purpose of the rule, arguing that "very often consideration of the purpose of a legal rule will show that certain kinds of harm alleged to have been caused by a breach of the rule are altogether outside its scope, since it is obvious that the rule is not concerned to give protection against that sort of harm." See (n 25) 109.

impact on what consequences are determined to be sufficiently proximate or foreseeable.[51] In relation to transatlantic enslavement, this inquiry must be situated in the ambiguous legal territory of the fifteenth to nineteenth centuries, acknowledging the changing understanding of enslavement's position in positive international law and countervailing considerations of its place in naturalist frameworks.

The tests of the sufficiency of the causal connection in question, foreseeability, and proximity are descriptive rather than instructive. Further attempts to elaborate on the substance of the inquiry, for instance the observation that the "injury must flow from the wrongful conduct as a matter of course and in natural sequence," likewise offer limited additional support for a determination on the facts.[52] Absent a comprehensive framework of legal rules and guidance, it is the nature of the circumstances at hand that is determinative.

In considering directness in the causal relationship, the contribution of alternative causes is crucial. Harms may be severed from the conduct attributed to the responsible state through the intervention of third parties.[53] In other words, causation may be altered, superseded, or suspended in ways that impact on the liability of the original wrongdoer for subsequent consequences. In instances of historical wrongdoing, the period of time during which external factors have the opportunity to intervene is extended, often resulting in a more complex causal chain. It is this state of affairs that led Jeremy Waldron to conclude that historical injustices will often be superseded as time passes.[54]

The degradation of the causal chain connecting contemporary individual suffering with historical enslavement makes determining the degree to which the wrongdoing may be considered causative problematic. On this micro level, many other factors can be seen to directly contribute

[51] Brownlie recognized the significance of both the relationship between the primary rule and the determination of the question of legal causation, and the circumstances of the breach, stating that "[t]he particular context of a breach of duty, i.e. the nature of the duty itself and the mode of breach, may determine the approach to the question of damages." Ian Brownlie, *Principles of Public International Law* (6th edn, OUP 2003) 447. The International Law Commission articulates this point in the commentary to the Articles on State Responsibility by suggesting that the deliberateness of causing harm and the intended scope of the rule are relevant to considerations of legal causation (n 22) 93.

[52] Castellanos-Jankiewicz (n 7) 46.

[53] The Articles on State Responsibility allow some parts of the injury pleaded to be severed in causal terms from the conduct attributed to the state. Deliberateness of causing harm and the intended scope of the rule are relevant to considerations of legal causation. Commentaries to the Articles on State Responsibility (n 22) 93.

[54] Jeremy Waldron, "Redressing Historic Injustice" (2002) 52 University of Toronto Law Journal 135; Jeremy Waldron, "Superseding Historic Injustices" (1992) 103 Ethics 4.

to the harms, including conscious actions of third parties. Thus, finding a sufficiently strong relationship between historical enslavement and the present suffering of individual people of African descent—and in particular the descendants of enslaved people—to satisfy the legal test is difficult. Yet, despite the increased probability of supersession in the case of historical abuses, the rupture of the causal chain should not be presumed. In cases of massive and widespread injustices, the greater level of abuse may result in a more robust chain because of the degree to which future outcomes are impacted by the wrongdoing. Thus, severe breaches may make a stronger case for continuing causation given the degree to which they are associated with harmful consequences. Moreover, wrongdoing need not be the only causative factor contributing to harm in order to found liability.

The responsibility of states to make reparation does not require sole causation; international law allows for situations in which multiple actors contribute to an injury, at which point the state in question may remain liable for the damage in whole or in part.[55] International jurisprudence is ambiguous as to when a state might be held liable for the entirety of conduct to which another state or other third party contributed. For instance, in *Corfu Channel*, the International Court of Justice found Albania liable for the entirety of the damage caused to British vessels by mines in the Corfu Channel between Albania and Greece, despite finding that a third party had substantially caused the damage. The court did not find that Albania had laid the mines, and in fact suggested that Albania did not have the capacity for such, but nonetheless required Albania to pay the full damages.[56]

Despite the determination in *Corfu Channel*, the Articles on State Responsibility recognize the possibility of some part of the injuries caused being severable from the responsibility of the state, suggesting the state is responsible "for all the consequences, not being too remote, of its wrongful conduct" unless "some part of the injury can be shown to be severable in causal terms from that attributed to the responsible State."[57] The provision for responsibility for aiding, assisting, directing, controlling, and coercing breaches by third states entails a division of liability for the consequences of such breaches, including recognizing the dual responsibility of states in

[55] See (n 33).

[56] *Corfu Channel Case* (n 33). Likewise, in *Case Concerning United States Diplomatic and Consular Staff in Tehran* (n 33), Iran was held responsible for damage primarily related to the conduct of militant students, who were not agents of the state, on the basis of its failure to protect the embassy.

[57] Commentaries to the Articles on State Responsibility (n 22) 93.

such circumstances.[58] It is therefore possible for alternative causative factors to contribute to the injury without breaking the chain of causation between the conduct of the state in question and identified harms. This is significant in the context of widespread historical injustices, for it allows the recognition of causation in relation to a proportion of contemporary harms, acknowledging interventions and contributions of external factors without completely dismantling the connection between historical wrongdoing and contemporary harms.

6.4. The harms of transatlantic enslavement

The Declaration of the World Conference Against Racism, Racial Discrimination, Xenophobia and Related Violence in 2001 (Durban Conference) concluded by recognizing the contemporary impacts of transatlantic chattel enslavement and colonialism:

> historical injustices have undeniably contributed to poverty, underdevelopment, marginalization, social exclusion, economic disparities, instability and insecurity that affect many people in different parts of the world, particularly in developing countries.[59]

Yet, despite this recognition, teasing out the causal relationship between the transatlantic system of chattel enslavement and contemporary harms is mired with difficulty. Relevant contemporary harms are not merely a result of discrete historical injustices but a continuous history of racialized systems of discrimination and oppression. Across the African diaspora, similar evolution of abuses can be seen in "ex-slave states," whose histories of racial discrimination and institutionalized disadvantage occupy the nexus of a plethora of different factors, constituted by both deliberative actions and environmental conditions.[60] Racialized social relations and structures of power, as well as the economic systems put in place to enable enslavement, serve as the foundation for a continuum of interrelated harms and abuses.

[58] Articles on State Responsibility (n 3) Chapter IV.

[59] United Nations, *Durban Declaration and Plan of Action, Adopted at the World Conference Against Racism, Racial Discrimination, Xenophobia and Related Violence* (September 8, 2001), endorsed by UNGA Res 56/266 (May 15, 2002).

[60] See, for instance, Beckles; Hassankhan and others; Shumway and Getz—n 43.

Thus, the entrenchment of plantation economies overly reliant on single commodities, early systems of prison labor and convict leasing, segregation, lynching, "red-lining," intergenerational trauma, wealth disparities, education and health issues, and other forms of racial discrimination that continue to manifest in old and new forms are characterized as the "strange fruit" of the transatlantic system.[61]

Consistent with the requirements of the causal inquiry in international law considered in sections 6.1–6.3, in considering historical injustices associated with transatlantic enslavement, it is necessary to define the exact wrongs to which responsibility attaches, the parties allegedly suffering harms, and the nature of that harm before causation may be engaged. Although this requires consideration on the facts of the specific case, some general observations may be made based on predominant ways of framing reparations claims. These different formulations raise different issues in establishing an unbroken chain of causation based on whether harms are characterized as individual or collective and whether standing relies on contemporary suffering or the inheritance of historical entitlements.

Inheritance-based claims rely on the transmission of a claim to redress from a wronged party to the beneficiaries of their estate. This presents little challenge in establishing causation, as enslaved people themselves suffered a range of direct harms connected to their enslavement.[62] The difficulty of such claims lies in connecting historical harm to enslaved persons to those alive today through a contemporary right to inheritance. While the transmission of judicial damages through awards to the victims' estate is possible, courts may distinguish between the different kinds of damages that may be transmitted.[63] For instance, while the Inter-American Court of Human Rights permits the automatic transmission of a deceased or disappeared

[61] See Blackmon; Link and Broomall; Fernandes Dias—n 43. See further section 1.6.

[62] For an inheritance-based argument for reparations, see Stephen Kershnar, "Are the Descendants of Slaves Owed Compensation for Slavery?" (1999) 16 Journal of Applied Philosophy 95.

[63] Both the Inter-American Court of Human Rights and the European Court of Human Rights have granted awards for breaches committed against a person who was deceased at the time of the ruling to the victim's estate—the victim's entitlement is thereby transmitted to their heirs by succession. In *Keenan*, for instance, the European Court of Human Rights awarded £7,000 in damages for suffering associated with the breach of the right to be free from inhuman and degrading treatment to the estate of the victim who had committed suicide in custody—*The Case of Keenan v The United Kingdom* (Merits and Just Satisfaction) App No 27229/95 (ECtHR March 4, 2001). In the *Aloeboetoe Case*, the Inter-American Court recognized the transmission of entitlements through succession—n 45 [54]. See also *Godínez Cruz Case* (Compensatory Damages) IACHR Series C No 8 (July 21, 1989) [51–53]; *Case of Velásquez Rodríguez v Honduras* (Compensatory Damages), IACHR Series C No 7 (July 21, 1989) [56–58].

victims' entitlement, the European Court of Human Rights exercises discretion over whether nonpecuniary damages are transmitted, only finding in favor of succession where such is necessary to advance "the cause of justice."[64] This might, in turn, infuse international judicial approaches to the consideration of suffering that may be the subject of reparations orders, despite this being mediated through the state as recipient. Furthermore, this case law only considers whether entitlements can be passed through one level of succession—specifically to the spouses and children of direct victims—leaving the question of how far entitlements might be transmitted unresolved. Bernard Boxill's presumption that enslaved persons would have conferred their rights to ownership over the products of their labor to their descendants cannot therefore stand unquestioned ad infinitum.[65]

Individualized harms, on the other hand, construct a claim for contemporary claimants distinct from that of those directly enslaved based on their own experience of harms arising from transatlantic enslavement. This may be premised on contemporary suffering causally connected to ancestry or systems of racial oppression connected to chattel enslavement.[66] They might also be related to the denial of intergenerational wealth, a claim connected to inheritance but not based on the passing down of an entitlement as in the case of claims relating to historical suffering.[67]

A growing body of literature supports the existence of intergenerational trauma—psychological suffering transmitted from parent to child through multiple generations. For instance, an increase in depressive and anxiety disorders has been found among survivors of the Shoah, which can result in damage to the coping strategies and an increase in such disorders among children of survivors. This can impact on the structure and mental health of families across generations.[68] In the context of Northern Ireland, research

[64] *Aloeboetoe and Ors v Suriname* (n 45) [54]. In the European Court of Human Rights, pecuniary damages are automatically passed on to the victim's successors, while nonpecuniary damages are presumed to be personal to the victim unless transmitting to successors is necessary to advance the cause of justice. Montserrat Enrich Mas, "Right to Compensation under Article 50" in Ronald St J Macdonald, Franz Matscher, and Herbert Petzold (eds), *The European System for the Protection of Human Rights* (Martinus Nijhoff 1993) 775, 782.

[65] Bernard Boxill, "Morality of Reparation" (1972) 1 Social Theory and Practice 113, 120.

[66] See J Angelo Corlett, *Heirs of Oppression* (Rowman & Littlefield 2010) 163–65.

[67] For analysis of the impact of slavery and racial discrimination on intergenerational wealth, see Darrell Gaskin, Alvin Headen Jr, and Shelley White-Means, "Racial Disparities in Health and Wealth: The Effects of Slavery and Past Discrimination" (2005) 32 The Review of Black Political Economy 95.

[68] Pierre Fossion and others, "Transgenerational Transmission of Trauma in Families of Holocaust Survivors: The Consequences of Extreme Family Functioning on Resilience, Sense of Coherence, Anxiety and Depression" (2015) 171 Journal of Affective Disorders 48.

recognizes that the transgenerational effect of conflict can manifest in the form of economic hardship and psychological impact, as well as affect care responsibilities for parents and grandparents of direct victims.[69] The structures of transatlantic enslavement often relied upon the fracturing of family relationships, fundamentally changing the family dynamics of people of African descent in the diaspora.[70]

Intervening factors and issues of attenuation may be less persuasive with regard to collective claims to reparations, for suffering operates on a systemic level rather than concerning discrete instances of racial injustice perpetrated by a multiplicity of different actors. In this case, unlike in relation to individual harms, collective identity must first be established, and subsequently contemporary harms suffered by that collective causally connected to historical injustices committed against that same collective.[71] In the initial interrogation finding and defining collective identity, victimization itself can operate as a collectivizing force.[72]

While injury alone may be insufficient to create a collective, the notion of common bonds between victims and the destruction of common identity may distinguish between those victim groups that may be collectivized and those that may not.[73] Thus, the racialized nature of the *maangamizi*—manifested in "Black Codes," presumptions of slave status, segregation laws, antimiscegenation laws, lack of capacity to testify in a court of law, lack of judicial protection, and a slew of other race-based distinctions constructed not only within the social consciousness but also within the law—reinforces the notion of people of African descent as a legally definable collective for the purpose of constructing reparations.[74]

[69] Emily Fitzgerald and others, "The Transgenerational Impact of 'The Troubles' in Northern Ireland" (*Queen's University Belfast School of Psychology* 2017) <www.qub.ac.uk/schools/psy/files/Filetoupload,784073,en.pdf> accessed May 8, 2018;, Damien McNally, "Transgenerational Trauma and Dealing with the Past in Northern Ireland" (*WAVE Trauma Centre*, March 2014).

[70] See, for instance, Wilma A Dunaway, *The African-American Family in Slavery and Emancipation* (CUP 2003).

[71] See, for instance, Diana Contreras-Garduño and Sebastiaan Rombouts, "Collective Reparations for Indigenous Communities before the Inter-American Court of Human Rights" (2011) 27 Utrecht Journal of International and European Law 4.

[72] See Mari Matsuda, "Looking to the Bottom: Critical Legal Studies and Reparations" (1987) 22 Harvard Civil Rights-Civil Liberties Law Review 323, 76.

[73] Friedrich Rosenfeld, "Collective Reparations for Victims of Armed Conflict" (2010) 92 International Review of the Red Cross 731, 743.

[74] Magee highlights the fact that people of African descent in the Unites States were marginalized from the legal system both on the terms of legal texts and in practice, noting that "With rare and less than satisfying exceptions, eighteenth century African-Americans found the legal system essentially closed to them. Enslaved Blacks generally were denied jury trials; often they were punished differently for crimes, based on their race; they were not permitted to testify against a white defendant; and free Blacks were permitted to offer evidence against whites in only one state, Louisiana." Rhonda

Despite the broad, racialized collective harms imposed upon African people and people of African descent by the system of transatlantic enslavement, formulations of collective remedies are often disparaged for clashing with traditional, individualistic rights theory.[75] However, they are increasingly finding a place in international law to recognize the harms committed against victim communities, particularly indigenous communities. The rise of collective remedies in the Inter-American Court of Human Rights and the International Criminal Court serves as a testament to the increasing recognition of the complexity of harms associated with wrongdoing, particularly when considering widespread abuses.[76] Such reparations may be awarded in response to collective harms, even where the wrongdoing does not constitute a breach of collective rights; the cultural bonds or collective experience of victims, as opposed to the specific right breached, may justify collective awards.[77]

Claims concerning collective victimization and harm may weather the storm of history more intact than individualized claims, for the collective entity may continue in existence from the time of enslavement to the present. In this way, collective victims are analogous to the state, moral harm to which may be easier to establish where continuity or succession is found. Furthermore, the possibility of awarding responsive reparations packages tailored to the case at hand—including community-based and symbolic measures—mitigates the difficulties associated with recognizing collective harms. In relation to both individualized and collective contemporary claims, the possibility for reparations awards specifically targeted toward multifaceted and often symbolic harms, in conjunction with the recognition that causation may be established in relation to only a proportion of the contemporary injuries, may expand possibilities for recognition of causation.

In considering the strength of chains of causation over time, the distinction between different categories of harm and different modalities of redress

Magee, "The Master's Tools, from the Bottom Up: Responses to African-American Reparations Theory in Mainstream and Outsider Remedies Discourse" (1993) 79 Virginia Law Review 863, 892.

[75] ibid 907.

[76] Under Rule 97(1) of the International Criminal Court's Rules of Procedure and Evidence, the court may award reparations on a collective basis where it deems appropriate. International Criminal Court, "Rules of Procedure and Evidence" (2000) UN Doc PCNICC/2000/1/Add.1. The Inter-American Court of Human Rights has granted collective reparations in a range of cases, particularly in relation to indigenous communities—see Contreras-Garduño and Rombouts (n 71).

[77] See, for instance, *Case of the Moiwana Community v Suriname* (Preliminary Objections, Merits, Reparations and Costs) IACHR Series C No 124 (June 15, 2005).

considered in chapter 5 substantially impacts the analysis. Moral damage under Article 31(b) of the Articles on State Responsibility was conceived not only to respond to immaterial harms to victims but also to the legal injury suffered by states by virtue of the breach of international obligations owed to them.[78] Thus, even where establishing a sufficient causal link between historical wrongdoing and contemporary material suffering is impossible or unlikely, the same conclusion need not automatically be reached for the moral implications of the abuses in question. It is possible to conclude that claims in relation to material damage have attenuated over time to such a degree that the legal connection between wrongful conduct with present harms has broken, yet still find the connection to continuing moral harms sufficiently direct and proximate. This is true for both moral harms suffered by a state and those experienced by individual and collective victims. Thus, the multiple modalities of reparations considered in chapter 5 can influence not only the construction of responsive reparations but also the consideration of causation.

6.5. The role of judicial discretion in causation

Despite the possibility of framing arguments for contemporary redress within the confines of existing international legal frameworks, any attempt to achieve redress faces substantial barriers in obtaining judicial support. Because issues of causation in law are determined at the discretion of judges in the circumstances of the case, a legal environment hostile to reparations claims is likely to influence the practical outcomes of any attempt to litigate historical enslavement, as well as legal reasoning in commentaries considering the claims.[79] Causation in law necessarily involves questions of legal policy that judges are expected to resolve. Yet, the basis on which these decisions are made in the corpus of international jurisprudence remains ambiguous.[80] Thus, the determinations of legal policy required by these

[78] Proposed Draft Articles (n 6) 388. See also Stern, "The Obligation to Make Reparation" (n 7) 569.

[79] The fact that "slippery slope arguments" are commonly premised on a continuum fallacy has done little to deter the propensity of commentators to situate them at the core of reparations denials in relation to a range of historical injustices.

[80] See Plakokefalos (n 19) 473; Straus (n 19) 894; Castellanos-Jankiewicz (n 7) 16.

considerations represent a "value-laden inquiry," the product of "cultural as well as intellectual developments."[81]

The scant domestic jurisprudence on the matter does not provide a promising foundation for the preservation of the causal chain in relation to historical enslavement. *In Re African-American Slave Descendants*, a case that attempted to hold private companies liable for their role in North American enslavement, the court declared that the plaintiffs could not "establish a personal injury sufficient to confer standing by merely alleging some genealogical relationship to African-Americans held in slavery over one-hundred, two-hundred, or three-hundred years ago."[82] This argument not only dismisses the inheritance-based claim in this case, but, in declaring that the plaintiffs "cannot" establish relevant injury, denies the possibility of such a claim in any case on the subject. The appellate court, upholding this determination, suggested that the causal chain was too long and had too many "weak links for a court to be able to find that the defendants' conduct harmed the plaintiffs at all, let alone in an amount that could be estimated without the wildest speculation."[83]

In the decision at first instance, causation served as a question of standing and operated as a bar to judicial consideration. This approach does not translate to international law given the positioning of causation on this level as a concern for determining reparations rather than wrongdoing. However, it is indicative of a judicial approach to causation in cases of historical enslavement that might be mirrored in considering the consequences of wrongful conduct at the international level. In the determination on appeal, the court indicated not only that the causal chain had been fatally weakened in the case but also that the intervening factors contributing to harms were so extensive as to make a determination of measures of redress for slavery inappropriate or impossible.[84] This interrogation fits within the parameters of the causal inquiry in international law, and thus may shape the approach taken by international judicial bodies on the issue.

Although *In Re African-American Slave Descendants* is a domestic case brought against private corporations, operating on a specific set of facts, and in a particular national environment, it provides insight into the way judges

[81] Martha Chamallas, "Questioning the Use of Race-Specific and Gender-Specific Economic Data in Tort Litigation: A Constitutional Argument" (1994) 63 Fordham Law Review 73, 74.
[82] *In Re African-American Slave Descendants Litigation* (2005) 375 F Supp 2d 721 (ND Ill).
[83] *In Re African-American Slave Descendants Litigation* (2006) 471 F Supp 3d 754 (7th Cir).
[84] See (n 83).

may approach the question of causation for widespread historical injustices. The limited tapestry of cases in which judges have had to engage with historical enslavement indicates that a conservative approach to all questions of justiciability and causation may prevail.[85] Furthermore, international jurisprudence involving the determination of nonpecuniary reparations and the prevailing commentary concerning the justiciability of historical injustices in international law indicate a propensity for fidelity to classical understandings of the extent of causal relationships.[86] Yet, to suggest that past judicial choices determining what circumstances break the causal connection between wrongdoing and its consequences are immutable is to entrench past understandings of the relationships between actions and reactions.

Antecedent interpretations of reality and legality are not inherently perspicacious and in fact often replicate the dynamics of power of an international legal system premised on inequality. New and alternative understandings of what constitutes injury caused by the breach ought to be possible, for there is no objectively discernible distinction between those injuries caused in fact and those that are reparable as a question of law. The latter half of the bifurcated causal inquiry involves the consideration of legal policy and not the application of a clear legal framework. The causal chain is a metaphor, not a material reality, and is thus determined by the interpretation of judges in the context of specific cases.

The inclusion of the intended scope of the primary obligation as a factor in the determination of legal causation significantly impacts on the nature of the assessment undertaken, requiring that decisions in the case account for the range of possible cases that might be allowed in light of the ruling. Inherent in this understanding is the assumption that not only are conceptions of appropriate remedies determined by the category of injuries, but also the formulation of reparable injuries itself is constituted by some notion of what ought to be redressed. Marc Galanter suggests that the first part of this proposition—that the determination of appropriate remedies is a reflection of a system of values—is widely accepted:

[85] American courts have been similarly conservative in other cases on the question. In *Johnson v McAdoo*, the court concluded that the US government was the only appropriate defendant in a case brought by formerly enslaved persons seeking an equitable lien on funds drawn from cotton taxes held by the US Treasury, and thus that the suit was barred on the basis of sovereign immunity—*Johnson v McAdoo* 45 App DC 440 (1916). In *Cato v United States* the claim against the US government was similarly barred on the basis of both sovereign immunity and statute of limitations grounds—*Cato v United States* (1995) 70 F 3d 1103 (9th Cir).

[86] On awards of satisfaction in international law, see section 5.1.

> We recognize that remedies are cultural constructs: it is not a natural given that an injury is adequately erased or cancelled or balanced by revenge, payment, condemnation, or apology. What satisfies our sense of an appropriate and adequate remedy clearly depends on the cultural presuppositions that we bring to the question.[87]

However, Galanter also suggests that injury and remedy both constitute "moving frontiers" that change over time with the changing capabilities and sensibilities of human society.[88] Thus, injury too is a social construct often determined by those in a position to influence legal frameworks with the result being that "injuries affecting the powerful are exaggerated while those affecting the marginalized are downplayed."[89] Wenger therefore suggests that the claim for reparations for transatlantic enslavement is rendered impossible by the legal system, for the system itself was constructed to protect the interests of those against whom the claim must be brought.[90] In Wenger's words: "the blind spots line up with the power gaps."[91]

Recognition of the "moving frontiers" of injury and remedy in the legal system nonetheless provides the potential for the "master's tools" to dismantle the "master's house." As the capabilities and sensibilities of the international community change, it is possible they could accommodate an understanding of injury maintaining the causal chain between transatlantic enslavement and its contemporary legacies. Advocating consideration of the legal claim to reparations for historical enslavement may require modification of the existing, dominant legal understanding of causation in order to allow for reparations claims, to account for new statistical methods of connecting cause and effect, to recognize the possibility of collective suffering, or to acknowledge more remote harms.[92] This need not involve a change to the relevant legal frameworks but merely a reconsideration of causation in light of new understandings of the relationships between actions and outcomes.

[87] Marc Galanter, "The Dialectic of Injury and Remedy" (2010) 44 Loyola Los Angeles Law Review 1, 2.

[88] ibid 3–6.

[89] Mary Anne Francks, "Injury Inequality" in Anne Bloom (ed), *Injury and Injustice* (CUP 2018) 231.

[90] Kaimipono David Wenger, "The Unconscionable Impossibility of Reparations for Slavery; Or, Why the Master's Mules Will Never Dismantle the Master's House" in Bloom (n 89).

[91] ibid 9.

[92] See, for instance, Matsuda (n 72); Kaimipono David Wenger, "Causation and Attenuation in the Slavery Reparations Debate" (2006) 40 University of San Francisco Law Review 279.

Yet, possibility and probability are not synonymous, and the likelihood of such occurring is questionable—particularly if domestic judicial responses to legal claims are taken as an indicator of international reception.[93] What then is the value of determining that the harms of historical slavery are potentially classifiable as causally relevant injury in the legal context?

The value of a finding of the international wrongfulness of transatlantic enslavement and associated brutality, and the recognition of causal connections between this injustice and contemporary suffering, are not premised on the capacity of states to invoke responsibility or on particular reparatory obligations accruing. The characterization of conduct as wrongful has value in itself. The probability that courts will not find in favor of the survival of a sufficient causal chain linking historical injustices to contemporary suffering does not entirely obviate the value of the recognition that legal arguments are possible and perhaps plausible. Recognizing the contested nature of causation, and thus the definition of reparable legal injury, acknowledges both the existing biases of the legal system and the ways in which this has assisted, or been complicit in, the injustices in question. Given the significance of recognition and cognitive justice within the framework of reparatory justice, even this small step ought to be valued.

It is not only within judicial mechanisms that legal reasoning and the construction of causally connected suffering holds sway. Such conclusions may have social or political value beyond the confines of international legal thinking. As Wenger identifies:

> Because remedy and injury are mutually constitutive, people will to some extent define injury backward from the existence of a legal remedy. Under that definition, an injury is something that the legal system addresses. Thus, if there is no legal harm, then there was no foul to begin with. . . . When a society decides that an injury really needs to be compensated, it will generally find a way to provide restitution. . . . Ultimately, then, society makes policy choices about that exactly is too big to remedy.[94]

Identifying a relationship between historical injustice and contemporary suffering consistent with (or at least not contradicting) legal frameworks

[93] See for instance *Cato v United States* (n 85); *In Re African-American Slave Descendants Litigation* (n 82).

[94] Kaimipono David Wenger, "'Too Big to Remedy?': Rethinking Mass Restitution for Slavery and Jim Crow" (2010) 44 Loyola Los Angeles Law Review 177.

of causation may change prevailing presumptions concerning historical enslavement and provide a lever for extralegal action. Ultimately, the conceptualization of harms as causally connected, reparable consequences may open a door for states and other actors to make the political choice that such injuries ought to be remedied. The capacity for multimodal and symbolic awards responding to a broader range of harms expands the possibilities in recognizing causal connections between past and present. While time may influence the construction of causal relationships, this should not be presumed. "[Q]uibbles about contingencies" should not outweigh the demands of justice, and the lived experiences of those suffering should be placed at the center of consideration.[95]

[95] Janna Thompson, "Historical Injustice and Reparations: Justifying Claims of Descendants" in Ronald Salzberger and Mary Turck, *Reparations for Slavery: A Reader* (Rowman & Littlefield 2004) 248.

7

Reparatory Justice in Transition

Injustices demanding redress may fall outside the judicial paradigm, necessitating a more tailored approach that marries legal and moral justice with the peculiarities of the situation at hand. The instability of the legal territory governing the claim to reparations for historical enslavement, the priorities embedded in the construction of international law, and the limitations of judicial mechanisms indicate that a positive legal conclusion on the matter may be unlikely in the foreseeable future. Yet, simultaneously, impetus to reckon with past injustices continues to take hold. Private institutions are increasingly interrogating their histories to expose connections to enslavement, including undertaking reparatory measures.[1] A growing number of churches have begun to engage with their connections to the transatlantic system.[2] A range of political bodies, at all levels, have grappled with, and apologized for, their role in transatlantic enslavement.[3] Furthermore, the rise in memorialization and commemoration marks the upturn in attempts to reckon with past injustices and signals the demand for reparative action (although not uncontested).[4] Thus, taking no action to deal with the past is becoming

[1] Universities in particular are engaging in this process, setting up centers and institutes for the study of their histories, making the connections to enslavement public, adopting some forms of redress, and targeting the issues of race and inequality that are the legacies of enslavement. The Universities Studying Slavery Consortium, currently involving forty-six member institutions, is a testament to the rise in this movement—"Universities Studying Slavery" (*University of Virginia*) <slavery.virginia.edu/universities-studying-slavery/> accessed November 17, 2018.

[2] For instance, the Church of England in 2006 voted to apologize for its involvement in the transatlantic system—"Church Apologises for Slave Trade" *BBC News* (February 8, 2006) <news.bbc.co.uk/1/hi/uk/4694896.stm> accessed November 17, 2018.

[3] See generally Mark Gibney and others (eds), *The Age of Apology: Facing up to the Past* (University of Pennsylvania Press 2008).

[4] See, for instance, Alice Bellagamba, Sandra Greene, and Martin Klein (eds), *African Slaves: African Masters: Politics, Memory, Social Life* (Africa World Press 2017); Ana Lucia Araujo (ed), *Politics of Memory: Making Slavery Visible in the Public Space* (Routledge 2012); Ana Lucia Araujo, *Public Memory of Slavery: Victims and Perpetrators in the South Atlantic* (Cambria Press 2010); Elisa Bordin and Anna Saachi (eds), *Transatlantic Memories of Slavery: Reimagining the Past, Changing the Future* (Cambria Press 2015); Katie Donington, Ryan Hanley, and Jessica Moody (eds), *Britain's History and Memory of Transatlantic Slavery: Local Nuances of a "National Sin"* (Liverpool UP 2016).

Reparations for Slavery in International Law. Katarina Schwarz, Oxford University Press. © Oxford University Press 2022.
DOI: 10.1093/oso/9780197636398.003.0008

increasingly unpalatable, regardless of whether formalistic legal mechanisms accommodate claims.

In shifting beyond the boundaries of legality, transitional reparatory practices provide a framework for the consideration of processes that may or may not be legally required but for which there is a strong moral imperative. If the historical nature of wrongdoing presents a barrier to reparatory justice, experiences of transition may provide valuable guidance for the moral imperative to redress. If the scale of abuse makes repair incomprehensible, the practice of past processes engaging with widespread abuse may supply a roadmap for some degree of reconciliation. If the ambiguous legal grounding of the wrongdoing stymies attempts to achieve justice, states and other actors may follow in the footsteps of transitional reparatory justice to acknowledge the suffering of victims in a meaningful way.

Although transitional justice may not deliver on strict legal requirements or impose legal obligations on states responding to serious abuses of rights, it nonetheless offers guidance for a theory of reparatory justice. A desire to learn from past reparations practice and the outcomes these have precipitated demands consideration of transitional justice, for it is in this context that the majority of large-scale reparations processes have taken place, and it is through this lens they are most frequently considered. Therefore, this chapter considers the contribution the practice of redress in transition makes to the broader theory of reparatory justice articulated in chapter 4. It situates the claim to reparations for historical enslavement within the context of the *maangamizi*, recognizing the centrality of enslavement in the development of modern international law, and the impact of this upon the legitimacy of the international legal system. Thus, the international legal system itself is understood as transitional.

7.1. Framing transitional justice

Transitional justice is a field of study largely shaped by the context in which it takes place—seeking to uncover the particular requirements of justice arising in situations of transition.[5] Despite this reliance on conditions to shape the discipline, the exact meaning of transition has been problematized since its

[5] See generally Ruti Teitel, *Transitional Justice* (rev edn, OUP 2002); Christine Bell, Colm Campbell, and Fionnuala Ní Aoláin, "Justice Discourses in Transition" (2004) 13(3) Social and Legal Studies 305; International Center for Transitional Justice, "What is Transitional Justice?" (International Center for Transitional Justice 2017) <www.ictj.org/about/transitional-justice> accessed September 28, 2017.

inception; the limitations and horizons of what qualifies as "transitional" have always been elusive and contested.[6] While paradigmatic transition moves from violent conflict toward peace and democracy, the relationship between conflict and resolution is fluid and changes over time, a dynamic increasingly recognized in transitional justice scholarship.[7]

In perhaps the first comprehensive formulation of transitional justice, Neil Kritz in 1995 articulated a conception of justice targeted toward states that had ousted brutal, repressive regimes and subsequently had to cope with the legacies of their predecessors' abuse.[8] The context and primary objective of transitional justice at this time were defined in the subtitle of his three-volume series: emerging democracies reckoning with former regimes. This conception of transition represents the paradigm against which other scenarios are assessed. Establishing sufficient similarity assures the application of transitional justice theories, while deviating too far from the prototypical case leads to the conclusion that a situation can no longer be considered transitional.

Despite this initially narrow scope, the development of the field demonstrated increasing recognition of the fluid boundaries of transitional justice, adaptation over time, and less selective application of transitional justice theories.[9] In 2003, Ruti Teitel characterized transitional justice as "the conception of justice associated with periods of political change, characterized by legal responses to confront the wrongdoings of repressive predecessor regimes."[10] Prima facie, Teitel requires the same kind of regime change demanded by Kritz. However, it is the notion of radical political transformation, rather than replacement, which serves as the threshold for Teitel's transition—transformation from conflict, authoritarian rule, or significant state repression in a "liberalizing direction."[11] This formulation allows for the

[6] See Bronwyn Leebaw, "The Irreconcilable Goals of Transitional Justice" (2008) 30(1) Human Rights Quarterly 101.

[7] On paradigmatic transition, see Bell, Campbell, and Ní Aoláin (n 5) 310. See also Neil Kritz (ed), *Transitional Justice: How Emerging Democracies Reckon with Former Regimes*, vol 1 (United States Institute of Peace Press 1995). On evolution, see James Gallen, "Jesus Wept: The Roman Catholic Church, Child Sexual Abuse and Transitional Justice" (2016) 10 International Journal of Transitional Justice 332; Stephen Winter, "Towards a Unified Theory of Transitional Justice" (2013) 7(2) International Journal of Transitional Justice 224; Fionnuala Ní Aoláin and Colm Campbell, "The Paradox of Transition in Conflicted Democracies" (2005) 27 Human Rights Quarterly 172.

[8] Kritz (n 7).

[9] Bell, Campbell, and Ní Aoláin (n 5) 310.

[10] Ruti Teitel, "Transitional Justice Genealogy" (2003) 16 Harvard Human Rights Journal 69.

[11] Teitel, *Transitional Justice* (n 5).

application of still evolving theories of transitional justice in a wider range of circumstances.

Echoing Teitel's broader definition, then UN Secretary General Kofi Annan in 2004 asserted the United Nations' normative conception of transitional justice as:

> the full range of processes and mechanisms associated with a society's attempts to come to terms with a legacy of large-scale past abuses, in order to ensure accountability, serve justice and achieve reconciliation.[12]

Like an echo, this understanding of transition is a somewhat altered representation of the prevailing understandings of the time, incorporating the objectives of accountability, justice, and reconciliation (with stability and democracy unarticulated but presumed). Annan's scale argument finds further elaboration in the observations of Pablo de Greiff, previous UN Special Rapporteur on the promotion of truth, justice, reparation and guarantees of non-recurrence, although de Greiff ties this to the extent of change underway, rather than the scale of abuses. Like Teitel, de Greiff relies on the idea of a shift in the liberal or democratizing direction but eschews prescription in relation to prior context. Thus, de Greiff's transition is not premised upon a shift from conflict or authoritarianism; a significant shift in a liberalizing or democratizing direction may itself constitute transition.[13]

Basing theories on a normative shift rather than on specificities of the prior regime allows for the expansion of transitional justice into previously excluded territory, namely the application of transitional justice in so-called settled democracies.[14] Such reasoning displaces the notion that established democracies are sites of "nontransition" and acknowledges the possibility of radical normative and political metanoia in the legitimating regime of democratic states.[15] An excessive focus on paradigmatic transitions overlooks the potential for grave abuses in situations where liberal democratic norms

[12] UNSC, "Report of the Secretary-General on the Rule of Law and Transitional Justice in Conflict and Post-Conflict Societies" (2004) UN Doc S/2004/616 [8].

[13] Pablo de Greiff, "A Normative Conception of Transitional Justice" (2010) 50(3) Politorbis 17.

[14] King and Page, for instance, apply transitional justice theory to the consideration of black reparations in the American domestic context—Desmond King and Jennifer Page, "Towards Transitional Justice? Black Reparations and the End of Mass Incarceration" (2018) 41 Ethnic and Racial Studies 739. See also (n 7): Gallen; Winter; Ní Aoláin and Campbell.

[15] Winter (n 7).

and accountability mechanisms are established.[16] Stephen Winter thus contends that transitional justice frameworks ought to be applied in such circumstances, as "grievous wrongdoing by a state burdens its legitimacy" and "transitional justice works to resolve that burden" regardless of whether the wrongdoing culminates in or necessitates complete transformation of systems of government.[17] This expansion remains consistent with the fundamental drive of transitional justice. Despite varying definitions, "all view transitional justice as the attempt to deal with past violence in societies undergoing or attempting some form of political transition."[18]

Although the application of transitional justice in settled states may deviate from the paradigm, it nonetheless relies on the same kind of transformation both Teitel and de Greiff's formulations highlight: "a normative shift in the principles underlying and legitimating the exercise of state power."[19] The end goal in both contexts is stable democracy, while the starting point is a state recovering from past violence.[20] Yet, despite this parity, conflicted democracies (as Ní Aoláin and Campbell title these atypical transitional states) may pose additional challenges to those advocating reparations and other transitional measures. The international human rights system may have "blind spots" (or at least a greater margin of appreciation) for violations occurring in established democracies, the appearance of the rule of law may mask the extent of state dysfunction, and legal and political institutions may be better able to resist reform or responsibility because of their democratic credentials.[21] Although these realities may decrease impetus for the enactment of transitional measures, they also underscore the necessity of such. Where accountability mechanisms suffer from system malfunction, democratic principles are severely undermined, and the need for transitional reparatory justice becomes more acute.

The expansion of transitional justice beyond the original paradigm and the development of an organizing principle based upon a shift toward more

[16] Patricia Lundy and Mark McGovern, "The Role of Community in Participatory Transitional Justice" in Kieran McEvoy and Lorna McGregor (eds), *Transitional Justice from Below: Grassroots Activism and the Struggle for Change* (Hart Publishing 2008) 101.

[17] Winter (n 7) 226.

[18] Christine Bell, "Transitional Justice, Interdisciplinarity and the State of the 'Field' or 'Non-Field'" (2009) 3 International Journal of Transitional Justice 5, 7.

[19] Teitel, *Transitional Justice* (n 5) 213.

[20] Ní Aoláin and Campbell (n 7) 174; Bell, "Transitional Justice, Interdisciplinarity and the State of the 'Field' or 'Non-Field'" (n 18) 7.

[21] Fionnuala Ni Aoláin, "The Emergence of Diversity: Differences in Human Rights Jurisprudence" (1995) 19 Fordham International Law Journal 101; Ní Aoláin and Campbell (n 7) 176, 189.

stable and democratic governance not only allow for its application in settled democracies but also allow for a wider chronology of transition. A state might uncontroversially be characterized as transitional for a matter of years while reckoning with the atrocities of a civil war or significant internal conflict, but what about states decades or even centuries removed from the primary atrocities giving rise to the potential transitional period? Given that transition is not defined by a specific set of events or contexts, but rather by the scale of abuses and the nature of necessary transformation, time alone is insufficient to satisfy the requirements of transition. Scholars advocate and accept the relevance of transitional justice discourse in considering historical abuses—including the claims of indigenous peoples for wrongful appropriation of land, genocide, and other harms associated with settler colonialism.[22] Where the legacies of these injustices persist, and failures in recognition and accountability continue to fuel instability and undermine democracy, transition remains a prima facie imperative.[23]

The expansion of the boundaries of transitional justice both in terms of scope and time, and the permeability of definitional borders, makes it vulnerable to the criticism that there is no meaningful distinction between transitional justice and ordinary justice.[24] Eric Posner and Adrian Vermuele suggest that the so-called "dilemmas of transitional justice" conceived in this broader sense are in fact simple but more extreme manifestations of the quandaries of all criminal justice systems, and thus that transitional justice does not have a distinct identity.[25] However, ideas of scale and a particular kind of transformation nonetheless provide a meaningful basis for differentiation. The nature, objectives, and characteristics of reparations in transition deviate from the standard legal frameworks, in part because they serve a broader range of functions not required in situations of nontransition and in part because they do so within a particular climate of large-scale abuse and

[22] See Rosemary Nagy, "The Scope and Bounds of Transitional Justice and the Canadian Truth and Reconciliation Commission" (2013) 7 International Journal of Transitional Justice 52; Jeff Corntassel and Cindy Holder, "Who's Sorry Now? Government Apologies, Truth Commissions, and Indigenous Self-Determination in Australia, Canada, Guatemala and Peru" (2008) 9 Human Rights Review 465.

[23] For transitional reparations programs enabling claims across multiple generations, see, for instance, the Czech Republic, Brazil, and Argentina, enabling reparations awards up to fourth kin. Law on Extrajudicial Rehabilitation (Large Restitution Law) 1991 (Czech and Slovak Federal Republic); Ignacio Cano and Patrícia Salvão Ferreira, "The Reparations Program in Brazil" in Pablo de Greiff (ed), *The Handbook of Reparations* (OUP 2006) 114; José María Guembe, "Economic Reparations for Grave Human Rights Violations: The Argentinean Experience" in de Greiff, ibid 36.

[24] Eric Posner and Adrian Vermuele, "Transitional Justice as Ordinary Justice" (2004) 117 Harvard Law Review 761.

[25] ibid.

atrocity. If responsiveness is truly a central feature of transitional justice, then it would be imprudent to overlook the significance of the context in shaping transitional justice.[26]

This narrative of transition, based on the specific context, encompassing a range of different circumstances, and premised on the presumption that mass atrocities demands a particular kind of transformation, speaks to the case for reparations for transatlantic enslavement in two key ways. First, it provides an alternative framework for achieving justice internally, where victim communities seek justice against the states in which they live. The application of transitional justice in "settled" democracies that nonetheless have histories of enslavement within their borders follows the pathways explored by Winter, Ní Aoláin, and Campbell.[27] Second, the expanded chronology of transition enables consideration of a broader range of historical cases.[28] Beyond this relatively established application of transitional justice within states, this understanding of the transitional imperative also supports a more novel approach.

For centuries, the international legal system systematically excluded African and indigenous peoples, supporting and legitimizing the imposition of enslavement, exploitation, and colonization.[29] European colonial and enslaver states wrought significant violence against those deemed "uncivilized," marginalizing them from an international system that purported to encompass all of humanity. Although a gradual process of emancipation, decolonization, and representation developed in the twentieth century, this did not substantially break from the past or reckon with injustices as transition demands.[30] Substantial attempts to reckon with this history have remained, for the most part, marginal. Thus, theories designed to grapple with officially mandated injustices on a large scale may be applied on the global level for analogous injustice. In other words, the international legal system as a whole may be characterized as transitional. For this reason, the following analysis takes both individual states and the international community as transitional

[26] On the centrality of responsiveness in transitional justice, see de Greiff, *The Handbook of Reparations* (n 23); Pamina Firchow and Roger Mac Ginty, "Reparations and Peacebuilding: Issues and Controversies" (2013) 14(3) Human Rights Review 231, 235.

[27] See (n 7).

[28] See (n 22).

[29] See chapter 2.

[30] On the need for a break from the past, see Bronwyn Leebaw, *Judging State-Sponsored Violence, Imagining Political Change* (CUP 2011).

units of measurement, and the reparations frameworks provided may be applied at both the national and international level.

7.2. The nature of reparatory justice in transition

Reparations are one constituent element of a broader selection of reforms associated with transitional justice processes and are now recognized as a normative part of transitional justice.[31] Reparations in international law strike a balance between the significance of retrospective and prospective objectives. With the predominance of the corrective paradigm, retrospectivity and the return to equality are favored over transformation.[32] Private law achieves a similar equilibrium, ruled by principles of restitution, rather than foregrounding future relations. Transitional justice, on the other hand, tips the scales toward prospectivity by centering, and in many cases prioritizing, the achievement of peace and democracy over corrective justice.[33] Dealing with the past in transition thus consists of two dimensions: undoing the past and accounting for the past.[34]

The efficacy of transitional justice processes is measured by their ability to serve the multiple interests of transition—interests that go beyond corrective justice to achieve broader peace, democracy, reconciliation, and transformation. Affirming this broader social and political function, de Greiff suggests, "transitional justice measures work—to the extent that they do—only in virtue of their capacity for norm-affirmation."[35] Like other mechanisms adopted in the transitional context, reparations are employed to serve the transitional agenda. That is, reparations are undertaken and constructed to

[31] Luke Moffett, "Reparations for Guilty Victims: Navigating Complex Identities of Victim-Perpetrators in Reparation Mechanisms" (2016) 10 International Journal of Transitional Justice 146, 166. See also Rama Mani, "Reparations as a Component of Transitional Justice: Pursuing 'Reparative Justice' in the Aftermath of Violent Conflict" in Koen de Feyter and others (eds), *Out of the Ashes: Reparation for Victims of Gross and Systematic Human Rights Violations* (Intersentia 2005) 79.

[32] See chapter 4.

[33] de Greiff highlights the importance of contributing to the "reconstitution or the constitution of a new political community" through measures designed to remedy past violations and prevent future victimization. Pablo de Greiff, "Justice and Reparations" in de Greiff, *The Handbook of Reparations* (n 23) 454. Teitel likewise highlights the "multiple purposes" of transitional reparatory practices, labeling them "backward-looking, in repairing victims of past state wrongdoing, but also forward-looking, in advancing the purposes of peace and reconciliation in the transition." Teitel, *Transitional Justice* (n 5) 127.

[34] See Bell, Campbell, and Ní Aoláin (n 5) 314.

[35] de Greiff, "A Normative Conception" (n 13) 22.

assist in establishing or improving democracy and ensuring a stable, peaceful state. Thus, the very objectives of reparations are altered by their implantation in transitional justice contexts. Pamina Firchow and Roger Mac Ginty evidence this shift by framing the goals of effective reparations in transition as providing structural and restorative elements to "facilitate the process of reconciliation and the consolidation of peace," as well as being important in terms of direct impact upon victims—goals not inherent to reparations as a broader category of redress measures but fundamental to the transitional project.[36]

In early transitional justice processes, consideration of reparations was overshadowed by discussions of amnesty and reconciliation. The South African case is a paradigm example of reparations following on the heels of alternative processes, manifesting the gradual displacement of the forward-looking approach with a bifurcated perspective acknowledging and addressing the past as well as tending to the future. Excepting the Interim Constitution, none of the documents produced during negotiations (including the new democratic constitution) made even passing reference to reparations.[37] It was not until the passing of the Promotion of National Unity and Reconciliation Act creating the Truth and Reconciliation Commission that reparation and rehabilitation were finally recognized as one of three primary concerns.[38] Yet, despite the supposed centrality of these issues, the recommendations of the Committee on Reparations and Rehabilitation submitted in the Truth and Reconciliation Commission's 1998 report were not met by policy until 2003 when the government enacted a reduced version of the committee's proposal.[39] Reparations were, at this time, coming to the fore as a central measure in situations of democratic transition.[40] Despite the initial prioritization of truth processes, most victims appearing before the Truth and Reconciliation Commission indicated that money or compensation was their primary need and first priority, with investigations into abuses ranking second.[41] Reparations and rehabilitation, and truth processes alone,

[36] Firchow and Mac Ginty (n 26) 234. This further displaces Posner and Vermuele's critique of transitional justice as "ordinary justice"—n 24.

[37] Christopher J Colvin, "Overview of the Reparations Program in South Africa" in de Greiff, *The Handbook of Reparations* (n 23).

[38] Promotion of National Unity and Reconciliation Act (No 34 of 1995) (South Africa).

[39] Colvin (n 37).

[40] See Aurélien Pradier, Maxine Rubin, and Hugo van der Merwe, "Between Transitional Justice and Politics: Reparations in South Africa" (2018) 25 South African Journal of International Affairs 301.

[41] Colvin (n 37) 191.

were necessary in order to counterbalance amnesties as well as being a prerequisite for reconciliation.[42]

In defining reparations, many authors within the transitional justice field consider only measures of compensation for victims, separate to trials, truth commissions, and other measures that might be adopted in transition.[43] However, bearing in mind the wider definition of reparations espoused in international law discussed in chapter 5, the following analysis favors the formulation of mechanisms offered by Luke Moffett, who identifies courts, truth commissions, reparation programs, and interstate procedures as key reparatory measures in transitional settings.[44] Thus, this chapter considers both the reparations programs adopted to provide direct benefits to victims of abuses and/or victim communities and additional measures to the extent that these alternative processes form an element of reparatory justice as conceived in chapter 4.

7.3. The objectives of reparations in transition

The importance of responsiveness in transitional reparations programs belies the attempt to make sweeping generalizations about the requirements of these measures.[45] It is nonetheless possible to identify a series of objectives that generally shape transitional reparations programs. These objectives contribute to the broader transitional justice agenda of promoting peace and democracy, serving all three of Rama Mani's "dimensions of justice in transition"—legal justice, rectificatory justice, and distributive justice—to varying degrees.[46] Yet, as goals in their own right, they are not exclusively concerned with the macro-objectives of transition, but instead build an understanding of reparatory justice in transition that contributes to the broader scheme of

[42] Truth and Reconciliation Commission of South Africa, *Final Report*, vol 5 (Truth and Reconciliation Commission 1998) 170.

[43] See for instance de Greiff, *The Handbook of Reparations* (n 23); Firchow and Mac Ginty (n 26) 235.

[44] Luke Moffett, "Transitional Justice and Reparations: Remedying the Past?" in Cheryl Lawther, Luke Moffett, and Dov Jacobs (eds), *Research Handbook in Transitional Justice* (Edward Elgar Publishing 2017) 35.

[45] Richard Falk, "Reparations, International Law and Global Justice: A New Frontier" in de Greiff, *The Handbook of Reparations* (n 23).

[46] On this account, legal justice is concerned with the restoration of the rule of law; rectificatory justice addresses specific abuses committed against individuals; and distributive justice grapples with structural and systematic inequalities. Rama Mani, *Beyond Retribution: Seeking Justice in the Shadows of War* (Polity Press 2002).

transitional justice itself. These objectives mimic international and private legal frameworks in many ways while also diverging in some key respects. Thus, it is not sufficient to conflate such measures with judicial reparatory justice.

This section posits six primary objectives drawn from transitional justice scholarship dealing with reparations:

(a) Responding to the suffering of victims of specific abuses of rights;
(b) Preventing future marginalization or abuse of victimized communities;
(c) Disrupting cycles of violence that might transform victims into perpetrators;
(d) Reconciling victims with perpetrators;
(e) Reconciling victims with society at large; and
(f) Sending a message to society as a whole about the new regime.

These objectives, though not exhaustive, frame the meaning and function of reparatory justice in transition.

Wendy Orr suggests that the understanding of reparations initially adopted by the Committee on Reparations and Rehabilitation in South Africa was drawn from the common international definitions of reparations and considered in terms of the "5 R's: redress, restitution, rehabilitation, restoration of dignity, and reassurance of non-recurrence."[47] Although these objectives are central to the understanding of reparations both in international law and in transition, they fail to fully encapsulate the multifaceted aims of reparatory justice in transition more generally. This analysis seeks to address not only the victim centricity of reparations as manifested in the "5 R's" but also their role in relation to perpetrators and society at large, encompassing both their backward- and forward-facing dimensions. Thus, the following analysis moves from the more traditional reparatory objectives considered in chapter 4 to the transitional, expanding the theory of reparatory justice accordingly.

[47] Wendy Orr, "Reparations Delayed is Healing Retarded" in Charles Villa-Vicencio and Wilhelm Verwoerd (eds), *Looking Back, Reaching Forward: Reflections on the Truth and Reconciliation Commission of South Africa* (University of Capetown Press 2000) 240–41.

7.3.1. Responding to wrongful suffering

Despite being shaped by context and divergent objectives, reparations in transitional justice are still fundamentally defined by wrongdoing—that is, the effort to redress specific abuses of rights. The essence of this objective is twofold: first, reparations are victim-centric measures targeted toward victims of wrongdoing; and second, they respond to harms associated with that wrongdoing.[48] Thus reparations, even in transition, represent an adherence to notions of corrective justice through the separation of victims of specific wrongdoing from those suffering for other reasons.

While distributive justice may have a place in transitioning states, such measures remain severed from those mechanisms tailored toward redress. This is consistent with the place of corrective justice, responsibility, and violation in international legal reparations frameworks.[49] However, reparations programs in transitional justice are abstracted from the victim-perpetrator relationship that forms the premise of redress in international law in several ways. Transitional reparations may therefore be viewed as existing along a spectrum within which corrective justice bears more or less relevance depending on the context of the abuses. It is the wrongdoing committed against victims and concomitant suffering (rather than the victim-perpetrator relationship) that remains constant, and thus ought to be seen as the more universal reparatory objective in situations of transition.

Although the line between reparations and assistance in transitional justice is often blurred in practice, recognizing the distinction is nonetheless crucial to understand their purposes and functions. This divergence is consistently reaffirmed in scholarship and practice.[50] While the rights-based approach of reparations is often framed as indifferent to suffering and need, this ought to be caveated by recognizing that such measures may be indifferent to suffering in an absolute sense but are responsive to the harms and needs connected to wrongdoing.[51] Moreover, distributive justice programs providing aid and support on the basis of need are not precluded by the

[48] Moffett's definition frames this dual focus in labeling reparations as victim-centered measures targeted toward redressing harms caused to victims of wrongdoing. Luke Moffett, "Transitional Justice and Reparations" (n 44) 1.

[49] See sections 4.2 and 4.3.

[50] Peter Dixon, "Reparations, Assistance and the Experience of Justice: Lessons from Colombia and the Democratic Republic of the Congo" (2015) 10 International Journal of Transitional Justice 88.

[51] Critiquing the rights-based approach, see Emily Camins, "Needs or Rights? Exploring the Limitations of Individual Reparations for Violations of International Humanitarian Law" (2016) 10 International Journal of Transitional Justice 126, 140.

existence of reparations programs, nor are they undermined by such. Rather, reparations respond to the specific moral dimension and unique status of suffering caused by wrongdoing as opposed to that resulting from more generalized situational factors.[52]

Although reparations in international law generally demand full and proportionate redress for all violations, reparations programs in transitional states often define eligibility requirements on the basis of certain abuses of rights, thus providing only partial recognition of wrongdoing and victimization.[53] In Argentina, the process of instituting, developing, and amending reparations programs that incrementally addressed different abuses without ever dealing with all violations is indicative of both the nature and flaws of this process. Between 1986 and 2004, eligibility requirements delimiting abuses targeted by reparations, and to whom they were directed, changed at least five times.[54] Each successive expansion improved the comprehensiveness of reparations but never encompassed the full universe of beneficiaries—a reality not unique to the Argentinean experience. The eligibility limits imposed on transitional mechanisms may undermine its efficacy with regard to the requirements of reparatory justice. However, the evolution of measures over time demonstrate the capacity of transitional reparations to respond to the context in which redress is sought and expand to redress lacunae in ways that judicial mechanisms may not.

Not only is wrong responsiveness compromised where eligibility is built only upon selected violations but the corrective justice paradigm is also complicated by the transitional context. While some situations may be characterized by the discrete victim-perpetrator relationships traditionally remedied by reparations, more often wrongdoing is complex, responsibility is dispersed, and public/private distinctions begin to collapse. In particular, the extent of state complicity in abuses, and subsequently the degree to which they monopolize reparations processes, can muddy the waters of a clean definition of the relationships that must be corrected. Thus, transitional countries might adopt reparations programs funded and administered entirely by the state, rather than constructed within a binary victim-perpetrator relationship and administered by courts.[55] In all such cases, the state bears

[52] See Dixon (n 50).

[53] The need for compromise in the scope of reparations, see sections 7.4.5 and 7.4.6.

[54] See Guembe (n 23) 30.

[55] South Africa, Chile, and Argentina are examples of this practice. See Colvin (n 37); Elizabeth Lira, "The Reparations Policy for Human Rights Violations in Chile" in de Greiff, *The Handbook of Reparations* (n 23); Guembe (n 23).

some degree of responsibility for the wrongdoing. However, there may also be individual perpetrators responsible for decisions leading to and enacting the violations.[56] This framework enables redress in a broader range of circumstances involving third-party contributions and interventions and, thus, may more readily capture cases of widespread historical abuse with greater complexity in the causal chains.

7.3.2. Combatting marginalization

Because transitional justice reparations cover widely varying scenarios, they cannot be defined purely in terms of corrective justice (righting a discrete relationship between victim and perpetrator). Instead, reparations in transition may be targeted toward the victims to restore their status in a more general sense—that is, to return them to a position of equality vis-à-vis society as a whole. As Jaime Malamud-Goti and Lucas Grosman highlight:

> in the context of a transitional democracy, the specific goal of compensation to victims of human rights abuses is to restore their dignity and to reintegrate them into society as equal citizens.[57]

The restoration of the dignity of victims in this context—characterized by complex and ambiguous abuses—prioritizes repairing victims as individuals and citizens over the correction of a binary relationship between victim and perpetrator.

Widespread abuses are neither merely the result of a specific set of acts contravening the rights of a group of individuals nor do they simply manifest the ill intentions of a limited number of perpetrators.[58] Rather, these violations frequently reflect wider prevailing conditions within a state caused or enabled by structures of marginalization and exclusion.[59] Although

[56] On complex violations, see South Africa, Truth and Reconciliation Commission (n 42) 170. cf abuses entirely committed by the state in the case of Japanese American internment—see Eric Yamamoto, *Race, Rights and Reparation: Law and Japanese American Internment* (Wolters Kluwer Law & Business 2013).

[57] Jaime E Malamud-Goti and Lucas Sebastián Grosman, "Reparations and Civil Litigation: Compensation for Human Rights Violations in Transitional Democracies" in de Greiff, *The Handbook of Reparations* (n 23) 541.

[58] See, for instance, Lauren Marie Balasco, "Reparative Development: Re-Conceptualising Reparations in Transitional Justice Processes" (2017) 17(1) Conflict, Security and Development 1.

[59] Paul Farmer, for instance, frames grave violations of human rights as "symptoms of deeper pathologies of power and are linked intimately to the social conditions that so often determine who

judicial redress may evidence elements of a transformational objective, the prevailing philosophy is one of return—putting victims back in the position that they were in prior to the wrongdoing.[60] With the introduction of peace building and democracy building as broader objectives to which reparations contribute within the transitional context, transformation becomes a much more significant aspect of reparatory justice.[61] In this context, reparations may be a vehicle for transformation through the subversion of preexisting structural inequalities, addressing past injustice and working to prevent repetition through the recognition of victims as human beings and rights bearers.[62] Thus, transitional reparatory justice may prioritize the symbolic, continuing harms of widespread historical abuses that contribute to structural inequalities in a manner excluded from legal considerations.

Constructing "fair, nondiscriminatory redress" that responds to victims' experience "as far as possible" is an important backward-looking dimension of reparations programs targeted toward ensuring appropriate and proportional responses to abuses.[63] By addressing the marginalization lying at the root of the atrocities, reparations deal with an important dimension of the abuse itself and take a more nuanced approach to categorizing wrongdoing.[64] This simultaneously reinforces the transformative dimension of reparatory justice, looking forward to prevent atrocity recidivism and ensure stability. Thus, combating marginalization can be seen as both transformative and traditionally reparatory, serving the dual aims of transition by combating the disunity that arises from inequality and marginalization and by ensuring the inclusion of previously excluded communities in the society of the state and political processes.

Combating and preventing marginalization creates the preconditions for civic involvement of citizens, contributing to the consolidation of an

will suffer abuse and who will be shielded from harm." Paul Farmer, *Pathologies of Power: Health, Human Rights and the New War on the Poor* (University of California Press 2003) 7.

[60] Transformative justice in international legal reparations is considered in section 4.2.3.

[61] See for instance Uprimny Yepes who articulates a transformative reparatory justice process that overcomes the limits of corrective justice by advocating the deepening of democracy through reparations. Rodrigo Uprimny Yepes, *Between Corrective Justice and Distributive Justice: Reparations of Human Rights Violations in Times of Transition* (Utrecht University 2009) 5.

[62] Ruth Rubin-Marín, "The Gender of Reparations in Transitional Societies" in Ruth Rubin-Marín (ed), *The Gender of Reparations: Unsettling Sexual Hierarchies while Redressing Human Rights Violations* (CUP 2009) 66.

[63] ibid 101.

[64] See UNSC, "The Rule of Law and Transitional Justice in Conflict and Post-Conflict Societies: Report of the Secretary-General" (2004) UN Doc S/2004/616, 8.

inclusive democratic regime.[65] By recognizing the entitlement to a remedy rather than merely some form of eligibility for support, victims' status as citizens is affirmed, promoting social solidarity and inclusion as features of the new political community.[66] In redressing specific instances of wrongdoing, reparations are framed as rights rather than assistance, thus affirming the equality and dignity of citizens vis-à-vis the rest of the society. Moreover, the significance of the majority in power "standing by" marginalized communities post-atrocity can have reconstructive force, building trust within the political community. Absent reparatory measures, reconstruction in this sense may be hindered, particularly where abuses center on dehumanization and denial of citizenship as in the case of transatlantic enslavement.[67] As de Greiff argues, the political perspective can construct citizenship through social solidarity, civil trust, and recognition.[68]

Despite their capacity for transformation, reparations should not be viewed as the primary vehicle for social transformation, nor should this objective drive the construction of reparations programs. Moffett warns against a preoccupation with transformation when formulating reparations programs, concluding that systematic reform requires other measures and mechanisms—for instance, educational and employment law reform.[69] To over-state the transformational potential of reparations is to detract from the impetus for broader systemic change beyond the group of victims eligible for reparatory redress. Moreover, it might also degrade the reparatory objective of such programs, which focus on repairing and recognizing victims as "human beings, whose fundamental rights have been violated."[70]

The transformational dimension of reparations in transition must be recognized, without treating reparatory and distributive justice as synonymous. Reparations provide a foundation for distributive justice policies and programs by mediating the "repair of victims and communities,

[65] Rubin-Marín (n 62) 66.

[66] Moffett, "Transitional Justice and Reparations" (n 44) 7.

[67] Reparations advocates stress the continued marginalization of people of African descent as central to reparations claims. See sections 1.6 and 6.5.

[68] de Greiff, "Justice and Reparations" (n 33).

[69] Moffett, "Transitional Justice and Reparations" (n 44) 9.

[70] CVR Final Report, cited and translated in Lisa Magarrell, "Reparations for Massive or Widespread Human Rights Violations: Sorting Out Claims for Reparations and Social Justice" (2003) 22 Windsor Yearbook of Access to Justice 85, 95.

past and present," redressing past violence that cannot be entirely severed from broader marginalization, but which also cannot represent the totality of exclusion.[71] While "the transformation of social relations" may be a "central objective of building peace," it should not be considered the guiding aim of reparatory justice processes, even in the context of transition.[72] However, combating forms of marginalization intimately connected to the abuses—unlike transformation in general—is critical in constructing reparatory justice that grapples with the specific harms of the wrongdoing and guaranteeing non-recurrence.

7.3.3. Disrupting cycles of violence

Pablo de Greiff connects transformation both to the prevention of future marginalization and to the advertence of cycles of violence.[73] While combating marginalization serves to ensure victims are not re-victimized in the future and disrupts patterns of violence recidivism, another cycle of violence can arise whereby past victims become future perpetrators. The often repeated aphorism "violence begets violence" can become a reality in situations of widespread atrocity and complex conflict; old wounds left untreated may heal in time but may also fester into new grievances used to justify the continuation or resurgence of violence.[74] Recognition, acknowledgment, and other measures to disrupt the underlying structures that contributed to the violence are crucial in the attempt to interrupt cycles of violence, whereas continued polarization sparks disunity and increases the risk of future conflict.[75] As measures capable of combating marginalization, prioritizing recognition and acknowledgment, reparations may serve, in part, to disturb these processes of violent retaliation.

[71] Teitel, *Transitional Justice* (n 5) 119–20.

[72] Andries Odendaal, "An Architecture for Building Peace at the Local Level: A Comparative Study of Local Peace Committees" (United Nations Development Programme 2010) 4.

[73] Pablo de Greiff, "Articulating the Links between Transitional Justice and Development: Justice and Social Integration" in Pablo de Greiff and Roger Duthie (eds), *Transitional Justice and Development: Making Connections* (Social Science Research Council 2009) 29.

[74] Moffett, "Reparations for Guilty Victims" (n 31) 167.

[75] Work Group of the International Work Group on Death, Dying and Bereavement, "Breaking Cycles of Violence" (2005) 29 Death Studies 585.

7.3.4. Reconciling victims and perpetrators

Particularly in situations where victims and perpetrators remain living in close proximity, interpersonal reconciliation for victims and their families is often vital to transition.[76] Without reconciliation, communities are far more likely to revert to situations of abuse, conflict, and instability. However, without some form of reparatory or restitutionary justice, efforts targeted toward reconciliation, including truth commissions and apologies, are unlikely to be successful.[77] Andrew Rigby labels such measures, offered alone, "cheap reconciliation" wherein the victim is expected to reconcile with their losses without the foundations of a sustainable settlement between the parties.[78] Reparations, on the other hand, enrich reconciliatory activities, ensuring that suffering and victimization are not only recognized but redressed.

Forgiveness processes alone may perpetuate existing power imbalances that led or contributed to violence, as it is often the state that determines whether such measures are adopted and on what terms.[79] Kanien'kehaka scholar Taiaiake Alfred highlights the potential for these mechanisms to overwrite a history of unaddressed wrongdoing in relation to indigenous peoples:

> The logic of reconciliation as justice is clear: without massive restitution, including land, financial transfers and other forms of assistance to compensate for past harms and continuing injustices committed against our peoples, reconciliation would permanently enshrine colonial injustices and is itself a further injustice.[80]

Where truth and apology mechanisms are set up to neutralize historical abuses, they not only neglect an opportunity to transform relationships between victims, perpetrators, and society but also fail victims by detracting from the impetus for other responses.[81] Thus, the restoration of the dignity

[76] See, for instance, the example of Rwanda, Daniel Bar-Tal and others, "A Sense of Self-Perceived Collective Victimhood in Intractable Conflicts" (2009) 91(874) International Review of the Red Cross 229.

[77] See Moffett, "Reparations for Guilty Victims" (n 31) 166.

[78] Andrew Rigby, *Justice and Reconciliation: After the Violence* (Lynne Rienbner Publishers 2001) 142.

[79] Mark Gibney and Erik Roxstrom, "The Status of State Apologies" (2001) 23 Human Rights Quarterly 911, 935.

[80] Taiaiake Alfred, *Wasáse: Indigenous Pathways of Action and Freedom* (Broadview Press Ltd 2005) 152.

[81] See Corntassel and Holder (n 22).

of victims and reaffirmation of their status as rights bearers may require a more complex understanding of the form of "citizenship" that ought to be advanced by reparatory measures founded on procedural justice principles.[82]

A positive process of collaborative reparations building is required to ensure reconciliation. Engagement with victims in reparations processes is vital to ensure conflicts of meaning and representation do not replace original divides.[83] Failures of acknowledgment and a lack of responsiveness to victim and survivor perspectives in particular may substantially hinder reconciliation. Where states fail to meaningfully engage with victims and construct reparations in such a way as to legitimize or sanitize abuses, victims are unlikely to accept them as measures of justice and a foundation for moving forward. For the *Madres de Plaza de Mayo* in Argentina and surviving victims of Japanese sexual enslavement during World War II, such failures precipitated the rejection of reparations by victims and survivors.[84] Although it is important that reparations are not premised on reconciliation, they can be a prerequisite to it. In this way, legitimate grievances are dealt with, closing off potential avenues for future conflict and providing for more peaceful coexistence of victims and perpetrators.

7.3.5. Reconciling victims and society

In transitional contexts, the broader objectives of peace, stability, and the inculcation of democracy require reconciliation not only within the direct victim-perpetrator relationship but also between victims as persecuted groups and society as a whole. This is evidenced in "ex-slave states," wherein racial tensions continue to fuel social and cultural conflicts. Reparations can assist in serving this largely political function by reaffirming the dignity and equal status of victims vis-à-vis mainstream society, recognizing their suffering as deserving of response and rebuilding the civic trust of victims.[85] The division and marginalization of victims severs them not only from the perpetrators but also from wider society, particularly where official actors

[82] On procedural justice, see section 4.3.3.

[83] Colvin (n 37) 208.

[84] Claire Moon, "'Who'll Pay Reparations on My Soul?' Compensation, Social Control and Social Suffering" (2012) 21(2) Social and Legal Studies 187, 194; Mariko Izumi, "Asian-Japanese: State Apology, National *Ethos*, and the 'Comfort Women' Reparations Debate in Japan" (2011) 62(5) Communication Studies 473.

[85] Lisa Magarrell, "Reparations for Massive or Widespread Human Rights Violations" (n 70) 91.

have been complicit in the abuses, turned a blind eye, or perpetuated the conditions leading to the violations. Symbolic reparations can have a "constitutive effect on improving community relations" and affirm broader human rights values.[86]

The signaling functions of reparations programs are central to their general acceptance within victim communities and society at large. Poorly designed and implemented reparations have the potential to increase conflict within victimized communities, thereby fueling further antagonism between victims and the state administering the program.[87] However, creating comprehensive and complete reparations programs that cover, so far as possible, the "whole universe of potential beneficiaries" and the whole range of relevant crime offsets the potential for such conflicts.[88] Ensuring public education programs and a consistently fair narrative of the atrocities and responses to them, as well as increased engagement of society might further interrupt tensions between victim and nonvictim communities.

7.3.6. Sending a message to society at large

An important element of transitional justice is the ability to draw a line between past and future—to signal a break between prior wrongs and present values without denying the past.[89] Reparations may send such messages about the new regime by recognizing the accountability of the state for antecedent failures, performing "the acts and rituals associated with the legal system of the liberal state" and rectifying the "derogation from equal protection under the law."[90] Thus, reparations may simultaneously sever the new regime from its predecessor, while creating legal continuity in recognizing rights and obligations that arose in the past. The re-establishment of the rule of law is a central feature of transition and must be accomplished in a myriad

[86] Kris Brown, "Commemoration as Symbolic Reparation: New Narratives or Spaces of Conflict" (2013) 14(3) Human Rights Review 273.

[87] See, for instance, the tensions fueled by urgent interim reparations in South Africa—Anna Crawford Pinnerup, "An Assessment of the Impact of Urgent Interim Reparations" in Brandon Hamber and Tlhoki Mofokeng (eds), *From Rhetoric to Responsibility: Making Reparations to the Survivors of Past Political Violence in South Africa* (Centre for the Study of Violence and Reconciliation 2000) 2.

[88] de Greiff identifies "completeness" and comprehensiveness' as two challenges of, or ways of assessing, reparations programs. Pablo de Greiff, "Repairing the Past: Compensation for Victims of Human Rights Violations" in de Greiff, *The Handbook of Reparations* (n 23).

[89] Leebaw, *Judging State-Sponsored Violence, Imagining Political Change* (n 30).

[90] Teitel, *Transitional Justice* (n 5) 134.

of ways, including structural and institutional reform.[91] Reparations signal the effective rehabilitation of the system through the practical application of justice. Reparations might also, however, challenge the attempt to create social harmony and entrench divisions by separating victim populations and perpetrators from the rest of society.[92] Careful negotiation of conflicts and the education of society are therefore crucial to ensure the efficacy of reparations.

Signaling functions operate not only internally, within the transitional state but also externally in its international relations. The notion of "moral deficit" has weight at both of these levels, and in many cases the satisfaction of reparatory requirements is seen as necessary to "recover" the morality of the nation. For instance, in the newly created Federal Republic of Germany, reparations were a way to demonstrate atonement to the international community and secure entrance into the international community.[93] Regaining this international credibility was vital to Germany's recovery from the atrocities committed in the eyes of the concert of nations.[94] Likewise, the potential for international condemnation is often recognized as an important causal factor in the establishment of a law on reparations in Brazil.[95] Nation building, both domestically and globally, is often a central element of transition. Reparations in this context can help address the moral shortfall of abuses, signaling to citizens and other states that the past has not only been recovered from but also redressed.

7.4. The elements of reparatory justice in transition

The ways in which reparations programs achieve the objectives identified in section 7.3 involve valuing certain ideas within transitional processes,

[91] See Agnes Hurwitz and Reyko Huang (eds), *Civil War and the Rule of Law: Security, Development, Human Rights* (Lynne Rienner Publishers 2008); Catherine Turner, "Delivering Lasting Peace, Democracy and Human Rights in Transition: The Role of International Law" (2008) 22 International Journal of Transitional Justice 126; Charles Call (ed), *Constructing Justice and Security after War* (United States Institute of Peace Press 2008); Elizabeth Andersen, "Transitional Justice and the Rule of Law: Lessons from the Field" (2015) 47 Case Western Reserve Journal of International Law 305.

[92] Rama Mani, "Rebuilding an Inclusive Political Community after War" (2005) 36(4) Security Dialogue 511.

[93] Ariel Colonomos and Andrea Armstrong, "German Reparations to the Jews after World War II: A Turning Point in the History of Reparations" in de Greiff, *The Handbook of Reparations* (n 23) 392–93.

[94] Teitel, *Transitional Justice* (n 5) 124.

[95] Cano and Salvão Ferreira (n 23) 112.

focusing on particular values, and featuring certain traits. Thus, the elements of reparatory justice in transition may be separated both from the objectives discussed in section 7.3 and from the elements of redress in international law considered in chapter 4. Six key characteristics of reparations in transition can be identified from both the literature and practice of these processes; namely, victim centricity, recognition, accountability, responsiveness, political compromise, and practical compromise.

The first three identified elements are encapsulated within the international legal scaffold for reparations discussed in chapter 4 and in Margaret Urban Walker's understanding of reparations as expressing acknowledgment, affirming responsibility, and rendering just treatment for victims.[96] Transformation and compromise, on the other hand, represent characteristic features of reparations in transition not prioritized within the traditional remedial framework, building instead upon the unique objectives and demands of transition. Optics and acoustics are central to reparatory justice that achieves the objectives in section 7.3; the impact of reparations programs is often contingent upon how they are perceived both by victims and by society at large.[97] Thus, the identified elements of reparations in transition prioritize the affective dimensions of practical measures as well as material relief.

7.4.1. Victim-centric redress

One of the primary features of reparations in transitional justice is a multifaceted concern with victims—the very notion of reparations in transitional contexts is defined by the centrality of victims in measures of redress.[98] Unlike criminal justice responses or economic and political reforms, reparations are primarily concerned not with the perpetrators of abuse but with those who suffered from it. As de Greiff frames the dynamic: reparations are an effort on behalf of victims while criminal justice is, in the end, a struggle against perpetrators.[99] Approaches that place victims at the heart of reparatory

[96] Margaret Urban Walker, *What is Reparative Justice?* (Marquette UP 2010) 19.
[97] Firchow and Mac Ginty (n 26) 233.
[98] Moffett, "Transitional Justice and Reparations" (n 44) 1. See also UN Commission on Human Rights, "Study Concerning the Right to Restitution, Compensation and Rehabilitation for Victims of Gross Violations of Human Rights and Fundamental Freedoms: Final Report Submitted by Mr Theo van Boven, Special Rapporteur" (UN Doc E/CN.4/Sub.2/1993/8 1993) paras 133, 137.
[99] de Greiff, "Repairing the Past" (n 88) 2.

measures in a meaningful, rather than merely tokenistic, way are crucial in marrying victim centricity with the objectives of transitional reparatory justice for which procedural justice is fundamental. As Mckay advises, it "is not simply a question of whether any remedy or outcome is produced, but whether that remedy or outcome is the right one for the victim."[100] By engaging victims in decision-making processes, official actors affirm their status and identity as actors and subjects rather than as objects that are acted upon, conveying public acknowledgment of suffering and adding to the symbolism attached to reparations.[101]

To realize victim centricity, reparations must be conceived both in terms of processes and outcomes. Victims should be enabled to assist in determinations of eligibility, apportionment of awards, and forms reparatory measures ought to take to be responsive to harms and needs.[102] The inclusion of victims in the processes through which redress is determined and delivered can improve the efficacy and efficiency of chosen programs, as well as bearing psychological significance.[103] The views and concerns of victims, directly engaged, can impact the substantive outcomes of reparations, increasing their capacity to understand and respond to the specific needs of victims in context.[104] Conversely, the effectiveness of reparations mechanisms and their ability to achieve the desired outcomes can be undermined when they fail to meaningfully engage victims in decision-making and negotiation.[105] Although it is often impossible to satisfy the needs and wishes of all victims in all situations, meaningful measures ensuring procedural justice can assist both in ensuring the best possible programs are implemented in the interests

[100] Fiona McKay, "What Outcomes for Victims?" in Dinah Shelton (ed), *The Oxford Handbook of International Human Rights Law* (OUP 2013) 922.

[101] Brandon Hamber, "The Dilemmas of Reparations: In Search of a Process-Driven Approach" in de Feyter and others (n 31) 135, 141.

[102] Moffett, "Transitional Justice and Reparations" (n 44) 34. The Brazilian Special Commission, protecting representation of the relatives of the victims, provides an example of such practice, wherein procedural justice measures had tangible impacts on reparatory processes. See Cano and Salvão Ferreira (n 23) 114–18.

[103] See Edgar Lind and Tom R Tyler, *The Social Psychology of Procedural Justice* (Springer 1988) 31–34.

[104] See Lind and Tyler (n 103) 31–34.

[105] Carlton Waterhouse, "The Good, the Bad, and the Ugly: Moral Agency and the Role of Victims in Reparations Programs" (2009) 31 University of Pennsylvania Journal of International Law 257, 258. On the impact of failures in procedural justice in practice, see the disappointment of victims in the *Duch Case* before the Extraordinary Chambers in the Courts of Cambodia, and the rejection of reparations by the so-called comfort women—Phuong Pham and others, "Victim Participation and the Trial of Duch at the Extraordinary Chambers in the Courts of Cambodia" (2011) 3 Journal of Human Rights Practice 264; Izumi (n 84).

of victims and that victims might accept the justice of the process, even where they dispute the substantive outcomes.[106]

To ensure the full participation and inclusion of victims in reparations processes, outreach, support, and education programs are essential. The presence of NGO networks and civil society actors supporting civilians can be a central feature in victims' capacity to claim reparations and to ameliorate the risks associated with making claims in situations following instability and conflict.[107] Without the operation of these mechanisms, victims might be unable or unwilling to make claims because of lack of knowledge, understanding, or support. As REDRESS highlights in their report on torture survivors:

> without a fuller understanding of survivors' perceptions and without the necessary support structures in place we are in danger of encouraging people whose lives have been traumatized to exercise rights they are unclear about, through processes that they are not actively involved in and do not understand, which then produce outcomes that do not match their expectations.[108]

Beyond improving the responsiveness of reparations to victims' injuries and needs, procedural involvement of victims in peacebuilding and reparations processes can deepen democratic engagement, assist in transforming social relations, and help address the structural causes of conflict, constructing a "peace infrastructure" for the future.[109] By placing victims at the center of transitional reparatory processes and ensuring their involvement at all levels of decision-making, participatory reparations can transform the lives of survivors and rebuild their civic identities.[110]

106 See Hamber, "The Dilemmas of Reparations" (n 101).

107 Prakesh Adhikari, Wendy Hansen, and Kathy Powers, "The Demand for Reparations: Grievance, Risk, and the Pursuit of Justice in Civil War Settlement" (2012) Journal of Conflict Resolution 183.

108 REDRESS, "Torture Survivors' Perceptions of Reparation: Preliminary Survey" (The REDRESS Trust 2001) <www.redress.org/downloads/publications/TSPR.pdf> accessed October 10, 2017, 9.

109 Roddy Brett and Lina Malagón, "Overcoming the Original Sin of the 'Original Condition': How Reparations May Contribute to Emancipatory Peacebuilding" (2013) 14(3) Human Rights Review 257.

110 See Margaret Urban Walker, *Moral Repair: Reconstructing Moral Relations after Wrongdoing* (CUP 2006).

7.4.2. Recognition

Victim centricity and procedural justice are intimately connected to the recognition of victims, their suffering, and the wrongdoing as central to individual and national recovery from abuses. Recognition can be viewed as a necessary condition for the satisfaction of all six objectives of reparations in transition identified in section 7.3, affirming acknowledgment of abuses and resultant suffering as a prerequisite for healing, reconciliation, and prevention.[111] Recognition relates not only to the atrocities themselves but also to the status of victims as citizens and human beings. The dominance of truth commissions in transitional settings marks the weight of recognition as a central value and feature of reparatory justice in transition.[112] As Jonathan Allen highlights, the truth and reconciliation commission "embodies a commitment to the recognition of the equal dignity of all citizens."[113] This element also manifests in memorialization and commemoration measures targeted toward the recognition of victims and their experiences, which are increasingly adopted in both public and private sector reparatory efforts.[114]

In practice, truth is sometimes considered more important than accountability or justice, although the two are intertwined.[115] For instance, Alan Terakawa suggests that hearings for Japanese American survivors of internment during World War II meant more to victims, their families, and communities than monetary compensation.[116] Similarly, in South Africa, negotiations focused on creating spaces for storytelling by victims and truth telling by perpetrators, considering such to be vital to the process of rehabilitation and reconciliation because they offered recognition, psychological healing, and the reparatory opportunity to hear the truth.[117] Nonetheless,

[111] See, for instance, the Chilean draft reparations Bill, defining transitional reparatory justice by recognition—*Diputados* cited in Lira (n 55) 58.

[112] Truth Commissions have been created in a wide range of transitional situations across the globe. See Priscilla Hayner, "Truth Commissions: A Schematic Overview" (2006) 88(862) International Review of the Red Cross 295.

[113] Jonathan Allen, "Balancing Justice and Social Unity: Political Theory and the Idea of a Truth and Reconciliation Commission" (1999) 49(3) University of Toronto Law Journal 331.

[114] Cheryl Lawther and Luke Moffett, "Researching Transitional Justice: The Highs, the Lows and the Expansion of the Field" in Lawther, Moffet, and Jacobs (n 44) 1, 2.

[115] Lawrence Weschler, "A Miracle, A Universe: Settling Accounts with Torturers" in Kritz (n 7) 491, 491.

[116] Alan Terakawa, "Commission Hearings Probe Reparations for Japanese-American WWII Internment" (1981) 67 American Bar Association Journal 1439, 1439.

[117] Graeme Simpson and Paul van Zyl, "South Africa's Truth and Reconciliation Commission" (1995) 585 Temps Moderne 394, 398.

the practice of the South African Commission demonstrated that truth alone is insufficient in ensuring recovery and reconciliation.

The official status of truth commissions—having been sanctioned, authorized, or empowered by the state—ensures the narrative of the conflict or abuses is given special status and recognition.[118] Such official recognition embodies the difference between "knowledge and acknowledgment," whereby the official sanctioning of knowledge—making it part of the "public cognitive scene"—becomes a positive act of affirmation.[119] This recognition is both a feature of, and prerequisite to, reparations, as victims are unable to assert rights or claim remedies for breaches when they are unheard, unseen, or not recognized as rights bearers.[120] Truth processes provide a platform for the acknowledgment of suffering and wrongdoing, presuming the equal status and dignity of victims, which may serve as the foundation of further redress.

Truth processes ensure not only that the perspective of victims is incorporated into the narrative of the conflict but can also provide for a more unified theory of the abuses.[121] Conversely, the existence of a multiplicity of different versions of events can undermine efforts to repair wrongs and create a stable state. The risk of continuing a "conflict-about-the-conflict" and thereby failing to recognize the experience of victims is acute in divided societies.[122] For instance, in Northern Ireland, Christine Bell and others critique state narratives as having "obscured evaluation of the extent to which the State in Northern Ireland was not simply a bystander or referee in the conflict but a participant in it."[123] Official, but at least partially independent, truth commissions can offset this danger of recognition deficit.

Despite their centrality in transitional reparatory processes, truth and apology alone are insufficient to ensure proper recognition and pave the way for reconciliation, stability, and democracy. Symbolic gestures require

118 Priscilla Hayner, *Unspeakable Truths: Transitional Justice and the Challenge of Truth Commissions* (2nd edn, Routledge 2011) 14.

119 Weschler (n 115) 492.

120 Patrick Hayden, "The Human Right to Health and the Struggle for Recognition" (2012) 38 Review of International Studies 569, 576.

121 ibid.

122 Such tension has manifested in the Northern Irish context, and in many ethic and quasi-ethnic conflicts. See John McGarry and Brendan O'Leary, *Explaining Northern Ireland: Broken Images* (Blackwell 1995); Christine Bell, *Peace Agreements and Human Rights* (OUP 2000); Colm Campbell, Fionnuala Ní Aoláin, and Colin Harvey, "The Frontiers of Legal Analysis: Reframing the Transition in Northern Ireland" (2003) 66 Modern Law Review 317. On other ethic or quasi-ethnic context, see Bell, Campbell, and Ní Aoláin (n 5) 316.

123 Bell, Campbell, and Ní Aoláin (n 5) 311.

"concrete action" if they are "to be part of a lived relationship."[124] As the South African Truth and Reconciliation Commission acknowledged in its final report:

> The granting of reparation awards to victims of gross violations of human rights adds value to the "truth-seeking" phase by:
>
> (a) enabling survivors to experience in a concrete way the State's acknowledgement of wrongs done to victims and survivors, family members, communities and the nation at large;
> (b) restoring the survivors' dignity;
> (c) affirming the values, interests, aspirations and rights advanced by those who suffered;
> (d) raising consciousness about the public's moral responsibility to participate in healing the wounded and facilitating nation-building.[125]

Often it is not the provision of financial reparations itself that is the issue but the failure on the part of the state to provide them.[126] In other words, a government's persistent refusal to provide any form of material redress in the face of requests or demands for such can undermine their sincerity, turning monetary payments into a moral indicator of commitment to victims. This is particularly true when money is considered as more than simply a material demand. As Moffett notes, "money changes the nature of dealing with victimization, connoting material and symbolic messages about the worth and deservingness of, and social solidarity with, the victim."[127] Thus, compensatory or material measures can be just as concerned with recognition of wrongdoing and the associated harms as they are with dealing with material consequences.

While truth processes without concrete action are generally insufficient in satisfying the requirements of both individual and collective recognition, the converse is also true—reparations programs unaccompanied by "steps to ascertain the truth about past violations" tend to be counterproductive as they "may be perceived as an effort to buy victims' silence."[128] In Chile,

[124] Nagy (n 22) 59.
[125] Truth and Reconciliation Commission (n 42) 312.
[126] Colvin (n 37) 206.
[127] Moffett, "Reparations for Guilty Victims" (n 31) 166.
[128] Lisa Magarrell, *Reparations in Theory and Practice* (International Center for Transitional Justice 2007) 2.

beneficiaries emphasized this demand for a holistic approach, declaring their appreciation for the economic reparations provided and received but demanding "further recognition for the harms they had suffered, as well as vindication of the dignity and good names of their families. They emphasized that no benefits would appease the need for 'justice and truth.'"[129] Truth, without action, is thus conceived as only partial recognition, and insufficient in satisfying the objectives of transitional reparatory justice. In the context of historical injustices, this speaks to the need for action beyond apologies and expressions of regret, not only to combat the continuing marginalization of victim communities but also to indicate the sincerity of attempts at redress and reconciliation.

7.4.3. Accountability

Although most transitional justice scholars sever accountability mechanisms from consideration of reparations, accountability is an important element of reparatory processes not limited to criminal justice and individual penalties.[130] Through direct apologies and reparations payments, states may be held accountable for abuses even absent criminal prosecution of individual perpetrators. Even where monetary payments are offered and available, failure on the part of the state to recognize responsibility and connect material measures to wrongdoing in this way can undermine reparatory justice.[131] It is not only the recognition of suffering that affirms the status of victims but also the recognition of wrongdoing, necessitating responsibility be acknowledged or imposed.

Direct accountability mechanisms most frequently take the form of criminal prosecutions, with individual perpetrators being held accountable for the abuses in which they participated.[132] International criminal prosecutions

[129] Lira (n 55) 62.

[130] Severing accountability mechanisms from reparations, see for instance de Greiff, *The Handbook of Reparations* (n 23); Firchow and Mac Ginty (n 26) 235.

[131] See, for instance, the rejection of reparations by the "comfort women" on the basis of the state's vague and evasive approach to the matter of responsibility—Urban Walker, *What is Reparative Justice?* (n 96) 23–24; Nishino Rumiko, Kim Puja, and Onozawa Akane, *Denying the Comfort Women: The Japanese State's Assault on Historical Truth* (Routledge 2018).

[132] Prosecutions have been pursued in Argentina, Chile, Colombia, Guatemala, Peru, and Rwanda—see Mark Drumbl, *Atrocity, Punishment and International Law* (CUP 2007). Prosecutions were also an element of Ugandan processes—see Sarah Nouwen, *Complementarity in the Line of Fire: The Catalysing Effect of the International Criminal Court in Uganda and Sudan* (CUP 2013). Peruvian President Alberto Fujimori was also arrested, tried and convicted by the Peruvian Supreme Court for crimes of corruption and human rights abuses occurring during his government—Jo-Marie

and domestic civil actions both possess the capacity to order reparations and damages paid directly to victims by perpetrators. However, in the consideration of historical cases, criminal responsibility is no longer engaged. While the liability of continuing entities may still be established, this is often complicated by contested legal terrain and issues in establishing causation. State responsibility might alternatively be recognized through administrative reparations programs that, though not occurring within the judicial framework, connect official responsibility to various forms of redress. Such programs rely on political will but may nonetheless provide for a measure of accountability in complex historical cases.

Despite their potential to overcome technical legal barriers, administrative reparations evidence limitations in their capacity for affirming accountability. Entirely state administered and state provided redress can fail to capture the lived reality of collective violence, which is often committed by private individuals, groups, or corporations, as well as the state.[133] Beyond affirming the corrective paradigm, accountability procedures and legal or quasi-legal mechanisms for engaging civil responsibility of perpetrators can be important in rebuilding civic identity and legal personhood. As Winter proposes, to "be a legal person is to have the claim to be dealt with according to the law."[134] In the context of historical enslavement, this might involve the assertion of responsibility against continuing private entities that maintain connections to the profits of enslavement. Reparations constitute a form of accountability on the part of the entity obliged to pay by affirming a legal relationship of responsibility between that entity and beneficiaries. Gaps in accountability can be created where significant perpetrators escape any form of culpability.

7.4.4. Responsiveness

Despite being shaped by international and private law frameworks, reparations in transitional contexts are sculpted within their particular political environment, with objectives extending beyond traditional legal

Burt and Carlos Rivera (eds), *The National and International Significance of the Trial and Conviction of Alberto Fujimori* (Instituto de Defensa Legal 2011).

133 Moffett, "Transitional Justice and Reparations" (n 44) 8.
134 Winter (n 7) 238.

relationships—what Moffett brands "bespoke reparation programs."[135] The importance of responsiveness in reparations programs and their victim centricity are interconnected. Yet, responsiveness goes further than simply focusing on the needs and desires of victims and victim communities. Because transitional reparatory justice is concerned not only with redressing wrongdoing for victims but also doing so within the broader scheme of transition, the shape of reparations must respond to victims, to the context in which they are embedded, and to the vision of society to which the state aspires.[136] Teitel encapsulates the complexity of this dynamic:

> The conception of justice that emerges is contextualized and partial: What is deemed just is contingent and informed by prior injustice. Responses to repressive rule inform the meaning of adherence to the rule of law. As a state undergoes political change, legacies of injustice have a bearing on what is deemed transformative.[137]

Determining what combination of measures are appropriate is a matter of responding to the circumstances of the violations. The transformative potential of symbolic measures and commemoration (in particular) is contingent upon context, presentation, and the manner of introduction of these elements into the society.[138]

As in international law, reparations in transition may take a variety of forms depending on the requirements of a given situation; they may be individual or collective, material or symbolic, and involve a multitude of different measures targeting different dimensions of the wrongdoing and suffering.[139] Although Emily Camins suggests there is a conceptual distinction between material and symbolic reparations, monetary payments themselves may have affective dimensions.[140] Thus, the variety of reparations modalities ought to

[135] Moffett, "Transitional Justice and Reparations" (n 44). See also Quirine Eijkman, "Recognising the Local Perspective: Transitional Justice and Post-Conflict Reparations" (2010) 10(3) Global Jurist 1.

[136] See Jemima Garcia-Godos, "Victim Reparations in Transitional Justice—What Is at Stake and Why" (2008) 26 Nordisk Tidsskrift for Menneskerettigheter 111, 112.

[137] Teitel, *Transitional Justice* (n 5) 6.

[138] Brown (n 86).

[139] Reparations in transition mimic the multiple modalities of redress considered in chapter 5.

[140] Camins (n 51) 129. Camins relies upon Mégret's conclusions concerning reparations in the International Criminal Court, which were subsequently disproved by the court in *Lubanga*. Frédéric Mégret, "The International Criminal Court Statute and the Failure to Mention Symbolic Reparations" (2009) 16 International Review of Victimology 127; *Situation in the Democratic Republic of the Congo in the Case of the Prosecutor v Thomas Lubanga Dyilo* (Decision establishing the principles and

be considered in context and in dialogue with one another, and the symbolic potential of material redress should not be overlooked.

Measures of direct restitution are the simplest form of responsive reparation, returning dispossessed property to victims and thereby directly repairing the substance of abuses.[141] Such measures may not only represent the best way of returning victims to something approximating the status quo ante but also serve as a means of transforming legal institutions and structures.[142] Thus restitution can serve not only as the closest possible solution in returning victims to the position that they would have been in absent the wrongdoing but also as a means of addressing broader challenges of the transition.[143] However, restitution is not the only form of reparation that may be tailored to meet the specificities of a particular situation; all choices regarding the form and substance of reparatory processes may be sculpted to respond to the demands of justice and the needs of victims within their unique transitional context.[144]

The capacity to engage both collective and individualized reparatory mechanisms enables responsive programs responding to collectivized harms and capitalizing on the symbolic value of certain collective modalities of redress. For instance, in both Morocco and Peru, collective reparations programs were developed to address suffering arising from abuses committed against individual members of specific groups with an additional cumulative effect. By ensuring that the basic needs of these groups were met where previously they had gone unfulfilled by the state, these mechanisms addressed the collective dimensions of the wrongdoing committed as a distinct feature

procedures to be applied to reparations) ICC-01/04-01/06 (August 7, 2012). For discussion of "other modalities" see paras 237–41 of the judgment.

[141] See, for instance, Law 1448 Concerning Victims and Restitution of Land (2011) (Colombia); Czech Law on Extrajudicial Rehabilitation (n 23).

[142] Land restitution in the Czech Republic, for instance, privatized the system of property ownership in the aftermath of imposed communist rule. Teitel, *Transitional Justice* (n 5) 129.

[143] Restitution is further considered in sections 4.2.1 and 5.2.

[144] See, for instance, the multiple responsive modalities of redress adopted in the Chilean reparations processes, including six distinct programs initiated by the National Corporation for Reparations and Reconciliation, and ultimately additional memorial activities undertaken by the government. Law 19.123 "Establishes the National Corporation for Reparation and Reconciliation and Grants other Benefits to Persons as Indicated" enacted February 8, 1992 (Official Gazette No. 34,188) in de Greiff, *The Handbook of Reparations* (n 23) 748; Lira (n 55) 60–62. Such measures might also respond to divergent short-term and long-term needs, particularly in relation to especially vulnerable victims whose harms may be compounded without immediate support. See, for instance, measures adopted in South Africa under the Promotion of National Unity and Reconciliation Act (n 38) ss 4(f), 1(1)(xix)(a), and 1(1)(ix). On failures in Urgent Interim Reparations, and the impact of delay on transition, see Colvin (n 37) 187–89.

of targeted abuses.[145] Nonetheless, it remains important that symbolic and collective measures do not eclipse individual and material benefits—which in many cases are prioritized by victims—where these are required by the circumstances of the wrongdoing and the suffering of victims.[146]

Preferences between individualized material redress and collective symbolic measures can manifest substantial divergence between victims themselves and society as a whole.[147] Procedural justice mechanisms can therefore be vital in the initial design of reparations programs, allowing for potential disjunct between victim perspectives and outside opinions to be reconciled. The influence of such processes are evident in the practice of the South African Committee on Reparations and Rehabilitation, which after a year-long consultative process incorporated monetary redress as a central element of their recommendations, despite initially favoring collective and symbolic measures over financial provisions.[148] Direct payments and individualized measures not only respond to the wishes of victims in many cases but also empower victims by allowing them to take control of their own recovery and channel resources to the things that are most suitable for them in their individual circumstances. Broader programs are seldom able to directly target the needs of individuals and are far more likely to generalize the needs and desires of survivors.

Arguments supporting monetary payments to victims run counter to those situations in which payments are perceived as blood money and an insult to the victims, suggesting that what is most crucial is a process that includes victims in decision-making processes and ultimately formulates measures of redress on the basis of the views, needs, and wishes of survivors. Victim centricity, procedural justice, and the inclusion of victims are vital to

145 See Lisa Laplante and Kimberly Theidon, "Truth with Consequences: Justice and Reparations in Post-Truth Commission Peru" (2007) 29(1) Human Rights Quarterly 228; Bettina Dennerlein, "Remembering Violence, Negotiating Change: The Moroccan Equity and Reconciliation Commission and the Politics of Gender" (2012) 8(1) Journal of Middle Eastern Women's Studies 10. See also the provision empowering the Committee on Reparations and Rehabilitation in South Africa, allowing the Committee to consider community reparations—Promotion of National Unity and Reconciliation Act (n 38) s 4(h).

146 On the overlooking of victims' needs in transitional justice processes, particularly trials and truth commissions, see Simon Robins, "Failing Victims? The Limits of Transitional Justice in Addressing the Needs of Victims of Violations" (2017) 11 Human Rights and International Legal Discourse 41. On the preference for compensation see (n 37).

147 For instance, Wendy Orr, a Commissioner of the Committee on Reparations and Rehabilitation in South Africa, noted that while non-victims may have been reluctant to frame reparations in terms of monetary redress, victims themselves seemed to prefer direct compensation—Orr (n 47) 241–42.

148 See Brandon Hamber, "Repairing the Irreparable: Dealing with the Double-Binds of Making Reparations for Crimes of the Past" (2000) 5 Ethnicity and Health 221.

responsiveness, ensuring measures adopted respond to the lived experiences and suffering of victims rather than their wants and needs perceived through the lens of the dominant majority. Empowering victims to engage in the construction of the programs targeted toward them enables them to "enact visions of state, society and government that respond directly to their self-defined and differential needs, priorities and cultural values."[149] Where victims represent a particular political, cultural, or ethnic group, this direct engagement can additionally ensure that measures adopted complement their belief systems rather than representing an additional majority-centric approach to minority issues.[150] Thus, responsive consultation can help ensure that the approach taken does not affirm status quo policies of the state marginalizing victim communities and failing to account for the nature of majoritarian injustices.[151]

7.4.5. Political compromise

The principle of *resitutio in integrum* targeted toward returning victims to the status quo ante or providing proportionate redress dominates reparations in international and private law, leaving little room for compromise or extraneous considerations. Transitional justice, on the other hand, often demands an accounting of a range of external factors, both political and practical.[152] Paul Gready therefore paints transitional measures as the "art of imperfect solutions and difficult choices, in the context of competition for finite resources and delicate political dynamics."[153] The pressing demand for peace and democracy often overrides corrective justice, requiring concessions and sacrifices be made by victims to ensure the success of transition. As Bell, Campbell and Ní Aoláin frame it, "the question of law's relationship to

[149] Brett and Malagón (n 109) 259.

[150] See, for instance, Nagy's critique of the Truth and Reconciliation Commission addressing the treatment of indigenous peoples in residential schools that highlights the potential for "liberal democracy building" to entrench structural violence against indigenous victims and ignore the colonial dimensions of abuses. Nagy (n 22).

[151] Corntassel and Holder suggest that political/legal rights-based approaches to reparations can reward, rather than redress, colonial injustices. Corntassel and Holder (n 22).

[152] Teitel highlights the external political aims advanced by transitional reparatory justice removing such measures from conventional corrective justice principles. Teitel, *Transitional Justice* (n 5) 132.

[153] Paul Gready, *The Era of Transitional Justice, the Aftermath of the Truth and Reconciliation Commission in South Africa and Beyond* (Routledge 2011) 1, 6–7.

political accommodation revolves around the issue of how to reconcile normative legal demands with the pragmatics of peace-making."[154]

Amnesties, pardons, and the retention of official positions within a regime represent measures of political compromise often considered necessary for the establishment and maintenance of peace in transition—measures directly contradicting the need for accountability and redress. Mark Freeman highlights amnesties as an area of significant contestation, suggesting that there are "few issues of law and policy as complex and divisive as the question of when and whether to grant amnesties for atrocities."[155] Amnesties and similar concessions are not only the price paid for the wider objectives of transition but can also represent the clash between different transitional goals and measures. Truth telling in particular can require some diminution in accountability processes to incentivize perpetrators to share their knowledge.[156] As Christine Bell recognizes in relation to the Truth and Reconciliation Commission in its inception, justice and reconciliation may be balanced as "both necessary to the stability of any new political order."[157]

By protecting those individuals directly responsible for atrocities, amnesties, pardons, and the protection of official positions within the new regime can undermine the recognition of wrongdoing and acknowledgment of responsibility. When constructed to protect high-level perpetrators from accountability, amnesties may be framed as an affront to justice not justified by the demands of transition.[158] Such measures may constitute a breach of a state's continuing duty to prevent, investigate, and punish human rights violations—a duty that legally cannot be sacrificed to transitional interests, even where truth and reparations processes had been extensive.[159] Thus, the

[154] Bell, Campbell, and Ní Aoláin (n 5) 317.

[155] Mark Freeman, *Necessary Evils: Amnesties and the Search for Justice* (CUP 2009) 1.

[156] See Martha Minow, *Between Vengeance and Forgiveness: Facing History after Genocide and Mass Violence* (Beacon 1998). Minow suggests that these trade-offs are widely recognized as an aspect of truth commissions.

[157] Bell, "Transitional Justice, Interdisciplinarity and the State of the 'Field' or 'Non-Field'" (n 18) 14.

[158] For instance, Argentinean laws pardoning members of the military *juntas* and select high-ranking officials and guerrilla leaders, as well as members of the military and armed forces under prosecution, were denounced by the Inter-American Commission on Human Rights as violations of the right to justice as well as the right to fair trial, and the right to judicial protection. Guembe (n 23) 27; IACHR, "Report No. 28/92, Cases 10.147, 10.240, 10.262, 10.309, and 10.311, Argentina" (October 2, 1992) IACHR 1992-3 OEA/Ser.L/V/II.83 Doc 14 (March 12, 1993), forty-four petitioners, including the Fundación Servicio Paz y Justicia representing ninety cases, in six separate cases were considered by the Commission—highlighting the extent to which victims felt wronged by the enacted amnesties and pardons—see [40], [42]–[50].

[159] IACHR (n 158) [40], [42]–[50].

demand for legal reparatory justice and transitional objectives may conflict. However, in such cases, the legal imperative is not usurped or replaced by transitional measures that lack equivalence.

Although international and regional courts may be willing to rule amnesties and pardons a breach of the relevant conventions, domestic courts may struggle to do so given their more limited relationship to the national parliament. For instance, where the Inter-American Commission denounced Argentinean amnesties as violations of the rights to justice, fair trials, and judicial protection, the Constitutional Court of South Africa upheld the constitutionality of the amnesty provisions of the Promotion of National Unity and Reconciliation Act.[160] The South African claim was dismissed by Judge Mahomed on three grounds: the cost of subjecting the state to civil claims for apartheid-era violations was prohibitive as it harmed the social welfare of the country; victims who could file a provable claim against the government were limited in comparison to the total pool of victims; and removing amnesty would withdraw the incentive for truth telling.[161] Judge Didcott in his separate but concurring opinion upheld the amnesty provisions on the basis of the constitutionally enshrined aims of reconciliation, which would be harmed by long-running civil litigation against the state and the associated negative publicity.[162] Thus, while international law may not consider transitional objectives as a relevant consideration in assessing the legality of amnesties, national courts embedded in the transitional context may be more likely to do so—particularly where those objectives have been implanted into national legislation. Thus, international frameworks and oversight remain crucial in ensuring reparatory justice in transition.

Both wrongdoing and victimhood may be abstruse, particularly where legality and morality are contested and the lines between victims and perpetrators are blurred. Perpetuation of confusion over right and wrong can give rise to continuing violence as different sides fight for the dominance of their narrative of the conflict.[163] Stabilizing society in the aftermath of conflict can therefore demand concessions to the absolute conception of justice advanced in the context of international and private law reparations. As Firchow and Mac Ginty identify, the degree to which reparations are

[160] ibid.
[161] Judge Mahomed, *Judgment in Case CCT 17/96*, Constitutional Court of South Africa (1996) [42]–[45].
[162] Judge Didcott, ibid [55], [57], [59].
[163] Moffett, "Reparations for Guilty Victims" (n 31) 167.

retributive as opposed to restorative—that is, focused on punishment versus reconciliation—affects their capacity to ameliorate the effects of conflict and prevent conflict recidivism.[164]

7.4.6. Practical compromise

It is not only political compromises that must be made in transitional states to protect the interest of peace and stability; often severe resource constraints in the aftermath of atrocity affect what is reasonably possible for a state to provide by way of reparations. Particularly in situations of widespread abuse and protracted conflict, transition often requires extensive rebuilding of institutions and infrastructure to ensure the wellbeing of citizens and the reestablishment of functioning democracy. The extent of injustices committed in the centuries of transatlantic enslavement compound this problem.[165] Resource constraints manifest in transitional reparatory projects in various ways, shaping what victims and wrongs are recognized as deserving of redress, the munificence of awards granted, and the effectiveness of the administering body. These limits are manifestations of the need for pragmatic compromise in transitional contexts, where the very ability to construct reparations programs can be contingent upon the perceived feasibility of proposals for redress from the perspective of society as a whole.[166]

In many ways, the aggregation of victims' claims into administrative rather than judicial procedures represents a compromise between the ideals of reparatory justice and pragmatism. Aggregating claims through specialized bureaucratic processes can provide a range of practical benefits: a greater number of victims may receive redress; benefits may be obtained with less delay; barriers to entry, procedural, and evidentiary requirements may be lightened; the expense of procedures can be massively reduced through economies of scale; and a single administering body can ensure greater parity

[164] Firchow and Mac Ginty (n 26) 234.

[165] This is further demonstrated in the figures advanced by reparations advocates as the sum of redress due, ranging between $500 million and $777 trillion—James Forman, "The Black Manifesto" (1970) 1(1) Review of the Black Political Economy 36; Afrikan World Reparations and Repatriation Truth Commission, "The Accra Declaration on Reparations and Repatriation" *The African Descent International Diaspora* (August 12, 1999) <http://estooks.wixsite.com/the-adid/black-power-and-reparations> accessed June 1, 2018.

[166] Katherine B Starzyk and others, "Framing Reparation Claims for Crimes against Humanity" in Jo-Anne Wemmers (ed), *Reparation for Victims of Crimes against Humanity: The Healing Role of Reparation* (Routledge 2014) 118.

between awards granted to different victims.[167] However, the benefits of such processes for victims are contingent upon the terms of the reparations program in question and not inherent in administrative processes.[168]

The structural limitations of judicial systems can significantly interfere with the achievement of reparatory justice in transition. In Chile, the inability to identify specific perpetrators often made judicial action impossible, for Chilean law requires actions to be addressed against a specific person, thus requiring investigation, which was barred by the Self-Amnesty Decree of 1978.[169] In Argentina, claims demanding indemnification for harms and damages resulting from wrongful detention were frequently rejected by courts on statute of limitations grounds.[170] Judicial processes may also be entirely inadequate to deal with reparations claims for widespread abuse in transitional states—in Guatemala, for instance, the victims of state-sponsored violence reached hundreds of thousands.[171] Although class actions and aggregation of claims may be used to streamline redress in such cases, the structural limitations of judicial institutions make dealing with the sheer volume of claims in such circumstances problematic. In relation to widespread historical injustices, these problems with judicial mechanisms are further compounded.

The scale of suffering alone may be used to deny the call for specific reparations, not just in the courts, but more generally, with some—particularly those from societal majorities—claiming that everyone suffers during a war or conflict, and thus no one ought to be singled out.[172] The degree

[167] See de Greiff, "Justice and Reparations" (n 33) 458. On reduced evidentiary burdens, see, for instance, Argentinean Law 23.466 (n 54). The treaty establishing the sovereignty of the Federal Republic of Germany likewise highlighted the need to account for evidentiary difficulties, many of which were created by the violations themselves—see Christian Pross, *Paying for the Past: The Struggle over Reparations for the Surviving Victims of the Nazi Terror* (Johns Hopkins UP 1998) 20.

[168] The Brazilian Law of Victims of Political Assassination and Disappearance, for instance, was criticized for pushing the burden of proof onto victims' families—Cano and Salvão Ferreira (n 23) 116.

[169] For fifteen years this decree was interpreted as preventing both the punishment of perpetrators and the investigation of cases. Only in the mid-1990s was this interpretation challenged and a duty to investigate affirmed. Malamud-Goti and Grosman (n 57) 545.

[170] Guembe (n 23) 28–29. This approach is also evident in American jurisprudence on the question of reparations for historical enslavement—see *Cato v United States* (1995) 70 F Supp 3d 1103 (9th Cir); *In Re African-American Slave Descendants Litigation* 375 F Supp 2d 721 (ND Ill 2005).

[171] Malamud-Goti and Grosman (n 57) 542–43.

[172] For instance, in *Lubanga*, the International Criminal Court noted that reparations programs' meaningfulness may be contingent on the inclusion of all members of the community, regardless of their connection to the crimes for which the person was convicted—*Prosecutor v Thomas Lubanga Dyilo* (Judgment on the Appeals against the "Decision Establishing the Principles and Procedures to be Applied to Reparations" of August 7, 2012 with Amended Order for Reparations (Annex A) and Public Annexes 1 and 2) ICC-01/04-01/06-3129 (March 3, 2015) [215]. Furthermore, polls conducted in post–World War II Germany suggested that the majority of Germans considered

to which governmental reparations rely on popular support makes them more susceptible to populist understandings of widespread injustices, where judicial bodies may be insulated from such by institutional protections. In response to the challenge of societal perceptions of victimization, reparations are frequently targeted toward those perceived to have suffered the most.[173] The report of the Truth and Reconciliation Commission in Timor-Leste acknowledged both the universality of suffering and the prioritization of certain abuses in declaring "[w]e are all victims but not all victims are equal. We must acknowledge this reality and lend a hand to those who are most vulnerable."[174] However, majoritarian understandings of transition and political processes may skew the prioritization of suffering against minority groups who have often suffered the most.[175]

The choice of restitutionary baseline—the wrongs or harms deemed compensable under state programs—involves choosing between victims who have suffered varying kinds of persecution, to varying degrees and at varying times, as well as balancing the demands of political interest groups.[176] Often the basis for differentiating between reparable harms and harms victims are simply expected to bear is the civil or political dimension of the atrocities in question.[177] The state targets those wrongs that most severely undermine democracy and political inclusion to set the stage for the rebuilding of such.

The tendency to prioritize civil and political rights can reduce the transformative potential of reparations by failing to account for the social and economic violations at the root of the conflict.[178] Moreover, it can overlook significant violations of rights that impact individuals and communities in devastating ways, thereby inhibiting the successful recovery of those victims.[179] However, where social and economic sufferings are targeted by social and economic reforms and support packages, a compromise on the scope of reparations is unlikely to have overwhelming practical effects. The

themselves victims of the war entitled to government assistance—Kurt Grossman, *Germany's Moral Debt: The German-Israeli Agreement* (Public Affairs Press 1954) 18–19.

[173] In the cases of Sierra Leone and Timor-Leste, amputees, orphans, widows, victims of sexual violence, and victims of torture were prioritized as the most vulnerable victims—see *Lubanga* (n 172).

[174] Commission for Reception, Truth and Reconciliation in East Timor, "Chega! The Report of the Commission for Reception, Truth, and Reconciliation Timor-Leste" (KPG 2005) section 12.1.

[175] For instance, on Germans creating a hierarchy post–World War II that ranked Jewish victims well below a range of other beneficiaries, see Grossman (n 172) 18–19.

[176] ibid 135.

[177] Teitel, *Transitional Justice* (n 5) 134.

[178] Brett and Malagón (n 109) 258.

[179] ibid.

burden of transition is not borne by reparations alone but rather comprises an interwoven series of measures targeted toward different levels of injustice and suffering in post-abuse societies, including both reparatory and distributive justice measures.

The selection of certain wrongs and exclusion of others in official reparations programs can create problematic lacunae in the application of justice, with the potential to further marginalize victimized communities. Reparations programs with a severely limited scope run the risk of harming the credibility of the new regime and its attempt to establish rule of law by enlarging the gap between law and practice.[180] The signaling functions of reparations can be undermined where specific victimized groups are inadequately redressed through official channels, particularly given that official recognition in itself has symbolic dimensions.[181] The veneer of legal rights and recognition attaching to comprehensive reparations programs transcends sides of a conflict, helping to legitimize the outcomes as measures associated with a sense of justice beyond the conflict, even where practical compromises must be made. Where reparations make a sincere and concerted attempt at recognition, they may be seen as "good enough," even where they do not fully repair the suffering caused by wrongdoing for the entire universe of possible beneficiaries.[182] Thus, a compromise may still satisfy the psychological needs of victims and serve as a prelude to recovery.

The impossibility, insufficiency, and inadequacy of any attempt to return victims to the position they were in prior to grave abuses make any redress to some degree partial and symbolic.[183] Thus, there will always be an element of compromise in the acceptance of reparations. As Lawther and Moffett conclude:

> Regardless of resources, rhetoric or expertise, transitional justice mechanisms will not be acceptable to all and cannot offer the magic silver bullet of political harmony, full truth, complete physical and psychological healing or socio-economic rejuvenation.[184]

[180] Camins (n 51) 144.
[181] Urban Walker, *What is Reparative Justice?* (n 96) 19.
[182] Hamber "The Dilemmas of Reparations" (n 101) 137.
[183] See *Blake v Guatemala* (Reparations and Costs) IACHR Series C No 48 (January 22, 1999).
[184] Lawther and Moffett, "Researching Transitional Justice" (n 114) 4.

Even where reparations programs are unable to redress the entire potential universe of beneficiaries and where awards cannot measure up to the scale of suffering inflicted upon victims, partial ameliorative acts and processes are an integral feature of corrective reparatory projects.[185] Thus, although the historical case manifests a more extreme example of resource limitations, transitional reparatory justice already accounts for the difficulties of constructing reparations for irreparable injustices.

That some degree of compromise on the basis of resource limitations may be acceptable to victim populations does not provide a state with blanket permission to decrease redress as it sees fit. Reparations programs are unlikely to be accepted as "good enough" when there is a failure in recognition. In particular, when the state instituting the program continues to deny or underplay its role in the conflict, refusing to accept responsibility for atrocities committed, victims are unlikely to find solace in compensation programs.[186] The range of options available for pursuing reparatory justice makes failure to provide such measures even more unacceptable—symbolic gestures in particular (where these are sincere and responsive) can account for resource constraints while still ensuring the recognition of victims.[187] Responsive forms of reparation can also offset the resource drain on recovering states.[188] While compromises on the basis of resource limitations may be an accepted feature of reparations in transition, willingness to accept less fair and meaningful redress is limited. As de Greiff underlines:

> a state cannot simply ignore the claims of victims with the argument that there are no resources to cover the corresponding costs, or alleging that there is simply no way to overcome the problems described. This would be tantamount to acknowledging that it is in no position to sustain a fair regime.[189]

[185] Teitel, *Transitional Justice* (n 5) 132.

[186] The *Madres de Plaza de Mayo* of Argentina, for instance, rejected reparations for this very reason, labeling compensation "blood money" in the absence of accountability and recognition—Moon (n 84) 194. See also Akane (n 131) with regard to the "comfort women."

[187] Theo van Boven and others, "Seminar on the Right to Restitution, Compensation and Rehabilitation for Victims of Gross violations of Human Rights and Fundamental Freedoms: Summary and Conclusion" in Kritz (n 7) 500.

[188] See, for instance, Argentina's distribution of government bonds to distribute the economic burden of reparations over time, thus postponing a portion of the costs while the costs of reconstruction were acute—see Guembe (n 23) 33.

[189] de Greiff, "Justice and Reparations" (n 33) 459.

7.5. Positioning reparations in transition

Transition paradoxically demands the re-establishment and bolstering of the rule of law while also necessitating that justice for victims be curtailed to some extent. Reparations exist and are enacted at the cusp of this dilemma. While carrying out many of the objectives of traditional reparatory justice, reparations in transition are servants not only of the corrective justice framework but also of the transition, seeking to restore the dignity of victims and achieve their reintegration into society as equal citizens, as well as supporting the establishment of long-term stability.[190] Thus, transitional reparatory justice may directly grapple with the legacies of massive historical injustice, without being tethered to formal legal requirements. The practice of reparatory justice in transition provides guidance for the enactment of measures of redress for transatlantic enslavement.

The solutions found in transitional reparatory processes to contextual legal challenges highlight the potential for justice that engages with the lived experiences of victims and institutional limitations, without sacrificing the need for action. Furthermore, transitional reparatory justice provides a call for justice in the face of massive and widespread injustice, where legal mechanisms fall short. In the context of transatlantic enslavement, occurring across multiple centuries, involving several states, featuring African complicity, and embedded in the foundations of the international legal system, judicial reparations may not sufficiently respond to the complexities of the case. Moreover, the contestation of the fundamental question of illegality identified in chapter 2 complicates attempts to achieve legal redress. However, transitional reparatory justice—in accepting the need for context-responsive processes as well as awards—may enable the reckoning reparations advocates seek.

[190] Malamud-Goti and Grosman (n 57) 541.

Conclusion

The Reparations Debate beyond International Law

International law is not a neutral system built upon a foundation of the rule of law, justice, or equality. Centuries of enslavement, colonialism, and imperial expansion constitute the bedrock of the modern international legal system.[1] Contemporary claims to universality may draw support from the notion of a global community of nations with equal participation and representation—of shared interests based on the precepts of shared humanity—however, the oscillations of power have substantially influenced the operation of international law from its inception. The founders of the system of European international law, purporting universality, created a jurisprudence of injustice, legitimizing the marginalization of African, indigenous, and aboriginal people, and the exploitation of their lands, their lives, and their labor. Thus, transatlantic enslavement and the *maangamizi* are interwoven with the construction and evolution of international law.

For many years, scholars have questioned these foundations and the inequalities embedded in the international legal order.[2] These commentators grapple with the historical development of international law, and how these anachronistic perspectives continue to permeate and shape international law in theory and in practice. Yet, the restructuring of the international system in response to this history remains elusive. The transition from hegemonic European dominance supported by violence, coercion, and the

[1] This was recognized at Abuja in 1993, calling for the restructuring of the international system in pursuit of justice. "The Abuja Proclamation" adopted at the Abuja Pan-African Conference on Reparations for African Enslavement, Colonization and Neo-colonialism (Abuja, April 27–29, 1993).

[2] See Anne Orford (ed), *International Law and Its Others* (CUP 2006); Antony Anghie, *Imperialism, Sovereignty and the Making of International Law* (CUP 2007); Antony Anghie and others (eds), *The Third World and International Order: Law, Politics, and Globalization* (Kluwer Law International 2003); Bhupinder Chimni, *International Law and World Order: A Critique of Contemporary Approaches* (Sage 1993); Gerry Simpson, *Great Powers and Outlaw States: Unequal Sovereigns in the International Legal Order* (CUP 2004); Martti Koskienniemi, *The Gentle Civilizer of Nations: The Rise and Fall of International Law, 1870–1960* (CUP 2002); Makau Mutua, *Human Rights: A Political and Cultural Critique* (University of Pennsylvania Press 2009); Sundhya Pahuja, *Decolonising International Law: Development, Economic Growth and the Politics of Universality* (CUP 2011).

Reparations for Slavery in International Law. Katarina Schwarz, Oxford University Press. © Oxford University Press 2022.
DOI: 10.1093/oso/9780197636398.003.0009

marginalization of non-European peoples remains incomplete despite the move toward decolonization in the twentieth century.[3] International law has neither drawn a line in the sand, signaling a break from the prior regime, nor has it given effect to the requirements of reparatory justice in the aftermath of widespread abuse.[4]

Absent remedies in the instance of a breach, the meaning of legal norms degrades. Reparations, therefore, cannot be severed from the normative legal order.[5] In conjunction with obligations of cessation and guarantees of non-repetition, reparations are the means by which international law gives effect to justice internally in direct response to wrongful conduct. As a normative system lacking centralized institutions possessing coercive power, the significance of normative legitimacy in international law is even greater than in the context of domestic systems. Reparations in this context affirm the validity of norms absent strict enforcement mechanisms or centralized legal sanctions.[6] Thus, the impact of widespread, unaddressed injustice within international law poses an existential problem for the system itself. With the continuation of harms through time and a failure to effect a transition from a system of law premised on imperialism and European domination, this problem continues to manifest in international law despite its historical roots.

The frameworks of the international legal system present significant barriers to attempts to achieve justice internally. Within the framework of positivist international legal thought, the doctrine of intertemporal law alone destabilizes reparations claims. The historical ubiquity of enslavement creates a platform for conclusions of legality, calls for moral relativity, and accusations of "presentism." On these accounts, crystallization of international law prohibiting enslavement at the time European states were involved in the forced migration and exploitation of twelve million African people

[3] See Dianne Otto, "Subalternity and International Law: The Problems of Global Community and the Incommensurability of Difference" (1996) 5 Social and Legal Studies 337; Nathaniel Berman, *Passion and Ambivalence: Nationalism, Colonialism, and International Law* (Brill 2011); Sundhya Pahuja, *Decolonising International Law: Development, Economic Growth and the Politics of Universality* (CUP 2011); Sundhya Pahuja, "The Postcoloniality of International Law" (2005) 46(2) Harvard Journal of International Law 459.

[4] On the need for a break from the past in transition, see Bronwyn Leebaw, *Judging State-Sponsored Violence, Imagining Political Change* (CUP 2011).

[5] See *Case Concerning the Factory at Chorzów (Germany v Poland)* (Jurisdiction) PCIJ Rep Series A No 9, 21. See further section 4.1.

[6] See Brigitte Stern, "The Elements of an Internationally Wrongful Act" in James Crawford, Alain Pellet, and Simon Olleson (eds), *The Law of International Responsibility* (OUP 2010) 193, 194; Dionisio Anzilotti, *General Theory of State Responsibility in International Law* (Firenze 1902); UNGA, "Report by Mr R Ago, Chairman of the Sub-Committee on State Responsibility" (1963) UN Doc A/CN.4/152, 250.

would be central to the construction of the reparations case. Yet, the evolution of international law with regard to enslavement fails to provide clear answers on this most basic question.

In the long history of global enslavement, jurists have evidenced substantial fluctuation in their understandings of the positioning of the institution of slavery within the dominant legal frameworks. For centuries, enslavement was permitted in restricted circumstances within jus gentium, despite its recognized contravention of *jus naturale.* In the medieval period, restrictions on enslavement were seen to increase both within states and regionally, as the law of Christian and Islamic nations came to bar the enslavement of coreligionists, while maintaining existing permissions for those outside the religious order.[7] The transatlantic system fundamentally altered the nature and scope of enslavement and its positioning within jurisprudential thought. However, the claimed universality of this reasoning was primarily premised on European expansion and the exclusion of peoples in the "New World" from international legal personality.

The problematic imperial foundations of international legal thought with regard to enslavement, combined with preceding limitations, the understanding of enslavement in general as a contravention of *jus naturale*, and the predominant naturalist international jurisprudence of the time, destabilize the claim to historical legality. Thus, the conclusion that transatlantic enslavement was definitively "legal at the time" fails to account for the realities and evolutions of the international legal system at the time. This does not lead to the converse conclusion that a general prohibition against enslavement was an unchanging and established element of universal law prior to, or throughout, the period of transatlantic chattel enslavement.[8] However, it does frustrate claims that reparations are not morally mandated on the basis of the positive legality of enslavement at the time. In other words, the argument that enslavement was "legal at the time" as a defense against the moral and political case for reparations is overthrown.

Despite the uneven legal terrain on which the reparations case stands with regard to the establishment of a breach, the frameworks of responsibility provided by international law offer insight and guidance for the moral and political case for reparations for transatlantic enslavement. Moreover, these

[7] See section 2.4.

[8] Such a position may be arguable on the basis of prevailing natural law principles of the time, although the likelihood of a successful legal claim on this ground is reduced by the oscillations of international norms and practice related to enslavement through history.

elements are frequently utilized in reparations denials to refute claims for extralegal reparatory processes. Thus, the additional elements of responsibility in international law remain relevant to the consideration of claims. Acquiescence, limitation, and attribution, considered on the facts of the case, and not on the presumption that historicity in itself will frustrate claims, can be eliminated as bars to recovery in relation to historical enslavement.[9] Yet, the international legal frameworks governing reparatory justice have more to offer the consideration of reparations claims than the deconstruction of obstructions to justice.

Reparations are inherent in, and fundamental to, the international legal system.[10] Reparatory justice, as a theoretical paradigm, grapples with injustices and their legacies within a framework shaped by wrongdoing, recognition, and responsibility—of setting wrongs to right. Thus, the centuries of jurisprudence regarding remedies speaks to the objectives that ought to be pursued in redressing the past. The international legal frameworks themselves provide comprehensive guidance on the forms reparations might take. The multiple modalities of redress available in international law and the different harms these target enable a dialectic between theory and practice, cultivating a broader understanding of reparability itself. Thus, the potential for nuanced, responsive reparations programs addressing a variety of harms may, in turn, influence the kinds of harms considered reparable.

In considering historical injustices, it is often the universe of potential claims, and not simply the case at hand, that shapes understandings of what ought to be redressed. Yet, in reframing reparations as not simply individualized, monetary payments but also as collective and symbolic measures, the nature of the causal inquiry may change. Consideration of what harms must be redressed within the consideration of causation may be expanded to account for these existing frameworks, recognizing a broader range of injuries within the determinations of legal policy already occurring.[11] The limits of the law in such cases ought to respond to the legal frameworks themselves, in this case requiring greater attention on the moral and symbolic injuries addressed through satisfaction.

The impetus for the application of reparatory justice in the case of historical enslavement is not drawn from the legal frameworks alone, and thus may be informed by a broader range of justice mechanisms. Historical injustices

[9] See chapter 3.
[10] See chapter 4, section 4.1.
[11] See chapter 6.

present challenges for legal mechanisms that may require the engagement of alternative processes. Thus, transitional justice provides a lens through which to consider the transformational demands on the international legal system as a whole, as well as in specific cases relating to transatlantic enslavement. These processes enable the balancing of competing interests, while upholding the fundamental need for responsibility, recognition, and reconciliation. Thus, transitional justice, in combination with the international legal frameworks, provides a rubric for the realization of justice in the case of historical enslavement.

Massive and widespread injustices have significant impact on the way people formulate their identities, and as time goes on, their histories.[12] The centrality of large-scale abuses makes the refusal to grapple with the past not only an act of obfuscation or avoidance but also a form of violence. The lack of redress may entrench the "nonpersonhood" of victims, cementing the affective dimensions of injustice through time and constituting an injury in itself.[13] As Jeremy Waldron articulates:

> To neglect the historical record is to do violence to this identity and thus to the community that it sustains. And since communities help generate a deeper sense of identity for the individuals they comprise, neglecting or expunging the historical record is a way of undermining and insulting individuals as well.[14]

Thus, the refusal to grapple with the past becomes unacceptable from the perspective of reparatory justice. Where legal frameworks themselves are the mechanisms through which injustice is realized, the moral weight of purported legality ought not to be determinative.[15] Reparations overthrow the marginalization and dehumanization of victims of wrongdoing by recognizing their humanity and status as rights bearers.[16] This remains

[12] Thompson, for instance, identifies that "Members of nations whose ancestors were the victims of unrequited historical wrongs often suffer from despair, depression and loss of both confidence and hope for the future." Janna Thompson, *Taking Responsibility for the Past: Reparation and Historical Injustice* (Polity 2002) 66.

[13] Mari Matsuda, "Looking to the Bottom: Critical Legal Studies and Reparations" (1987) 22 Harvard Civil Rights-Civil Liberties Law Review 323, 390.

[14] Jeremy Waldron, "Superseding Historical Injustice" (1992) 103(1) Ethics 4, 6.

[15] On the potential for law to legitimate abuse of power and violence, see Bronwyn Leebaw, "The Irreconcilable Goals of Transitional Justice" (2008) 30 Human Rights Quarterly 95.

[16] Yael Danieli, "Massive Trauma and the Healing Role of Reparative Justice" in Carla Ferstman, Mariana Goetz, and Alan Stephens (eds), *Reparations for Victims of Genocide, War Crimes and Crimes against Humanity: Systems in Place and Systems in the Making* (Martinus Nijhoff 2009) 66.

true irrespective of whether the case engages five years or five centuries of discrimination.

Claims to reparations for historical enslavement face a plethora of challenges in both legal and political arenas. The extent to which the *maangamizi* was foundational to the international system, and remains central to international relations, presents a challenge to reparatory justice through official channels in the upcoming years, despite increasing global attention and support. Yet, even if legal and political systems remain silent, reparations discourse has broader value, particularly in the context of immaterial harms demanding symbolic or cognitive justice. As Ta-Nehisi Coates opines in relation to the question of reparations for the African American experience of enslavement and its aftermath:

> No one can know what would come out of such a debate. Perhaps no number can fully capture the multi-century plunder of black people in America. Perhaps the number is so large that it can't be imagined, let alone calculated and dispensed. But I believe that wrestling publicly with these questions matters as much as—if not more than—the specific answers that might be produced. An America that asks what it owes its most vulnerable citizens is improved and humane. An America that looks away is ignoring not just the sins of the past but the sins of the present and the certain sins of the future. More important than any single check cut to any African American, the payment of reparations would represent America's maturation out of the childhood myth of its innocence into a wisdom worthy of its founders.[17]

There is value in considering and speaking about reparations even absent legal and political conclusions. Affirming the foundations of claims contributes to reparatory justice through broader societal acknowledgment and recognition, even absent official action. The movement for reparatory justice, shaped by marginal and subaltern perspectives, is not denied value simply by virtue of mainstream denials. Yet, the affective dimensions of reparatory justice are premised not only on resistance but also on the society in which injustices were embedded listening. Thus, creating space in which

[17] Ta-Nehisi Coates, "The Case for Reparations" *The Atlantic* (June 2014) <www.theatlantic.com/magazine/archive/2014/06/the-case-for-reparations/361631/> accessed June 25, 2018.

the perspectives of those people previously marginalized may speak for themselves, and in which their voices are heard, is a reparatory act in itself.

> Yes we hold the most spectacular Survival Record.
> But we must hasten to remind ourSelves
>
> that just to survive
> simply to survive
> merely to survive
> barely to survive
> is not & can
> never be enough.
>
> *And so still we stand so tall among the cannonades*
> *We smell of mists and of powdered memories*
>
> *And those who took away our Voice*
> *They are now surprised*
> *They couldnt take away our Song.*[18]

[18] Kofi Anyidoho, "MEMORY & VISION" in Alice Bellagamba, Sandra Greene, and Martin Klein (eds), *African Voices on Slavery and the Slave Trade* (CUP 2013) xxii; originally published in Kofi Anyidoho, *Praise Song for the Land* (Sub-Saharan Publishers 2002), emphasis in original.

Work Cited

"14 Caribbean Nations Sue European Countries for Slavery Reparations" *Aljazeera* (September 27, 2013) <http://america.aljazeera.com/articles/2013/9/27/14-caribbean-nationssueeuropeancountriesforreparationsoverslaver.html> accessed November 19, 2018

"CARICOM Nations Unanimously Approve 10 Point Plan for Slavery Reparations" (*Leigh Day*, March 11, 2014) <www.leighday.co.uk/News/2014/March-2014/CARICOM-nations-unanimously-approve-10-point-plan> accessed June 1, 2018

"Church Apologises for Slave Trade" *BBC News* (February 8, 2006) <news.bbc.co.uk/1/hi/uk/4694896.stm> accessed November 17, 2018

"Universities Studying Slavery" (*University of Virginia*) <slavery.virginia.edu/universities-studying-slavery/> accessed November 17, 2018

Ade Ajayi JF, "The Policy of Reparation in the Context of Globalization" (2004) *African Studies Papers* <journals.openedition.org/etudesafricaines/4524> accessed October 31, 2018

Adelman J, *Colonial Legacies: The Problem of Persistence in Latin American History* (Routledge 1999)

Adhikari P, Hansen W, and Powers K, "The Demand for Reparations: Grievance, Risk, and the Pursuit of Justice in Civil War Settlement" (2012) 56(2) Journal of Conflict Resolution 183

Afrikan World Reparations and Repatriation Truth Commission, "The Accra Declaration on Reparations and Repatriation" *The African Descent International Diaspora* (August 12, 1999) <http://estooks.wixsite.com/the-adid/black-power-and-reparations> accessed June 1, 2018

Akwagyiram A, "Poignant Site to Remember Slave Trade" *BBC News* (March 26, 2007) <http://news.bbc.co.uk/1/hi/uk/6494097.stm> accessed October 25, 2018

Aleinikoff TA, "A Case for Race-Consciousness" (1991) 91 Columbia Law Review 1060

Alfred T, *Wasáse: Indigenous Pathways of Action and Freedom* (Broadview Press Ltd 2005)

Allain J (ed), *The Legal Understanding of Slavery: From the Historical to the Contemporary* (1st edn, OUP 2012)

Allain J, *Slavery in International Law: Of Human Exploitation and Trafficking* (Martinus Nijhoff 2013)

Allain J, *The Law and Slavery: Prohibiting Human Exploitation* (Brill Nijhoff 2015)

Allen J, "Balancing Justice and Social Unity: Political Theory and the Idea of a Truth and Reconciliation Commission" (1999) 49(3) University of Toronto Law Journal 331

Anaya SJ, *Indigenous Peoples in International Law* (2nd edn, OUP 2004)

Andersen AN, "'We Have Reconquered the Islands': Figurations in Public Memories of Slavery and Colonialism in Denmark 1948–2012" (2013) 26(1) International Journal of Politics, Culture and Society 57

Andersen E, "Transitional Justice and the Rule of Law: Lessons from the Field" (2015) 47 Case Western Reserve Journal of International Law 305

Anghie A, "Finding the Peripheries: Sovereignty and Colonialism in Nineteenth-Century International Law" (1999) 40 Harvard International Law Journal 1
Anghie A, *Imperialism, Sovereignty and the Making of International Law* (CUP 2007)
Anghie A, "LatCrit and TWAIL" (2011–12) 42 California Western International Law Journal 311
Anghie A, "International Law and the Pre-History of Globalisation" (2015) 33 Singapore Law Review 3
Anghie A and others (eds), *The Third World and International Order: Law, Politics, and Globalization* (Kluwer Law International 2003)
Antunes NSM, "Acquiescence" *Max Planck Encyclopedia of Public International Law* (2006) <opil.ouplaw.com/view/10.1093/law:epil/9780199231690/law-9780199231690-e1373> accessed April 18, 2018
Anyidoho K, *Praise Song for the Land* (Sub-Saharan Publishers 2002)
Anzilotti D, *General Theory of State Responsibility in International Law* (Firenze 1902)
Anzilotti D, "La responsabilité internationale des Etats à raison des dommages soufferts par des étrangers" (1906) 8 Revue Générale de Droit International Public 5
Aptheker H, *American Negro Slave Revolts* (Columbia UP 1943)
Araujo AL, *Public Memory of Slavery: Victims and Perpetrators in the South Atlantic* (Cambria Press 2010)
Araujo AL (ed), *Politics of Memory: Making Slavery Visible in the Public Space* (Routledge 2012)
Araujo AL, *Shadows of the Slave Past: Memory, Heritage, and Slavery* (Routledge 2014)
Araujo AL, *Reparations for Slavery and the Slave Trade: A Transnational and Comparative History* (Bloomsbury Academic 2017)
Aristotle, *The Ethics* (JA K Thompson tr, Penguin Books 1955)
Aristotle, *The Nicomachean Ethics* (David Ross tr, OUP 2009)
Asare WK, *Slavery Reparations in Perspective* (Trafford 2002)
Austin J, *The Province of Jurisprudence Determined* (2nd edn, J Murray 1861)
Ayala B, *De Jure et Oficiis Bellicis et Disciplina Militari, 1582* (Carnegie Institution of Washington 1912)
Balasco LM, "Reparative Development: Re-Conceptualising Reparations in Transitional Justice Processes" (2017) 17(1) Conflict, Security and Development 1
Baptist EE, *The Half Has Never Been Told: Slavery and the Making of American Capitalism* (Basic Books 2014)
Baptist EE and Camp SMH (eds), *New Studies in the History of American Slavery* (University of Georgia Press 2006)
Bar-Tal D and others, "A Sense of Self-Perceived Collective Victimhood in Intractable Conflicts" (2009) 91(874) International Review of the Red Cross 229
Bassiouni MC, "Enslavement as an International Crime" (1991) 23 New York University Journal of International Law and Politics 45
Baxter RR, "Multilateral Treaties as Evidence of Customary International Law" (1965–1966) 41 British Yearbook of International Law 275
Beauchamp G, "Apologies All Around: Today's Tendency to Make Amends for the Crimes of History Raises the Question: Where Do We Stop?" (2007) 76(4) The American Scholar 83
Beckles H, *Britain's Black Debt: Reparations for Caribbean Slavery and Native Genocide* (University of the West Indies Press 2013)
Beckles H and Shepherd V, *Trading Souls: Europe's Transatlantic Trade in Africans* (Ian Randle 2007)
Bell C, *Peace Agreements and Human Rights* (OUP 2000)

Bell C, "Transitional Justice, Interdisciplinarity and the State of the 'Field' or 'Non-Field'" (2009) 3 International Journal of Transitional Justice 5

Bell C, Campbell C, and Ní Aoláin F, "Justice Discourses in Transition" (2004) 13(3) Social and Legal Studies 305

Bellagamba A, Greene S, and Klein M (eds), *African Voices on Slavery and the Slave Trade* (CUP 2013)

Bellagamba A, Greene S, and Klein M (eds), *African Slaves: African Masters: Politics, Memory, Social Life* (Africa World Press 2017)

Belli P, *De Re Militari et Bello Tractatus* (Clarendon Press 1936)

Bentrovato D, Korostelina K, and Schulze M (eds), *History Can Bite: History Education in Divided and Postwar Societies* (V&R Unipres 2016)

Berman N, *Passion and Ambivalence: Nationalism, Colonialism, and International Law* (Brill 2011)

Berry MF, *My Face Is Black Is True: Callie House and the Struggle for Ex-Slave Reparations* (Alfred A Knopf 2005)

Bîrzu B, "Considerations Regarding the Non-Applicability of Statutory Limitations to Genocide, Crimes against Humanity and War Crimes" (2015) 11 Acta Universitatis Danubius Juridica 96

Bittker B, *The Case for Black Reparations* (Beacon Press 2003)

Blackmon D, *Slavery by Another Name: The Re-enslavement of Black Americans from the Civil War to World War II* (Icon Books 2012)

Blair T, "PM's Article for the New Nation Newspaper" (November 27, 2006) <webarchive.nationalarchives.gov.uk/20040105034004/http://number10.gov.uk/page10487> accessed November 1, 2016

Blair T, "The Shame of Slavery" *New Nation* (November 27, 2006) 2 <www.ligali.org/truth2007/learning/tony_blair_statement_of_sorrow_new_nation_27_nov_06.pdf> accessed March 2, 2018

Bloom A (ed), *Injury and Injustice* (CUP 2018)

Bolivar S, "Message to the Congress of Bolivia (Lima, 25 May 1826)" quoted in Carozza, "From Conquest to Constitutions: Retrieving a Latin American Tradition of the Idea of Human Rights" (2003) 25 Human Rights Quarterly 281

Borchard E, "Important Decisions of the Mixed Claims Commission, United States and Mexico" (1927) 21 American Journal of International Law 516

Borchard E, *Declaratory Judgements* (reprint, W S Hein 1941)

Bordin E and Saachi A (eds), *Transatlantic Memories of Slavery: Reimagining the Past, Changing the Future* (Cambria Press 2015)

Boxill B, "Morality of Reparation" (1972) 1 Social Theory and Practice 113

Boxill B, "Black Reparations" *Stanford Encyclopaedia of Philosophy* (Winter edn, 2011) <https://stanford.library.sydney.edu.au/archives/win2011/entries/black-reparations/> accessed November 13, 2018

Bradley K (ed), *The Cambridge World History of Slavery: The Ancient Mediterranean World*, vol 1 (CUP 2011)

Branch W, "Reparations for Slavery: A Dream Deferred" (2002) 3 San Diego International Law Journal 177

Brett R and Malagón L, "Overcoming the Original Sin of the 'Original Condition': How Reparations May Contribute to Emancipatory Peacebuilding" (2013) 14(3) Human Rights Review 257

Brooks R, *Atonement and Forgiveness: A New Model for Black Reparations* (University of California Press 2004)

Brophy A, "The World of Reparations: Slavery Reparations in Historical Perspective" (2002) 3 Journal of Law in Society 105

Brown K, "Commemoration as Symbolic Reparation: New Narratives or Spaces of Conflict" (2013) 14(3) Human Rights Review 273

Brown W, *States of Injury* (Princeton UP 1995)

Brownlie I, *Principles of Public International Law* (6th edn, OUP 2003)

Bryant-Davis T, "Healing Requires Recognition: The Case for Race-Based Traumatic Stress" (2007) 35 The Counselling Psychologist 135

Buckland WW, *The Roman Law of Slavery: The Condition of the Slave in Private Law from Augustus to Justinian* (CUP 1908)

Buckland WW, *A Text-Book of Roman Law: From Augustus to Justinian* (Peter Stein ed, 3rd edn, CUP 1963)

Bulmer-Thomas V, *The Economic History of Latin America since Independence* (2nd edn, CUP 2003)

Burdick W, *Principles of Roman Law* (Lawyers Cooperative Publishing Co 1938)

Burt J and Rivera C (eds), *The National and International Significance of the Trial and Conviction of Alberto Fujimori* (Instituto de Defensa Legal 2011)

Buser A, "Colonial Injustices and the Law of State Responsibility: The CARICOM Claim for Reparations" KFG Working Paper Series No. 4, Berlin Potsdam Research Group, "The International Rule of Law: Rise or Decline?" (August 2016)

Buser A, "Colonial Injustices and the Law of State Responsibility: The CARICOM Claim for Reparations" (2017) 2 Heidelberg Journal of International Law 409

Call C (ed), *Constructing Justice and Security after War* (United States Institute of Peace Press 2008)

Cameron D The Rt Hon, "PM's Speech to the Jamaican Parliament" (*UK Government*, September 30, 2015) <https://www.gov.uk/government/speeches/pms-speech-to-the-jamaican-parliament> accessed March 14, 2018

Camins E, "Needs or Rights? Exploring the Limitations of Individual Reparations for Violations of International Humanitarian Law" (2016) 10 International Journal of Transitional Justice 126

Campbell C, Ní Aoláin F, and Harvey C, "The Frontiers of Legal Analysis: Reframing the Transition in Northern Ireland" (2003) 66 Modern Law Review 317

Campbell G and Alpers EA, "Slavery, Forced Labour and Resistance in Indian Ocean Africa and Asia" (2004) 25(2) Slavery and Abolition ix

CARICOM Reparations Commission, "CARICOM Ten Point Plan for Reparatory Justice" (*CARICOM*, March 2014) <www.caricom.org/caricom-ten-point-plan-for-reparatory-justice/> accessed November 19, 2018

Cassese A, "The International Criminal Tribunal for the former Yugoslavia and Human Rights" lecture delivered to the British Institute of Human Rights on May 1, 1997, published in 4 European Human Rights Law Review (1997) 329

Castellanos-Jankiewicz L, "Causation and International State Responsibility" (2012) *SHARES Research Paper 07*, ACIL 2012-07 <papers.ssrn.com/sol3/papers.cfm?abstract_id=2419913> accessed April 10, 2018

Catron JW, "Evangelical Networks in the Greater Caribbean and the Origins of the Black Church" (2010) 79(1) Church History 77

Chamallas M, "Questioning the Use of Race-Specific and Gender-Specific Economic Data in Tort Litigation: A Constitutional Argument" (1994) 63 Fordham Law Review 73

Chandler ND (ed), *The Problem of the Color Line at the Turn of the Twentieth Century: The Essential Early Essays* (reprint, Fordham UP 2015)

Cheng B, *General Principles of Law as Applied by International Courts and Tribunals* (Cambridge 1953)

Chimni B, *International Law and World Order: A Critique of Contemporary Approaches* (Sage 1993)

Clarence-Smith WG, *Islam and the Abolition of Slavery* (OUP 2006)

Clarkson T, *The History of the Rise, Progress, and Accomplishment of the Abolition of the African Slave-Trade by the British Parliament* (New impression, Frank Cass & Co Ltd 1968)

Clayton L, *Bartolomé de Las Casas and the Conquest of the Americas* (John Wiley & Sons 2010)

Coates R, "If a Tree Falls in the Wilderness: Reparations, Academic Silences, and Social Justice" (2004) 83 Social Forces 841

Coatsworth J, "Inequality, Institutions and Economic Growth in Latin America" (2008) 40 Journal of Latin American Studies 545

Collins W and Wanamaker M, "Up from Slavery? African American Intergenerational Economic Mobility since 1880" (2017) <https://www.nber.org/papers/w23395> accessed October 31, 2018

Contreras-Garduño D and Rombouts S, "Collective Reparations for Indigenous Communities before the Inter-American Court of Human Rights" (2011) 27 Utrecht Journal of International and European Law 4

Corlett JA, *Heirs of Oppression* (Rowman & Littlefield 2010)

Corntassel J and Holder C, "Who's Sorry Now? Government Apologies, Truth Commissions, and Indigenous Self-Determination in Australia, Canada, Guatemala and Peru" (2008) 9 Human Rights Review 465

Craton M, *Testing the Chains: Resistance to Slavery in the British West Indies* (Cornell UP 2009)

Craven M, *The Decolonization of International Law: State Succession and the Law of Treaties* (OUP 2007)

Crawford J, Pellet A, and Olleson S (eds), *The Law of International Responsibility* (OUP 2010)

Crooks JJ, *A History of the Colony of Sierra Leone, Western Africa* (reprint, Brown & Nolan 1903)

Croucher R and Michel D, "'Legal at the Time'?: Companies, Governments and Reparations for Mauritian Slavery" (2014) 58(1) Journal of African Law 89

Curran AS, *The Anatomy of Blackness: Science and Slavery in an Age of Enlightenment* (Johns Hopkins UP 2011)

Curto J, "Experiences of Enslavement in West Central Africa" (2008) 41(82) Histoire Sociale/Social History 381

Dagan H, "Restitution and Slavery: On Incomplete Commodification, Intergenerational Justice, and Legal Transitions" (2004) 84 Boston University Law Review 1139

Dal Lago E and Katsari C (eds), *Slave Systems: Ancient and Modern* (CUP 2008)

Dampha LF, *Reparation for Slavery and Colonialism: The Teachings of Durban* (CreateSpace 2015)

Davis DB, *Inhuman Bondage: The Rise and Fall of Slavery in the New World* (OUP 2006)

de Feyter K and others (eds), *Out of the Ashes: Reparation for Victims of Gross and Systematic Human Rights Violations* (Intersentia 2005) de Greiff P (ed), *The Handbook of Reparations* (OUP 2006)

de Greiff P, "A Normative Conception of Transitional Justice" (2010) 50(3) Politorbis 17

de Greiff P and Duthie R (eds), *Transitional Justice and Development: Making Connections* (Social Science Research Council 2009)

de las Casas B, *A Short Account of the Destruction of the Indies* (Nigel Griffin tr, Penguin 1992)

de las Casas B, *History of the Indies* (Andrée M Collard tr, Harper & Row 1971)

de Vattel E, *The Law of Nations* (Béla Kapossy and Richard Whatmore eds, Liberty Fund 2012)

Dennerlein B, "Remembering Violence, Negotiating Change: The Moroccan Equity and Reconciliation Commission and the Politics of Gender" (2012) 8(1) Journal of Middle Eastern Women's Studies 10

Dias MSF, *Legacies of Slavery: Comparative Perspectives* (Cambridge Scholars Publishing 2007)

Dixon P, "Reparations, Assistance and the Experience of Justice: Lessons from Colombia and the Democratic Republic of the Congo" (2016) 10 International Journal of Transitional Justice 88

Dockès P, *Medieval Slavery and Liberation* (Arthur Goldhammer tr, University of Chicago Press 1982)

Dolezalek G, "The Moral Theologian's Doctrine of Restitution and Its Juridification in the Sixteenth and Seventeenth Centuries" [1992] Acta Juridica 104

Dominicé C and Šahović M (eds), *Droit International 2* (Pedone 1982)

Donington K, Hanley R, and Moody J (eds), *Britain's History and Memory of Transatlantic Slavery: Local Nuances of a "National Sin"* (Liverpool UP 2016)

Drumbl M, *Atrocity, Punishment and International Law* (CUP 2007)

Dugan C and others, *Investor State Arbitration* (OUP 2008)

Du Plessis M, "Historical Injustice and International Law: An Exploratory Discussion of Reparation for Slavery" (2003) 25(3) Human Rights Quarterly 624

Du Plessis P, *Borkowski's Textbook on Roman Law* (4th edn, OUP 2010)

Dumberry P, *State Succession to International Responsibility* (Martinus Nijhoff 2007)

Dunaway WA, *The African-American Family in Slavery and Emancipation* (CUP 2003)

Dupuy PM, "The International Law of State Responsibility: Revolution or Evolution?" (1989) 11(1) Michigan Journal of International Law 105

Edmondson L, "Trans-Atlantic Slavery and the Internationalization of Race" (1976) 22 Caribbean Quarterly 5

Edwards C, *The Hammurabi Code, and the Sinaitic Legislation; with a Complete Translation of the Great Babylonian Inscription Discovered at Susa* (Kennikat Press 1971)

Eijkman Q, "Recognising the Local Perspective: Transitional Justice and Post-Conflict Reparations" (2010) 10(3) Global Jurist 1

Eltis D and Engerman SL (eds), *The Cambridge World History of Slavery*, vol. 3 (CUP 2011)

Emory University, "Estimates Tables" (*The Transatlantic Slave Trade Voyages Database* 2013) <http://slavevoyages.org/assessment/estimates> accessed October 27, 2018

Emory University, "Timeline: Number of Captives Embarked and Disembarked per Year" (*The Transatlantic Slave Trade Voyages Database* 2013) <http://slavevoyages.org/assessment/estimates> accessed October 27, 2018

Encarnación O, *Democracy without Justice in Spain: The Politics of Forgetting* (University of Pennsylvania Press 2014)

Equiano O, *The Interesting Narrative of the Life of Olaudah Equiano, or Gustavus Vassa, The African* (8th edn, Norwich 1794)

Erdozain D, "The Secularisation of Sin in the Nineteenth Century" (2011) 62(1) The Journal of Ecclesiastical History 59

Evans M (ed), *International Law* (4th edn, OUP 2014)

Fage JD, *Introduction to the History of West Africa* (CUP 1955) 48

Fage JD, "Slavery and the Slave Trade in the Context of West African History" (1969) 10(3) Journal of African History 393

Fage JD, "Slaves and Society in Western Africa, c. 1445–c. 1700" (1980) 21 Journal of African History 289

Farmer P, *The Uses of Haiti* (3rd edn, Common Courage Press 2005)

Fassbender B and others (eds), *The Oxford Handbook of the History of International Law* (OUP 2012)

Ferstman C, Goetz M, and Stephens A, *Reparations for Victims of Genocide, War Crimes and Crimes against Humanity: Systems in Place and Systems in the Making* (Martinus Nijhoff 2009)

Finkenbine RE, "Belinda's Petition: Reparations for Slavery in Revolutionary Massachusetts" (2007) 64(1) William and Mary Quarterly 95

Finley M, "Slavery" in *Encyclopaedia of the Social Sciences*, vol 14 (Macmillan Co and Free Press 1968)

Finley M, *Ancient Slavery and Modern Ideology* (Brent D Shaw ed, expanded edn, Markus Wiener Publishers 1998)

Finley M, *Classical Slavery* (Taylor & Francis 2014)

Finney P, "The Ubiquitous Presence of the Past? Collective Memory and International History" (2014) 36(3) The International History Review 443

Firchow P and Mac Ginty R, "Reparations and Peacebuilding: Issues and Controversies" (2013) 14(3) Human Rights Review 231

Fisher NRE, *Slavery in Classical Greece* (Bristol Classical Press 1993)

Fitzgerald E and others, "The Transgenerational Impact of 'The Troubles' in Northern Ireland" (*Queen's University Belfast School of Psychology* 2017) <www.qub.ac.uk/schools/psy/files/Filetoupload,784073,en.pdf> accessed May 8, 2018

Foner PS (ed), *Frederick Douglass: Selected Speeches and Writings* (Chicago Review Press 2000)

Forman J, "The Black Manifesto" (1970) 1(1) Review of the Black Political Economy 36

Fossion P and others, "Transgenerational Transmission of Trauma in Families of Holocaust Survivors: The Consequences of Extreme Family Functioning on Resilience, Sense of Coherence, Anxiety and Depression" (2015) 171 Journal Of Affective Disorders 48

Freeman M, *Necessary Evils: Amnesties and the Search for Justice* (CUP 2009)

Frith N, "Saving the Republic: State Nostalgia and Slavery Reparations in Media and Political Discourses" (2015) 23(2) Modern and Contemporary France 213

Galanter M, "The Dialectic of Injury and Remedy" (2010) 44 Loyola Los Angeles Law Review 1

Galindo GRB and Yip C, "Customary International Law and the Third World: Do Not Step on the Grass" (2017) 16 Chinese Journal of International Law 251

Gallen J, "Jesus Wept: The Roman Catholic Church, Child Sexual Abuse and Transitional Justice" (2016) 10 International Journal of Transitional Justice 332

García Amador FV, "Fourth Report on State Responsibility" (1959) UN Doc A/CN.4/119, 2 Yearbook of the International Law Commission 1

García Amador FV, *The Changing Law of International Claims*, vol 2 (Oceana Publications 1984)

Garcia-Godos J, "Victim Reparations in Transitional Justice—What is at Stake and Why" (2008) 26 Nordisk Tidsskrift for Menneskerettigheter 111

Gaskin D, Headen Jr A, and White-Means S, "Racial Disparities in Health and Wealth: The Effects of Slavery and Past Discrimination" (2005) 32 The Review of Black Political Economy 95

Gattini A, "The UN Compensation Commission: Old Rules, New Procedures on War Reparations" (2002) 13 European Journal of International Law 161 Gemery H and Hogendorn J (eds), *The Uncommon Market: Essays in the Economic History of the Atlantic Slave Trade* (Academic Press 1979)

Genovese E, *From Rebellion to Revolution: Afro-American Slave Revolts in the Making of the Modern World* (Louisiana State UP 1979)

Gentili A, *De Iure Belli Libri Tres, 1612* (Clarendon Press 1933)

Gibney M and Roxstrom E, "The Status of State Apologies" (2001) 23 Human Rights Quarterly 911

Gibney M and others (eds), *The Age of Apology: Facing up to the Past* (University of Pennsylvania Press 2008)

Gifford A, "Pipe Dream or Necessary Atonement" (2007) 36 Index on Censorship 89

Gifford A, "The Legal Basis of the Claim for Reparations" First Pan-African Congress on Reparations (Abuja, April 1993) <http://www.shaka.mistral.co.uk/legalbasis.htm> accessed June 4, 2018

Gillies J (ed), *Aristotle's Ethics and Politics*, vol 2 (A Strahan, T Cadell and W Davies 1797)

Girard PF, *Manuel Élémentaire de Droit Romain* (A Rousseau 1929)

Glancy J, *Slavery in Early Christianity* (OUP 2002)

Goldenberg D, *The Curse of Ham: Race and Slavery in Early Judaism, Christianity, and Islam* (Princeton UP 2005)

Gong G, *The Standard of "Civilization" in International Society* (OUP 1984)

Gordon-Reed A, "America's Original Sin: Slavery and the Legacy of White Supremacy" (2018) 97(1) Foreign Affairs 2

Gould S, *The Mismeasure of Man* (2nd edn, WW Norton & Co 1996)

Graefrath B, *Responsibility and Damages Caused: Relationship between Responsibility and Damages* (Nijhoff 1985)

Graham L, "Reparations, Self-Determination, and the Seventh Generation" (2008) 21 Harvard Human Rights Journal 47

Gray C, *Judicial Remedies in International Law* (Clarendon Press 1987)

Gready P, *The Era of Transitional Justice, the Aftermath of the Truth and Reconciliation Commission in South Africa and Beyond* (Routledge 2011) 1

Green T, *The Rise of the Trans-Atlantic Slave Trade in Western Africa, 1300–1589* (CUP 2012)

Grossman K, *Germany's Moral Debt: The German-Israeli Agreement* (Public Affairs Press 1954),

Grotius H, *The Rights of War and Peace, in three books. Wherein are explained, the law of nature and nations, and The Principal Points relating to Government. Written in Latin by the learned Hugo Grotius, and translated into English. To which are added, all the large notes of Mr. J. Barbeyrac, Professor of Law at Groningen, and Member of the Royal Academy of Sciences at Berlin* (London 1738)

Grotius H, *The Freedom of the Seas or the Right Which Belongs to the Dutch to Take Part in the East Indian Trade* (Batoche Books 1999)

Grotius H, *The Rights of War and Peace*, vol 2 (Richard Tuck tr, Liberty Fund 2005)

Hair PEH, "Sources on Early Sierra Leone: Barreira on Just Enslavement, 1606" (1975) 6 Africana Research Bulletin 52

Haldemann F, "Another Kind of Justice: Transitional Justice as Recognition" (2008) 41(2) Cornell International Law Journal 678

Hamber B, "Repairing the Irreparable: Dealing with the Double-Binds of Making Reparations for Crimes of the Past" (2000) 5 Ethnicity and Health 221

Hamber B and Mofokeng T (eds), *From Rhetoric to Responsibility: Making Reparations to the Survivors of Past Political Violence in South Africa* (Centre for the Study of Violence and Reconciliation 2000)

Hamel CE, *Black Morocco: A History of Slavery, Race, and Islam* (CUP 2013)

Hart HLA, *The Concept of Law* (2nd edn, OUP 1994)

Hart HLA and Tony Honoré, *Causation in the Law* (2nd edn, OUP 1985)

Hart R, *Slaves Who Abolished Slavery: Blacks in Rebellion* (University of the West Indies Press 2002)

Hassankhan MS and others (eds), *Legacy of Slavery and Indentured Labour: Historical and Contemporary Issues in Suriname and the Caribbean* (Routledge 2016)

Hauser-Schäublin B (ed), *World Heritage Angkor and Beyond: Circumstances and Implications of UNESCO Listings in Cambodia* (Göttingen UP 2011)

Hawthorne W, *From Africa to Brazil: Culture, Identity, and an Atlantic Slave Trade, 1600–1830* (CUP 2010)

Hayden P, "The Human Right to Health and the Struggle for Recognition" (2012) 38 Review of International Studies 569

Hayner P, "Truth Commissions: A Schematic Overview" (2006) 88(862) International Review of the Red Cross 295

Hayner P, *Unspeakable Truths: Transitional Justice and the Challenge of Truth Commissions* (2nd edn, Routledge 2011)

Hayward J and Wheen N (eds), *Treaty of Waitangi Settlements* (Bridget Williams Books 2015)

Heinl RD and Heinl NG, *Written in Blood: The Story of the Haitian People 1492–1995* (rev edn, UP of America 2005)

Henry CP, *Long Overdue: The Politics of Racial Reparations from Forty Acres to Atonement and Beyond* (New York UP 2009)

Heuman G and Burnard T (eds), *The Routledge History of Slavery* (Routledge 2011)

Heuman G and Walvin J, *The Slavery Reader* (Routledge 2003)

Heywood L, "Slavery and Its Transformation in the Kingdom of Kongo: 1491–1800" (2009) 50(1) The Journal of African History 1

Heywood L and Thornton J, *Central Africans, Atlantic Creoles, and the Foundation of the Americas, 1585–1660: The First Generation of African Americans in North America and the Caribbean, 1619–1660* (CUP 2007)

Higgins R, *Problems and Process: International Law and How We Use It* (Clarendon Press 1994)

Hockett J and Saucier D, "A Systematic Literature Review of 'Rape Victims' versus 'Rape Survivors': Implications for Theory, Research, and Practice" (2015) 25 Aggression and Violent Behaviour 1

Honoré A, "Linguistic and Social Context of the Lex Aquilia" (1972) 7 Irish Jurist 138

Horowitz D, "Ten Reasons Why Reparations for Slavery Is a Bad Idea—and Racist Too" (2001) 31(2) The Black Scholar 48

Horowitz D, *Uncivil Wars: The Controversy over Reparations for Slavery* (Encounter Books 2002)

Howard-Hassmann R, "Reparations to Africa and the Group of Eminent Persons" (2004) 173–74 Cahiers d'études africanes 81

Howard-Hassmann R and Lombardo A, *Reparations to Africa* (University of Pennsylvania Press 2008)

Hurwitz A and Huang R (eds), *Civil War and the Rule of Law: Security, Development, Human Rights* (Lynne Rienner Publishers 2008)

Ibbetson D, "How the Romans Did for Us: Ancient Roots of the Tort of Negligence" (2003) 26 University of New South Wales Law Journal 475

Inikori J (ed), *Forced Migration: The Impact of the Export Slave Trade on African Societies* (Hutchinson & Co 1982)

Inter-American Commission of Human Rights, "Uruguay Report" (1992) 13 Human Rights Law Journal 340

International Center for Transitional Justice, "What is Transitional Justice?" (International Center for Transitional Justice 2017) <www.ictj.org/about/transitional-justice> accessed September 28, 2017

International Committee of the Red Cross, "Rule 160/ Statutes of Limitation" *Customary IHL Database* <ihl-databases.icrc.org/customary-ihl/eng/docs/v1_rul_rule160> accessed April 23, 2018

International Court of Justice, "Declarations Recognizing the Jurisdiction of the Court as Compulsory" (International Court of Justice 2018) <www.icj-cij.org/en/declarations> accessed March 14, 2018

International Law Commission, "Draft Articles on the Responsibility of States for Internationally Wrongful Acts, with commentaries" (2001) 2(2) Yearbook of the International Law Commission 31

International Law Commission, "Draft Articles Proposed by the Drafting Committee on Second Reading" (2000) 1 Yearbook of the International Law Commission 386

International Law Commission, "Report of the International Law Commission on the Work of its Fifty-Third Session" (2001) 2(2) Yearbook of the International Law Commission 31

International Law Commission, "Summary Record of the 2392nd Meeting" (1995) 1 Yearbook of the International Law Commission 88

International Network of Scholars and Activists for Afrikan Reparations, "Public Report: Launch of the International Network of Scholars and Activists for Afrikan Reparations (INOSAAR)" (London, October 2016) <http://www.inosaar.llc.ed.ac.uk/sites/default/files/atoms/files/public_report_21_oct_2017.pdf> accessed May 23, 2018

International Steering Committee for Stop the Maangamizi: We Charge Genocide/Ecocide, "About" (*Stop the Maangamizi*) <stopthemaangamizi.com> accessed June 1, 2018

Izumi M, "Asian-Japanese: State Apology, National *Ethos*, and the 'Comfort Women' Reparations Debate in Japan" (2011) 62(5) Communication Studies 473

Jaffrey P, *The Nature and Scope of Restitution: Vitiated Transfers, Imputed Contracts and Disgorgement* (Hart 2000)

Jalloh A and Maizlish S (eds), *The African Diaspora* (Texas A&M UP 1996),

James F and Perry R, "Legal Cause" (1951) 60 Yale Law Journal 761

Johnson AC, Coleman-Norton PR, and Bourne FC, *Ancient Roman Statutes: Translation with Introduction, Commentary, Glossary and Index* (Clyde Pharr ed, University of Texas Press 1961)

Jones H, *Mutiny on the Amistad: The Saga of a Slave Revolt and Its Impact on American Abolition, Law, and Diplomacy* (OUP 1987)

Joshel SR, *Slavery in the Roman World* (CUP 2010)

Kaddhouri M, *The Islamic Law of Nations: Shaybani's Siyar* (Johns Hopkins UP 1966)

Kaplow L and Shavell S, "Accuracy in the Assessment of Damages" (1996) 39 Journal of Law and Economics 191

Kapur R, *Erotic Justice: Law and the New Politics of Postcolonialism* (Glasshouse 2005)

Karenga M, "The Ethics of Reparations: Engaging the Holocaust of Enslavement" (Coalition of Blacks for Reparations in America Conference, Baton Rouge, June 22–23, 2001)

Karenga M, "The Ethics of Reparations: Engaging the Holocaust of Enslavement" (The National Coalition of Blacks for Reparations in America Convention, Baton Rouge, June 2001) <http://www.ncobraonline.org/wp-content/uploads/2016/02/Karenga-THE-ETHICS-OF-REPARATIONS.pdf> accessed October 23, 2018

Kendall EL, *A Living Sacrifice: A Study of Reparation* (Westminster Press 1960)

Kern HL, "Strategies of Legal Change: Great Britain, International Law, and the Abolition of the Transatlantic Slave Trade" (2004) 6 Journal of the History of International Law 233

Kershnar S, "Are the Descendants of Slaves Owed Compensation for Slavery?" (1999) 16 Journal of Applied Philosophy 95

King D and Page J, "Towards Transitional Justice? Black Reparations and the End of Mass Incarceration" (2018) 41 Ethnic and Racial Studies 739

Klein H, *African Slavery in Latin America and the Caribbean* (2nd edn, OUP 2007)

Klimchuk D, "Unjust Enrichment and Reparations for Slavery" (2004) 84 Boston University Law Review 1257

Kohler L and Saner H (eds), *Hannah Arendt—Karl Jaspers Correspondence 1926–1969* (Robert Kimber and Rita Kimber tr, Harcourt Brace and Jovanovich 1992)

Kooy DV and Cox JN, "Melodramatic Slaves" (2012) 55(4) Modern Drama 459

Koskienniemi M, *The Gentle Civilizer of Nations: The Rise and Fall of International Law, 1870–1960* (CUP 2002)

Koskenniemi M, Rech W, and Fonseca MJ (eds), *International Law and Empire: Historical Explorations* (OUP 2017)

Kritz N (ed), *Transitional Justice: How Emerging Democracies Reckon with Former Regimes*, vol 1: *General Considerations* (US Institute of Peace Press 1995)

Laccino L, "Stop the Maangamizi: Africans 'Never Received Even an Apology for Slavery'" (August 2, 2016) <http://www.ibtimes.co.uk/stop-maangamizi-africans-never-received-even-apology-slavery-1573817> accessed November 1, 2016

Laing AG, *Travels in the Timammee, Kooranko and Soolima Countries* (William Clowes, Northumberland Court 1825)

Lambert D, "Black-Atlantic Counterfactualism: Speculating about Slavery and Its Aftermath" (2010) 36 Journal of Historical Geography 286

Laplante L and Theidon K, "Truth with Consequences: Justice and Reparations in Post-Truth Commission Peru" (2007) 29(1) Human Rights Quarterly 228

Law R, *The Slave Coast of West Africa 1550–1750: The Impact of the Atlantic Slave Trade on an African Society* (Clarendon Press 1991)

Lawrence T, *The Principles of International Law* (D C Heath 1895)

Lawther C, Moffett L, and Jacobs D (eds), *Research Handbook on Transitional Justice* (Edward Elgar Publishing 2017) League of Nations, "Draft Convention on Slavery Recommended by the Sixth Assembly: Reply from the British Government" (1926) A.10.1926.VI; 8 League of Nations Official Journal 1031

Leebaw B, "The Irreconcilable Goals of Transitional Justice" (2008) 30(1) Human Rights Quarterly 101

Leebaw B, *Judging State-Sponsored Violence, Imagining Political Change* (CUP 2011)

da Legnano G, *Tractatus De Bello, De Represaliis et De Duello, 1390* (Thomas Erskine Holland ed, OUP 1917)

Lemski N and Cameron CM (eds), *What Is a Slave Society? The Practice of Slavery in Global Perspective* (CUP 2018)

Lesaffer R, *Peace Treaties and International Law in European History* (CUP 2004)

Letschert R and others (eds), *Victimological Approaches to International Crimes: Africa* (Intersentia 2011)

Leyh BM, *Procedural Justice? Victim Participation in International Criminal Proceedings* (Intersentia 2011)

Lind E and Tyler TR, *The Social Psychology of Procedural Justice* (Springer 1988)

Link W and Broomall J (eds), *Rethinking American Emancipation: Legacies of Slavery and the Quest for Black Freedom* (CUP 2015)

López R, "The (Re)collection of Memory after Mass Atrocity and the Dilemma for Transitional Justice" (2015) 47 New York University Journal of International Affairs and Politics 799

Lott E, *Love and Theft: Blackface Minstrelsy and the American Working Class* (OUP 2013)

Lovejoy P, *Transformations in Slavery: A History of Slavery in Africa* (CUP 2011)

Lovejoy PE (ed), *Africans in Bondage: Essays Presented to Philip D Curtin on the Occasion of the 25th Anniversary of the African Studies Program* (University of Wisconsin Press 1986)

Lowenthal D, "On Arraigning Ancestors: A Critique of Historical Contrition" (2009) 87(3) North Carolina Law Review 901

Macdonald R St J, Matscher F, and Petzold H (eds), *The European System for the Protection of Human Rights* (Martinus Nijhoff 1993)

Mackie JL, *The Cement of the Universe: A Study of Causation* (Clarendon Press 1980)

Magarrell L, "Reparations for Massive or Widespread Human Rights Violations: Sorting Out Claims for Reparations and Social Justice" (2003) 22 Windsor Yearbook of Access to Justice 85

Magarrell L, *Reparations in Theory and Practice* (International Center for Transitional Justice 2007)

Magee R, "The Master's Tools, from the Bottom Up: Responses to African-American Reparations Theory in Mainstream and Outsider Remedies Discourse" (1993) 79 Virginia Law Review 863

Mancall P (ed), *Travel Narratives from the Age of Discovery* (OUP 2006)

Mani R, *Beyond Retribution: Seeking Justice in the Shadows of War* (Polity Press 2002)

Mani R, "Rebuilding an Inclusive Political Community after War" (2005) 36(4) Security Dialogue 511
Manning P, *Slavery and African Life* (CUP 1990)
Manning P (ed), *Slave Trades, 1500–1800: Globalization of Forced Labour* (Variorum 1996)
Mannix D, *Black Cargoes: A History of the Atlantic Slave Trade, 1518–1865* (Longmans, Green and Co 1962)
Marty P, "Islam in French Guinea" (1936) 29 Sierra Leone Studies 49
Matsuda M, "Looking to the Bottom: Critical Legal Studies and Reparations" (1987) 22 Harvard Civil Rights-Civil Liberties Law Review 323
Matthews J, *A Voyage to the River Sierra Leone* (B White & Son 1788)
Mazrui AA, *Black Reparations in the Era of Globalization* (Institute of Global Cultural Studies 2002)
McCrudden C, "Human Dignity and the Interpretation of Human Rights" (2008) 19 European Journal of International Law 655
McCrudden C (ed), *Understanding Human Dignity* (OUP 2013)
McEvoy K and McGregor L (eds), *Transitional Justice from Below: Grassroots Activism and the Struggle for Change* (Hart Publishing 2008)
McGarry J and O'Leary B, *Explaining Northern Ireland: Broken Images* (Blackwell 1995)
McKeown N, "Greek and Roman Slavery" in Nicolas Ralph Edmund Fisher, *Slavery in Classical Greece* (Bristol Classical Press 1993)
McNally D, "Transgenerational Trauma and Dealing with the Past in Northern Ireland" (WAVE Trauma Centre, March 2014)
Mégret F, "The International Criminal Court Statute and the Failure to Mention Symbolic Reparations" (2009) 16 International Review of Victimology 127
Mehren Av and Gordley J, *The Civil Law System: An Introduction to the Comparative Study of Law* (2nd edn, Little, Brown & Co 1977)
Meillassoux C, *The Anthropology of Slavery: The Womb of Iron and Gold* (University of Chicago Press 1991)
Miers S and Kopytoff I, *Slavery in Africa: Historical and Anthropological Perspectives* (University of Wisconsin Press 1977)
Miller JC, *Way of Death: Merchant Capitalism and the Angolan Slave Trade, 1740–1830* (University of Wisconsin Press 1988)
Miller M, "Land and Racial Wealth Equality" (2011) 101 American Economic Review 371
Minow M, *Between Vengeance and Forgiveness: Facing History after Genocide and Mass Violence* (Beacon 1998)
Mintz S, *Caribbean Transformations* (Aldine Publishing 1974)
Mirandola Pd, *On the Dignity of Man* (C Glenn Wallis tr, Hackett Publishing Company 1965)
Mitchell R, "Compensate Us for Slavery—Robinson" *The Gleaner* (Kingston, March 3, 2015) <jamaica-gleaner.com/article/lead-stories/20150303/compensate-us-slavery-robinson> accessed March 2, 2018
Moffett L, *Justice for Victims before the International Criminal Court* (Routledge 2014)
Moffett L, "Reparations for Guilty Victims: Navigating Complex Identities of Victim-Perpetrators in Reparation Mechanisms" (2016) 10 International Journal of Transitional Justice 146
Moon C, "'Who'll Pay Reparations on My Soul?' Compensation, Social Control and Social Suffering" (2012) 21(2) Social and Legal Studies 187
Moore F, *Travels into the Inland Parts of Africa* (London 1738)

Muchlinski P, Ortino F, and Schreuer C (eds), *The Oxford Handbook of International Investment Law* (OUP 2008)

Muhammad PM, "The Trans-Atlantic Slave Trade: A Forgotten Crime against Humanity as Defined by International Law" (2004) 19 Amherst University Law Review 883

Mullin M, *Africa in America: Slave Acculturation and Resistance in the American South and the British Caribbean, 1736–1831* (University of Illinois Press 1992)

Muraszkiewicz J, "Article 12 of the EU Human Trafficking Directive: Fulfilling Aspirations for Victim Participation in Criminal Trials?" (2016) 7(3) New Journal of European Criminal Law 331

Mutua M, *Human Rights: A Political and Cultural Critique* (University of Pennsylvania Press 2009)

Nagy R, "The Scope and Bounds of Transitional Justice and the Canadian Truth and Reconciliation Commission" (2013) 7 International Journal of Transitional Justice 52

Neff S ed, *Hugo Grotius on the Law of War and Peace* (CUP 2012)

Nehisi-Coates T, "The Case for Reparations" *The Atlantic* (Washington DC, June 2014) <https://www.theatlantic.com/magazine/archive/2014/06/the-case-for-reparations/361631/> accessed June 1, 2018

Nesiah V, "Placing International Law: White Spaces on a Map" (2003) 16 Leiden Journal of International Law 1

Neuborne B, "Holocaust Reparations Litigation: Lessons for the Slavery Reparations Movement" (2003) 58(4) NYU Annual Survey of American Law 615

Ni Aoláin F, "The Emergence of Diversity: Differences in Human Rights Jurisprudence" (1995) 19 Fordham International Law Journal 101

Ní Aoláin F and Campbell C, "The Paradox of Transition in Conflicted Democracies" (2005) 27 Human Rights Quarterly 172

Nicholas B, *An Introduction to Roman Law* (OUP 1962)

Niem C, Keo D, and Putheary S, *Behind the Darkness: Taking Responsibility or Acting under Orders?* (Youth for Peace 2011)

Nolte G (ed), *European and US Constitutionalism* (Council of Europe 2005)

Nouwen S, *Complementarity in the Line of Fire: The Catalysing Effect of the International Criminal Court in Uganda and Sudan* (CUP 2013)

Nozick R, *Anarchy, State and Utopia* (Basic Books 2013)

Nussbaum A, "The Significance of Roman Law in the History of International Law" (1951–2) 100 University of Pennsylvania Law Review 678

O'Connell DP, *State Succession in Municipal Law and International Law*, vol 2 (CUP 1967)

Odendaal A, "An Architecture for Building Peace at the Local Level: A Comparative Study of Local Peace Committees" (United Nations Development Programme 2010)

Oldfield J, *"Chords of Freedom": Commemoration, Ritual and British Transatlantic Slavery* (Manchester UP 2007)

Oppenheim L, *International Law: A Treatise, Volume 1, Peace* (H Lauterpacht ed, 8th edn, Longmans, Green and Co 1955)Orakhelashvili A (ed), *Research Handbook on the Theory and History of International Law* (Edward Elgar Publishing 2011)

Orford A (ed), *International Law and Its Others* (CUP 2006)

Otto D, "Subalternity and International Law: The Problems of Global Community and the Incommensurability of Difference" (1996) 5 Social and Legal Studies 337

Pahuja S, "'This Is the World: Have Faith'" (2004) 15(2) European Journal of International Law 381

Pahuja S, "The Postcoloniality of International Law" (2005) 46(2) Harvard Journal of International Law 459

Pahuja S, *Decolonising International Law: Development, Economic Growth and the Politics of Universality* (CUP 2011)
Parisi F, "Alterum non Laedere: An Intellectual History of Civil Liability" (1994) 39 American Journal of Jurisprudence 317
Pasqualucci J, "Victim Reparations in the Inter-American Human Rights System: A Critical Assessment of Current Practice and Procedure" (1996) 18 Michigan Journal of International Law 1
Patterson O, *Slavery and Social Death: A Comparative Study* (Harvard UP 1982)
Paul Farmer, *Pathologies of Power: Health, Human Rights and the New War on the Poor* (University of California Press 2003)
Personnaz J, *La Reparation du Prejudice en Droit International Public* (Librairie du Recueil Sirey 1939) 298
Pham P and others, *So We Will Never Forget: A Population-Based Survey on Attitudes about Social Reconstruction and the Extraordinary Chambers in the Courts of Cambodia* (Human Rights Centre, University of California 2009)
Pham P and others, "Victim Participation and the Trial of Duch at the Extraordinary Chambers in the Courts of Cambodia" (2011) 3 Journal of Human Rights Practice 264
Plakokefalos I, "Causation in the Law of State Responsibility and the Problem of Overdetermination: In Search of Clarity" (2015) 26(2) European Journal of International Law 471
Plessis Md, "Historical Injustice and International Law: An Exploratory Discussion of Reparations for Slavery" (2003) 25 Human Rights Quarterly 624
Posner R, *Economic Analysis of Law* (2nd edn, Little, Brown and Co 1977)
Posner E and Vermuele A, "Transitional Justice as Ordinary Justice" (2004) 117 Harvard Law Review 761
Postma J, *The Atlantic Slave Trade* (ABC-CLIO Inc 2003)
Pradier A, Rubin M, and Merwe Hvd, "Between Transitional Justice and Politics: Reparations in South Africa" (2018) 25 South African Journal of International Affairs 301
Price GN, "How Long Are the Chains of Slavery in the United States? Estimates of the Intergenerational Effects for Black Males between 1880–1930" (2019) 68 Social and Economic Studies 147
Pross C, *Paying for the Past: The Struggle over Reparations for the Surviving Victims of the Nazi Terror* (Johns Hopkins UP 1998)
Pufendorf S, *De Jure Naturae et Gentium Libri Octo, 1672* (Clarendon Press 1934)
Quinn K and Sutton P (eds), *Politics and Power in Haiti: Studies of the Americas* (Palgrave Macmillan 2013)
Ramji J, "Reclaiming Cambodian History: The Case for a Truth Commission" (2000) 24(1) Fletcher Forum of World Affairs 137
Rana R, "Symphony of Decolonisation: Third World and Human Rights Discourse" (2007) 11(4) International Journal of Human Rights 367
REDRESS, *Reparation: A Sourcebook for Victims of Torture and Other Violations of Human Rights and International Humanitarian Law* (REDRESS 2003)
REDRESS, "Collective Reparations: Concepts & Principles" (The REDRESS Trust, 2015)
REDRESS, "Torture Survivors' Perceptions of Reparation: Preliminary Survey" (The REDRESS Trust, 2001) <www.redress.org/downloads/publications/TSPR.pdf> accessed October 10, 2017
Reese T, "'Sheep in the Jaws of So Many Ravenous Wolves': The Slave Trade and Anglican Missionary Activity at Cape Coast Castle, 1752–1816" (2004) 34(3) Journal of Religion in Africa 348

Reid A, *Slavery, Bondage and Dependency in Southeast Asia* (University of Queensland Press 1983)

Reitzer L, *La Reparation Comme Consequence De L'Acte Illicite en Droit International* (Librairie du Recueil Sirey 1938)

Reparations Scholar, "What Is the International Social Movement for Afrikan Reparations (ISMAR)?" (February 20, 2015) <reparationsscholaractivist.wordpress.com/2015/02/20/what-is-the-ismar/> accessed October 21, 2016

Rice A and Kardux JC, "Confronting the Ghostly Legacies of Slavery: The Politics of Black Bodies, Embodied Memories and Memorial Landscapes" (2012) 9(3) Atlantic Studies 245

Richardson D, "Shipboard Revolts, African Authority, and the Atlantic Slave Trade" (2001) 58(1) The William and Mary Quarterly 69

Rigby A, *Justice and Reconciliation: After the Violence* (Lynne Rienbner Publishers 2001)

Roberts J, *Slavery and Enlightenment in the British Atlantic* (CUP 2013)

Robertson G, *Crimes against Humanity: The Struggle for Global Justice* (Penguin 1999)

Robins S, "Failing Victims? The Limits of Transitional Justice in Addressing the Needs of Victims of Violations" (2017) 11 Human Rights and International Legal Discourse 41

Robinson R, *The Debt: What America Owes to Blacks* (Dutton 2000)

Robinson R, "African Americans Are Owed for Years of Bottomness" *LA Times* (Los Angeles, February 6, 2000) <articles.latimes.com/2000/feb/06/opinion/op-61518> accessed October 23, 2018

Rodney W, "African Slavery and Other Forms of Social Oppression on the Upper Guinea Coast in the Context of the Atlantic Slave-Trade" (1966) 2(3) Journal of African History 431

Rosenfeld F, "Collective Reparations for Victims of Armed Conflict" (2010) 92 International Review of the Red Cross 731

Rubin-Marín R (ed), *The Gender of Reparations: Unsettling Sexual Hierarchies while Redressing Human Rights Violations* (CUP 2009)

Rumiko N, Puja K, and Akane O, *Denying the Comfort Women: The Japanese State's Assault on Historical Truth* (Routledge 2018)

Rustad M and Koenig T, "The Historical Continuity of Punitive Damages Awards: Reforming the Tort Reformers" (1993) 42 American University Law Review 1269

Sabahi B, "A Concise History of the Law of State Responsibility and Reparation in International Law" in Borzu Sabahi, *Compensation and Restitution in Investor-State Arbitration: Principles and Practice* (OUP 2011)

Sale MM, *American Slave Ship Revolts and the Production of Rebellious Masculinity* (Duke UP 1997)

Sales J and Cole K, "Punitive Damages: A Relic That Outlived Its Origins" (1984) 37 Vanderbilt Law Review 1117

Salzberger R and Turck M (eds), *Reparations for Slavery: A Reader* (Rowman & Littlefield 2004)

Sanders A, *The Evil Within: Genocide, Memory and Mythmaking in Cambodia* (Radboud University 2006)

Santos MSD, "The Repressed Memory of Brazilian Slavery" (2008) 11(2) International Journal of Cultural Studies 157

Sarat A, Douglas L, and Merrill M (eds), *The Limits of the Law* (Stanford UP 2005)

Sartre JP, *Anti-Semite and the Jew* (George J Becker tr, Schocken Books 1974)
Savage E (ed), *The Human Commodity: Perspectives on the Trans-Saharan Slave Trade* (Frank Cass 1992)
Schacht J, *An Introduction to Islamic Law* (Clarendon Press 1982)
Schlueter L and Redden K, *Punitive Damages* 3 (3rd edn, Butterworth Legal Publishers 1995)
Schrage E (ed), *Negligence: The Comparative History of the Law of Torts* (Duncker & Humblot 2001)
Scott JB (ed), *The Spanish Origins of International Law: Francisco de Vitoria and His Law of Nations* (Clarendon Press 1934)
Sebok A, "Two Concepts of Injustice in Restitution for Slavery" (2004) 84 Boston University Law Review 1405
Sensbach JF, "Charting a Course in Early African-American History" (1993) 50(2) The William and Mary Quarterly 394
Shafy S, "Caribbean States Call for Slavery Reparations" *Spiegel Online* (March 21, 2014) <www.spiegel.de/international/world/caribbean-states-want-reparations-for-western-europe-slave-trade-a-960109.html> accessed November 19, 2018
Shaw M, *International Law* (8th edn, CUP 2017)
Shelton D, *Remedies in International Human Rights Law* (1st edn, OUP 1999)
Shelton D, "Righting Wrongs: Reparations in the Articles on State Responsibility" (2002) 96 American Journal of International Law 833
Shelton D (ed), *The Oxford Handbook of International Human Rights Law* (OUP 2013)
Shelton D, *Remedies in International Human Rights Law* (3rd edn, OUP 2015)
Shepherd V, "Slavery, Shame and Pride: Debates over the Marking of the Bicentennial of the Abolition of the British Trans-Atlantic Trade in Africans in 2007" (2010) 56 Caribbean Quarterly 1
Sher G, "Ancient Wrongs and Modern Rights" (1981) 10 Philosophy and Public Affairs 3
Sherwin E, "Reparations and Unjust Enrichment" (2004) 84 Boston University Law Review 1443
Shklar J, "Giving Injustice Its Due" (1989) 98 Yale Law Journal 1135
Shumway R and Getz T (eds), *Slavery and Its Legacy in Ghana and the Diaspora* (Bloomsbury Academic 2017)
Simons S, "French City Confronts its Brutal Past" *Spiegel Online* (Nantes, April 24, 2012) <www.spiegel.de/international/europe/nantes-opens-memorial-to-slave-trade-a-829447.html> accessed October 25, 2018
Simpson G and van Zyl P, "South Africa's Truth and Reconciliation Commission" (1995) 585 Temps Moderne 394
Simpson G, *Great Powers and Outlaw States: Unequal Sovereigns in the International Legal Order* (CUP 2004)
Sinha M, *The Slave's Cause: A History of Abolition* (Yale UP 2016)
Smith M and Paquette R (eds), *The Oxford Handbook of Slavery in the Americas* (OUP 2010)
Sohm R, *The Institutes: A Textbook of the History and System of Roman Private Law* (James Crawford Ledlie tr, Clearendon Press 1907)
Soyinka W, *The Burden of Memory, the Muse of Forgiveness* (OUP 1999)
Spiegel H, "Origin and Development of Denial of Justice" (1938) 32 American Journal of International Law 63

Stanford-Xosei E, "What is the *Maangamizi*" (From the Transatlantic Slave Trade to Engaging the Maangamizi: Historical Injustice and Reparations Conference, Belfast, June 29–30, 2016)

Stanford-Xosei E, "'Stop the Maangamizi!' Campaign Message" (*Vimeo*, July 3, 2018) <https://vimeo.com/278175852> accessed October 29, 2018

Starke JG, *Starke's International Law* (IA Shearer ed, 11th edn, Butterworths 1994)

Steckel RH and Jensen RA, "New Evidence on the Causes of Slave and Crew Mortality in the Atlantic Slave Trade" (1986) 46(1) Journal of Economic History 57

Strand P, "Inheriting Inequality: Wealth, Race, and the Laws of Succession" (2010–2011) 89 Oregon Law Review 453

Strand PJ, "Inheriting Inequality: Wealth, Race, and the Laws of Succession" (2010–2011) 89 Oregon Law Review 453

Straus M, "Causation as an Element of State Responsibility" (1984) 16 Law and Policy in International Business 893

Stringer R, *Knowing Victims: Feminism and Victim Politics in Neoliberal Times* (Routledge 2014)

Suárez F, "*De Legibus, Ac Deo Legislatore, 1612*" in *Selection from Three Works of Francisco Suárez*, vol 2 (William S Hein & Co 1995)

Sweet JH, "The Iberian Roots of American Racist Thought" (1997) 54 William and Mary Quarterly 159

Taliadoros J, "The Roots of Punitive Damages at Common Law: A Longer History" (2016) 64 Cleveland State Law Review 251

Tams CJ, "Recognizing Guarantees of Non-Repetition: LaGrand and the Law of State Responsibility" (2002) 27 Yale Journal of International Law 441

Taylor ER, *If We Must Die: Shipboard Insurrections in the Era of the Atlantic Slave Trade* (Louisiana State UP 2006)

Teitel R, *Transitional Justice* (OUP 2002)

Teitel R, "Transitional Justice Genealogy" (2003) 16 Harvard Human Rights Journal 69

Tenaglia-Webster M (ed), *Slavery* (Greenhaven Press 2009)

Terakawa A, "Commission Hearings Probe Reparations for Japanese-American WWII Internment" (1981) 67 American Bar Association Journal 1439

Thomas JAC, "Review" (1964) 54 Journal of Roman Studies 211

Thompson J, *Taking Responsibility for the Past: Reparation and Historical Justice* (Polity 2002)

Thompson KD, *Ring Shout, Wheel About* (University of Illinois Publishing 2014)

Thornton J, *Africa and Africans in the Making of the Atlantic World, 1400–1800* (2nd edn, CUP 1998)

Thornton J, *A Cultural History of the Atlantic World, 1250–1820* (CUP 2010)

de Tocqueville A, *Democracy in America* (JP Mayer and Max Lerner eds, George Lawrence tr, Harper & Row 1966)

Törnblom K and Vermunt R, *Distributive and Procedural Justice* (Taylor & Francis 2007)

Torpey J (ed), *Politics and the Past: On Repairing Historical Injustices* (Rowman & Littlefield 2004)

Torpey J, *Making Whole What Has Been Smashed: On Reparations Politics* (Harvard UP 2006)

Truth and Reconciliation Commission of South Africa, *Final Report*, vol 5 (Truth and Reconciliation Commission 1998)

Torpey J (ed), *Politics and the Past: On Repairing Historical Injustices* (Rowman & Littlefield 2003)
Tsri K, *Africans Are Not Black: The Case for Conceptual Liberation* (Routledge 2016)
Tunc A (ed), *International Encyclopedia of Comparative Law* (Mohr 1983)
Turner C, "Delivering Lasting Peace, Democracy and Human Rights in Transition: The Role of International Law" (2008) 22 International Journal of Transitional Justice 126
Tylor H, *A Treatise on International Public Law* (Calaghan & Company 1901)
Tyman WF, "We Must Let Go of Grudges from Slavery" *Chicago Tribune* (November 6, 2017) <www.chicagotribune.com/news/opinion/commentary/ct-perspec-slavery-reparations-white-supremacy-1107-20171106-story.html> accessed April 23, 2018
UNSC, "Report of the Secretary-General on the Rule of Law and Transitional Justice in Conflict and Post-Conflict Societies" (2004) UN Doc S/2004/616
Urban Walker M, *Moral Repair: Reconstructing Moral Relations after Wrongdoing* (CUP 2006)
Urban Walker M, *What is Reparative Justice?* (Marquette UP 2010)
Vagts DF, "Hegemonic International Law" (2001) 95 Amherst Journal of International Law 843
van den Anker C (ed), *The Political Economy of New Slavery* (Palgrave Macmillan 2004)
Van Dijk J, "Free the Victim: A Critique of the Western Conception of Victimhood" (2009) 16 International Review of Victimology 1
Verdeja E, "A Normative Theory of Reparations in Transitional Democracies" (2006) 37 Metaphilosophy 449
Verdun V, "If the Shoe Fits, Wear It: An Analysis of Reparations to African Americans" (1993) 67 Tulane Law Review 597
Villa-Vicencio C and Verwoerd W (eds), *Looking Back, Reaching Forward: Reflections on the Truth and Reconciliation Commission of South Africa* (University of Cape Town Press 2000)
Villiger M, *Customary International Law and Treaties: A Study of Their Interactions and Interrelations* (Brill 1985)
Waldron J, "Superseding Historic Injustice" (1992) 103(1) Ethics 4
Waldron J, "Redressing Historic Injustice" (2002) 52 University of Toronto Law Journal 135
Walvin J, *Atlas of Slavery* (Taylor & Francis 2014)
Waterhouse C, "The Good, the Bad, and the Ugly: Moral Agency and the Role of Victims in Reparations Programs" (2009) 31 University of Pennsylvania Journal of International Law 257
Waterhouse C, "Total Recall: Restoring the Public Memory of Enslaved African-Americans and the American System of Slavery through Rectificatory Justice and Reparations" (2011) 14 The Journal of Gender, Race and Justice 703
Watson A, *Roman Slave Law* (Johns Hopkins UP 1987)
Watson A (ed), *The Digest of Justinian* (University of Pennsylvania Press 2011)
Watson J (ed), *Asian and African Systems of Slavery* (University of California Press 1980)
Weedon C and Jordan G, "Collective Memory: Theory and Politics" (2012) 22(2) Social Semiotics 143
Weeramantry CG, *Universalising International Law* (Brill 2004)
Wemmers J-A (ed), *Reparation for Victims of Crimes against Humanity: The Healing Role of Reparation* (Routledge 2014)

Wenger KD, "Causation and Attenuation in the Slavery Reparations Debate" (2006) 40 University of San Francisco Law Review 279

Wenger KD, "'Too Big to Remedy?': Rethinking Mass Restitution for Slavery and Jim Crow" (2010) 44 Loyola Los Angeles Law Review 177

Westley R, "Many Billions Gone: Is It Time to Reconsider the Case for Black Reparation?" (1998) 40 Boston College Law Review 429

Whatley W, "The Transatlantic Slave Trade and the Evolution of Political Authority in West Africa" (2012) IDEAS Working Paper Series from RePEc <ideas.repec.org/p/pra/mprapa/44932.html> accessed October 29, 2018

Wheaton H, *Elements of International Law* (Little, Brown and Co 1866)

Winbush RA (ed), *Should America Pay?: Slavery and the Raging Debate on Reparations* (Harper Collins 2003)

Winter S, "Towards a Unified Theory of Transitional Justice" (2013) 7(2) International Journal of Transitional Justice 224

Wittmann N, "Slavery Reparations Are a Must" (2009) 488 New African 24

Wittmann N, *Slavery Reparations Time Is Now: Exposing Lies, Claiming Justice for Global Survival, an International Legal Assessment* (Power of the TrInIty Publishers 2013)

Work Group of the International Work Group on Death, Dying and Bereavement, "Breaking Cycles of Violence" (2005) 29 Death Studies 585

Wright RW, "Causation, Responsibility, Risk, Probability, Naked Statistics, and Proof: Pruning the Bramble Bush by Clarifying the Concepts" (1987–1988) 73 Iowa Law Review 1001

Wright S, *International Human Rights, Decolonisation and Globalisation: Becoming Human* (Routledge 2001)

Wylie G and McRedmond P (eds), *Human Trafficking in Europe: Character, Causes and Consequences* (Palgrave Macmillan 2010)

Yamamoto E, *Race, Rights and Reparation: Law and Japanese American Internment* (Wolters Kluwer Law & Business 2013)

Yepes RU, *Between Corrective Justice and Distributive Justice: Reparations of Human Rights Violations in Times of Transition* (Utrecht University 2009)

Yudoff M, "Liability for Constitutional Torts and the Risk-Averse Public School Official" (1976) 49 Southern California Law Review 1322

Zimmermann A, "Continuity of States" *Max Planck Encyclopedia of Public International Law* (2006) <http://opil.ouplaw.com/view/10.1093/law:epil/9780199231690/law-9780199231690-e1389> accessed May 2, 2018

Zimmermann R, *The Law of Obligations: Roan Foundations of the Civilian Tradition* (Juta 1990)

Index

For the benefit of digital users, indexed terms that span two pages (e.g., 52–53) may, on occasion, appear on only one of those pages.

Figures are indicated by *f* following the page number